D0999809

Pennsylvania

WESTHOLME STATE MILITARY HISTORY SERIES

Pennsylvania

A Military History

The Second State of the Union

William A. Pencak

Christian B. Keller

Barbara A. Gannon

WESTHOLME
Yardley

©2016 William A. Pencak, Christian B. Keller, Barbara A. Gannon
Maps by Paul Dangel
Maps © 2016 Westholme Publishing

All rights reserved under International and Pan-American Copyright
Conventions. No part of this book may be reproduced in any form or by any
electronic or mechanical means, including information storage and retrieval
systems, without permission in writing from the publisher, except by a
reviewer who may quote brief passages in a review.

Westholme Publishing, LLC
904 Edgewood Road
Yardley, Pennsylvania 19067
Visit our Web site at www.westholmepublishing.com

First Printing October 2016
ISBN: 978-1-59416-251-0
Also available as an eBook.

Printed in the United States of America

Contents

Authors' Note and Dedication

We dedicate this volume to the memory of our co-author, mentor, and friend William A. Pencak, who suddenly passed away on December 9, 2013, while the manuscript for the book was in preparation. One of the leading international scholars of the American colonial period and early Republic, author of countless publications, former editor of *Pennsylvania History*, and an oracle of knowledge on Pennsylvania history, Bill was a professor at Penn State when we were graduate students. Without his tutelage and encouragement, neither of us would have likely finished our degree programs. In every sense of the word, Bill selflessly and cheerfully took on the role of mentor, helping us navigate the murky waters of graduate school and overseeing our first formal publications. A friend to students everywhere, he took a special interest in our careers and introduced us to the right people at the right time, threw impromptu parties, and celebrated every milestone with us. All these years after our graduation from Penn State we look back at our times with Bill, smile, and gratefully remember his generosity and excellence.

This book will unfortunately be his last, and it is a great honor for us to have our names listed next to his. Farewell, dear friend, and thank you.

Christian B. Keller
Barbara A. Gannon

List of Maps

Introduction

Pennsylvania was founded in 1682 by William Penn and the Quakers as a "Holy Experiment" to determine whether a society that had no military, eschewed violence as a means of solving conflicts, and tolerated a wide variety of religions could survive. It could: Pennsylvania existed as a "peaceable kingdom"—to use the title of Quaker Edward Hicks's numerous paintings of Penn's treaty with the Indians—until 1754.[1] This prompted the French philosopher Voltaire to comment in his *Letters on the English* that "William Penn might glory in having brought down upon earth the so much boasted golden age, which in all probability never existed but in Pennsylvania."[2]

But war was essential to both Pennsylvania's founding and its history. William Penn was only able to begin his experiment because of the wealth and prestige he inherited from his father, Admiral William Penn, who fought for both king and Parliament most of the years from 1645 to 1665. The younger Penn hoped to call his new colony "Sylvania"—meaning, simply, woods —as Quakers disdained naming places after human beings as irreligious vanity (hence the numerous Walnut, Market, Chestnut, and other such streets at the center of old Pennsylvania towns). Yet King Charles II insisted on adding "Penn" to honor William Penn *Sr.*, a man who had loaned him money, helped him return to his throne in 1660, and defeated a Dutch invasion at the Battle of Lovestoft in 1665.[3]

The long peace Penn initiated in 1682 was also deceptive. Beginning with the "Walking Purchase" of 1737 if not earlier, Pennsylvania's Indian policy involved removing people from their traditional homelands through questionable treaty purchases backed up by threats from the powerful, pro-English Iroquois against their weaker native neighbors. The Indians' pent-up anger was responsible for the outbreak of the bloodiest war in early America, which became the global French and Indian War.

These frontier struggles continued throughout the American Revolution and into the new republic until Anthony Wayne finally secured the western frontier at the Battle of Fallen Timbers in 1794.

Pennsylvania was also the site of two of the American Revolution's greatest battles with the British— Brandywine and Germantown outside Philadelphia in 1777—and of intense guerrilla warfare. Unlike the relatively united colonies of New England and Virginia, Pennsylvania, like the other middle colonies, was deeply divided. Loyalists, revolutionaries, Indians, Pennsylvanians, and Virginians, along with British, French, and German soldiers, fought over who would possess most of a new state whose boundaries were yet to be determined. Virginia ceded the southwest to Pennsylvania in 1781, and Connecticut's claim to its northern third was only denied by Congress in 1786. During the War of 1812, too, the major inland naval battle was fought on Lake Erie where American forces based in Erie, Pennsylvania, defeated a British squadron.

The best-known military event in Pennsylvania's history, however, was the Battle of Gettysburg, fought from July 1–3, 1863, and considered by many scholars the turning point of the American Civil War. Termed "the Arsenal of the Union," Pennsylvania played a crucial role in the entire Northern war effort, however. From the citizens of Pittsburgh who prevented the federal government from shipping arms to the South in December 1860; to the First Defenders of Central Pennsylvania who rushed to Washington, D.C., immediately after the attack on Fort Sumter; to the 360,000 Pennsylvania soldiers (second only to New York) who fought for the Union, the Keystone State was key to Union victory. Two Philadelphians, George B. McClellan and George G. Meade, between them commanded the Army of the Potomac, the Union's main field army in the East, for nearly the entire war and marshaled the Union through the great tests of Antietam and Gettysburg. African-, Irish-, and German-American troops flocked in great numbers to the state's colors, adding a distinctly multicultural flavor to Pennsylvania's volunteer regiments, and the vaunted Pennsylvania Reserves division, unique in the Federal Army, participated in nearly every major campaign against Robert E. Lee's army. The southern tier counties also played host to Confederate invaders several times during the conflict, giving Pennsylvania the unenviable distinction of being the only Northern state to be occupied by the enemy for any significant period of time.

Pennsylvania was also a leader in America's twentieth century wars. During World War I, the Pennsylvania-based 28th Division, which appeared on the western front only in June 1918, achieved heroic stature as 14,000 of its 25,000 men were killed or wounded in the five months before the war ended. Charles Schwab, president of Bethlehem Steel, led the Emergency Fleet Corporation and used his company to build from scratch a large percentage of the vastly expanded United States Navy. Pittsburgh produced four-fifths of the military's steel, and Pennsylvania overall contributed three-quarters of the nation's wartime coal requirements. In World War II, Pennsylvanian dominance in heavy industry began to decline as western states industrialized, but it was still responsible for 31 percent of the nation's steel production. The Philadelphia Navy Yard employed 58,000 people and built over 1,200 ships; the Frankford Arsenal in that city had over 20,000 workers. The army jeep was invented and first produced in Butler, Pennsylvania. General George C. Marshall, who strategically directed the national war effort in World War II, was a native of Uniontown, and Dwight D. Eisenhower, who in 1950 thought he established his retirement home in Gettysburg, had to wait another ten years until the conclusion of his second term as president to become a full-time Pennsylvanian.

With the decline of its heavy industry and military conflict shifting from Europe to Asia, Pennsylvania's role in the Korean and Vietnam wars, interventions in Latin America, and recent wars in the Middle East has primarily been to provide soldiers and train military leaders. With its numerous small towns, Pennsylvania has more American Legion posts than any other state, testifying to the state's strong community ties, patriotism, and military commitment. Prominent late twentieth-century Pennsyl-

vania generals include Alexander Haig and Charles Joulwin, who were the supreme commanders of NATO from 1974 to 1979 and 1993 to 1997, respectively. Haig, like Marshall, later served as secretary of state. Beginning in 1951, the Army War College—which had been opened and closed in different locations since 1901—found its permanent home in Carlisle, Pennsylvania. Here, scholars and high-ranking military officers prepare for future conflicts by studying the theory, history, strategy, and practice of war and the the creation of national security policy.

During the Gulf War of 1989–1990, the Fourteenth Quartermaster Corps from Greensburg, Pennsylvania, had the highest casualty rate of any American or allied unit: on February 25, 1990, thirteen of its members were killed and forty-three wounded during a Scud attack. Pennsylvania again took on importance in the war on terror when on September 11, 2001, passengers took control and downed Flight 93 outside of Shanksville, a plane terrorists probably intended to crash into the White House. Former Pennsylvania governor Tom Ridge then served a term as the nation's first secretary for homeland security from 2003 to 2005.

Like all military histories, Pennsylvania's is a tale of destruction, suffering, and humiliation as well as glory. Torture and killing of prisoners, women, and children were common in the French and Indian War and American Revolution. During the Civil War approximately twice as many Union soldiers died from disease—especially dysentery, diarrhea, or gangrene—than in combat. With its strong Quaker tradition, Pennsylvanians have also been in the forefront of conscientious objection to war, such as the Philadelphia-based, Nobel Peace Prize–winning American Friends Service Committee, the nation's leading organization representing the rights of pacifists. The Keystone State also looms prominently in active opposition to American wars: it shared with New York the dubious honor of having the most opponents of the American Revolution, and during the Civil War Irish draft resisters in the coal regions formed the Molly Maguires and attacked leading Republicans and army conscription officers. Considered the most important Supreme Court case limiting free speech in wartime, the Charles Schenck case began with the arrest of a Philadelphian in 1917.

Pennsylvania's diverse military history, encompassing conventional and guerrilla warfare, strong patriotic participation and equally strong dissent, agricultural and industrial production, reflects the state's geographical and ethnic diversity.[4] Unlike Texas or Virginia, states with great collective pride, Pennsylvania is a series of regions that have little in common, divided up by mountains. The southeastern quadrant of the state, from Chester and Philadelphia, north to Easton on the Delaware River and the mountains that begin there, and westward to the Susquehanna, is, after more than three hundred years of intense use, still some of the most fertile, nonirrigated soil in the world. Today, in an era of deindustrialization, agriculture is again Pennsylvania's leading industry, as it was in the Colonial era. Here colonists also discovered more raw iron than anywhere else in the British Empire—the numerous forges and furnaces that remain place names in the state attest to this historical reality. The colony, especially Lancaster and Berks counties, was the home of the famed and deadly Pennsylvania long rifle and the sturdy Conestoga wagon; the latter was used by thousands of settlers after 1740, some of whom moved on to populate the South and Midwest.

Most of the rest of Pennsylvania consists of range after range of mountains that once contained greater resources for manufacturing than anywhere else in the nation. The state's northeast was the source of nearly all the United States' hard, or anthracite, coal, mined extensively beginning in the 1820s. Similarly, southwestern Pennsylvania marked the northernmost limit of a huge field of soft, or bituminous, coal that stretches through West Virginia and Kentucky south to Alabama. Not only Pittsburgh, but also smaller cities such as Aliquippa, Homestead, and Donora flourished as that coal was combined with the region's plentiful supplies of coke to make steel, a product in which Pennsylvania led the nation from the late nineteenth to the mid-twentieth century. In 1859, Edward Drake discovered oil in northwestern Pennsylvania, the center of the world's first oil boom and the intial source of John D.

Rockefeller's great wealth. Used to light lamps, the wells became too deep to be profitable just as large quantities of oil were discovered in Texas and the automobile was invented at the turn of the twentieth century. Pennsylvania's immense forests—suggested by the English translation of their name as "Penn's Woods"—made it the number one producer of lumber in the United States in the 1860s; it ranked at least fourth until 1900. Wagons, railroad cars and ties, gun carriages, and buildings were among the forests' chief military uses. With the exception of a few small stands of wood (such as the 150-acre Alan Seeger Park in Centre County) the magnificent forests that now fill much of the state are almost all second growth, less than a century old. In 2008, geologists discovered that Pennsylvania was at the center of a huge deposit (estimated at over 400 trillion cubic feet) of natural gas that could be extracted from Marcellus Shale that extended from New York into Ohio and West Virginia. The state's aggressive mining of shale, at a moment when the United States seemed to be running low on energy supplies, suggests that if there are wars in the future, Pennsylvania's natural resources will continue to fuel them.[5]

Pennsylvania has also been the center of more ethnic and religious diversity than arguably any other state. Several Pennsylvania groups have made distinctive contributions to the nation's wartime experience. William Penn made a point to attract pacifists from Germany—the Moravians, Mennonites, and Amish being the most prominent—who have joined with the Quakers as the most noticeable religious objectors to war throughout American history. But most of the early Pennsylvania Germans were Lutheran or Reformed (now United Church of Christ) Protestants who would fight for land on the frontier. There, those who could not find land east of the Susquehanna joined the Scots-Irish (Presbyterians from northern Ireland) and headed west. These settlements, opposed by the Quaker government in the interest of keeping the peace, led the Indians to turn on the settlers in the French and Indian War. A century later, working-class Irish Roman Catholic draft resisters from the anthracite coal region were the most violent Pennsylvania opponents of a Civil War from which the Republican, Anglo-Saxon Protestant bosses who ran the coal mines profited greatly. In the twentieth century, Pennsylvania Germans were among the last Americans to support World War I, as they considered their ethnic homeland the victim of French and British propaganda and American businessmen who made millions supporting those nations' interests.

In American military as in political history, Pennsylvania deserves the title of the "Keystone State." Its central position in the nation, like the keystone at the top of a constructed arch, held the nation together in the revolution and connected East and West in the Civil War. Its men and industrial might have been the key to American success in its pre-1950 wars and significant contributors to the conflicts thereafter. As a leader in dissent, Pennsylvania has also been prominent in questioning both the motives and consequences of the resort to arms. The military history of the Keystone State, much as its entire historical background, is in many ways representative of the nation's as a whole.

1. Before Pennsylvania

William A. Pencak

William Penn was fortunate when he brought the first settlers to Pennsylvania in 1682. The land he settled first, around Philadelphia, was inhabited by the Leni Lenape (translation: "Original People") Indians, better known to Europeans as the Delaware. They lived in small groups, and based on archaeological evidence had dwelled peacefully—few graves gave evidence of violent deaths—in the Delaware Valley for at least a century. Penn purchased land from a dozen sachems in the area immediately around Philadelphia; they represented a population numbering no more than a few thousand. The Lenape had suffered extremely from European diseases, especially smallpox: few remained alive after epidemics in 1654, 1663, 1677, and 1688–1691.[1]

The Lenape had probably encountered Europeans as early as the Verrazzano voyage to North America in the 1520s, but regular contact began when the Dutch began trading with New Amsterdam as their base in the 1620s. Early contact with the Dutch led to violence; in 1632 Indians destroyed the small Dutch whaling station at Swanandael at the mouth of the Delaware River, killing all thirty inhabitants as they worked in the fields. It occurred over a misunderstanding—an Indian removed a tin plate with a Dutch standard on it. Seeing how angry the Dutch were, some Indians killed the man and brought his body to the settlement. The Dutch explained that was an extreme response, but the dead indian's friends surprised and destroyed the Dutch, believing they were responsible for the execution.[2]

The Swedes were the next to come to the Delaware Valley, in 1638. They had hoped to grow silk and tobacco and trade for furs. Johan Printz, the colony's six-foot-eight-inches-tall, four-hundred-pound governor from 1643 to 1654, was a soldier and advised the New Sweden Company that "nothing would be better than to send over here a couple of hundred soldiers" to "break the necks of all of them [the Indians] in this River." But

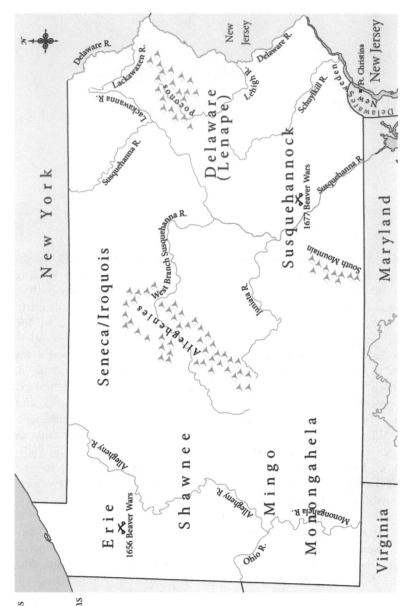

Map 1: Native Peoples of Pennsylvania. This map shows the lands of Pennsylvania's historic Native Americans at the time of the Beaver Wars. Also shown is the nascent permanent European presence in Pennsylvania of New Sweden.

his handful of soldiers were insufficient for any offensive operations,
and in spite of himself Printz inaugu-
rated the peace with the Lenape that
would continue with William Penn.
Instead, Printz did most of his fighting with his own people (he executed
a soldier for mutiny in 1653 after
twenty-two inhabitants petitioned
against his one-man rule) and against
the nearby Dutch in New Amsterdam.
Besides its farms and hamlets, New
Sweden consisted of a number of
small forts along the Delaware, the
northernmost at the juncture of the
Schuylkill and Delaware rivers at the
present city of Philadelphia. But the
colony was too tiny to survive any
attack: Sweden rarely sent reinforcements to a colony whose inhabitants
kept deserting to Maryland or New
Netherland. Several of the Swedish
ships, sent out only every year or two
in any case, were lost in storms or
decimated from disease. New Sweden
never had more than 368 settlers. In
1655, seven Dutch warships and three
hundred soldiers from New
Amsterdam appeared and forced the
Swedes to surrender. The Dutch and
later the English (who took over New
Netherland in 1664), however, left the
Swedes alone to practice their
Lutheran religion and continue their
peaceful agricultural ways. The Finns
who constituted much of New
Sweden's population left the log cabin
as their legacy.[3]

Warfare among the Indians was
endemic in the land that would
become Pennsylvania's hinterland. It
was first observed by Europeans as
early as 1608, when John Smith

A Delaware/Lenape family drawn by
Thomas Campanius Holm for
*Description of the Province of New
Sweden, Now Called, by the English,
Pennsylvania, in America,* first published in Swedish in Stockholm in
1702. Thomas based his drawing on
the description provided by his grand-
father, John Campanius, who was a
missionary to the Lenape in the 1640s.

explored the northern reaches of
Chesapeake Bay. There he encountered:

a people called Susquehannock. . . . 60
of those Susquehannocks came to the
discoverers with skins, bows, arrows,
targets, beads, swords, and tobacco
pipes for presents. Such great and well
proportioned men are seldom seen, for
they seemed like giants to the English,
yea and to the neighbors [other
Indians], yet seemed of an honest and
simple disposition, with much ado
restrained from adoring the discoverers
as gods. Those are the most strange
people of all those countries, both in

language and attire; for their language it may well beseem their proportions, sounding from them, as it were a great voice in a vault, or cave, as an echo. Their attire is the skins of bears and wolves; some have cassocks made of bear heads and skins that a man's neck goes through the skin's neck, and the ears of the bear fastened to his shoulders behind, the nose and teeth hanging down his breast, and at the end of the nose hung a bear's paw; the half sleeves coming to the elbows were the necks of bears and the arms through the mouth with paws hanging at their noses. One had the head of a wolf hanging in a chain for a jewel, his tobacco pipe three quarters of a yard long, prettily carved with a bird, a bear, a deer, or some such device at the great end, sufficient to beat out the brains of a man, with bows and arrows and clubs suitable to their greatness and conditions. These [Indians] are scarce known to Powhatan. They can make near 600 able and mighty men and are palisaded in their towns to defend them from the Massawomeks, their mortal enemies.[4]

Who the Massawomeks were remains a mystery. They only appear in European sources from 1608 to 1634 and then disappear. Other Indians reported that the Massawomeks "eat men," had "many boats and so many men they made war upon the entire world," and "came from beyond the mountains," near "a great salt lake." The best guess is they were Iroquois, or a people related to them, based on the small amount of linguistic evidence that survives, and lived along the south shores of Lakes Erie and Ontario. In any event, even before Jamestown and Quebec were settled

in 1607 and 1608, respectively, the European demand for furs and the Indian demand for alcohol, guns, and other goods resulted in a fierce competition for trade. The Massawomeks were enemies of both the Powhatans in Virginia and the Susquehannocks in Pennsylvania.[5]

The Susquehannocks themselves were recent arrivals. They had lived in the northern region of the river valley that still bears their name until about 1580. Then the Iroquois pushed them south into what is now Lancaster County, Pennsylvania, where most of their archaeological sites are found. As trade increased with the founding of New Amsterdam (1624) and New England (1620s) in addition to Quebec, the Iroquois sought to expand the territory in which they hunted for furs. Thus began the Beaver Wars, which lasted from about 1610 until the Peace of Albany in 1677.[6]

THE BEAVER WARS

The Beaver Wars altered the nature of Indian society and warfare. Before the introduction of European trade goods, the Native Americans hunted primarily for their own needs. Wars with neighbors were limited as was the depletion of the supply of beaver. Once the Europeans' demand for furs increased, so did hostilities among the Indians. Along with the deadly epidemics, this led to great demographic decline. As they had on a limited scale in the past, Indians replaced lost members with those captured from other people. The Beaver Wars then turned into the Mourning Wars, in

A copper engraving published in 1613 of an Iroquois fort under attack, witnessed by Samuel de Champlain. Following European contact, fighting increased among the native tribes in an attempt to control the fur trade. The Beaver Wars, as they were named, resulted in Iroquois domination of much of the mid-Atlantic.

which captives who were not killed were adopted by the conquerors.[7]

The Iroquois were the greatest winners in the Beaver Wars. These five nations—Ondondaga, Cayuga, Mohawk, Seneca, and Oneida (a sixth, the Tuscarora, joined in 1722 after being expelled from North Carolina)—who lived mostly in what is now central New York, were with the French and English the most important military power in the northern colonies from the mid-1600s until the American Revolution. Each nation handled its own domestic affairs but they united on issues of foreign policy, frequently with different nations adopting what appeared to be pro-French or pro-British policies to convince both European powers they were indeed their allies. This strategy also enabled them to obtain the frequent presents the Europeans offered to obtain their friendship—clothing, blankets, alcohol, but most especially the guns that enabled the Iroquois to exert their influence south into the backcountry of Pennsylvania, Maryland, and Virginia and westward to what are today the states of Kentucky, Illinois, and Michigan. Some scholars have even seen the Iroquois federal system as a model for the United States Constitution, but in fact, while occasionally admired by colonial leaders from the abortive Albany Plan of Union in 1754 until the mid-1780s, discussion or influence of the Iroquois model was almost nonexistent during discussions over what system of union to adopt.[8]

The Iroquois's greatest victory came in 1656, when, using guns obtained from the French, Dutch, and English, they defeated their closest southern neighbors, the Erie. The Erie ceased to exist as a viable nation in what is now Pennsylvania and their surviving members headed west. In 1661, mutual fear of the Iroquois led the Susquehannocks to ally with Maryland (founded in 1629). They managed to defeat the Iroquois in 1663. The two Indian nations then warred inconclusively for a decade as Maryland and Virginia began to fear the nearby Susquehannocks more than the distant Iroquois. In 1674 the two colonies made peace with the Iroquois and the following year attacked the Susquehannocks. Nathanael Bacon's Rebellion of 1676 in Virginia began when he hoped to expel the Susquehannocks because they stood in the way of westward set-tlement. Most of the Susquehannocks then joined the Iroquois for protection. (A handful of Susquehannocks continued to live independently in Pennsylvania as the Conestogas in the vicinity of present-day Harrisburg. In the 1740s the Moravians converted them to Christianity, and the twenty survivors were massacred in 1763 by the Paxton Boys.) In 1677, in negotiations at Albany directed by New York governor Edmund Andros, the Iroquois established the Covenant Chain, or peace with the English colonies and various Indian peoples to the south.[9] Thus, when William Penn began his "Holy Experiment" in 1682, in neither the Delaware Valley nor the fertile country of southeastern Pennsylvania, no strong or war-like Indian societies lived who could pose a threat to the peace the Quaker leader hoped to establish.

2. Pennsylvania's Early Defense Policy, 1682–1730

William A. Pencak

Contrary to the common belief, fostered by Benjamin West's famous 1771 painting known as *Penn's Treaty with the Indians*, William Penn made not one but a dozen treaties between 1682 and 1684 with the various small groups of Indians who lived in the region around Philadelphia. History, however, has remembered them simply as "the" treaty with the Indians—to guarantee "forever hereafter a firm and lasting peace" for which he spent over £1,200 in presents. Penn also took care that no threats would come to his colony from the sea. First, he positioned Pennsylvania "in the center of the English colonies, for if the French come by land, they must come through several of them before they can well annoy" it. Second, he made sure Philadelphia, the major oceangoing port, was over a hundred miles from the mouth of Delaware Bay and possible depredations from England's enemies. Deepwater vessels could only navigate the Delaware's tricky channels with the aid of river pilots who knew its obstructions and cur-

rents well. Thus, Penn felt reasonably secure that "there is not any one province lies higher from the ocean, and therefore not easy to be surprised by the enemy in any way."[1] Penn may have relied on God's assistance for his new society to succeed, but he carefully chose its geographical location so that divine intervention would be kept to a minimum.

Although long praised as a model for Native American–colonial relations, Penn's treaties contained in embryo the causes that would transform Pennsylvania from the most peaceful and admired of the American colonies to the most war-torn and unstable place on the continent from 1754 until the mid-1790s. The Indians whom the colonists believed "surrendered" their land thought they were only giving the settlers permission to use land they would physically occupy and farm, and that they retained the right to joint use of any other land—especially for hunting. The Pennsylvanians, of course, believed in European notions of absolute property ownership guaranteed by officially registered paper deeds—they could stake out absolute claims to land whether they were using it at present or not.

Thus, as early as 1684, colonists were reporting to Penn that the Indians were "much displeased at our English settling upon their land, and seem to threaten us, that William Penn hath deceived them," and that "William Penn shall be brother no more." Penn, who was back in England, responded that if the Indians were "rude and unruly" and "will not punish" those who resisted European occupation, "we will and must, for they must never see you afraid of executing the justice they ought to do." Pennsylvania may have eschewed military force, but sheriffs and other local magistrates enforced penalties—including execution—for murder and burglary, with lesser punishments for theft and disorderly behavior. By 1695, Tammamend, the chief whose initial friendship with the whites led to the fraternal Societies of St. Tammany in Philadelphia and New York in his honor, bowed to the inevitable and canceled "any farther claims, dues and demands whatever, concerning the said lands or any other trace of land claimed by us from the beginning of the world."[2]

Henceforth, settlers swarmed onto land where few Indians remained, and obliged them to move west or north, either accepting or refusing the presents offered in return. Disputes, of course, occurred between Indians who had not yet left and settlers who had moved in ahead of official pur-

One of only two life images of William Penn (1644–1718), this sketch was done when the founder of Pennsylvania was middle-aged.

chases. These usually involved disputes over trade goods, murder, assault, and rape and occurred when some or all of those involved were intoxicated. But both Pennsylvania and the Indians worked to settle these quarrels, even if it meant that sometimes the culprits went free, so that the peace was kept between the larger communities.[3]

The first defense crisis Pennsylvania faced, however, came from the sea and France, not the land and Indians. In 1689, war broke out between Britain and France when Penn's former patron, James, the Duke of York, who had become King James II, was ousted from his throne in the Glorious (meaning bloodless) Revolution of 1688. King Louis XIV of France hoped to restore the Roman Catholic James to the throne. In the colonies, the conflict was known as

King William's War (1689–1697) after James's successor. Exposed to attacks from privateers, the three largely Anglican Lower Counties—New Castle, Kent, and Sussex—which Penn had created in 1682 demanded autonomy and provisions for defense that the Quaker majority, sitting in Philadelphia and representing the three Upper Counties of Chester, Philadelphia, and Bucks, was unwilling to grant. Penn himself became a champion of military preparedness, realizing he might otherwise lose his colony for displeasing the British. He appointed Captain John Blackwell, a Puritan with military experience, to govern his colony in September 1688, but the Pennsylvania Provincial Assembly refused to cooperate with him. Penn's worst fears were realized in 1693 when the British government attempted to spur the colony into action by removing William Penn as proprietor after Pennsylvania failed to provide the requested eighty men or any money to assist New York in defending itself against the French Canadians and their Huron allies. The Crown proceeded to extend the authority of New York's governor Benjamin Fletcher to Pennsylvania as "Captain General and Vice Admiral."[4]

For three years, Fletcher had no more success than Blackwell or Penn in trying to get something out of the assembly. Finally, in 1696, he obtained a mere £300 "for the supply and relief of those Indians of the Five Nations that are in friendship with the English the necessaries of food and raiment." Although meager, this sum set a precedent that would last until the French and Indian War. Pennsylvania would pretend it was giving the British money for other purposes, knowing full well it would be absorbed into the military budget.[5]

In 1699 William Penn returned for the second time to Pennsylvania, where he remained until 1701. (He only spent four out of the last thirty-six years of his life in the land he hoped would be a model to the world.) His quarrels over the refusal of the Quaker assembly to cooperate with English defense policy led him to appoint as his successor, for the second time, a governor with a reputation for military efficiency. Andrew Hamilton was a Presbyterian who as governor of both East and West Jersey from 1692 to 1697 and again from 1699 to 1702 had successfully persuaded West Jersey's numerous Quakers to permit the sizable non-Quaker population to organize a militia and other defenses. Hamilton argued in vain that in Pennsylvania, too, if "such of the people as are inclined to" would "enlist themselves and form a militia, [then] all pretences of defense may be removed." But even the outbreak of Queen Anne's War (1702–1713) failed to move the Quaker-dominated assembly to more than token efforts. They built some watchtowers on Delaware Bay and voted more "gifts to the British monarch" that allowed them to support defense without compromising their pacifist principles. Realizing that they would bear the brunt of any attack and were also anxious to create a militia and coastline fortifications, the Lower Counties seceded from the Pennsylvania Assembly in 1703 when the Quaker majority refused to defend them. To keep them from being taken over by the Crown, Penn acceded to their demands and created the separate colony of Delaware with its own legislature. Unlike Pennsylvania it was willing to defend itself, and the Penn family would remain its proprietors until the American Revolution.[6]

When Hamilton died in 1704, Penn replaced him with John Evans, whom he ordered to start a militia. The assembly refused; Evans organized a "Governor's Guard" on his own that he claimed consisted of ten companies, whereas the assembly stated it only numbered "some forty bedraggled men." That year, French privateers destroyed Lewes, Delaware. Evans tried to spur the lawmakers on by telling them an entire enemy fleet was upon them; they didn't bite. Instead, Philadelphia Quakers refused to stop their ships for inspection when they entered Delaware Bay, prompting Delaware batteries to fire on them. In 1709, Penn tried Charles Gookin as his governor, with instructions for the colony to provide £4,000 and 150 men for a British-colonial expedition to seize Canada. The assembly responded with a gift for the queen of £500, later augmented by an additional £300. Gookin went insane, and the British expedition that arrived in Boston was too decimated by smallpox to attempt an invasion. In 1711, the assembly again voted £2,000 for yet another massive expedition to Canada, but it was devastated on the rocks beneath Quebec. Only money (and not much, and no troops) was forthcoming from Pennsylvania.[7]

Peace finally came to Pennsylvania and the other American colonies in 1713 when France and Britain were exhausted after more than a decade of fighting over who would become king of Spain. But the first thirty years of colonial Pennsylvania witnessed the transformation of William Penn—in England most of the time and more aware of the pressures of a nation fighting for its survival than of a Pennsylvania assembly fighting to maintain Quaker principles—into a supporter of military defense. Although it managed to avoid sending troops into battle for many years, Pennsylvania's history was already being shaped by the military context of the wider world that it tried to ignore, but in which it had to survive.

3. Wars in Pennsylvania, 1731–1748

William A. Pencak ✦ Christian B. Keller

CRESAP'S WAR, 1731–1738

Pennsylvania escaped military conflict in Queen Anne's War, but troubles on the border with Maryland led to frontier skirmishes known as Cresap's War in the 1730s. (The conflict is also known as the Conojocular War, after the Conojohela Valley, which marked the western border of the disputed area.) Settlement from Maryland and Pennsylvania was converging. In 1731, Governor Samuel Ogle of Maryland granted Thomas Cresap land west of the Susquehanna River beyond Lancaster and commissioned him a justice of the peace. In the ensuing quarrels, Cresap claimed that nearby Pennsylvanians' livestock tore down his fences and ate his corn, and that the farmers threw him in the Susquehanna River when he was operating his ferry service for the benefit of Maryland newcomers. Marylanders in turn shot horses belonging to Pennsylvanians that they claimed trespassed on their lands. Pennsylvania's justices of the peace termed Cresap and his followers "men

of desperate fortunes" and "loose moral and turbulent spirits." The war's only death came in 1734, when land Cresap issued to William Glaspil was deeded by Pennsylvania to John Hendricks. As the Lancaster County sheriff and six deputies attempted to arrest Cresap, ten Marylanders attacked them and mortally wounded Knowles Daunt.[1]

In July 1735, Cresap and a band of about twenty men threatened to shoot a Lancaster justice of the peace, John Wright. The same year, Pennsylvania deputies attempted to arrest two Marylanders who owed them money and were beaten up. Governor Ogle sent surveyors, protected by armed guards, and in September 1736 about three hundred militiamen commanded by Colonel Nathanael Rigby to drive out the Pennsylvanians. In response, Wright (at Wrightsville, which still bears his name) gathered 150 Pennsylvanians to confront them. Over the objections of Cresap, who stormed that the Marylanders were "afraid of their

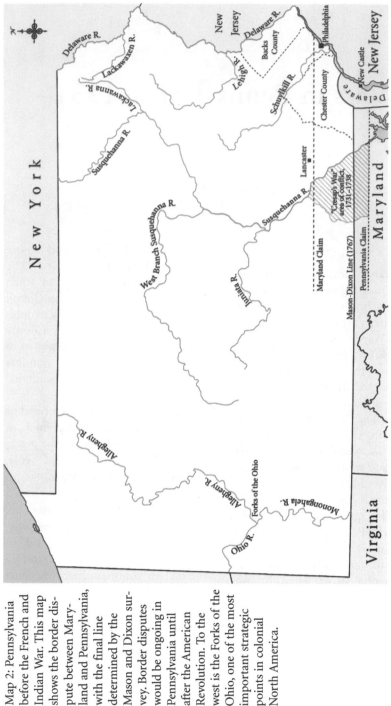

Map 2: Pennsylvania before the French and Indian War. This map shows the border dispute between Maryland and Pennsylvania, with the final line determined by the Mason and Dixon survey. Border disputes would be ongoing in Pennsylvania until after the American Revolution. To the west is the Forks of the Ohio, one of the most important strategic points in colonial North America.

own mothers' calf skins," the two sides negotiated a truce, in part because both colonies courted new immigrants to America, some of whom had learned how to play the two authorities against each other in search of better land deals.

After Rigby's men returned to Maryland in November 1736, Pennsylvania proceeded to arrest "the Maryland Monster," as they referred to Cresap, and sent him in irons to Philadelphia, where he would be secure from rescue attempts. Cresap did not go down without a fight; he was assisted in his struggle by his formidable wife, who fought at his house and rode on horseback by his side. When Cresap was jailed, she built both a house and some flatboats to take possession of Hendricks's land. When Pennsylvanians tried to recapture it, she rode to the nearby Maryland militia camp and returned at their head to drive them off. In an era when every able-bodied person on the frontier counted, many of the area's women took part in the contest. Ogle responded by sending a group of about twenty militiamen, whom Pennsylvanians termed "Irish ruffians," led by Charles Higginbotham, who proceeded to chase out the Pennsylvanians. For the first time, the Pennsylvania Assembly, approved by Lieutenant Governor Patrick Gordon, did what the English had previously requested in wartime: they officially called for volunteers to serve under the auspices of the colony. Higginbotham's attacks sharply diminished.

British intervention brought the struggle to an end. Both the Penns and the Calverts (Lord Baltimore's family) had no desire for a fight. When the government of King George II warned them to settle their differences and ordered Cresap freed, they realized that failure to reach an agreement might jeopardize their lucrative proprietorships. So in 1738 they agreed on a boundary fifteen miles south of Philadelphia to be extended farther westward, although it was not finalized until 1750, after both sides had appealed to British courts. The land had been disputed since William Penn had arrived and settled Philadelphia in what was technically part of the original land grant to Maryland of 1629. Although it was not marked out until 1763, when Charles Mason and Jeremiah Dixon undertook a four-year expedition that erected 244 milestones along what is known as the Mason-Dixon Line, Pennsylvania's southeastern border was finally fixed.

THE WAR OF JENKINS' EAR, KING GEORGE'S WAR, AND FRANKLIN'S ASSOCIATION, 1739–1748

No sooner had the troubles with Maryland ended than the British colonies were again at war. The War of Jenkins' Ear, begun with Spain in 1739 over an ear in a bottle that the British Parliament was told a Spanish official had hacked off an English captain, became King George's War in 1744 when France joined the struggle. Pennsylvania's Quaker merchants entered the fray when they allowed Governor George Thomas to authorize their ships (manned by non-

"The Prospect of Philadelphia from Wickacove, exactly delineated by G. Wood," 1735. Note the battery of cannon guarding the waterfront to the left of center near the flag.

Quakers) to serve as privateers that attacked Spanish and later French shipping. But the assembly refused to vote money for defense or authorize militia companies, adding to their pacifist principles the argument that the Penn family, who were the largest landowners in the British Empire if not the world, would have to allow their lands to be taxed as well.[2]

When the assembly refused to vote money, beginning in 1740 Governor Thomas permitted servants to enlist in military expeditions, the first being taken by the British navy to the West Indies. The assembly claimed servants were their masters' property and that they were being unlawfully taken away. It then voted £1,600 to compensate masters for the losses of 188 servants in Philadelphia County, 58 in Chester, and 19 in Bucks. The servant population of Philadelphia decreased from over 900 to under 400 during the 1740s, both through enlistments and the fact that warfare prevented importation of more servants.[3]

Pennsylvania changed its tune after the French entered the war. On his own authority, in December 1744, Governor Thomas appointed William Moore of Chester County colonel of a Pennsylvania regiment and Thomas Edwards and Reece Morgan captain and lieutenant of a company in Lancaster County. The Pennsylvania Assembly voted £4,000 in 1745 and £5,000 1746 for supplies, wheat, and "other grain" to assist intercolonial expeditions projected to attack French Canada. The language the Quaker majority used to avoid voting military supplies fooled no one: "Other grain means gunpowder," Thomas remarked as he accepted the funds. Benjamin Franklin added humorously that if all else failed, the assembly could vote to purchase a fire

engine, then nominate him as a committee of one to purchase it and "buy
a great gun, which is certainly a fire
engine."[4]

In February 1746, the assembly
authorized and funded four companies (nearly four hundred men) of
volunteers and dispatched them to
Albany in anticipation of a campaign
that year. They remained in service
until November 19, 1747, when they
were finally discharged after more
than a year and a half of waiting in
vain. The names, occupations, birthplaces, and ages of the men who
enlisted confirm the conclusions of
early American military historians
that poor young men, many of whom
were recent immigrants to the Middle
Colonies, constituted the bulk of the
recruits. A company raised in
Lancaster County numbered fifty-
nine laborers (probably farmworkers
although some possibly worked in
town) with tailors (7), bricklayers (5),
shoemakers (4), smiths (4), coopers
(3), weavers (2), wheelwrights (2),
millers (2), bakers (2), and a barber,
joiner, and sawyer also being represented. Nineteen of the men were
born in Germany, eleven in Ireland
(Scots-Irish), eight in England, and
only three in Pennsylvania and one in
Maryland. Most of the recruits were
young: ten under age twenty, fifty-five
in their twenties, nineteen, ages thirty
to thirty-nine, and eight in their for-
ties, the oldest man being forty-six.[5]

Men raised in the longer-settled
eastern counties reflected more economic differentiation. The regiment
raised in Philadelphia by William
Trent, who later became an important

western trader, consisted of fifty-five
laborers but also mariners (one each
from Denmark, Barbados, Ireland,
and England), tailors (5), cordwainers
(that is, shoemakers, 5), smiths (4),
sawyers (3), and weavers (3), along
with a gardener, clothier, trader, sad-
dler, baker, joiner, husbandman,
cooper, collier, house carpenter, carpenter, and two wool combers. Forty-
one of the enlistees were (mostly
Scots-Irish) born in Ireland, suggesting that they had just arrived and
were either employed as servants or
had not yet immigrated to the frontier. Twenty-three were English, two
Scots, only one German (demonstrat-
ing Germans had ceased to arrive in
large numbers due to the war in
Europe and earlier arrivals had
moved out to the western counties),
and one from St. Christopher.
Virginia and Maryland each furnished a recruit, and New Jersey two.
Two were nineteen, fifty-six in their
twenties, twenty-seven in their thirties, and six over forty, the oldest
being forty-three. Ten men deserted
and three died during their year and a
half in service.

Similar patterns emerge in the regiment Delaware raised. Sixty-six
laborers were joined by six coopers,
four tanners, four cordwainers, two
weavers, and a wigmaker, tinner,
planter, stocking weaver, blacksmith,
whitesmith (who worked in pewter
and tin), mariner (from South
Carolina), and a surgeon. Along with
forty-eight Irish (that is, Scot-Irish)
immigrants, England (13), Scotland
(40), Wales (1), and other colonies
were the birthplaces of these men.

Fifteen came from Delaware, four from New Jersey, one from Long Island, two from Maryland, two from New England, and one from Pennsylvania. Ten men were under twenty, fifty-four were in their twenties, twenty-nine in their thirties, and two over forty, the oldest being forty-five.

The fourth regiment, raised primarily in Bucks County, included sixty-five laborers, nine weavers, three blacksmiths, two tailors, two saddlers, and a barber, locksmith, glove maker, cooper, wheelwright, butcher, bricklayer, and bottle maker. Fifty-nine were born in Ireland, twenty-four in Germany, four in England, two in New Jersey, and one each in Scotland, Maryland, and Sweden. Only one was a native Pennsylvanian. Eleven had no occupation or birthplace listed. Twelve were under twenty, seventy-three were in their twenties, nine in their thirties, and five over forty, the oldest being forty-three.

Unlike these poor volunteers who had no property to abandon when they left the province for a lengthy period, Pennsylvania attracted a much broader cross section of the population when defenders were needed close to home. In the summer of 1747, French and Spanish privateers—"pirates," the Pennsylvanians called them—began to attack ships and settlements on the Delaware River. With no governor currently in the province, the Pennsylvania Provincial Council implored the assembly that "the boldness of our enemies and the knowledge they have gained of our bay and river"—by visiting Philadelphia under flags of truce to trade illegally and exchange prisoners—"gives us great reason to apprehend an attack on this city unless some provision be speedily made to discourage them." The assembly, however, unlike the council, was dominated by pacifist Quakers. They commented that "it will be difficult, if not impossible, to prevent such accidents; the length of the bay and river and the scatteringness of the settlements below . . . render them liable to depradations."[6]

At this point, Benjamin Franklin entered the controversy. At the time, he was the province's best-known printer and creator of Philadelphia voluntary associations such as a fire company, street paving society, and library company to aid in civic improvement. He published a pamphlet, *Plain Truth*, arguing that the defenseless state of the province would suggest to the enemy that the people were all Quakers and invite further plundering. "Who can, without utmost horror, conceive the miseries . . . when your persons, fortunes, wives, and daughters, shall be subject to the wanton and unbridled rage, rapine, and lust of *Negroes*, *mulattoes*, and others, the vilest and most abandoned of mankind." Franklin was here referring to the mixed-race crews of privateers raised in the Caribbean.

Franklin's solution was the voluntary association that had proven so successful in the past. He appealed primarily to "the middling people, the traders, shopkeepers, and farmers of this province" to fill his ranks. Indeed,

Benjamin Franklin (1706–1790) painted by Robert Feke in 1746 when Franklin was forty years old. This is the earliest portrait of Franklin.

over half of Philadelphia's recruits belonged to one of the five fire companies, two libraries, or sixteen other societies that had flourished in the city. Pennsylvania, Franklin claimed, with some exaggeration, had "60,000 men acquainted with firearms, many of them hunters and marksmen hardy and bold." Within a week, a thousand Philadelphians, or at least half the adult men in the city, had volunteered. To manage this newly organized militia group, which Franklin termed the Association, on January 12, 1748, the old sage announced he was retiring from the printing business. His career in politics that would culminate in the independence of the United States began with his efforts to persuade Pennsylvanians to defend themselves.

United in companies of fifty to a hundred men, Pennsylvania raised 124 companies or somewhere between five thousand and ten thousand men by the end of 1748: 20 companies from Philadelphia (city and county), 16 from Chester, 19 from Bucks, 26 from Kent and New Castle in Delaware, and 32 from Lancaster, which at the time encompassed all of Pennsylvania beyond Philadelphia, Bucks, and Chester counties. Consisting largely of Germans with few Quakers and pacifists, Lancaster's inhabitants were eager to join: in January 1746, they had petitioned the Pennsylvania Assembly, "setting forth their want of arms and ammunition." Franklin also formed an artillery company and raised the money through a lottery and donations from local merchants. With added cannons from the governors of New York and Massachusetts, two batteries were in place to defend the city by April 1748.

Franklin's concentration on recruiting the middle class was more than an appeal to the most numerous and likely volunteers. He had to defend this extra-governmental action from both of Pennsylvania's political groups—the proprietary and the Quaker factions. Proprietor Thomas Penn complained that "this association is founded on a contempt of government, and cannot lead to anything but anarchy and confusion." He thought it "a military Commonwealth," "little short of treason," and feared that "when they know they may act in a military manner . . . independent of this government . . . why should they not act against it." And while some Quakers contended it was acceptable for others to defend them, others agreed with an anonymous Quaker who argued: "for upwards of sixty years," Pennsylvania "had been preserved from the barbarous and cruel usage of the natives of this land" thanks to "the peculiar blessings of Providence" that rewarded the colony for its pacifism. The Philadelphia Quaker Meeting threatened to disown (although ultimately it did not) the sixty-three Quakers who were willing to permit others to defend them!

Presbyterian clergyman William Tennent and Anglican William Currie—representatives of the two other major English-speaking denominations in Pennsylvania—rebutted the Quakers. In Currie's words, a government "that under any pretext whatsoever, shall absolutely refuse to make any provision for the defense of the [people's] lives and fortunes, when in the most imminent danger, must certainly be out of their way of duty." He also disputed with the Quakers who maintained that Christians had to follow the example of a New Testament Christ who did not use violence. Currie insisted that because Christ did not specifically prohibit war, and it was allowed in the Old Testament, people could engage in defensive struggles. He also blessed a soldier and instructed people to "render unto Caesar those things which are Caesar's." Franklin, for his part, did not overlook the irony that in August 1747, the Pennsylvania Assembly had spent £130 to hire privateers from Massachusetts and Connecticut to defend Delaware Bay.

The Association seemed to be moot when King George's War ended in August 1748. But it had transformed Franklin from the force behind uncontroversial public projects into "a sort of tribune of the people" who had to be "treated with regard," in the words of Thomas Penn. And no one believed the peace would be permanent. As the Pennsylvania frontier continued to expand, so did its encounters not only with Native Americans but also with the French.

4. Pennsylvania in the French and Indian Wars, 1748–1766

William A. Pencak ✦ Christian B. Keller

THE STRUGGLE FOR THE OHIO VALLEY, 1748–1754

The French and Indian War, known in Europe as the Seven Years War, pitted England and its colonies and allies against France and its colonies and allies around the world. Between 1754 and 1763 the two greatest powers squared off in North America in a bid for control of the continent. At stake was nothing less than the future government and culture of America. The name of the war is important: previous colonial wars, King William's (1689–1697), Queen Anne's (1702–1713), and King George's War (1744–1748) were named after monarchs; these wars began in Europe over causes unrelated to the British colonies in North America. British colonists were told to begin fighting their French and Spanish counterparts when war broke out and told to lay down their weapons when Europeans decided to make peace. The name "French and Indian War" implies that the primary cause for this war happened in America itself.

But it was more than a war involving the British with the French and Indians. Historian Lawrence Henry Gipson, who covered its events in a fifteen-volume *History of the British Empire Before the American Revolution* that took him over forty years (1928–1970) to write, believed "The Great War for Empire" was a better term. What began as a frontier skirmish in what is now western Pennsylvania turned into a world war in which both Britain and France, for the first time, made a colonial incident a cause for a major war that was ultimately fought on every inhabited continent (except the unsettled Australia) and drew in all of Europe's leading powers. Historian Fred Anderson, in his superb history published in 2006, prefers to call the conflict *The War That Made America*. The issues of British taxation and regulation of colonial commerce, the frontier, and government that led to the American Revolution arose because of problems stemming from the war.

This world-shattering and world-shaping event could not have had

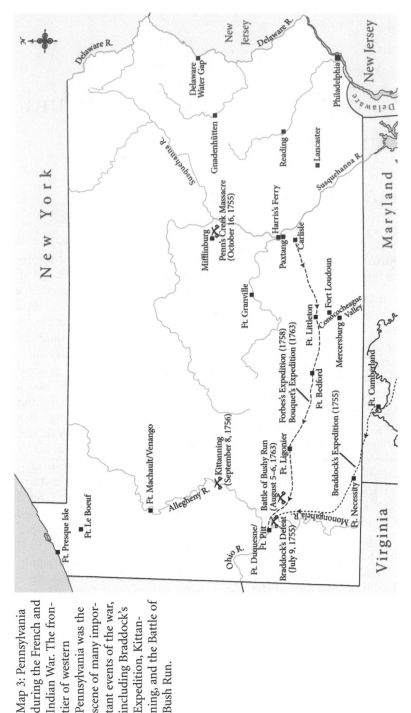

Map 3: Pennsylvania during the French and Indian War. The frontier of western Pennsylvania was the scene of many important events of the war, including Braddock's Expedition, Kittanning, and the Battle of Bush Run.

more humble origins. By the late 1740s, the rapidly expanding populations of Virginia and Pennsylvania, preceded by land speculators and Indian traders, eagerly eyed the lands of the eastern Ohio River valley. So did French fur traders and the government of what was alternately called Quebec, New France, or Canada. This land is now in western Pennsylvania and (later) Ohio, but it only became so in 1781 when the United States Congress ruled in favor of Pennsylvania's claims over Virginia's.

Pennsylvania-based, Irish-born fur trader George Croghan, who learned Indian languages and lived comfortably among them, was the first colonial to establish friendly relations with the Ohio Valley Indians. In 1747, he persuaded the Wyandots and Senecas to murder five French fur traders who were his competition. He next encouraged Pennsylvania to secure the Indians' loyalty through presents of ammunition, as his letter (original spelling retained) suggests: "The Ingans att this side of Lake Eary is Makeing warr very Briskly Against the French, Butt is very impatiant To hear from there Brothers, ye English, Expecting a Present of power & Lead, which if they Don't gett, I am of Opinion, By the Best Accounts I can gett, That they will Turn to the French, which will be very willing to make up with them again."[1]

Two years later, the French countered by sending an expedition of about three hundred French, French Canadians, and Indians under the command of Pierre-Joseph Céloron

de Blainville that descended from Lake Erie, to what is now present-day Pittsburgh, and down the Ohio River. Céloron informed the Indians that the land belonged to the French, evicted English traders, and complained to Pennsylvania's governor that his people were trespassing. Céloron planted at least six lead plates that were inscribed (in French) as "monuments" to the "possession we have taken of the said river Ohio and of all those which empty into it, and of all the lands on both sides as far as the sources of the said rivers." The area's Indians, who were pro-British at the time, were not happy to know their lands belonged to the king of France. They dug up the plates and sent one to Virginia.[2]

In 1749, the Virginians entered the fray. None other than Thomas Cresap, the Maryland settler ejected from Lancaster County during "Cresap's War," and Hugh Parker, agents for Virginia's Ohio Company that claimed the region, toured it with guide Christopher Gist.[3] Favorably received by the Indians, in 1752 they negotiated a treaty at Logstown, today a suburb of Pittsburgh. The British guaranteed the Indians' independence; in return, they promised not to disturb British settlements and gave the Virginians permission to build a fort at the Forks of the Ohio, which they hoped would protect them from the French.[4]

The first forts, however, were built by the French. Beginning in May 1753, they constructed Fort Presque Isle (present-day Erie, Pennsylvania), Fort Le Boeuf (Waterford), and Fort

Machault (Franklin).[5] As Governor Robert Hunter Morris of Pennsylvania would later write: "The conduct of the assemblies on this continent almost without exception has been so very absurd that they have suffered the French to take quiet possession of the most advantageous places, not only to answer the purposes of a very extensive Indian trade, but to enable them to protect their settlements and annoy ours." The Indians had asked for British assistance but received none.[6]

The Indians kept trying, and turned from pacifist Pennsylvania to meet with Virginia's governor Robert Dinwiddie at Winchester to ask for help in ejecting the French. His first measure was to send twenty-one-year-old George Washington, an experienced frontier surveyor and eager volunteer, to confront the French commander and demand he evacuate land supposedly belonging to Virginia. Washington was accompanied only by Christopher Gist as a guide. The French received him courteously but, unsurprisingly, refused to leave, telling him that Dinwiddie should have addressed his letter to the French governor-general who had the authority to decide such matters.[7]

Virginia soon responded. On January 26, 1754, Dinwiddie ordered the newly appointed captain William Trent to raise a hundred men. He was to build a fort at the Forks of the Ohio and, with the help of the Indians, to "dislodge and drive away, and in case of refusal or resistance, to kill and destroy, or take prisoners, all or every person and persons whatsoever, not

subjects of the King of Britain, who now are, or shall hereafter come to settle, and take possession of any lands on the said River Ohio." George Washington, himself a newly minted major, was to raise more troops and follow as soon as possible. On February 17, the first log of the fort was laid by Tanacharison, also known as the Half King, the Iroquois leader who was chief negotiator at the Treaty of Logstown, and who threatened to make war against anyone who tried to seize the new structure.[8]

He did not have long to wait. Although usually known as Trent's Fort, it did not even last long enough to be officially named. On April 17, about six hundred French soldiers arrived, forcing the forty-one Virginians present to surrender. They were treated courteously and released. The French even offered to buy their tools and allowed them to keep them when they refused. The French immediately tore down the stakes the British had erected and began to build a much larger edifice named after the governor-general of Canada, Fort Duquesne.[9]

Aware that Washington was approaching, the French commander Claude-Pierre Pécaudy de Contrecoeur sent out a small party of thirty-five men under Joseph Coulon de Villiers de Jumonville. Whether they were supposed to order Washington to leave or spy on his activities remains uncertain. What is certain is that the Half King insisted Washington attack Jumonville. He launched a surprise attack on the morning of May 27, quickly killing

A modern reconstruction of Fort Necessity at the Fort Necessity National Battlefield, Fayette County, Pennsylvania. Here, after a short battle, George Washington surrendered British colonial troops to the French on July 3, 1754. The Battle of Fort Necessity, or Great Meadows, was one of the first engagements in what would become the French and Indian War.

ten or twelve Frenchmen and capturing the rest. Jumonville was suddenly tomahawked to death by the Half King after he had surrendered and was negotiating with Washington. The first blood of the French and Indian War was shed.[10]

Washington realized his position was perilous, which is reflected in the name he gave the fort he rapidly constructed: Fort Necessity. A replica stands on its original location in present-day Fayette County. By June he commanded about three hundred militiamen and one hundred British regulars, who spent much of their time constructing a wilderness road to facilitate settlement. But their days were numbered. On July 3, the main French force from Fort Duquesne appeared; outnumbered by more than two to one, Washington surrendered. He was forced to take responsibility for Jumonville's "assassination" in the surrender terms, which he claimed he could not understand as

they were written in French.[11] The French allowed Washington and his troops to return to Virginia with the full honors of war. Although neither he nor anyone else knew it yet, the twenty-two-year-old George Washington had started a world war.

However, he might not have done so except for events taking place simultaneously at Albany, New York. The Board of Trade was headed by the Earl of Halifax, who had the approval of the Duke of Newcastle, the prime minister, to confront the French aggressively and oust them from North America.[12] Halifax had written to the governor of New York in September 1753, telling him to call a meeting of colonial representatives for the purpose of "burying the hatchet and renewing the Covenant Chain," or alliance between the Iroquois and the British colonies. The conference convened on June 14, 1754, and is most famous for the Albany Plan of Union, proposed by

Benjamin Franklin and Thomas Hutchinson of Massachusetts, that the delegates approved. An elected intercolonial parliament would decide on defense matters of mutual concern, including taxes, and a governor-general appointed by the Crown could veto or initiate legislation. In connection with the plan, the first American political cartoon— Franklin's snake warning the provinces to "Join, or Die" appeared. But neither the individual colonies nor Britain wanted to surrender their authority to such a body. It was the plan itself that died.[13]

The Albany Congress's main achievement, if it can be called that, was a final land purchase that provoked the all-out Indian war that began the following year. The required money came in a roundabout way. Pennsylvania's governor James Hamilton had asked the Pennsylvania Assembly for £20,000 for "the King's use"—that is, to prepare for war. However, the governor would not approve the legislature's bill that taxed the vast estates of the proprietors, the Penn family, and only voted £500 for presents to the Indians. That small sum of money enabled Pennsylvania to purchase much of the central part of the state from the Iroquois, although Delaware, Shawnee, and other peoples were in fact the land's inhabitants. While at the conference, on July 4, the day after Washington surrendered, Pennsylvania's leading Indian interpreter, Conrad Weiser, negotiated a treaty obtaining a huge tract of land. Pennsylvania's primary concern was to deprive the Susquehannah Company, recently formed in Connecticut, from claiming the region. The Iroquois were paid £400, and another £400 when the land was settled, for territory that was occupied by other Indians who had no desire to move.[14]

The Iroquois were continuing a pattern here they had established in the late 1730s. They exercised sovereignty over the Indians who inhabited much of Pennsylvania and forced their southern neighbors to make huge grants of land to the Quaker province. First came the infamous Walking Purchase of 1737. The Penn family produced a forged treaty from the 1680s granting territory from the forks of the Delaware (Easton) to Pennsylvania as far as a man could walk in a day. They then positioned swift runners at intervals to claim a large piece of northeastern Pennsylvania.[15] As Iroquois leader Canasatego had told a group of Delaware in 1742 who refused to vacate this land, "We conquered you; we made you women; we charge you to remove instantly." Although some historians have argued that traditionally the Iroquois valued women and intended merely that the Delaware were to be guardians of the Iroquois homeland, Canasatego's statement was clearly insulting and reflected the long-standing interaction of the colonies and the Iroquois, who had begun to adopt colonial agricultural techniques, weapons, clothing, and cultural practices.[16] Even larger purchases followed in 1744 and 1748.[17] The Iroquois sent representatives such as Shikellamy (who lived in what is present-day Sunbury) and Tanacharison (the Half King, who lived near Logstown, north of modern Pittsburgh in western Pennsylvania) to make sure these weaker tribes did their bidding.

Christian Frederick Post, a leading Pennsylvania Indian negotiator, summed up the Iroquois policy as follows: "They settle these new allies on the frontiers of the white people, and give them this as their instruction. 'Be watchful that no body of the white people may come to settle near you. You must appear to them as frightful men, and if notwithstanding they come too near give them a push. We will secure and defend you against them.'"[18]

Instead of purchasing peace, Pennsylvania's acquisition at Albany ensured that resentment was building up in their closest Indian neighbors. When the Iroquois failed to meet their promises "to secure and defend" them against Pennsylvania intruders, those they had forced to become their "new allies" would take matters into their own hands.

BRADDOCK'S EXPEDITION, 1755

The resentment of Pennsylvania's dispossessed Indians exploded following the disastrous expedition of General Edward Braddock. Early in 1755, the British government sent the sixty-year-old officer and two regiments, approximately 1,400 men, to coordinate a three-pronged offensive against the French. Braddock had served in the 1740s in Europe, but was chiefly valued for the administrative skills he

had demonstrated as commander of the fortress of Gibraltar. In a meeting held in Alexandria, Virginia, on April 14, 1755, with colonial governors and other notables, including Benjamin Franklin, he outlined his plans. Lieutenant Colonel Robert Monckton would conquer Fort Beauséjour, recently built by the French on the isthmus connecting Nova Scotia and what is now New Brunswick, that threatened the British port of Halifax; a second expedition under Sir William Johnson would seize Crown Point, the French fort that menaced the Hudson Valley. Braddock himself would lead his men plus about five hundred Virginia militiamen commanded by the newly promoted colonel George Washington to capture Fort Duquesne, and then march north to take Fort Niagara, which still exists as a historic site just north of Niagara Falls. All three forces would then converge on the Canadian capital of Quebec.[19]

Braddock did not think his own part of the campaign would be much trouble. As he told Benjamin Franklin, "after taking Fort Duquesne I am to proceed to Niagara; and, having taken that, to Frontenac, if the season will allow time; and I suppose it will, for Duquesne can hardly detain me above three or four days; and then I see nothing that can obstruct my march to Niagara."[20]

But Braddock encountered troubles from the start. Virginia voted £20,000 for the expedition, but failed to come through with wagons, wagon drivers, food, and other supplies, prompting Braddock to explode to

Franklin that these colonies "promised everything but delivered nothing." The Pennsylvania Assembly also voted £20,000, but Governor Robert Hunter Morris vetoed it on the proprietor's orders since issuing paper money was part of the appropriation. Earlier, he had described the province he had recently arrived to govern: "there was never a set of people in the world so stupidly infatuated, or so blind to their country's interest . . . [they] are rich, flourishing, and numerous, and not only decline taking up arms, but even refuse to supply the articles or offer the assistance expected from them."[21]

A concerned Benjamin Franklin swung into action with such effect that Braddock praised him for having "promised nothing but delivered everything." The general promised Franklin £800 sterling, which Franklin agreed to advance on his own credit, to obtain provisions, and when that proved insufficient, Franklin advanced another £200. Franklin obtained 150 wagons of provisions and men to transport them from Pennsylvania to the backcountry. Fortunately, Braddock signed an order that Franklin be reimbursed the full sum before his later demise, or Franklin would have been personally liable for the entire amount. Finally, in June 1755, after Braddock had been on the march for over two months, Governor Morris signed a bill authorizing £15,000 for the expedition, which left unanswered the assembly's demand that the Penn family lands be taxed.[22]

During the spring, Franklin stayed with Braddock "for several days,

Major General Edward Braddock (1695–1755), engraving after a lost portrait by an unknown artist.

dined with him daily, and had full opportunity of removing all his prejudices" against the assembly. However, Franklin was far less successful in dispelling Braddock's distrust of the Indians who assisted both him and the French.

This general was, I think, a brave man, and might probably have made a figure as a good officer in some European war. But he had too much self-confidence, too high an opinion of the validity of regular troops, and too mean a one of both Americans and Indians. George Croghan, our Indian interpreter, join'd him on his march with one hundred of those people, who might have been of great use to his army as guides, scouts, etc., if he had treated them kindly; but he slighted and neglected them, and they gradually left him.[23]

One oft-repeated story that should be doubted is the description given by Shingas, one of the Delaware Indian leaders, regarding why the Indians deserted Braddock. When they asked Braddock what would happen to the land once the French were driven out, Braddock replied that "no savage should inherit the land." They responded "that if they might not have liberty to live on the land they would not fight for it, to which General Braddock replied that he did not need their help and had no doubt of driving the French and their Indians away."[24] But why would Braddock have invited the Indians to discuss their participation if he would treat them so rudely? It is more probable that the Indians defected because the British and colonial officers believed the Indians could be ordered about like their own troops. The Half King, who was one of only eight Indians who ultimately accompanied the expedition as a scout, complained of a colonel who "was a good-natured man, but had no experience; he took upon him to command the Indians as his slaves, and would have them every day upon the scout, and to attack the enemy by themselves, but would by no means take advice from the Indians." This colonel was none other than George Washington, who had ample experience with the Indians before the war.[25]

Braddock had just as little use for the colonial troops. Franklin warned Braddock:

"The only danger I apprehend of obstruction to your march is from ambuscades of Indians, who, by constant practice, are dexterous in laying and executing them; and the slender line, near four miles long, which your army must make, may expose it to be attack'd by surprise in its flanks, and to be cut like a thread into several pieces, which, from their distance, can not come up in time to support each other."

He smil'd at my ignorance and reply'd, "These savages may, indeed, be a formidable enemy to your raw American militia, but upon the king's regular and disciplin'd troops, sir, it is impossible they should make any impression."[26]

Braddock's reputation as a disciplinarian did not endear him to the colonials, either. He sentenced one wagon driver, nineteen-year-old Daniel Morgan of Virginia, to 500 lashes (a number deemed lethal), for striking a British officer who had previously hit Morgan with the flat of his sword. The hearty Morgan survived, and boasted to his old age that they had miscounted the strokes and he only received 499. British cruelty would come back to haunt them: Morgan commanded the American army that annihilated Banastre "the Butcher" Tarleton's army at the Battle of Cowpens in 1781 during the American Revolution. Twenty-one-year-old Daniel Boone, another wagon driver who would confront the British in Kentucky twenty years later, had an uneventful time until he was forced to escape with his team during the battle itself.[27]

Braddock's army followed the Potomac River from Alexandria, Virginia, and on March 29 set out from Cumberland, Maryland, overland to Fort Duquesne. The column, four miles long, built a road as it went, as Braddock planned to use it to supply the fort once it was taken.

Horses died from want of forage and men were near starvation for want of food as they approached the Forks of the Ohio at about two miles per day. When they were about ten miles from the fort, on the morning of July 9, either on his own initiative or at the command of his superior Contre-couer, Captain Daniel Beaujeu led about two hundred French and six hundred Indians out of the fort to ambush the column.[28]

Before the British had a chance to deploy, Beaujeu's men encountered Braddock's advance guard of three hundred men commanded by Colonel Thomas Gage, who twenty years later, after being promoted to general, would command the British army in Boston that began the American Revolution. In charge of scouting the endless hills and valleys that compose much of western Pennsylvania, Gage had failed to send out pickets far enough to spot the enemy. The Indians who attacked quickly took cover; the British, as they were trained to do, formed a square. Soldiers would consecutively lie, kneel, and stand, with each rank firing smoothbore muskets in unison as the others reloaded in lockstep. The musket's effective range was no more than fifty yards, and it was very inaccurate, only effective if fired in volleys. Squares formed by men with muskets were very useful on open battlefields when facing a cavalry or infantry charge, but against enemies hidden behind rocks and trees, they were worse than useless. If the British had been less disciplined, they could have at least taken cover themselves.

The climax of the Battle of the Monongahela was the shooting of General Braddock. The fact that the commanding officer of such a large and formidable force was targeted and killed was one of the most dramatic events of colonial American history.

Some Americans did, in fact, disperse and fight the enemy on his own terms; they thereby also became targets of the British volleys.

As Gage's men were fighting, a wagon train bringing up supplies ran into them, creating more confusion. Braddock then arrived with the main force. He was almost immediately mortally wounded as were sixty-two of eighty-six officers, who could easily be picked off by rifles and arrows, which were far more accurate than muskets. The increasing absence of direction from their superiors added to the troops' confusion, and as the main army retreated, it ran into and became mixed up with Braddock's rear guard, which was just coming up. When the day was over, an astonishing 900 of the 1,400 troops who were engaged were killed or wounded as opposed to under thirty French and Indians; one of their casualties, who fell in the first few minutes of battle, was Captain Beaujeu. About a dozen soldiers were captured by the Indians and tortured to death. Under Washington's nominal command, the troops retreated on the road they had constructed. Braddock died four days later near Fort Necessity; he was buried in an unmarked grave to prevent hostile Indians from desecrating the body. In 1804, workers found a body with officer's buttons that has been presumed to be Braddock's. Or so it was told by the workers to Charles Willson Peale, who placed the remains in his Philadelphia Museum, some ultimately making their way to P. T. Barnum's Museum, and one vertebra going to the Walter Reed Army Hospital in Washington, D.C. What could be salvaged was reinterred in 1913 and the present monument erected.[29]

THE YEAR OF DISASTER: THE AFTERMATH OF BRADDOCK'S DEFEAT, 1755–1756

Braddock's defeat signaled the Indians of western Pennsylvania that the time was ripe to recover the lands that the Iroquois had forced them to surrender—especially with the purchase of 1754 fresh in their minds. The French at Fort Duquesne encouraged them and supplied them with weapons. At the moment no British or colonial troops guarded the thousands of mostly German and Scots-Irish migrants who had settled in small hamlets and on individual farmsteads in the valleys of the Susquehanna and Juniata rivers and their numerous tributaries.

Highly mobile Indian war parties struck out from the Delaware Water Gap in the northeast to the Juniata Valley on the scattered settlements Pennsylvanians had built. The first attack, known as the Penn's Creek Massacre, occurred on October 16, 1755, about two miles southeast of the present town of Mifflinburg.[30] Fourteen settlers, including leader Jacob Leroy, were killed and another eleven captured. At least six men from Paxton Township were killed later that month, as they were returning home from that area. On November 1, forty-seven people were killed at Great Cove in what is now Fulton County. The Indians ranged far to the east: twenty miles north of Reading, fifty people were killed in Bethel Township.[31] On November 24, eleven Moravian missionaries and Indian converts were killed at Gnadenhütten (Huts of Grace) at present-day Lehighton.[32]

By mid-1756, about three thousand inhabitants had been killed, captured, or displaced. The expanding Pennsylvania frontier was rolled back over a hundred miles. The towns were crowded with refugees. Bethlehem alone added more than two hundred to its population of less than six hundred in eight days in November 1755. Alarms rang out almost daily in

Lancaster and Carlisle for men to rush to defend the town. Indians even raided into northern New Jersey, making it hazardous to cross the Delaware River.[33]

Meanwhile, Governor Morris and the Pennsylvania Assembly blamed each other for failing to defend the frontier. The assembly agreed to raise £55,000 but only if the proprietor paid taxes, which Morris was forbidden to approve. Between 500 and 1,000 frustrated Pennsylvania Germans led by Conrad Weiser then marched on the capital of Philadelphia and demanded some sort of provincial defense. In response, on November 25, the assembly approved the first bona fide militia act in the province's history. Unlike the militias of other colonies, which required men between the ages of sixteen and sixty to muster for regular training, the Quaker-dominated assembly simply put its stamp of approval on those people who wished to muster. Quakers and other pacifists were exempt not only from service but from paying taxes for defense. Provincial secretary Richard Peters commented: "Perhaps there was never such a farce acted as . . . this Militia Law, and from first to last was never seen a greater scene of hypocrisy and dissimulation."[34] But as the Quakers were now very much a minority in the province, the law opened the way for the many who wished to fight the Indians to receive support from the government.

Two days later, the assembly finally voted to raise the £55,000 after word arrived that the proprietor had com-promised by offering a "free gift" of £5,000 that was not to be considered a precedent for taxation. The governor and legislature then authorized building a string of forts to protect the province and provided for recruiting the Pennsylvania Provincial Regiment, a full-time military force. About a week later, the Germans returned, this time depositing stinking, dead bodies on the State House steps to drive home the need for immediate action. Shortly thereafter, the assembly and governor agreed to place a bounty of £150 on every Indian captive, and £130 for the scalp of any Indian male and £50 for any female who appeared to be at least fifteen years old. The prospect of between one and three years' wages for taking a scalp was certainly a considerable incentive for volunteers.[35]

Pennsylvanians ultimately built about forty forts about twenty miles apart, with smaller blockhouses every five miles, on the frontier in an arc roughly from Easton on the Delaware River to Mercersburg on the southwest border with Maryland. A commission including Benjamin Franklin, accompanied by his son William, left Philadelphia on December 18, 1755, and spent about fifty days beginning work on the forts and recruiting men to guard them. Seventeen bore the names of the private individuals who constructed them—John Harris, who operated the ferry across the Susquehanna River at the site of present-day Harrisburg, turned his house into a fort where local inhabitants could take refuge. John Armstrong's west of

Carlisle, Dietz's, Doll's, and Dupui's were among other examples of smaller forts.

Most of these forts were erected on stilts, with only one entrance accessed by a ladder that could be pulled up. Small holes through which guns could be fired were the only other openings. The forts were constructed in meadows, or else nearby woods were cleared so Indians could not approach too closely. People only came to these forts when reports of Indian raids in the area required them to gather for their safety. Larger forts, named after colonial or British notables—Fort Franklin, Fort Halifax, Fort Shirley—were more substantial palisades built by the province and garrisoned. One of these, Fort Granville near present-day Lewistown, was attacked by a superior French and Indian force on August 3, 1756, when all but twenty-four of its men were out protecting settlers in the Juniata Valley; its commander, Edward Armstrong, was killed. The sergeant who surrendered the fort was tortured to death.[36]

The Fort Granville attack prompted Governor Morris to plan a secret expedition to Kittanning, the headquarters of the Delaware Indians who had carried out many of the raids. He chose militia lieutenant colonel John Armstrong, Edward's brother, to lead it.

RECOVERY: FROM KITTANNING TO THE FORBES EXPEDITION, 1756–1759

About three hundred men joined Armstrong at Fort Shirley, now Shirleysburg, in Huntington County. They left on August 30, and managed to reach Kittanning without being detected. On September 8, they launched a surprise attack. When the Delaware took cover in their cabins, inflicting heavy casualties, including wounding Armstrong, he ordered his men to set the compound on fire. This blew up a huge store of gunpowder that the French, located at Fort Duquesne forty miles to the south, had just delivered. As the Delaware fled the burning cabins, they were immediately shot down. Two versions exist of the death of Tewea (or Chief Jacobs, as the Pennsylvanians referred to the Delaware leader): the first is that he and his wife were slain as they attempted to escape through a cornfield; the second, reported by the Anglican priest Thomas Barton of Lancaster, is that he rushed out of his burning cabin, tomahawk in hand, and exclaimed that "he was born a soldier and would not die a slave."[37]

Armstrong was able to rescue fifteen captives (although four were lost on the route back) and estimated he killed about thirty or forty Indians, but the price was high. A roving party of Delaware attacked the small detachment he had left to guard his camp, killing six of its twelve men. The Delaware also harassed them on their return to Fort Lyttleton (now a town in Fulton County), and Armstrong reported his casualties as seventeen dead and thirteen wounded. However, Thomas Barton understood why Armstrong was received as a hero and a medal for bravery—the first ever struck in the colonies—was issued in his honor when he arrived in Philadelphia to collect the £600 bounty on Captain Jacobs's head: "though killing a few Indians and burning their huts at the Kittanning is an action not very considerable in itself, yet it is the best that has yet appeared for this province."[38]

Despite Armstrong's actions, Barton also predicted "that the approaching spring will again make us tremble." He was right: according to the best available statistics compiled by historian Matthew C. Ward, 484 Pennsylvanians were killed and 202 captured in the seventy-eight Indian raids in the fifteen months before Kittanning, and 228 killed and 173 captured in the eighty-eight raids in the fifteen months after. After the raid, Fort Shirley was abandoned, as almost no settlers remained that far west. John Armstrong himself had to refuse entry to refugees into his fort because it was too crowded. The raids ultimately declined by early 1758, partly because so few settlers remained in western Pennsylvania.[39]

Meanwhile, between June and October 1756, ten Quakers in the Pennsylvania Assembly either resigned or did not run for reelection, permitting others who were not pacifists—but still committed to maintaining the assembly's rights against the proprietor and thus preserving Quaker Party dominance—to take their place. In November, the new assembly voted to form the Pennsylvania Regiment, a permanent force to be stationed on the frontier to supplement the militia, who usually turned out only when there was an immediate danger in their locale. About nine hundred men joined in 1757. As in the mid-1740s, the average age was about twenty-five, only a year younger than the age of the average officer. About 45 percent of the men were laborers, 44 percent artisans, and only one in six was born in Pennsylvania, with Scots-Irish (40 percent), Germans (17 percent), and the rest of the British Isles (13 percent) being the most represented foreign birthplaces. As most of the recent immigrants to Philadelphia had been servants, at least one-half of those enlisted were probably servants escaping their terms.[40]

While Pennsylvania desperately tried to guard its frontier in the west, the Quakers launched a peace offensive in the east. In December 1756, Israel Pemberton, Philadelphia merchant and assembly leader, known colloquially as the "King of the Quakers," founded the Friendly Association for Preserving and Regaining Peace with the Indians by Pacific Measures. Taking advantage of the fact that the Indians in what is now north-central Pennsylvania were hungry, as the English traders in the area had left, they began talks with Delaware leader Teedyuscung, who rejected the Iroquois role of "woman" and spoke on his people's behalf. These talks culminated in negotiations at Easton between July 21 and August 8, 1757, in which Pennsylvania agreed to guarantee Delaware land in the Wyoming Valley, provide them with presents and teachers, and build them a town at Wyoming in

exchange for an alliance and acceptance of the Walking Purchase of
1737.[41]

Meanwhile, the British army and
the Pennsylvania Assembly were
quarreling. The Earl of Loudoun
arrived to command the forces in
North America in 1756. His army
needed winter quarters, and he decided to spread it among New York,
Boston, and Philadelphia, the
colonies' major ports where accom-
modations and supplies were most
plentiful. Colonel Henry Bouquet was
in charge of the more than six hundred men assigned to Philadelphia. At
first they were crowded into the 120
or so public houses—taverns that
usually had a room or two upstairs to
accommodate travelers—in the city.
But a smallpox epidemic and the
crowded conditions—over a hundred
soldiers were sleeping on straw on the
ground—caused Bouquet to demand
that they be dispersed among the
city's private homes. This upset the
citizens, of course, fearing misbehav-
ior by the (usually) young men who
would, among other things, become
acquainted with their daughters and
serving maids. Governor William
Denny approved the quartering, but
when the assembly learned of his
action, they sent a committee headed
by Benjamin Franklin to protest that
he had acted arbitrarily. Invoking the
"Turkish despotism" colonials and
Britons frequently used to describe
the worst form of tyranny, Franklin,
to Denny's face, called him "a meer
Bashaw, or worse than a Bashaw" and
"no Governor, as he did not protect
the people." Lord Loudoun, hearing

of the dispute and with another five
hundred troops on the way, gave
Pennsylvanians a stark alternative: "If
the number of troops now in
Philadelphia are not sufficient, I will
instantly march a number sufficient
for that purpose and find Quarter to
the whole." The assembly capitulated,
but the next year lost no time building barracks capable of holding five
thousand troops in the city's
Northern Liberties. Bouquet commented: "I detest this cursed city."[42]

The assembly did not take its
defeats easily. In February 1757, it
sent Benjamin Franklin to England
for the express purpose of removing
the Penn family for its refusal to pay
taxes as part of the amount the
province gave toward funding the
war. Whether because of Franklin's
absence or for other reasons,
Governor William Denny became
more pliable. In March, pleading that
if he followed the proprietor's
instructions the province would be
ruined, he signed a bill allowing the
Penn estates to be taxed. In return, the
assembly voted a stronger militia bill
that required all those except pacifists
and Roman Catholics (who presumably could not be trusted fighting the
Catholic French) from serving, and
placed the military under the governor's command. But it insisted the
governor could only choose militia
officers from lists it compiled.

Denny's willingness to compromise
did not receive much reciprocity. He
objected to the assembly sending its
wampum—tokens symbolizing
peace—rather than the governments
as a whole to the negotiations at

Easton; the assembly in turn protested when Denny on his own authority ordered two hundred Pennsylvanians to join forces fighting the Cherokees in South Carolina. The Penn proprietors, angered that Denny had violated their instructions, replaced him with James Hamilton. Until the end of the war, even after the British Privy Council decided in favor of the proprietor in 1760, the Pennsylvania Assembly refused to vote funds that did not tax the proprietor and permit it to decide how the governor ought to spend the money. So no further funds for the war came after 1760. Control of the military as well as of the purse had become a political football in the struggle between an assembly that hoped to replace the Penn family and a royal government and proprietors who insisted on retaining their privileges.[43]

British forces finally came to Pennsylvania's aid again in 1758. General Jeffrey Amherst was put in charge of Braddock's original strategy: as Nova Scotia had been taken in 1756, he was to capture Louisbourg where the St. Lawrence emptied into the Atlantic as prelude to an attack down the river on Quebec and Montreal; then take Fort Carillon (Ticonderoga) and drive the French from the Lake Champlain–Lake George area; and finally to seize the French forts from Duquesne to Presque Isle in Pennsylvania. Amherst sent General John Forbes to Philadelphia to execute the last of these schemes; he arrived in April 1758, and assembled a formidable force of seven thousand British sol-

diers (mostly Scots) along with provincial troops from Pennsylvania, Virginia, and North Carolina. Unlike Braddock, Forbes decided to strike at the French entirely through Pennsylvania. A road existed from Shippensburg to Bedford, where Forbes built a fort. He also constructed Fort Ligonier so that if he had to retreat, these two safe havens and supply bases would be available and the disaster that Braddock incurred would be avoided.[44]

Until the last moment, Forbes's expedition also seemed doomed. The Virginians in Forbes's column, headed by George Washington, were angry that Forbes was marching through Pennsylvania, which would help inhabitants of that colony pour into the region rather than Virginians. Washington intrigued with the Virginia government to replace Forbes, doubting that he had orders to undertake such an "impossible" expedition, and offered to go to England himself to explain how "grossly . . . the public money has been prostituted." The only Indians who accompanied the column, Cherokees and Catawbas from the south, demanded huge presents to remain and then deserted when their demands were not met.

Still, Forbes pressed ahead, over several ridges of the Allegheny Mountains and the Juniata River during the rainiest summer on record, losing dozens of wagons. Many soldiers became ill; a trained physician, Forbes also realized he himself was dying. In great pain, he had to be carried on a litter as Colonel Henry

Bouquet directed the day-to-day activities of the campaign.

Military setbacks also occurred. Forbes had been very careful to send out scouting parties to make sure he was not ambushed. On September 14, as he approached Fort Duquesne, he ordered Major James Grant to take eight hundred men and quietly check the surrounding area. Grant, hoping to win the campaign on his own, advanced with drums and fifes playing, splitting his force and hoping to trap the French. Instead, he was ambushed and over half his force killed or captured. Forbes withdrew to Fort Ligonier, presumably to retreat east or wait out the winter. As late as November 11, the French attacked Forbes's advance guard near the fort. Composed of Virginia troops led by Washington, the Virginians were firing at each other in the thick smoke and wilderness, killing about thirty of their own through friendly fire before Washington could stop them.

Prospects looked bleak, but then things changed. In Easton, Pennsylvania, the colony's leaders met with more than five hundred representatives of the Iroquois as well as the tribes that had revolted in 1755. Once again, Teedyuscung rather than the Iroquois took the lead. At the second Treaty of Easton, signed on October 26, the colony promised the Indians that all the lands beyond the Alleghenies would be theirs, nullifying the treaty made at Albany in 1754, and that colonials would only enter it if asked to establish trading posts. The Treaty of Easton's provisions were

Soldiers from the Forbes expedition entering the remains of Fort Duquesne on November 24, 1758. The French had abandoned and detonated the fort before the British arrival.

almost identical to those of the later British Proclamation of 1763, designed to keep the Indians and colonists apart.[45] In the meantime, Moravian missionary Christian Frederick Post, traveling with Forbes's column, made the same guarantee to the Indians near Fort Duquesne. Within sight of the fort, and over the objections of the French who demanded the Indians take him captive, he met with Tamaqua and Shingas (who along with Chief Jacobs had led the attacks from Kittanning) and informed them that Pennsylvania had restored much of the western part of the colony to the eastern Delaware the previous year and would be glad to guarantee their lands as well.[46]

Furthermore, the French at the fort were starving, forced to eat their horses for lack of supplies. To save lives in what he considered a hopeless situation, the French commander François-Marie Le Marchand De

Lignery dismissed his Indian allies and sent his militia home to Louisiana and Illinois, leaving only four hundred French troops to face the more than six thousand men Forbes now had available. Learning from deserting Indians of the fort's condition, Forbes prepared to attack. On November 24, his army heard a huge explosion: the French had retreated and blown up the fort. After noting with horror the bodies of tortured British soldiers, captured in Grant's futile attack, the British left two hundred men under the command of Pennsylvanian (and former escaped Highland Scot rebel) Hugh Mercer as a garrison, the rest of the army returning east. A letter from an anonymous individual in the army, published in the *Pennsylvania Gazette* on December 14, 1758, best summed up Forbes's triumph and the great hopes it inspired among Pennsylvanians:

I HAVE the Pleasure to write this Letter upon the Spot where Fort Duquesne once stood, while the British Flag flies over the Debris of its Bastions in Triumph.

Blessed by God, the long looked for Day is arrived, that has now fixed us on the Banks of the Ohio with great Propriety called La Belle Rivière, in the quiet and peaceable Possession of the finest and most fertile Country of America, lying in the happiest Climate in the Universe. This valuable Acquisition lays open to all his Majesty's Subjects a Vein of Treasure, which, if rightly managed, may prove richer than the Mines of Mexico, the Trade with the numerous Nations of Western Indians: It deprives our Enemies of the Benefits they expected from their deep laid Schemes, and breaks asunder the Chain of Communication betwixt Canada and Louisiana, a Chain that threatened this Continent with Slavery, and therefore, the chief Favourite and Mistress of the French Court. These Advantages have been procured for us by the Prudence and Abilities of General FORBES, without Stroke of Sword, tho' had they been purchased at the Price of so much Blood and Treasure, every Lover of his Country must have allowed that they would have been cheaply bought.

The Difficulties he had to struggle with were great. To maintain Armies in a Wilderness, Hundreds of Miles from the Settlements; to march them by untrodden Paths, over almost impassable Mountains, thro' thick Woods and dangerous Defiles, required both Foresight and Experience, especially if you consider the Efforts of an active Enemy, frequently attempting to cut off our Convoys; consider also his long and dangerous Sickness, under which a Man of less Spirits must have sunk; and the advanced Season, which would have deterred a less determined Leader, and think that he has surmounted all these Difficulties, that he has conquered all this Country, has driven the French from the Ohio, and obliged them to blow up their Fort (when we were within a few Miles of it we heard the Explosion) he has now reconciled the several nations of Indians at War with us and with one another, regained our lost Interest among them, and fixed it on so firm a Foundation, as not again to be shaken; so that our Back Settlements, instead of being frightful Fields of Blood, will once more smile with Peace and Plenty. These Things have rendered him the Delight of the Army, and must endear him to the Provinces.

All his Motions were narrowly watched by the Enemy, who, finding that he not only proceeded with Care and Circumspection, but with inflexible Steadiness, and that they could neither face him in the Field, retard his March, nor resist him in their Fort, retired to their Batteaus, and fell down the River, we hear, to a Fort, built two or three Years ago, near the Junction of the Ohio with the Cherokee River, where their united Stream falls into the Missisippi, Eight Hundred Miles from hence.

The Twenty sixth of this Month [November] was observed, by the General Orders, as a Day of publick Thanksgiving to Almighty God for our Success; the Day after we had a grand feu de Joye [celebration], and today a great Detachment goes to Braddock Field of Battle, to bury the Bones of our slaughtered Countrymen, many of whom were butchered in cold Blood by (those crueller than Savages) the French, whom to the eternal Shame and Infamy of their Country, have left them lying above Ground ever since. The unburied Bodies of those killed since, and strewed round this Fort, equally reproach them, and proclaim loudly, to all civilized Nations, their Barbarity.

Thanks to Heaven, their Reign on this Continent promises no long Duration! especially if Mr. PITT be preserved, whose great Soul animates all our Measures, infuses new Courage into our Soldiers and Sailors, and inspires our Generals and Admirals with the most commendable Conduct.

Forbes enjoyed his triumph only briefly. Deathly ill, he made his way back to Philadelphia in his litter; he died on March 11, 1759. After a mag-

nificent funeral, he was buried inside Christ Church, Philadelphia. The *Pennsylvania Gazette* wrote on March 15 that "he made a willing Sacrifice of his own life to what he valued more, the Interest of his KING and COUNTRY." The principal east-west street in Pittsburgh where his army advanced still bears his name, as did, for many years, the stadium where the Pittsburgh Pirates played baseball.

The French in the west were by no means finished. In the spring of 1759, seven hundred soldiers and eight hundred Indians left Fort Niagara and approached Mercer's garrison, which was saved because the force was recalled when the British attacked Niagara itself. The British then began to construct a much larger fort on the site of Fort Duquesne and replaced the colonial militia with British troops. This was Fort Pitt, the genesis of the city of Pittsburgh. Despite the success of James Wolfe in capturing Quebec, the capital of French Canada, in September 1759, it would be four years before the war officially ended. In the meantime, the British garrisoned the forts of western Pennsylvania, largely to keep peace with the Indians by preventing the settlers from transgressing the Treaty of Easton. By July 1760, 1,300 troops were stationed at Fort Pitt, 250 at Fort Ligonier, and 100 each at Forts Cumberland and Bedford.[47]

Peace seemed to have come to the frontier. But the English did not heed the warning of Teedyuscung, who had met with General Forbes shortly after the fall of Fort Duquesne: "If the English would draw back over the mountains, they would get all other nations into their interest; but if they stayed and settled there, all the nations would be against them; and he was afraid it would be a great war, and never come to peace again."[48]

PONTIAC'S WAR: ORIGINS, 1759–1763

Two interacting developments ensured that the peace that settlers enjoyed with the Indians of western and northern Pennsylvania at the end of the French and Indian War would be brief. First, despite the Treaty of Easton, settlers continued to swarm into territories guaranteed to the Native Americans. Second, Sir Jeffrey Amherst, commander of the British forces in North America, had only contempt for the natives. Thus, on May 9, 1763, scarcely three months after the Treaty of Paris was signed ending the French and Indian War and ceding Canada to Britain, a coalition of Indian nations led by Chief Pontiac attacked Fort Detroit and other British outposts.

As the British began constructing Fort Pitt in 1759, Pennsylvania and Virginia settlers started to gather in the area. By 1761 a town with 150 structures contained 219 men, 75 women, and 38 children. Traders led by George Croghan, who constructed Croghan Hall at the fort and claimed a large tract of land, supplied Indians who had become dependent on them with food, clothing, weapons, and liquor in return for furs. Indian women became the companions of traders and other settlers, and at the fort drunken brawls involving Indians and settlers became com-

monplace. Meanwhile, British soldiers stationed at Fort Burd on the Youghiogheny River reported frontier people planting fields and "such crowds of hunters . . . at which the Indians seem very much disturbed and say the white people kill all their deer." Colonel Henry Bouquet, the commander at Fort Pitt, citing the Treaty of Easton, threatened to expel these intruders and try them by court-martial. He was challenged by Governor Francis Fauquier of Virginia, who informed him he had no right to subject Englishmen to martial law and had no jurisdiction over territory that was part of Virginia and had been lawfully acquired by its inhabitants. Fauquier argued that Pennsylvania's Treaty of Easton did not apply to Virginia in any case.[49]

Meanwhile, Amherst consolidated his power and his intransigence. The British general had won three major campaigns—in 1758 capturing the French fortress at Louisbourg that guarded the St. Lawrence River; in 1759 against Fort Carillon (Ticonderoga) that enabled the British to approach Canada through New York; and finally in 1760 against Montreal, the final French stronghold on the continent. None of these achievements relied on Native Americans; Amherst had only observed them stealing supplies and deserting from his forces and beginning the Cherokee War in the Carolinas after they had previously been loyal to the British.[50]

Amherst's Indian policy was a combination of arrogance and stinginess: Indians, like soldiers and colonists,

An artist's interpretation of Fort Pitt in 1758. The fort stood near the site of the original French Fort Duquesne at the Forks of the Ohio, the confluence of the Allegheny (left) and Monongahela (right) rivers that merge to form the Ohio. The Forks was an important strategic position for access to the interior of North America.

ought to obey their superiors. "If they do not behave as good and faithful allies ought to do, and renounce all acts of hostilities against His Majesty's subjects I shall retaliate upon them, and I have the might so to do tenfold every breach of treaty they shall be guilty of and every outrage they shall commit." But in fact, Amherst's funds and forces were both depleted after 1760—Britain moved its resources to other theaters of the war. Amherst was left with about eight thousand men for all of North America. Regarding the French in Canada as his principal potential problem, the general stationed nearly two-thirds of his men there or in upstate New York, with barely five hundred distributed among the dozen forts on the western frontier. He also discontinued the practice of giving substantial presents to the Indians, who regarded these as fair rent for the forts and surrounding settlements constructed on their lands. As Amherst explained to New York's Sir William Johnson, who lived among the Iroquois and was the foremost distributor of presents:

I do not see why the Crown should be put to that expense. I am not . . . for giving them any provisions; when they find they can get it on asking for, they will grow remiss in their hunting, which should industriously be avoided; for so long as their minds are intent on business they will not have leisure to hatch mischief. . . . Services must be rewarded . . . but as to purchasing the good behavior either of Indians, or any others, is what I do not understand; when men of what race soever behave ill, they must be punished but not bribed.[51]

The Indians complained about encroachments without success. In November 1762, Seneca chief Kindrutie refused the request of Pennsylvania's governor James Hamilton to build another fort on the Susquehanna River by reminding him what was promised at Fort Pitt: "You promised to go away as soon as you drove the French away, and yet you stay there and build houses." At Detroit, Major Henry Gladwin, the commander, observed that the Indians "say we mean to make slaves of them, by taking so many posts in their country, and that they had better attempt something now to recover their liberty, than wait till we are better established."[52]

They did not wait long. During the war, Indians had sided with either the French or the British as suited their interests. Now, without the two powers contending against each other, they united to develop what might be called a sense of Native American nationalism, heavily based on the religious teachings of a prophet named Neolin. By November 1762, leaders at Fort Pitt learned that Neolin was circulating copies of a "plan" among the Indians of the Ohio Valley. According to the prophet, the Earth was a square box placed between the devil and hell on the left side and heaven on the right. To reach heaven, open only to Indians, people had to overcome "all the sins and vices . . . learned from the white people," and "learn to live without any trade or connections with the white people, clothing, and supporting themselves as their forefathers did." This especially included

relearning the use of bows and arrows, so as not to be dependent on guns, eschewing hard liquor, and growing their own food. A major part of Neolin's teachings concerned the English. Assuming the voice of the Master of Life who spoke to him in a dream, Neolin urged: "Drive them out, make war upon them; I do not love them at all; they know me not, and are my enemies. . . . Send them back to the lands which I have created for them and let them stay there."[53]

Although Ottawa chief Pontiac lent his name to the uprising, Neolin's teachings appear to have been the catalyst that united Indians of diverse nations in a huge confederacy from the shores of Lake Superior to the Susquehanna Valley. Historians previously termed the war "The Conspiracy of Pontiac" or "Pontiac's Rebellion," but both are misnomers. A conspiracy suggests something illegal, or secret, as well as a sinister event planned by a small group of people; a rebellion, as when Union leaders termed the Southern secession in 1860–61 a "rebellion," means an unlawful insurrection against legitimate authority. The term "war" dignifies both sides as combatants in a major conflict.[54]

The war began on May 9, 1763, when a large number of Indians who had gathered at Fort Detroit butchered the English who lived outside the fort and then laid siege to it. Forts Sandusky (in Ohio), St. Joseph (present-day Niles, Michigan), Miami (Fort Wayne, Indiana), and Ouitanon (Lafayette, Indiana) all fell in May, showing the extent of the union and the coordination of the Indians' plans. On June 2, Chippewa Indians used a game of lacrosse to capture Fort Michilimackinac, located at the strait separating the lower and upper parts of Michigan. Not having learned of the outbreak of hostilities, the British garrison left the fort as usual to watch and bet on the game. The Indians tossed the ball over the fort's wall, seized control of it, and massacred the garrison.[55]

War came to Pennsylvania on May 28. Shingas, the Delaware leader, warned his friend the western trader Thomas Colhoon to leave the village of Tuscarawas as an attack was imminent. Colhoon complied but was attacked and three of his party were killed as they headed for Fort Pitt. The same day, Indians killed Colonel William Clapham and destroyed his settlement on the Youghiogheny River. Captain Simeon Ecuyer, who commanded Fort Pitt's garrison of 145 men, prepared for a siege. He called all the local inhabitants into the fort, which meant more than five hundred people, including more than two hundred women and children, were crowded into its confines. He then burned any buildings outside in which the Indians could take cover, organized a militia company of about a hundred men, and sent word to Colonel Bouquet in Philadelphia to send reinforcements.[56]

Smaller forts in western Pennsylvania were less prepared. On June 16, Mingo Indians attacked Fort Venango, killing its garrison of about fifteen men and burning its commander, Lieutenant Francis Gordon,

Henry Bouquet (1719–1765) led a British force to victory at the Battle of Bushy Run and lifted the siege of Fort Pitt during Pontiac's War.

alive after he wrote a forced letter explaining that they were fighting because the British hoped "to possess all their country." Two days later, the Indians attacked Fort LeBoeuf. When he realized he could no longer hold out due to the flaming arrows the Indians shot, Ensign George Price and his thirteen men chopped a hole in the wall, and after eight days in the wilderness all except two safely reached Fort Pitt. On June 20, about 250 warriors surrounded Fort Presque Isle and set it on fire. After two days its commander, Ensign John Christie, surrendered his twenty-nine troops and some civilians on the condition they be allowed safe conduct to Pittsburgh. The Indians had no intention of honoring these terms: they divided up the captives, torturing two of them to death, and sent Christie to Detroit, where he was later released.

Indians also attacked Fort Ligonier and settlements located near Fort Bedford farther to the east in June, but reinforcements arriving at the last minute prevented their loss.[57]

Meanwhile, two Delaware leaders who had been friendly to the English hoped to talk Ecuyer into surrendering Fort Pitt. He refused but gave them provisions and liquor for their trip home. Included were two handkerchiefs and a blanket that had been used by Englishmen who had come down with smallpox. Ecuyer was the first European commander to use this tactic against the Indians. Without knowing of his action, on July 7 General Amherst suggested the same policy to Colonel Bouquet: "You will do well to try to inoculate the Indians, by means of blankets, as well as to try every other method, that can serve to extirpate this execrable race." Amherst's statement reflects the racial consciousness developing after the French and Indian War: with no need for Indian allies, the British and their American colonists began to group all Indians as a (red) "race" deemed to possess innately savage characteristics. Whether from the trade goods or from germs spread by settlers they raided and captured—no epidemic affected the Indians surrounding the fort—a smallpox epidemic did break out among the Ohio Valley Indians later that year. (Colonel Bouquet's own fate was ironic: sent in 1765 to command the British garrison at Pensacola, Florida, he died nine days after his arrival of yellow fever.)[58]

Upon hearing of the hostilities in western Pennsylvania, Amherst dispatched the closest British regulars, who were camped in Staten Island, New York, some ninety miles north of Philadelphia. On June 18, these five hundred men, many of whom were still sick from diseases contracted in the West Indies, reported to Bouquet in Philadelphia. Believing that even a small number of regulars could defeat the hostile Indians, Amherst did not remove any of the nearly six thousand troops from upstate New York or Canada. But Bouquet did not wait for them, nor did he wait and see if the Pennsylvania Assembly would raise and pay for provincial troops to help him. He went to Carlisle on June 28 and hoped to organize Pennsylvanians in their own defense. Instead of finding the munitions and provisions he had expected, the town "was crowded with miserable refugees, who were reduced to a state of beggary . . . the streets filled with people, in whose countenances might be discovered a mixture of grief, madness, and despair." Others lived outside the town around campfires. Bouquet immediately sent to Lancaster for provisions and dispatched soldiers to reinforce Forts Bedford and Ligonier as Indian parties continued to attack settlers who remained on their farms. The reinforcements from Staten Island arrived on July 10.[59]

Bouquet set out on July 15 to relieve Fort Pitt. He learned soon thereafter that the Pennsylvania Assembly would not assist him with the militia, which it planned to use in another campaign along the Susquehanna River. He reached Fort

Bedford on July 25, where he was joined by fourteen rangers who could handle the invaluable scouting duties to prevent an ambush. Following the Forbes Road, which had deteriorated over the past four years, and in a terrible heat wave, Bouquet's force arrived at Fort Ligonier on August 2, rested, and set out again on August 5. By midday, the army was about a mile away from a place called Bushy Run, where they could find cool water, when the advance guard was attacked. Bouquet sent reinforcements, which charged and dislodged the Indians, only to find them attacking his rear, where the pack animals laden with supplies were located. As some of his troops retreated, Bouquet had them use the sacks of flour that they carried to form defenses around the horses. Other soldiers continued to charge the Indians to keep them from approaching too close, as their arrows and rifles were more accurate than the British muskets. This close-order fighting continued until nightfall.

When the Indians attacked the next day, Bouquet put into effect a plan that he invented and had often suggested to other officers, which would be used by both friends and foes of Britain in the future. He had some men pretend to retreat, while others were stationed on their flanks and over a hill where the Indians did not see them. When the warriors charged, yelling and certain of easy victory, they were met by a withering volley followed by a bayonet charge. Bouquet lost fifty men killed and sixty wounded, but survived with his main force intact in an attack similar to the one unleashed against Braddock's in 1755. He praised the Scots Highlanders of the Forty-Third and Seventy-Seventh Regiments who had borne the brunt of the fighting as "the bravest men I ever saw." On August 11, carrying their wounded, Bouquet's column finally marched into Fort Pitt bringing much-needed food; the Indians, who had come out to fight at Bushy Run, had departed. Thanks to Bouquet's tactical use of flour sacks and his feigned retreat, the Indians would never again be in a position to threaten a major British fort.[60]

Two weeks after Bouquet relieved Fort Pitt, a group of over a hundred Pennsylvanians under Colonel John Armstrong, the commander at Kittanning in 1756, marched to confront the Indians who lived on Grand Island, in the west branch of the Susquehanna River. They were led by Captain Bull, Teedyuscung's son, who was retaliating against all white settlers for the recent murder of his father. The two forces fought an indecisive engagement at Muncy Creek Hill on August 27; the bloody raids continued, even against the pacifist Moravians who had been converting the Delawares to Christianity. On October 15, Captain Bull destroyed the Connecticut settlers' village that had been built on the ruins of his father's town and killed ten people. Two further expeditions, another under Armstrong and a second under Major Asher Clayton, were able to destroy some Indian villages, but the enemy fled before they could be engaged.[61]

While the Pennsylvania frontier continued to burn, Jeffrey Amherst was recalled because of anger at the war his confrontational policies had provoked. He sailed for England on November 18. When he arrived, he found that George Croghan had preceded him and submitted a memorial on behalf of the "suffering traders" of 1763 for royal compensation for their losses. "General Amherst's conduct is condemned by everybody and has been pelted away in the papers," Croghan reported. "The army curse him in public as well as the merchants." In Pittsburgh, learning of Amherst's departure, the officers drank toasts amid "universal cries of joy."[62]

THE PAXTON BOYS, 1763–1764

Joy turned to horror that December. On December 13, about thirty "Paxton Boys" who hailed from Paxtang, near present-day Harrisburg, and led by Lazarus Stewart, massacred six Conestoga Indians who had been converted to pacifism and Christianity by the Moravians. They then murdered fourteen more in the Lancaster workhouse, adjacent to the jail, where Pennsylvania officials had taken them for safekeeping. The Indians prayed and sang Christian hymns as they were being hacked to death.[63]

Indians friendly to Pennsylvania were in an especially difficult situation during Pontiac's War. Hostile Indians were pressuring them to join the uprising upon pain of death. As an Indian spokesman in Wyalusing who refused to join the fray stated:

Pontiac's followers "threatened me to . . . cut off my head for taking the White people's part." Some whites realized the best fate for friendly Indians was to remove them from the frontier. On September 13, 1763, Colonel John Elder had suggested relocating the Conestogas and placing a garrison at their settlement instead. Governor Penn responded that they had done nothing to deserve this: he had no reason to remove "innocent, helpless, and dependent" people who relied upon the governor for support." But when thirty-one Pennsylvanians were killed in present-day Northampton and Lehigh counties on October 8 and 9, Moravian Indians in the area received the blame for tipping off the murderers. An investigation revealed that Indians at Nain and Wichetunk had in fact traded guns to the hostiles, but the Pennsylvania Assembly believed they had only done so under duress and were "willing and desirous, from their attachment to the government, or regard for their own safety, to be removed." In November, the government relocated them to Philadelphia.

Given this background, the hostility of the frontiersmen to Moravian Indians can be understood if not justified. William Henry described the massacre in Lancaster, which only took the Paxton Boys ten minutes to finish before they rode away:

The first notice I had of this affair was, that while at my father's store, near the court house, I saw a number of people running down the street toward the jail, which enticed me and other lads to follow them. At about six or eight yards from the jail, we met from twenty-five to thirty men, well mounted on horses, and with rifles, tomahawks, and scalping knives, equipped for murder. I ran into the prison yard, and there, oh what a horrid sight presented itself to my view! Near the back door of the prison lay an old Indian and his squaw, particularly well known and esteemed by the people of the town on account of his placid and friendly conduct. His name was Will Soc; across him and squaw lay two children, of about the age of three years, whose heads were split with the tomahawk, and their scalps taken off. Towards the middle of the jail yard, along the west side of the wall, lay a stout Indian, whom I particularly noticed to have been shot in his breast; his legs were chopped with the tomahawk, his hands cut off, and finally a rifle ball discharged in his mouth, so that his head was blown to atoms, and the brains were splashed against and yet hanging to the wall, for three or four feet around. This man's hands and feet had also been chopped off with a tomahawk. In this manner lay the whole of them, men, women, and children spread about the prison yard; shot, scalped, hacked and cut to pieces.[64]

A company of British soldiers commanded by a Captain Robinson that supposedly protected the Lancaster Indians did nothing to stop the carnage. His reaction reflected the "only good Indian is a dead Indian" mentality then developing on the frontier: "Damn them I would not care if the whole race were slain, for my company has suffered enough by them already, I will not stir one step." The Pennsylvania Council urged Governor Penn to enlist the aid of

Colonel John Armstrong at Carlisle and the Reverend John Elder at Paxton to find the rioters and "suppress all such Insurrections among the People under their influence for the future." They placed a bounty of £200 per head on the murderers.[65]

But no force in western Pennsylvania dared challenge the Paxton Boys. Next they marched on Philadelphia, gathering inhabitants along the way, hoping to murder as well the Moravian Indians who were being protected there. Philadelphia, while reluctant to defend the frontier, had no qualms about defending itself. One inhabitant noted that "drums, colors, rusty halberds and bayonets, were brought forth from their lurking places; and as every good citizen who had a sword had it girded to his thigh, so everyone who had a gun had it placed on his shoulder." As Sally Potts remarked, the Quakers themselves "seem'd as ready as any to take up arms in such a cause to defend the laws and libertys of their country against a parcel of rebels."[66]

The Anglican clergyman Thomas Barton sarcastically noted that the Paxton Boys "have been able at last to lay bare the pharasaical bosom of Quakerism, by obliging the non-resisting quality to take up arms, and to become proselytes to the first great Law of Nature [self-defense]."[67]

On February 5, 1764, about 250 frontiersmen confronted nine companies of Philadelphia inhabitants in Germantown. Their leaders, including Benjamin Franklin, agreed to present the Paxton Boys' demands to the governor if they agreed to dis-

Cartoon described on page 47. Note the fox, symbolizing shrewdness, standing between Penn's legs, and the Indian hiding in the bushes in the foreground.

perse. Their "Declaration and a Remonstrance," as it was called, demanded that trade with the Indians cease, that all white captives be released, that the frontier receive more military protection, and, finally, that the western counties, which had only ten assemblymen as opposed to twenty-four for the three "old counties" of Bucks, Philadelphia, and Chester, be granted more representation. Confronted with force, they did not insist on an initial demand that the protected Indians be turned over to them or be expelled from the province.

The march of the Paxton Boys set off the greatest pamphlet controversy not only in Pennsylvania, but in pre-Revolutionary colonial history. Sixty-

three pamphlets appeared within a year, along with ten political cartoons—the first in the colonies except for the "Join or Die" snake Franklin prepared for the Albany Congress of 1754. Opponents of the Quakers and their unwillingness to defend the frontier accused them, literally, of sleeping with the enemy, questioning "whether the affection which some members of that sect have shown to Indians . . . can possibly be owing to the charms of their squaws." In one cartoon, the Quakers' leader in the assembly, wealthy merchant Israel Pemberton (referred to in several cartoons as "I.P."), is shown embracing a half-naked Indian woman. The caption reads:

She dives her hand into his Fob
And thence conveys as we are told
His watch whose cases are of Gold.

In another cartoon (opposite) "I.P."
is handing out tomahawks while:

The German bleeds & bears ye Furs
Of Quaker Lords & Savage Curs
The Hibernian frets with new Disaster
And kicks to fling his broad brim'd
Master
But help at hand Resolves to hold down
The Hibernian's Head or tumble all
down.

In the cartoon, a Quaker and an
Indian ride the backs of German and
Scots-Irish settlers as they try to
escape among the bodies of the
Indians' victims.

Benjamin Franklin, who had
assumed a leading position in the
Quaker Party's opposition to the
Penn family, was especially criticized
for his efforts to have the proprietor
removed and replaced by a royal governor—himself. (While in England
from 1757 to 1762, he had secured the
governorship of New Jersey for his
son William.) The proprietor's supporters tried to expose Franklin's
stance as pure opportunism: "Fight
Dog Fight Bear I am content/If I can
get the government," he says in one
cartoon where the Devil is whispering
in his ear. Another supporter of the
proprietor noted that   while the
Quakers would not defend the frontier, they nevertheless turned out
when the Paxton Boys marched on
Philadelphia: "Feuds and Quarrels
they abhor 'em/The Lord will fight
their Battles for 'em." But when the
Paxtonians threatened, "now the case

is alter'd quite./And what was wrong,
is chang'd to Right."

The Quakers and Franklin were just
as angry and sarcastic. One pamphlet
talks of "Waymode of Transylvania"
in which the proprietor, compared to
a Turkish overlord—always a sign of
extreme despotism in early American
writing—supported a "sect" called
the "Piss-Brutarians," or "Presbyterians," who massacred peaceful
Indians, which required the people to
have recourse to their emperor (the
king of England). Another tract spoke
of the self-government exercised by
Presbyterians in their churches as the
reason for their violent behavior:
"Owing to the Effect their Principles
have, . . . they are, and always have
been (tho' under the mildest of
Governments) a Set of uneasy, discontented, and innovating People"; "a
bigoted,   stiff-necked,   rebellious,
pedantic Crew." Taken as a whole, the
pamphlets exhibited three sets of
mutual disgust: western and eastern
Pennsylvania, the Quakers and their
Presbyterian/proprietary opponents,
and the ethnic English and the Scots-
Irish. In both Indian relations and
quarrels among its own inhabitants,
Penn's "Holy Experiment" had degenerated into the most bloody and conflicted province in mainland North
America.[68]

PONTIAC'S WAR: PHASE 2, 1764–1766

Fortunately for the colonists in gener-
al and Pennsylvania in particular,
Amherst's replacement, General
Thomas Gage, was willing to let New
York's Sir William Johnson, the
Indian agent for the northern

colonies, do his job. Owner of huge tracts of land, victor at the Battle of Crown Point in 1755 for which he was knighted, Johnson lived among the Iroquois. He wore their clothes, embraced their customs, and was married to Molly, the sister of Joseph Brant (Thayendanegea), an Iroquois leader educated at the school that became Dartmouth College. Johnson promptly recruited the Iroquois, who had remained loyal to the British but whom Amherst had refused to use, to bring the Delaware and other Pennsylvania Indians back into line. On February 27, 1764, mixed-blood interpreter Andrew Montour and about two hundred Iroquois, marching in snow up to three feet deep, surprised and captured Captain Bull and forty of his followers. Montour's column proceeded to destroy several villages, and the Delawares and their allies fled from central Pennsylvania into what is now eastern Ohio to be out of the Iroquois' range.[69]

In the Ohio River valley, however, the raids continued. On February 24, Indians attacked soldiers gathering wood outside the gates of Fort Pitt itself. On April 14, the British discovered a turncoat settler named Gershom Hicks scouting the terrain for a planned Delaware attack on Fort Pitt that never materialized. Thirteen settlers were killed near Fort Loudoun on June 14, and on July 26 nine children and their schoolmaster Enoch Brown were massacred inside his schoolhouse in the Conococheague Valley.[70]

These events finally mobilized the Pennsylvania Assembly to act by placing a bounty equal to $134 on each male Indian scalp and $50 for each female. But it also raised a thousand troops. General Gage approved a plan for the summer and fall of 1764: a force led by Colonel John Bradstreet would move on the Indian villages along the Scioto River, while Bouquet would leave Fort Pitt and attack those on the Muskingum. As Pontiac had failed to take Fort Detroit and win any support from the French in St. Louis—who urged him to make peace—the Ohio Valley Indians were willing to negotiate when finally confronted with forces of more than one thousand men each. In a meeting on October 20, Bouquet spoke from a position of strength, accusing the Indians of beginning "this war without the least reason or provocation whatsoever," reminding them of their atrocities, and insisting that they deliver all their captives.

Return of the captives was a major issue. Indians had seized about two thousand Pennsylvanians beginning in 1755, a significant addition to a native population estimated at about ten thousand. While a few prisoners, usually male, were either executed or tortured, the great majority were adopted into Indian families. There, they served the double purpose of filling the place of lost relatives and being human shields to discourage attacks on their settlements. Many, especially children, were happy living with their Indian families—who raised children more affectionately and with much more outdoor play time than Europeans—and developed loving relations with them. In addition, captives taught Indians to domesticate cattle, make butter and cheese, forge axes and farm implements, and build European-style houses. Nevertheless, not understanding how any European could possibly wish to live with the Indians, Bouquet insisted that all the captives be returned. About two hundred were released, although many escaped back to the Indians as soon as they could, especially those who had been taken as children.[71]

The two most famous captives had radically different experiences. Mary Jemison (1742–1833) related hers in a narrative that was published in 1824. She was taken prisoner in 1758 at her father's farm near present-day Chambersburg after the rest of her family was killed. She saw some fellow prisoners tortured to death at Fort Duquesne, which even after six decades "afforded a spectacle so shocking, that . . . my blood almost curdles in my veins when I think of them." But she herself was adopted by two Seneca women who had lost a brother; she learned their language and married a Delaware warrior who moved the family to the Genesee Valley in New York. She married twice, had several children, and refused to return to white society, even after the Sullivan expedition during the Revolutionary War devastated the Indians' territory. To this day, Jemison is a name found among the Seneca (Iroquois descent is matrilineal).[72]

Simon Girty, on the other hand, was considered by Moravian missionary John Heckewelder "as brutal, depraved, and wicked a wretch as ever lived." Girty was born in 1741; first his father and then his stepfather were killed by Indians. After several years in captivity, he was returned to Fort Pitt. Learning the Indians' languages and customs, dressing like an Indian and remaining pretty much a loner, he was in demand as a scout and interpreter. After supporting Lord Dunmore in his war against the Ohio Valley Indians in 1774, he switched to the patriot side in the revolution. Disgusted at their murdering Indian women and children, in 1778 he joined the British once again, leading frontier raids and participating in the torture and execution of the American colonel William Crawford when in 1782 the Delaware punished Crawford for the Gnadenhutten Massacre—the second of that name, this time in Ohio—where Crawford killed ninety-six pacifist Delaware Indians converted to Christianity by the Moravians. Girty led war parties and continued to plague the frontier until the British abandoned Fort Detroit in 1796, when he moved to Canada.[73]

Technically, Pontiac's War came to an end on July 23, 1766, when Pontiac came to Fort Oswego, New York, and signed a treaty with Sir William Johnson. Yet nothing concrete was settled: many Indians were disgruntled, and a Peoria Indian killed Pontiac on April 20, 1769. Skirmishing on the Pennsylvania frontier continued, and the Pennsylvania Assembly, hoping to stop settlers' encroachment on Indian lands, prescribed the death penalty for this offense. The most notorious incident occurred in January 1768, when Frederick Stump killed four Indian men and two women whom he claimed had become drunk and threatened him at his cabin on Middle Creek in Cumberland County. The next day Stump and his servant John Ironcutter (he had translated his last name from the German Eisenhower) walked fourteen miles to an Indian encampment and killed the four women and children they found there, claiming they might know of the murders and convey the information to other Indians. Stump and Ironcutter boasted of their accomplishment, and when Sheriff John Holmes of Cumberland County confined them in the county jail a local mob stormed it and freed them. They were never heard from again. Although General Gage feared that "there doesn't seem much probability, considering the present disposition of the Indians, that they can be pacified for the loss of their people," war did not break out again in the west for several years.[74]

PENNSYLVANIANS CONFRONT BRITISH SOLDIERS IN THE CONOCOCHEAGUE VALLEY, 1765

As a condition of keeping peace on the Pennsylvania frontier, commanding general Thomas Gage and Indian agent Sir William Johnson agreed that the Ohio Valley Indians needed to be retained as allies to work with British garrisons to prevent continued settler infiltration and the conflicts that would inevitably result. George Croghan was sent to negotiate a peace at a meeting in May 1765. He was suc-

cessful. More than four hundred warriors at Fort Pitt expressed a willingness "to comply with everything [the British] required of them," with the condition: "do not act as you have done for a year or two before those late troubles, when you prohibited the sale of powder, lead, and rum." Croghan had already begun to solve that problem. That January, as agent for the Philadelphia firm of Baynton, Wharton, and Morgan, his men set out for Pittsburgh with £15,000 of goods to trade for furs.[75]

George Croghan may have pacified the Indians when he began sending trade goods to the Ohio Valley, but he enraged the settlers when they found out he was supplying weapons that could not only be used for hunting but also for war. When in March 1765 a pack train took back roads rather than the Forbes Road to avoid detection, the settlers in the Conococheague Valley and its principal settlement, Mercersburg, suspected the worst. First, the settlers tried to persuade the leader of the eighty-one-horse train to turn back, as continuing on "would be a kind of murder, and would be illegally trading at the expense of the blood and treasure of the frontiers." When that failed, a band of frontiersmen headed by James Smith intercepted the column, discovered tomahawks and scalping knives, and burned or confiscated the goods. Smith and his eleven men were known as the "Black Boys" because they painted and disguised themselves as Indian warriors—who frequently wore black war paint—during the French and Indian War.[76]

Next, the British commander, Lieutenant Charles Grant, at nearby Fort Loudoun sent out a party to recover the goods and arrested six of the Black Boys. James Smith led over a hundred men, confronted the garrison of about a dozen, and successfully demanded the prisoners be released. Far from acting lawlessly, the Black Boys insisted that the civil power—which meant William Smith of Mercersburg, James's brother, the local justice of the peace—was superior to the military (a maxim of British law) and that the caravan was not taking Forbes Road, the British army road, but attempting to sneak by on highways constructed by the local inhabitants. The Pennsylvania government and British army investigated the situation, agreed that Croghan and his employers were indeed engaging in illegal trade, but then failed to stop it. Sticking to their notion of legality, the settlers at Conococheague then insisted that all trade caravans passing to Pittsburgh had to be inspected and obtain a pass from William Smith, stating that they were free of weapons. When on May 6 Ralph Nailer attempted to evade the inspection, the Black Boys seized him, whipped him, took his goods, and wounded one of the soldiers who came to arrest them. Later in May, they distributed notices asking the entire local population to turn out against the British:

These are to give notice to all our Loyal Volunteers, to those that has not yet enlisted, you are to come to our Town and come to our Tavern and fill your Bellys with Liquor and your

The "Black Boys" attacking a wagon train in the Conococheague Valley.

Mouth full of swearing . . . our Justice has wrote to the Governor and everything clear on our side and we will have Grant the officer whip'd or Hang'd, and then we will have orders for the goods so we need not stop, what we have a mind and will do, for the Governor will pardon our crimes, and the Clergy will give us absolution and the country will stand by us, so we may do what we please for we have Law and Government in our hands.

The crowd proceeded to seize Lieutenant Grant. When he accused them of being rebels, they answered that "they were ready for a rebellion." They released him on condition he return all the firearms he had seized from the inhabitants, but he broke his promise. A standoff remained until November when the settlers attacked Fort Loudon for two days. The battle ended when a column arrived from Pittsburgh relieving Grant of his command: Fort Loudon was closed. The Black Boys had won. They revived their system of inspection four years later when caravans again arrived suspected of transporting illegal goods. When the British garrison at Fort Bedford imprisoned some men who seized the goods, James Smith repeated his tactics, attacking the fort and forcing the tiny garrison of fourteen men to surrender the prisoners.[77]

The battle at Fort Loudon was the first confrontation between Americans and British troops in the years leading up to the Revolution. The only reason it is not better known is that historians more familiar with events in Boston have downplayed the importance of frontier expansion as a cause of the revolution as opposed to taxation and disputes over commercial regulations. Even in south-central Pennsylvania, in 2010, an effort to prevent the destruction of William Smith's house failed in his hometown of Mercersburg despite the efforts of several historians and a local committee. It now lies in ruins, its stones numbered and waiting to be rebuilt, as its site has become a parking lot of the local fire department. But the story lives on, or at least it should, in a song James Smith recorded in his memoirs:

Ye patriot souls who love to sing,
What serves your country and your king,
In wealth, peace, and royal estate,
Attention give whilst I rehearse,
A modern fact, in jingling verse,
How party interest strove what it cou'd,
To profit itself by public blood,
But, justly met its merited fate.

Let all those Indian traders claim,
Their just reward, inglorious fame,
For vile base and treacherous ends.
To Pollins, in the spring they sent,
Much warlike stores, with an intent,

To carry them to our barbarous foes,
Expecting that no-body dare oppose,
A present to their Indian friends.

Astonish'd at the wild design,
Frontier inhabitants combin'd,
With brave souls, to stop their career,
Although some men apostatiz'd,
Who first the grand attempt advis'd,
The bold frontiers they bravely stood,
To act for their king and their country's good,
In joint league, and strangers to fear.

On March the fifth, in sixty-five,
Their Indian presents did arrive,
In long pomp and cavalcade,
Near Sidelong Hill, where in disguise,
Some patriots did their train surprise,
And quick as lightning tumbled their loads,
And kindled them bonfires in the woods,
And mostly burnt their whole brigade.

At Loudon, when they heard the news,
They scarcely knew which way to choose,
For blind rage and discontent;
At length some soldiers they sent out,
With guides for to conduct the route,
And seized some men that were trav'ling there,
And hurried them into Loudon where
They laid them fast with one consent.
But men of resolution thought,
Too much to see their neighbors caught,
For no crime but false surmise;

Forthwith they join'd a warlike band,
And march'd to Loudon out of hand,
And kept the jailors pris'ners there,
Until our friends enlarged were,
Without fraud or any disguise.
Let mankind censure or commend,
This rash performance in the end,
Then both sides will find their account.

'Tis true no law can justify,
To burn our neighbors property,
But when this property is design'd,
To serve the enemies of mankind
It's high treason in the amount.[78]

As with "The Liberty Song" written by Philadelphia lawyer John Dickinson to encourage Bostonian resistance to the British, the Conococheague resisters had their own song. They insisted that their behavior was lawful—all their actions were authorized by Justice William Smith, the local magistrate—and that the real culprits were military officers who acted, contrary to British law, without the consent of civil authority in an area that was not a war zone. The real traitors were those who would "serve the enemies of mankind" and "burn our neighbors property"—the Indians and the traders/traitors who supplied them. It is no wonder that the American Revolution in Pennsylvania would be as much a struggle over who would rule the state as a war for independence against Britain.

Map 4: Pennsylvania during the American Revolution. Pennsylvania was the "Keystone State" many times in it history, but no more than when it witnessed the critical early battles for the survival of the Continental Army, and harbored George Washington and his beleaguered troops at Valley Forge. Pennsylvania also saw savage conflict along its frontier, and the major expeditions against Britain's Indian allies originated in Pennsylvania.

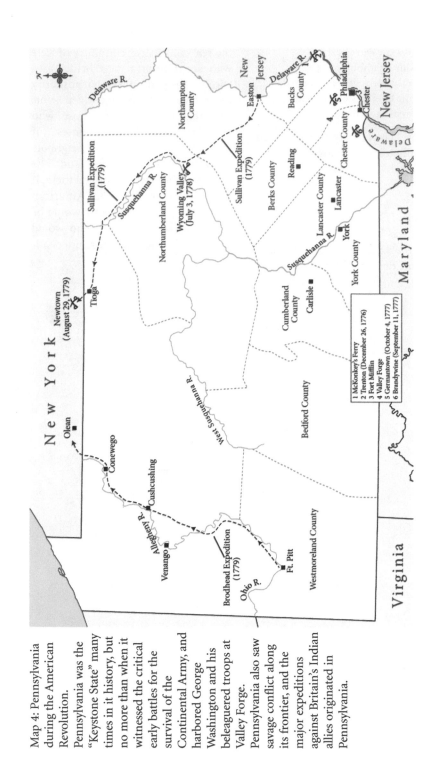

5. Pennsylvania in the American Revolution, 1765–1783

William A. Pencak ◆ Barbara A. Gannon

ORIGINS OF THE AMERICAN REVOLUTION, 1765–1775

Pennsylvania was not in the forefront of leading the colonies into the American Revolution. During the 1760s and early 1770s, the two contending groups in the legislature, the Quaker Party and the Proprietary Party, had been competing for the favor of the British government. The Quaker Party hoped to have the proprietor replaced with a royal governor—that was Benjamin Franklin's original goal when he went to Britain as the province agent in 1757, before he realized in the 1760s that British policy had become hostile to colonial interests. At the same time, the Penn family proprietors and their supporters sought to keep the colony in their hands. With that goal in mind the Penns commissioned Benjamin West—a native of Chester County who had moved to England where his fine work prompted King George III to appoint him the royal painter of history scenes—to paint the famous scene of *William Penn's Treaty with the Indians* in 1771. Using contemporary Quakers as his models—Penn only sat for a portrait once, before he became a Quaker, as a young man—West and the Penns hoped to remind the king of the family's contribution to the empire.[1]

A new party, led by Presbyterians and frequently called the Presbyterian Party, had emerged in Philadelphia to urge a more radical resistance. Their origins may be traced to the Paxton Boys, whose supporters adopted their general perspective that the only way the province would defend the west is if the newly settled regions received representation in the Pennsylvania Assembly proportionate to their population. While they finally obtained new counties with delegates—Bedford, Westmoreland, and Northumberland in the early 1770s—they had little effect because these huge and populous counties had only one vote each, compared to the eight apiece for the Quaker-dominated Bucks, Chester, and Philadelphia.[2]

Meanwhile, in Philadelphia, ordinary citizens became dissatisfied with the conservatism of both Quaker and Proprietary leaders to follow Boston. When in December 1773, a shipment similar to the tea that caused the Boston Tea Party came up the Delaware, an extralegal meeting of citizens persuaded the captain not to land his cargo as the assembly remained quiescent. Pennsylvania entered the intercolonial resistance movement in a major way on May 20, 1774, the day after Paul Revere arrived in Philadelphia with news of the Coercive (or, as the Americans called them, Intolerable) Acts. Massachusetts's elected upper house was to be appointed by the Crown, its town meetings limited to voting for officeholders, its resistance leaders (Samuel Adams and John Hancock in particular) sent to England for trial, and Boston Harbor closed until the town paid for the tea dumped into the harbor. (Later in the year, the Quebec Act gave all the land west of the Alleghenies—much of it claimed by Pennsylvania speculators and occupied by Pennsylvania squatters— to the province of Quebec.) Pennsylvania radicals led by Charles Thomson, Joseph Reed, and Thomas Mifflin joined forces with moderate John Dickinson to form a Committee of Correspondence to plan Pennsylvania's response. Correctly surmising the Quaker-dominated assembly would continue to do nothing, on June 11 the committee declared the Boston Port Bill unconstitutional, supported Virginia's call for a Continental Congress, and

authorized a committee of forty-three to coordinate policy with the county committees that were already forming.[3]

The Pennsylvania Assembly finally acted when it chose eight of its members to serve in the Continental Congress, which met in Philadelphia on September 5. None were from the Committee of Correspondence, and all were conservatives who hoped to keep any protest moderate and respectable. The other states were not pleased. They responded by refusing Assembly Speaker Joseph Galloway's offer of the State House for their meetings. They chose Carpenters Hall next door to signify approval of the more militant Philadelphia working classes who had spearheaded the city's resistance.

Pennsylvania's own Provincial Conference met again from January 23 to 28, 1775. Each county received one vote: the members realized that principal support for resistance would come from the backcountry (along with city workers) rather than the farmers of the "old counties" along the Delaware River and the urban elite. The conference approved of nonimportation, the Continental Congress's main response to the Coercive Acts, and urged the inhabitants to produce their own manufactures—most significantly, gunpowder for "defense."

ORGANIZING THE REVOLUTION, 1775–1777

Defense became a real issue in April 1775 when war broke out in Massachusetts. The hitherto backward colony quickly made up for lost time as people throughout the state converted their Committees of Correspondence into Committees of Safety and formed military units on their own. When radical Quaker Christopher Marshall of Lancaster went to visit James Cannon in Philadelphia on April 29, he discovered that "he was not there, being gone to the State House Yard to help consult and regulate the forming of a militia." On May 1, Marshall noted that "this day a number of the associators to the militia met in each of the wards of the city, to form themselves in suitable companies, and to choose their respective officers." Many Quakers joined in, especially a number of young men "who asked leave of the managers to learn the exercise in the factory yard." Wealthy citizens bought fancy horses and uniforms, earning the derisive nicknames of the "Silk Stocking Company" and the "Lady's Light Infantry" from those who could only bring their bodies and, perhaps, a gun. A broadside on May 18, 1775, asked that Philadelphians adopt "the cheapest uniform, such as that of a HUNTING SHIRT," so the militia would be free of class distinctions. The rank and file also demanded the important issues be decided by general meetings of the Associators so that "each man may have a voice in what so nearly concerns them."[4]

The presence of the Second Continental Congress in Philadelphia as of May 10, especially the more radical Virginians and Massachusetts delegates, encouraged these military preparations. Furthermore, Congress created the Continental army on June 14 and chose George Washington to lead it the next day. To join the New Englanders and New Yorkers who were gathering outside Boston (on June 17 they would fight the Battle of Bunker Hill and prevent the British from extending their control outside the city), Congress approved raising ten companies of riflemen, six from Pennsylvania, two from Maryland, and two from Virginia. Congress deliberately selected frontier men who knew how to use these weapons, far more effective at picking off targets at a distance. The three leaders of Pennsylvania's contingent—Colonel William Thompson, General John Armstrong, and General Hugh Mercer—were all involved in the Battle of Kittanning, fought extensively in the backcountry, and became community leaders after the war. (George Washington himself had commanded the Virginia frontier after Braddock's defeat.) The six companies of Pennsylvania Rifles came from Cumberland, Berks, York, Northampton, and Lancaster counties, all of which—with equal justice—claim the honor of supplying the first troops to the Continental army.[5]

In Cambridge, outside of Boston, the riflemen became equally well-known for their amazing shooting—the British pickets became afraid to show themselves—as well as their undisciplined behavior—naked bathing in the Charles River (showing off to the ladies), refusal to muster in military order or wear regular uniforms, drinking and fighting among themselves and with other Continentals, and wasting their ammunition in shooting contests that confused the rest of the army as to whether a skirmish was occurring or not. Washington sent many of the rifle companies on the expedition to conquer (or, as the Americans preferred, "liberate") Canada under Benedict Arnold that fall. Most of these were captured, including Thompson, who spent much of the war in captivity and died in 1781. He is depicted in John Trumbull's famous painting *The Death of General Montgomery*, based on Benjamin West's *Death of General Wolfe* (depicting Wolfe's death at Quebec in 1759).

The rest of the riflemen were attached to the main army. As British officers were accustomed to appearing visibly leading their men, they protested in vain that guns that could fire with such accuracy were an unethical form of warfare. Hugh Mercer died at the Battle of Princeton in January 1777. Only Armstrong survived the war and continued his career in western Pennsylvania.

While all sorts of people were Associators, turning out when the British were in the immediate area and keeping order and rounding up supplies and recruits in their community, the rank and file of the Continental army consisted of young, mostly single men, especially immigrants, according to the patterns discovered by Philip Swain in his study of the men who enlisted for Boston and Gregory Stiverson in his discussion of Maryland soldiers. (There is

This detail from a watercolor made by a young French officer in 1781 is probably the best surviving depiction of an American rifleman during the Revolutionary War. Note the characteristic fringed hunting shirt with cape, full length trousers, broad brimmed hat, hunting pouch with powder horn attached, a tomahawk, and a rifle equipped with a sling.

no systematic study of Pennsylvania's Continentals.) That much of western Pennsylvania became either "Depreciation Land" (given in lieu of cash to those to whom the state owed money, including Associators) or "Donation Land" (given by Pennsylvania to all members of the Continental line who remained for the duration of the war), and that after the war large numbers of soldiers moved west rather than selling their land, is strong evidence the average soldier was a poor man for whom military service was a way to get a start in life. The conflicts between Pennsylvanians, Virginians, Connecticut Yankees, and Indians on both the western and northern frontiers is further proof of the large migration following the war.[6]

Most Pennsylvanian men, as throughout the new nation generally, did not serve in the Continental army. They participated in the revolution as associators or were members of local committees, variously called Committees of Safety, Correspondence, or Observation among other things. In May 1775, the reluctant Pennsylvania Assembly, bowing to public pressure, authorized a Committee of Safety to direct the defense of the state, although that body's conservative Quaker majority made participation voluntary. On June 30, the assembly agreed to vote £50,000 for defense but not to organize a militia to put the money to use. But it did approve "the Association entered into by the good people of the province for the defense of their lives, liberty, and property," and recommended that the Board of Commissioners send "firelocks, with bayonets fitted to them, cartridge boxes . . . and knapsacks" to the local organizations. The assembly likewise recommended that all those opposed to bearing arms "cheerfully assist in proportion to their abilities": Philadelphia's committee began a voluntary collection among Quakers and other conscientious objectors.[7]

People of future importance led some of the committees. George Ross, signer of the Declaration of Independence, took the lead in Lancaster County, while the future general "Mad Anthony" Wayne headed the committee in Chester. Lawyer Edward Biddle (whose nephew Nicholas became president of the Second Bank of the United States), and iron manufacturer Mark Bird (namesake of Birdsboro, whose daughter married Declaration signer James Wilson) were principal leaders in Berks County. Cumberland's organizers included Wilson himself (a Scots-trained lawyer who lived at the time in Carlisle) and Robert Whitehill (leader of the Pennsylvania Anti-Federalists and Wilson's principal opponent when the federal constitution was debated at the Pennsylvania ratifying convention in 1788). Philadelphia leaders included newcomers to politics such as Charles Willson Peale, the artist, David Rittenhouse, the astronomer, James Cannon, a mathematics professor, Dr. Thomas Young, a New Yorker who had learned about popular mobilization in Boston, and Timothy Matlack, a lapsed Quaker, who along with Reed, Thomson, and Mifflin, would later be disowned by the Quaker meeting for becoming "Fighting Quakers." Matlack—who lived to be about ninety-nine years old—is an especially interesting person. The son of a merchant who associated in taverns with the lower classes, his is the only portrait in Charles Willson Peale's gallery of notable patriots—now at the Second Bank of the United States in Philadelphia—who sports a working man's cap. These leaders would be joined in spirit, if not on the committee itself, by English immigrant Thomas Paine, whose pamphlet *Common Sense* galvanized the movement for independence in January 1776, and Benjamin Franklin, arriving home from England after a decade, who repudiated the moderation of nearly all the established political leaders of both the Quaker and Proprietary parties—that is, nearly all the men of his own generation—having seen the arrogance of British power at first hand.

The main effect of this extra-governmental mobilization was to involve many more Pennsylvanians in military and political activity than ever before as Associators, public officeholders, and what later officially became the militia. Unlike in New England and the southern colonies, where the established local governments and colonial legislatures organized the resistance, Pennsylvania—as with all the colonies from Maryland north to New York—required a new political structure in a severely conflicted province to bypass a colonial legislature that never endorsed independence. With the exception of the small pacifist sects such as the Moravians, Amish, and Mennonites, the Germans—the vast majority of whom were Lutheran or Reformed (Calvinist)—repudiated the Quaker pacifism they had followed in the past, joined the revolutionary ranks, and began, for the first time, to elect each other to the committees, legislature, and military offices. Scots-Irish settlers, who had dominated local communities in the west, also won province-wide and military offices: James Taylor of Bucks County and James Smith of Cumberland were

elected to Congress and signed the Declaration of Independence; along with Scots-born James Wilson and Robert Morris, born in England, immigrants made up four of the seven Pennsylvania signers.

These leaders, however, had a hard time controlling their more extreme followers. A Committee of Privates formed in Philadelphia in the autumn of 1775 and was soon organizing rank-and-file militiamen throughout the colony to drive the revolution in a more radical direction. They insisted that certain political demands be met for their participation. First, anyone who was willing to fight ought to be entitled to vote, whereas in colonial Pennsylvania only men over twenty-one who owned fifty pounds' worth of property qualified. They also demanded that those who failed to volunteer pay a fine. On October 31, the Committee of Privates marched to the Pennsylvania Assembly and presented a petition declaring the Quakers (who still formed much of that body) "unfriendly to the liberties of America" since they would enjoy protection without contributing to the "common safety." The assembly passed a compromise that made military service mandatory in theory, although payment of a small fine excused any conceivable objector for religious, political, or personal reasons. The assembly also established "Rules and Regulations for the Better Government of the Military Association in Pennsylvania" on November 25, which it encouraged all the Associators to adopt.[8]

As Pennsylvania's Associators pushed the colony into the resistance movement, the assembly continued to oppose the movement toward independence that was gaining popularity everywhere in early 1776. Finally, after pacifists and moderates opposed to both independence and continued resistance were elected to the assembly in the election of May 1, 1776 (the old counties still dominated), the exasperated members of the Continental Congress adopted a resolution proposed by John Adams—for Pennsylvania's benefit. Congress proclaimed that "where no government sufficient to the exigencies of their affairs" existed, the representatives of the people should adopt one "best conducive to their happiness and safety." Seizing the initiative, the Committee of Privates in Philadelphia declared that the Pennsylvania Assembly, "like James II"—the British king who left the throne in 1688 when faced with a Dutch invasion—"have abdicated the government and by their acts of detestable cowardice have laid the Provincial Conference under the necessity of taking instant charge of affairs."

The Provincial Conference then ruled that only those who swore an oath of allegiance to the new government on a Christian Bible—which eliminated Quakers (who refused to swear oaths), loyalists, and (by accident) the handful of Jews in Pennsylvania—could vote and hold office. In September, a constitutional convention approved the most radical government of all the new states: it retained the oath of allegiance, making participation difficult for those who might approve of the revolution itself but not the state constitution; Pennsylvania kept its single-house assembly, but it was now to be elected by all adult male oath-swearing taxpayers and its apportionment favored the more revolutionary western counties; the nation's first experiment in rotation in office provided that each assemblyman could only serve four years out of any seven; all laws passed once (except emergency measures) had to be printed and referred back to the communities before they became law after they passed a second time after review by the voters; and a Council of Censors could declare laws unconstitutional. The state's governor was replaced by the Supreme Executive Council's president—a title deliberately chosen to indicate a weak officeholder who merely "presided," such as someone who presided over a club. Stimulated by the militia companies, organized in opposition to Pennsylvania's pre-Revolutionary leadership, Pennsylvania may have been (with New York) the last of the colonies to approve independence, but it enjoyed (or endured) the most radical internal upheaval of any of the states.[9]

The Associators, and their successors the militia, were not only expected to turn out as "Minutemen" if the British threatened Pennsylvania. Their principal ongoing functions were making sure their own numbers and the Pennsylvania contingent in the Continental army were supplied with uniforms, food, and weapons and that people opposed to the revolution were silenced and prevented from assisting the British.

As Associators mobilized throughout the state, they became increasingly angry with those who did not. When the British army marched on Philadelphia during December 1776, after chasing the Americans out of New York, the Committee of Privates threatened to disband unless all citizens were obliged to fight or pay a significant penalty: "All shall go, or none will go," they promised. The first Assembly of the state of Pennsylvania supported them and passed a meaningful tax—three pounds, ten shillings, or about a month's wages for a laborer—to be paid by those who would not serve.[10]

This fine was confirmed in the first state militia law, passed on March 17, 1777, after Washington had defeated the British at Trenton and Princeton between December 15 and January 1 and the emergency had abated. County lieutenants organized the militia and collected fines—amounting to over £6,000,000 in mostly inflated money before the end of the war—that they used to fund the state's war effort, as taxes were collected sporadically at best.

The war increased industrial productivity in the state, as the lieutenants' purchases demonstrate. For instance, one account of the lieutenant of the city of Philadelphia notes:

Paid sundry persons for 332 muskets, 278 bayonets, 532 cartridge boxes, 1530 bayonet belts, 2479 bayonet scabbards, 100 wooden bayonet tips, 44 sides and 178 1/2 lb. harness leather for making bayonet scabbards, belts, and slings, 14 lb. shoe thread, and 18 lb. flax and hemp, with spinning for same, one

wood horse for the saddlery, 19 1/2 lb. tent ropes, cutlass, 1 pair horse pistols, 1193 gun slings, 51 1/2 doz. brushes and wires, 18 rifle guns, 5 powder horns, 1 pouch, 15 knapsacks, 5 canteens, 2 halberds (axe-like blade and steel spike mounted on end of long staff), 48 hammers, 1 crowbar and 1 side of leather delivered for artillery, repair of ordinance store house, collecting, hauling, inspecting, repairing and storage of arms, lading and unlading when the enemy approached the city in 1777, and for hauling ordinance per accounts and receipts—£9,500.

Even before the revolution, furnaces and forges found throughout Pennsylvania, especially in Berks and Lancaster counties, produced guns, wagon frames, and farm tools. Mark Bird of Berks, James Wilson's father-in-law, owned perhaps the largest forge in the state and made more than forty cannons for the Continental army. To protect the productivity of Berks and its county seat, Reading, the army was stationed at Valley Forge during the winter of 1777 to 1778.[11]

SUPPRESSING OPPOSITION, 1775–1783

The Associators also began to suppress their critics. The usual response—as was true in many colonies—which generally worked, was simply to make the culprits confess and promise not to support the British anymore in either word or deed. For instance, one Isaac Hunt, who had attacked the Paxton Boys and opposed the Presbyterians for over a decade, was "persuaded" by thirty Associators, who showed up at his house, to "ask pardon of the public." The men placed him in a cart, wheeled him through the streets with drums beating and fifes playing the rogue's march, and forced him to confess in various locations. When they passed the house of Dr. John Kearsley Jr., he fired on them. Placed in the cart to replace Hunt, Kearsley remained adamant. As he was about to be deported to England it was discovered that he was suggesting to the British plans to invade Pennsylvania. He was imprisoned and died during the war. Others agreed to join or at least stop criticizing the militia after "being formally introduced to a tar barrel," while still others, like James Allen, son of the last provincial chief justice, joined in the hope that "discreet people mixing with [the Associators] may keep them in order."[12]

Rounding up loyalists (who actively supported Britain) and the disaffected (such as Quakers who refused to support the revolution) was one of the main tasks of the Committee of Safety, which supervised the province until the Supreme Executive Council took its place on March 4, 1777, under the new constitution. As with New York City and Charleston, South Carolina, the presence of a British army in the city with American forces nearby led to guerrilla warfare between the lines.

In Chester County, the chief loyalist "bandit" was one James Fitzpatrick. The *Pennsylvania Packet* reported on August 18, 1778, "that the infamous Fitch, alias Fitzpatrick, with his associate Dougherty, have been exceeding troublesome to travelers on the Lancaster road, frequently laying them under contribution, and some times offer gross insults and personal abuse to the friends of the United States." A deserter from the American army following the Battle of Long Island, Fitzpatrick (also known as "Fitz" or "Fitch") resisted attempts to make him rejoin his unit and joined the British when they arrived in Pennsylvania in September 1777. He then organized his band, called himself Captain Fitz, and made a special point of targeting army recruiters and tax collectors, frequently whipping them (the punishment that had caused him to desert) as well as taking their money. Since there was little support for the revolution in Chester County, Fitzpatrick had something of the reputation of a local hero. He was known for his bravado, walking through areas of patriot sentiment in broad daylight and even attending meetings where people were planning to capture him. He was finally seized by Captain William McAfee, who overpowered Fitz with the aid of a serving girl at his parent's house (the girl and McAfee then disputed the £1,000 reward, which they were compelled to split). Fitz was finally executed on September 26, 1778. He was so tall that his feet touched the ground as he was being hung, which required the executioner to press on his shoulders and strangle him to death. Fitz's chief lieutenant, William Dougherty, probably escaped to Canada.[13]

Bucks County was as hostile or indifferent to the revolution as Chester. There the chief guerrilla fighters were the Doans, who came from a Quaker farm family. Moses Doan turned against the patriot cause in 1774, as soon as collections were made in Pennsylvania to assist the Bostonians who had been cut off from the sea by the Boston Port Bill. Joined by his brothers Aaron, Levi, Mahlon, and Joseph as well as his cousin Abraham, he began to rob colonial tax collectors and wealthy revolutionaries, as well as steal their horses. In 1776, Moses Doan offered his gang's service as spies to General William Howe (who had taken New York), which Howe gladly accepted. Moses Doan was also probably the man who tried to warn Colonel Johann Rall, who commanded the Hessian force Washington surprised at Trenton, that the Americans were coming. But Rall refused to see him and stuffed the note Doan gave him in his pocket, where it was found after the colonel was mortally wounded.[14]

The Doans were active until the early 1780s, stealing £1,307 in public funds from the Bucks County treasury in Newtown on October 22, 1781. After General Charles Cornwallis's defeat, however, the patriots organized posses in earnest to capture them. On September 1, 1783, the gang was surprised near the Gardenville Tavern (still standing) and Moses was killed. His body was dumped in front of his parents. Of the other members, Mahlon, Aaron, and Joseph were all captured and sentenced to hang, but escaped. Levi and Abraham were finally captured and hanged in Philadelphia in July 1788.

The patriots were able to investigate and squelch the conspiracy of a group known as the Associated Loyalists who lived in York, Lancaster, and Cumberland counties and hoped to seize the United States arsenals at the towns of York, Lancaster, and Carlisle. Most of these were Anglicans of English descent in a heavily pro-revolutionary, German and Scots-Irish area, although some Quakers and German pietists south of Carlisle were also known as "the Bermudian Creek Tories." Once exposed, the perpetrators, especially Daniel Shelly and David Copeland, managed to pin most of the blame on the area's two Anglican priests, Thomas Barton of Lancaster and Daniel Batwell of York, who were sent back to the British lines.[15]

However, the vast majority of loyalists and disaffected citizens who attracted the state's attention were found in Philadelphia. Some were imprisoned there from other states or western Pennsylvania. By January 1776, Philadelphia housed the following collection: "Dr. John Connolly and his two confederates, Dr. John Ferdinand Dalziel Smyth of Maryland and Allen Cameron of the Cherokee country, besides Colonel Moses Kirkland of South Carolina," and "General Donald McDonald, chief of the North Carolina Tories," his subordinate Colonel Allen McDonald, and "twenty-five more of their set." In May, as the Continental Congress was debating independence, at least four loyalist clubs sprang up in the city itself. Investigated by a newly formed Committee of Secrecy, their leaders, including William Smith, the Anglican clergyman and vice-provost of the College of Philadelphia, and Tory poet Joseph Stansbury were imprisoned.

The greatest roundup of loyalists occurred in July and August 1777, as the main British army approached Philadelphia from the south. The first people to be deported were Governor John Penn—who tried to remain neutral during the revolution and succeeded to the extent that his heirs received compensation for their losses from the United States; Benjamin Chew, who had been a member of the Provincial Council and Pennsylvania's chief justice; James Tilghman, also a member of the Provincial Council; Jared Ingersoll, judge of admiralty; Dr. George Drummond, custom-house officer; and other lesser officials. Most were paroled—as officers and gentlemen usually were by the other side during the revolution—and promised on their word to remain in specific, restricted locations far from the city. Other people of loyalist sympathies, such as the Lutheran minister Henry Melchior Muhlenberg and the Allen family, retired to their country residences (Muhlenberg, in Trappe; the Allens, Bethlehem), where they remained unmolested as they did nothing to aid the British.

The forty-four additional accused loyalists, thirteen chosen by Congress and the rest by the Supreme Executive Council, were only banished on April 25 after word reached Philadelphia that the British had landed in Maryland. Like Ingersoll mentioned above, they were all ordered to be sent to Winchester, Virginia, "dragged into

wagons by force by soldiers," and "drove off surrounded by guards and a mob," as Elizabeth Drinker put it. They were a mixture of mostly Quakers—who had refused to support the revolution, urging others not to support it, and by refusing to accept Continental money—and Anglicans who tended to be more openly pro-British. The Quakers included three members of the Fisher family, six of the Pembertons, and Henry Drinker (husband of the famous diarist Elizabeth Sandwith Drinker). The Anglicans included William Smith and Thomas Coombe, two of the priests in the city, although William White, the only priest to remain loyal to the revolution, persuaded the authorities to let Smith and Coombe remain. Smith remained on friendly terms with the British, but removed to Chestertown, Maryland, where he founded Washington College in 1783. Coombe left with the British army, never to return.[16]

Their husbands' exiles offered the loyalist women of Philadelphia the opportunity for concerted political action. In April 1778, they signed a petition for their husbands' release; Elizabeth Drinker was one of four who went to Lancaster to meet with George Washington, Joseph Reed (president of the Supreme Executive Council), and Timothy Matlack (representing the city's Committee of Safety). For two weeks they negotiated, and finally, because "the zeal and tenderness of these good women are so great," Matlack noted, their husbands were returned to Philadelphia.[17]

Despite this show of mercy, the Supreme Executive Council continued to attaint traitors while the British occupied the city. The first to be condemned were Joseph Galloway, three members of the Allen family, the rector of Christ and St. Peter's Churches Rev. Jacob Duche—who had switched from being a patriot to urging George Washington to make peace when the British occupied the city. Thirteen men were named on March 6, 1778, fifty-seven on May 8, seventy-five on May 21, two hundred on June 15, and sixty-two on October 15, for a total of 407 for the year. Forty-six more were added between 1779 and 1781. Some loyalists left their wives in Philadelphia when they evacuated with the British army in the (vain) hope that they could conserve their property that way. Grace Galloway, for one, had to be forcibly ejected from her home by Charles Willson Peale. The College of Philadelphia, which was dominated by loyalists, lost its charter and property on November 27, 1779 (only restored on May 6, 1789) and was replaced by the State University of Pennsylvania, dominated by the new radical government. The two schools merged as the first institution to be entitled the University of Pennsylvania in 1791.

The geographic distribution of the "traitors" conforms roughly to the patterns of allegiance in Revolutionary Pennsylvania. The "old counties"—Philadelphia, Bucks, and Chester—which had dominated the assembly and were heavily Quaker and Anglican, were filled with loyalists and neutrals. Of those accused of treason, 109 were from Philadelphia City, 76 from Philadelphia County, 87 from Chester, and 75 from Bucks. The ring of counties surrounding them—Northampton, Berks, Lancaster, York, and Cumberland—were heavily German Reformed (Calvinist) and Lutheran and, except for Anglican priests and a few leading citizens, were some of the most staunchly revolutionary in the nation, as they had long-standing grievances against the political rule of the old counties. York had nine so-called traitors, Northampton thirty-five, and frontier Bedford County four. In general, although guerrilla warfare was endemic on the western and northern frontiers among Pennsylvanians, Indians, Virginians, and Connecticut settlers who disputed their claims, no one was accused of treason who took part in these struggles.[18]

The revolutionaries also had to deal with prisoners of war. The first British POWs began arriving in Pennsylvania late in 1775: the greatest number, now including hired German soldiers, was the 2,500 who came after General John Burgoyne surrendered at Saratoga in October 1777. They were sent to the interior of the province— the vicinity of Reading and Lancaster were two main areas—where Pennsylvanians noted two distinct behavior patterns. The British, especially the officers, were arrogant and dismissive of the rebels they considered "vagabonds" and "rascals." On June 4, 1777, the Lancaster prisoners celebrated King George III's birthday, became rowdy, and charged their guards, who killed a man and wounded three before order was restored. Unlike the Americans, who were confined in prison ships and other unpleasant, unhealthy, and deadly quarters, the revolutionaries gave the British considerable freedom, requiring them only to report to their barracks at night. But they responded by trying to escape and trying to persuade Americans to become loyalists. As John Nixon remarked: "the kind treatment given them meets with very improper and indecent return." By 1777, the Americans were forced to confine British prisoners in stockades and compel officers—who were allowed to live freely on their word of honor not to escape or take part in the war unless exchanged—to wear their uniforms at all times so Americans would know who was trying to change their allegiance.

German prisoners of war, however, responded well to the American's leniency. Sent to predominantly German-speaking areas in central Pennsylvania (there is still a neighborhood called Hessian Camp in Reading), the soldiers began working as farmers and in industry—Mark Bird employed a dozen in his ironworks. They refused to celebrate the king's birthday when the British did. For the most part, they melted into the general population, as did Isaac Klinkerfuss who married an American girl and ultimately obtained his own farm. They could not be exchanged as they were frequently impossible to locate.[19]

WASHINGTON CROSSES THE DELAWARE, 1776–1777

The first appearance of George Washington's Continental army in Pennsylvania in December 1776 was not a happy one. They had been defeated by the British at the Battle of Brooklyn and chased out of New York and New Jersey. Only by crossing the Delaware River and taking or destroying all the available boats could they find safety in Pennsylvania. General William Howe chose not to pursue Washington and set up posts throughout New Jersey from Perth Amboy across from Staten Island, to Burlington, just north of Philadelphia on the eastern side of the Delaware. Inhabitants reported there to take oaths of loyalty to the king and receive hard currency in exchange for the food and supplies the British, their German allies, and their horses needed to survive the winter.[20]

Washington had been preparing to defend Philadelphia from an expected attack, but when it did not materialize he realized that his main problem was keeping his army intact and the American cause alive after the disasters of 1776. Most of his troops' enlistments expired on January 1, 1777. He had between 2,000 and 4,000 soldiers fit for battle, with another 1,700 or so incapacitated by illness. In December, Washington positioned his army at McKonkey's Ferry, the present site of Washington Crossing, Pennsylvania. On December 19, Thomas Paine published a collection of articles entitled *The American Crisis* in Philadelphia. Washington had it read to the troops to improve morale. The following passage from his first article was especially inspiring and has become part of American history: "These are the times that try men's souls; the summer soldier and the sunshine patriot will, in this crisis, shrink from the service of his country; but he that stands it *now*, deserves the love and thanks of man and woman. Tyranny, like hell, is not easily conquered; yet we have this consolation with us, that the harder the conflict, the more glorious the triumph."[21]

Even more inspiring must have been the arrival of 3,600 more soldiers. On December 20, General John Sullivan appeared with the 2,000 men of General Charles Lee's division. Lee, who disliked Washington, had refused to join him, but on December 12 he was captured by the British with a small group of his men. Sullivan came at once to Washington's assistance with the main force. Horatio Gates supplied 600 soldiers from northern New York, and Colonel John Cadwalader led 1,000 men raised in Philadelphia.

With these reinforcements, Washington made his plans. He diverted over half of his 6,000 men to protect the ferries at Bristol and New Hope in Bucks County and to guard supplies and the wounded at Newtown, Pennsylvania. Then he planned to attack Trenton, New Jersey, where Colonel Johan Rall commanded about 1,500 Hessian troops. To do this successfully, Washington realized he needed to move the 2,000 enemy soldiers commanded by Colonel Carl von Donop out of nearby Borden-

A Durham boat reproduction used during the annual Washington's crossing of the Delaware event at Washington Crossing Historic Park, Pennsylvania. With a flat bottom and sides, these boats were probably about 60 feet long and were originally used to haul freight up and down the Delaware River. No plans or examples exist but the reproductions are based on what scant evidence we have.

town. This occurred on December 23, when Donop attacked a fort established at Mount Holly, New Jersey, containing about six hundred men commanded by Captain Samuel Griffin. Ironically, Washington was sending Griffin reinforcements to launch a diversionary attack, but Donop made his move before they arrived. Plundering Mount Holly and getting drunk, Donop's men were celebrating their nearly bloodless victory when the main attack at Trenton came. Griffin and his soldiers escaped to nearby Moorestown.

Washington's attack on Trenton required assembling a large flotilla of boats in Pennsylvania. He enlisted the local ferries, which had carried coaches across the Delaware and thus could handle horses and artillery. Most of the soldiers were transported in Durham boats. Invented about 1750 by Pennsylvania ironmaster Robert Durham to ship his goods on the Delaware River, these vessels were forty to sixty feet long, about eight feet wide, and yet displaced less than two feet of water. Sailors, ship-builders, and dockworkers from Philadelphia and other Pennsylvania towns joined in the rowing, and informed the experienced boatmen of John Glover's Marblehead Regiment —whalers who had saved Washington's army earlier in the year by rowing it from Brooklyn Heights to Manhattan—about currents and shoals.

The crossing, beginning at six o'clock on the evening of December 25 to take advantage of the cover of darkness, took place during a storm, which made it difficult to see the ice floating in the river. Only a few men fell overboard—almost no one could swim at the time—as artillery chief General Henry Knox shouted directions ensuring none of the eighteen cannons were lost. Originally, Washington planned a three-pronged attack on Trenton, but a column led by Pennsylvania general James Ewing could not cross opposite the river at Trenton, whereas Colonel John Cadwalader, crossing from Bristol, Pennsylvania, to Burlington, New Jersey, was able to ferry his men but not his cannon, causing him to order their retreat.

After being one of the first men to cross, Washington established a post on the New Jersey side, forbidding entry to his lines to anyone who did not know the password "Victory or Death." On the morning of December 26, Washington divided his army in two: he and General Nathanael Greene marched to Trenton on the Pennington Road, while General Sullivan commanded the troops on the River Road. Surprising the Hessian troops who were sleeping late following their Christmas celebra-tions, the Americans killed twenty-two Hessians, wounded ninety-eight, took one thousand prisoners, and obtained much-needed cannons, muskets, and powder. Three Americans were killed and six wounded. The mortally wounded Colonel Rall, who survived long enough to surrender, had received a written warning that a surprise attack was coming, but placed it in his pock-et without reading it.

We remember Washington's river crossing as the prelude to his famous victory as depicted in the famous 1851 painting *Washington Crossing the Delaware* by Emanuel Leutze found in New York's Metropolitan Museum of Art. The painting was designed to be inspirational and encapsulate the meaning of America and its Revolution, rather than to accurately portray the event. The crossing occurs under sunny skies rather than at night during a storm, as General Washington's face catches the rays more than any other. His boat and the figures in it are also propor-tionately larger than the others.

We don't know who accompanied Washington in his boat, but Leutze makes sure to include future president James Monroe (then an eighteen-year-old Virginia lieutenant) and Pennsylvania general Edward Hand, who received the sword at Yorktown when Cornwallis surrendered. Also in the boat are a Scotsman identifiable by his bonnet, an African American (an interesting touch as in 1851 the nation was being torn apart on the slavery question), two farmers (one of whom has been wounded), and possibly a Native American (toward the rear of the boat). A rower wearing a red shirt may possibly be a woman, painted three years after the Seneca Falls Convention demanded equal rights for women.

Other problems with the painting include the "Stars and Stripes," the American flag that flew for the first time over eight months later on September 3, 1777. The boat is far too small to be a Durham boat and for the number of people it contains. Horses and guns, an important part of the battle, crossed the rivers in the much larger and sturdier ferries that in peacetime handled coaches, rather than the smaller boats. Although historian David Hackett Fischer argues that everyone would have been standing to avoid icy water in the bottom of the boat, other scholars maintain that standing figures would have capsized the boat.

Most Americans would describe "Washington Crossing the Delaware" as a single event. But there were three crossings. The second occurred immediately after the battle, as the soldiers had to get back to Pennsylvania before nearby British garrisons counterattacked. This time,

they had about one thousand prisoners and the sizable quantity of muskets, artillery, and ammunition they had taken. More of them fell overboard on the way back because some celebratory drinking had occurred despite Washington's orders that they were to remain sober.

Washington could have remained in Pennsylvania but decided to press his advantage. Unaware of the nature of the attack, all the British and Hessians in the area had withdrawn to Princeton, about ten miles north of Trenton. After getting his men back to Pennsylvania on December 27, Colonel Cadwalader suggested that the British in the area could also be defeated. Washington agreed, and between December 29 and January 1 crossed the Delaware a third time. The weather had become colder, and some of the soldiers—who crossed at eight different points—could even march across on the ice. Upon reaching New Jersey, Washington had another problem: many of his men's enlistments, including the invaluable Marblehead men, had expired. Begging his men to stay and add to their laurels, Washington sweetened the pot with a bounty that persuaded them to remain another six weeks. On January 2, he won the Battle of Princeton. Among those killed was the Pennsylvania general Hugh Mercer, refugee from Bonnie Prince Charlie's army of 1745, participant in the Kittanning expedition of 1756, and namesake of the town of Mercersburg, where in 1765 the first American armed resistance to Britain occurred following the French and

Indian War. Later in 1777, the Americans named the Delaware River fort erected opposite Philadelphia in his memory. Both New Jersey's capital, Trenton, and Princeton are now located in Mercer County.

Immediately after the Battle of Princeton, Washington retired with his army to Morristown, New Jersey.

BRANDYWINE: THE BRITISH APPROACH PHILADELPHIA, SEPTEMBER 1777

Washington expected that General Howe would march on Philadelphia once campaigning weather arrived in the spring of 1777, but Howe intended instead to lure Washington out of this well-defended post in the mountains to fight in central New Jersey. When Washington refused to budge, instead dispatching units to harass Howe's scattered forces, the British general retreated to New York and planned to take Philadelphia later in the year. He hoped to repeat his success of 1776 in New York, where he had defeated the American army and attracted sizable numbers of loyalists. Joseph Galloway, the former Speaker of the Pennsylvania Assembly and one of Howe's chief American advisers, assured him that most of the inhabitants near Philadelphia were either loyal or, at worst, neutral Quakers and other pacifists. Timothy Pickering, the adjutant general of the Continental army, agreed. As he wrote to his brother: "I feel in some degree reconciled to Howe's entering Pennsylvania and Philadelphia, that the unworthy inhabitants (or which 'tis apparent a majority of the state is composed) may experience the calamities of war, which nothing but their own supineness and unfriendliness to the American causes would have brought on them. Possibly Heaven permits it in vengeance for their defection, that their country should be the seat of war."[22]

Howe left British general John Burgoyne, who was moving south from Canada in an effort to take Albany, New York, to his own resources, believing no sizable force could threaten him but, just in case, leaving his second in command, General Henry Clinton, in New York City with instructions to assist Burgoyne if necessary.

Howe rejected a march across New Jersey. His troops would have been strung out for miles along the only roads his artillery and wagons could use, subject to surprise attack, continual harassment, and massive desertions (especially on the part of the Germans, whom the Americans encouraged with promises of freedom and land of their own). General Howe hoped at first to sail up the Delaware River to Philadelphia. On July 21, 1777, his fleet of 267 ships departed New York Harbor with about 16,000 troops. On reaching the Delaware Bay, they met with Captain Andrew Hammond, who had commanded HMS *Roebuck*, a British ship that had patrolled the bay since the beginning of the war. Hammond warned them the Delaware was a tricky river filled with shoals and rocks: he himself had once been driven aground. It required knowledgeable pilots to guide ships from the Atlantic Ocean eighty miles upriver to Philadelphia. The city's southern approaches were filled with creeks, marshes, and woods, difficult for a large army to traverse but easy for it to be harassed and ambushed. Meanwhile, the Americans had fortified the Delaware just below the city at Fort Mifflin in Pennsylvania and Fort Mercer in New Jersey, which would have required British ships to survive a cannonade in order to pass. The revolutionaries had also had placed chevaux-de-frise (literally translated as "horses from Friesland," a region in Holland that developed them) to block the river. These thirty-foot-square wooden boxes were each weighted down in the riverbed with twenty to forty tons of stone; in them were placed underwater two or three large iron spikes facing downstream. Only pilots friendly to the patriots knew where the gaps between these devices could be found, and any attempt by the British to dismantle them would have subjected them to fire from the forts. The Americans had also prepared fireships, galleys, floating batteries, and other defenses that would have made taking the city from the river questionable at best.

Howe then decided his only option was to sail into Chesapeake Bay and take Philadelphia from the south. Unfortunately, his fleet was afflicted alternately with storms and calms, his horses were near starvation (170 had to be jettisoned), and his hungry men were confined in stifling, stinking, lice-ridden quarters. Not until August 25 did the troops begin to disembark at the Elk River in northern Maryland after more than a month at sea. The day before, Washington had marched his approximately 8,000-man army through the streets of Philadelphia to assure patriots that he could defend them and warn the loyalists that they and their British allies indeed faced formidable odds.

The British spent a week recuperating from their ocean ordeal and on September 3 began to march. At Cooch's Bridge, in Newark, Delaware, Washington's new corps of light infantry, commanded by William Maxwell of New Jersey, met the British advance guard and were repulsed. Howe made the risky decision to abandon his supply base at the Head of Elk and live off the land, hoping to meet up with the British fleet commanded by his brother Lord Richard Howe. Unfortunately for him, the fleet took a week to arrive, forcing the troops to live off the land and offend the local farmers. Howe's official policy was to hang soldiers who plundered civilians, but his officers looked the other way this time, given the desperate condition of their men.

After failing to provoke Washington—whose men were quartered near Wilmington, Delaware—into a battle, Howe and the Americans both headed north. Washington arrived at Brandywine Creek first and built earthen entrenchments near several fords where the British might cross. Two thousand Pennsylvania militiamen commanded by General John Armstrong, victor of the Battle of Kittanning, protected Gibson's Ford and Pyle's Ford. Nathanael Greene and 1,800 Virginians guarded Chad's

Ferry, south of Chad's Ford (now Chadds Ford). Sixteen hundred Pennsylvania Continentals commanded by General Anthony Wayne of Chester County defended Chad's Ford itself. Twelve hundred Maryland Continentals commanded by New Hampshire general John Sullivan covered Brinton's Ford a mile to the north. Only five hundred men covered the next three fords—Jones's, Wistar's, and Buffington's—farther up the river where Washington did not expect an attack. Washington kept 4,300 men in reserve behind Greene and Wayne, who he thought would bear the brunt of the assault. He then sent Maxwell's light infantry across the creek to provide intelligence of the British maneuvers.

Howe had twice before faced the Americans at entrenched positions. In June 1775, at the Battle of Bunker Hill, he sent wave after wave of troops up Breed's Hill (not Bunker Hill, the taller hill behind it) in Charlestown, Massachusetts, where he lost nearly a thousand men. The following year, at the Battle of Long Island in August 1776, he avoided this pitfall and sent a large force behind the American positions on the hills of Brooklyn and nearly destroyed the Continental army. At Brandywine, Howe opted for the latter alternative. Local loyalists told him exactly where Washington's men were positioned. They also gave him the crucial information that the creek could be crossed at Trimble's and Jeffries' fords, only two miles north of Buffington's, whereas the Americans believed the stream was impassible for another ten miles.

Howe divided his army in two and began to move at five o'clock on the morning of September 11. The Hessian general Wilhelm von Knyphausen and seven thousand men would "amuse" the Americans by attacking their front, while General Charles Cornwallis led another eight thousand men up the creek where he would surprise them from the rear. As the British marched through Kennett Square, the local Quakers continued to hold their scheduled meeting as American and British cavalry skirmished. Maxwell's light infantry inflicted considerable damage, killing or wounding two-thirds of a corps of British sharpshooters equipped with a new breech-loading rifle invented by their commander Captain Patrick Ferguson. The Americans withdrew to their defenses behind the creek as Knyphausen's and Washington's artillery pounded each other without much effect between noon and two o'clock in the afternoon.

Cornwallis, meanwhile, had crossed the creek at Trimble's Ford two miles away. There he met a patrol of Pennsylvania riflemen commanded by Lieutenant Colonel James Ross of Lancaster. Ross immediately sent off a dispatch to Washington:

Sept. 11 '77. Great Valley Road
Eleven o'clock A.M.
Dear General, A large body of the enemy—from every account 5000, with 16 or 18 field pieces, marched along this Road just now.

Someone recognized both General Howe and Joseph Galloway among the troops. General Sullivan had also heard from Colonel Moses Hazen, guarding Jones's Ford with eighty men, that the British were on the march. Washington thought about launching a full-scale attack on Knyphausen, but as he was beginning that assault he received contradictory information that Cornwallis was nowhere near his troops. Believing that it was Cornwallis who was feinting, rather than Knyphausen, Washington called off the attack. Had he continued it, he might have first defeated Knyphausen and then turned on Cornwallis.

At about half past two in the afternoon, the inhabitants of Sconnelstown suddenly spotted Cornwallis's army, led by the Hessian Jaegers in green uniforms and Scots Highlanders wearing their kilts. Twenty-four hundred British and Hessian grenadiers, tall men whose fifteen-inch bearskin hats added to their stature, followed them. Two young Quaker brothers, Joseph and William Townsend, were among those who warned General Washington of their approach. Washington sent his reserve troops, commanded by Generals William Alexander (who claimed to be the Scots nobleman Lord Stirling) and Adam Stephen, to confront them. They dug in on a hill near the Birmingham (Quaker) meetinghouse. John Sullivan's troops were also dispatched to join them.

At four o'clock the fighting began there as Captain Thomas Marshall's Third Virginia Regiment fired on the advanced guard of Hessian Jaegers about two hundred yards from the meetinghouse. As the British attacked, they surprised Sullivan's troops, moving into position on the American left; in their panic, two of Sullivan's divisions mistakenly fired at each other as they retreated from the field. The British were thus able to drive Sullivan from the battlefield and attack Stirling and Stephen from both the front and rear. Lieutenant Ebenezer Elmer of New Jersey described the progress of the battle:

We came in sight of the enemy who had crossed the river and were coming down upon us. We formed about 4 o'clock on an eminence, the right being in the woods. Presently a large column came on in front playing the grenadiers' march and now the battle began which proved excessive severe. The enemy came on with fury. Our men stood firing upon them most amazingly, killing almost all before them for near an hour till they got within six rods [thirty-three yards] of each other, when a column of the enemy came upon our flanks which caused them to give way which soon extended all along the line. We retreated and formed on the first ground and gave them another fire and so continued on all the way, but unfortunately for want of a proper retreat 3 or 4 of our [artillery] pieces were left on the first ground.[23]

Confusion reigned as hand-to-hand combat, artillery fire, and gunshots all rang out. Among those wounded in the fierce fighting was the nineteen-year-old Marquis de Lafayette, who saw his first combat. Although Congress appointed him a major general, he had no command and was fighting with General Stirling's division. Lafayette had arrived from France earlier that year,

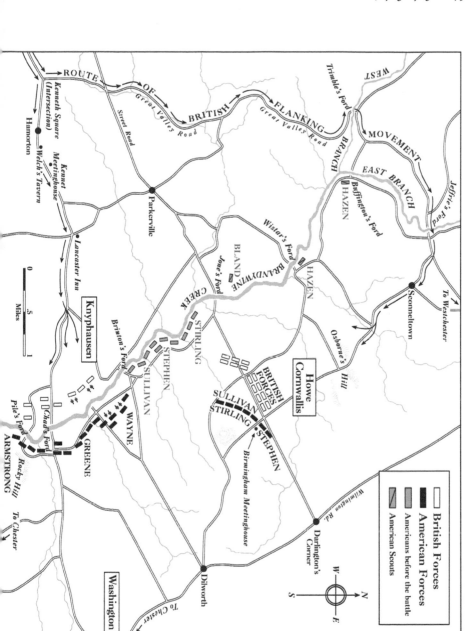

Map 5: The Battle of
Brandywine,
September 11, 1777.

leaving his new bride behind, and made his way north from Charleston, South Carolina, where he had landed. He offered to volunteer as a private soldier, which won the respect of Washington and other American leaders who were tired of European officers volunteering who insisted on high ranks and salaries. As with other casualties, Lafayette was taken to Bethlehem, where the Moravians, especially an attractive young woman he liked a great deal, cared for him in a hospital.

With the Americans on the verge of collapse, Washington dispatched General Nathanael Greene from his main force to assist his embattled right flank. Armstrong's Pennsylvania militia was too far away to be of help, and only Maxwell's light infantry and Anthony Wayne's troops remained to face Knyphausen. At about five o'clock the German general ordered his men to cross the creek, which they did under heavy fire, while wading in water up to their waists. Confronting what one American colonel described as "the most terrible fire I suppose ever heard in America," Wayne's men fought until darkness and Cornwallis's British grenadiers, having smashed the American right, began to join Knyphausen's troops and take positions on hills above his positions. Washington ordered a retreat to Chester; a charge by a troop of American cavalry commanded by the Polish officer Casimir Pulaski was one element that persuaded the exhausted British and Germans not to pursue their foes.

The Battle of Brandywine was the longest (from before dawn until nightfall) battle of the Revolutionary War. It was also the largest: Washington had a total of about 12,000 men at his disposal, the British 16,000. Washington and Greene estimated about 300 Americans were killed, 600 wounded, and 400 captured, while Howe reported 543 casualties to the British ministry, of whom 98 were deaths. Some 350 Americans deserted as well, to judge by postings in Philadelphia newspapers. Thanks to leaders like Wayne, Lafayette, and Pulaski, the Americans retreated in good order rather than being routed. Although national mythology emphasizes the forthcoming Valley Forge winter as decisive in training the American army, Washington and his officers had already accomplished much during 1777. General Howe had won an important victory, but it was not decisive. He failed to pursue the American army, and he had no wagons either to carry his supplies or to transport the wounded.

GERMANTOWN: THE BRITISH TAKE PHILADELPHIA, OCTOBER 1777

Washington had to decide on a course of action. He still hoped to protect Philadelphia and sought to replenish his own supplies from Reading, the nearest town with sizable quantities of munitions, some fifty miles northwest of Philadelphia. He crossed the Schuylkill River at Matson's Ford (Conshohocken), the first fordable site about ten miles north of Philadelphia, but when the British remained several days at Brandywine he crossed back, hoping to fight them again before they took the city. The two armies were ready to fight at Boot Tavern and Goshen Meeting House on September 16, but a heavy rainstorm prevented it. Washington again crossed the river, but left two units—General Anthony Wayne's Pennsylvania Division of about 1,500 men and the 1,200 soldiers in William Smallwood's Maryland militia—behind in Chester County to harass the British and, if possible, take their baggage train.

Wayne and Smallwood did not know the British were camped at Tredyffrin, only four miles from Wayne's camp at Paoli Tavern. This community had been recently named for Pasquale Paoli, the Corsican patriot who had tried to liberate his island from the French, who ironically had been granted sanctuary in Britain after he failed. The area's loyalists informed Howe of Wayne's position, and on September 20, at ten o'clock at night, General Charles Grey led 1,200 men on a surprise attack. They removed the flints from their muskets so the surprise would be complete: in a short time, Wayne suffered over 340 casualties—272 men killed, wounded, and missing, 71 taken prisoner—before fleeing, while the British lost only 4 men killed and 7 wounded. Grey then went on to defeat Smallwood's men as well.

The Americans were quick to term Paoli a "massacre" and spread the word that the British had killed men trying to surrender. But the sizable number of prisoners belies that. The British had basically done to Wayne what Washington had done to Colonel Rall at Trenton—surprised his force and inflicted great casualties. Congress investigated the disaster, and ruled that Wayne had failed to ensure his camp's security but was not guilty of misconduct. Living up to his nickname "Mad Anthony" off as well as on the battlefield, Wayne demanded a court-martial to clear his name, which a board of thirteen officers did on November 1.[24]

On September 23, the British crossed the Schuylkill without opposition at Fatland Ford near Valley Forge. They marched south and set up camp in Germantown, ten miles north of the city, on September 25. The following day, General Cornwallis marched triumphantly into Philadelphia with 3,000 men who occupied the city. By October 2, Howe also detached 1,000 men to Chester County and 2,000 to Wilmington, Delaware. He hoped to repeat the success he had enjoyed in New York the previous year—using the city as a base from which to gain support and supplies from the surrounding region. But in so doing, he reduced his main camp to under 8,000 men. Washington still had over 12,000 soldiers.[25]

On October 3, Washington determined to strike at Howe quickly, before he could build impregnable defenses. He planned to divide his army into four columns, with a fifth to provide a diversion to keep Cornwallis occupied in Philadelphia. The problem with the plan was its complexity. Four columns spread out over twelve miles had to march in silence in the night—and in the fog that typically occurs from Pennsylvania's numerous creeks and valleys—and then strike the British at the same time in the early morning.

Washington's troops began to march at six o'clock on the evening of October 3. General Armstrong's Pennsylvania militia formed the extreme right and was entrusted with attacking the Hessians on Wissahickon Creek. The right-center column, troops from Maryland and Pennsylvania led by Generals Thomas Conway, John Sullivan, and Anthony Wayne, headed down what is now Germantown Avenue toward the British light infantry stationed at Mount Airy, the country estate of William Allen, a prominent loyalist and the last chief justice of colonial Pennsylvania. There they were to meet William Smallwood's Maryland and David Forman's New Jersey militia, who were approaching from the left. Nathanael Greene commanded the far left column. The plan called for complete silence, no lights, and a concerted attack by four columns in the fog at five in the morning.

The Americans attacked first at Mount Airy at half past five. Shouting "Have at the Bloodhounds! Avenge Wayne's Affair [of Paoli]," they easily overwhelmed the 350 men there. Hearing the noise, General Howe rode up from Germantown and tried to rally the light infantry, a British force he had played a key role in founding and organizing. "For shame! For shame, light infantry! I never saw you retreat before! Form! Form! It's only a scouting party!" But as he himself came under fire, he retreated with the rest of the men to the main camp at Germantown.

Cliveden, the country house of loyalist Benjamin Chew, was on the way to the camp. Around quarter past six, about one hundred men of Colonel Thomas Musgrave's Fortieth Regiment fortified the house in an effort to divert the Americans from pursuing the fleeing light infantry, who heard Wayne's men shout that they would "give no quarter" or take no prisoners in revenge for Paoli. The Americans at first realized the ruse and bypassed the house. However, they then encountered British resistance from behind walls and trees, and in the fog; instead of pressing ahead they fired wherever they were fired upon, sometimes shooting at each other.

At the same time, the reinforcements expected to flank the main British camp failed to appear. Nathanael Greene's men took the wrong road, became confused in the fog, and arrived north of their goal. By seven o'clock in the morning, Washington (who followed the rear of the Conway/Sullivan/Wayne column) feared that his men would exhaust the forty rounds of ammunition they carried before they met the main British force. Washington sent his chief aide, Colonel Timothy Pickering of Massachusetts, to warn Sullivan's troops, who were in the rear of that column, to conserve their fire. On his way back, Pickering passed Cliveden where the British happened to fire at him; he proceeded to tell Washington there were still British troops in the rear of his own.

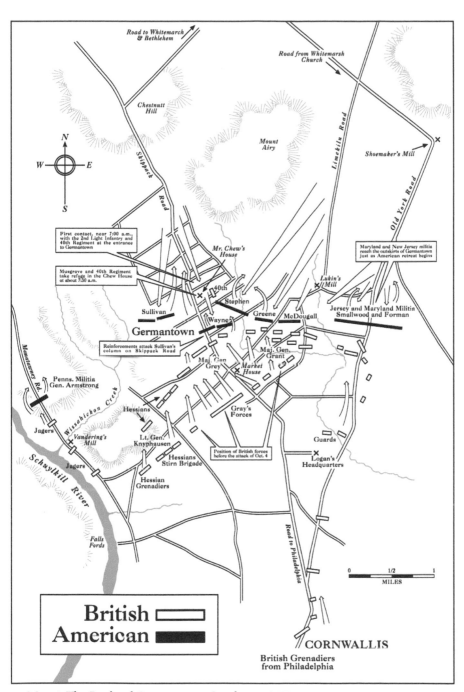

Road to Whitemarch
& Bethlehem

Road from Whitemarsh
Church

Chestnutt
Hill

Mount
Airy

Limekiln Road

Shoemaker's Mill

N
W — E
S

Skippack Road

Old York Road

First contact, near 7:00 a.m.,
with the 2nd Light Infantry and
40th Regiment at the entrance
to Germantown

Mr. Chew's
House

Maryland and New Jersey militia
reach the outskirts of Germantown
just as American retreat begins

Musgrave and 40th Regiment
take refuge in the Chew House
at about 7:30 a.m.

Lukin's
Mill

40th

Sullivan

Stephen

Greene   McDougall

Jersey and Maryland Militia
Smallwood and Forman

Wayne

Germantown

Reinforcements attack Sullivan's
column on Skippack Road

Maj. Gen.
Grey

Maj. Gen.
Grant

Market
House

Penns. Militia
Gen. Armstrong

Manatawny Rd.

Wissahickon Creek

Hessians

Gray's
Forces

Jagers

Vandering's
Mill

Lt. Gen.
Knyphausen

Guards

Schuylkill River

Jagers

Hessians
Stirn Brigade

Position of British forces
before the attack of Oct. 4

Logan's
Headquarters

Hessian
Grenadiers

Falls
Fords

Road to Philadelphia

0   1/2   1
MILES

British
American

CORNWALLIS
British Grenadiers
from Philadelphia

Map 6: The Battle of Germantown, October 4, 1777.

Washington received conflicting advice on what to do about Cliveden. His aide Alexander Hamilton urged that a small body of troops lay siege to it while the rest of the army headed toward the main camp. Artillery chief Henry Knox, however, compared this to leaving "a castle in the rear" and insisted on bombarding the house. Knox was also confident that the outnumbered British in the house commanded by Captain William Harris would realize the folly of resistance and respond to a request to surrender. Instead, the officer carrying the white flag, Lieutenant William Smith of Virginia, was shot and killed as Pickering predicted he would be. Whether responding in kind to the American shouts of "no quarter" or simply shooting, as they had been, at anyone who came close to the house, the British had no intention of giving up.

Knox's subsequent cannonade failed: Cliveden's sturdy stone walls and thick wooden doors, with all available furniture piled against shattered doors and windows, foiled the light six-pound artillery the Americans had brought with them. Next, two New Jersey regiments tried to storm the house under the cover of grapeshot; the British mowed them down at point-blank range and bayoneted the handful who reached the front door. Finally, four officers took some straw from a nearby barn and sneaked around the house in the hopes of setting fire to its kitchen. Two were killed, but Lieutenant Colonel John Laurens of South Carolina and a French volunteer,

Chevalier Thomas-Antoine du Plessis-Mauduit, almost miraculously preserved both their lives and their dignity: "it would have been ridiculous to return running. M. de Mauduit, like a true Frenchman, chose rather to expose himself to death rather than ridicule; but the balls respected our prejudices; he returned safe and sound, and Mr. Laurens, who was in no greater haste than he, escaped with a slight wound in his shoulder."

General Wayne's men, on their way to the main camp and hearing the fighting in their rear, turned back and also marched toward Cliveden. As the house was surrounded, Americans firing at it from both directions shot into each other, thinking the British had placed artillery in the house. Meanwhile, General Greene's forces finally arrived, but instead of encountering the British crashed into Wayne's men who were approaching Cliveden from the opposite side of Germantown Road. Adam Stephen, commanding one of Greene's two brigades, whose service with George Washington dated back to Fort Necessity and included much of the French and Indian War, ordered his troops to attack Anthony Wayne's men whom he thought were redcoats. He was later discovered asleep and drunk, for which he was dismissed from the army.

By eight o'clock in the morning the battle was over. The main British army arrived, along with reinforcements from General Cornwallis in Philadelphia—who had easily captured the "fifth column" sent to divert him—dispersing the Americans. John

British troops took refuge in Cliveden, the Benjamin Chew House, during the Battle of Germantown. The troops used the stone house as a fortress and successfully thwarted multiple attempts by Washington's army to remove them. By diverting the Continental army, the small force provided time for the main British army and reinforcements to arrive and disperse Washington's forces.

Armstrong's Pennsylvanians never reached the battlefield. Hessian troops perched high above Wissahickon Creek prevented them from advancing.

Three British soldiers stationed at Cliveden were killed and twenty-five wounded; the British army counted a total of 465 wounded and 70 killed. Among the dead was General James Agnew, who was shot by civilians firing out of the Germantown Mennonite Church as he led his troops toward Cliveden. The Americans officially listed 152 dead, 521 wounded, and over 400 missing. New Jersey's major James Witherspoon, son of John Witherspoon, signer of the Declaration of Independence and president of the College of New Jersey (later Princeton University) was killed along with General Francis Nash by a stray cannonball that careened to the rear of the field. The real heroes of the battle, as the British colonel Thomas Musgrave realized, were the men of his regiment who held off practically the entire American army at Cliveden. They received the thanks of King George, and in 1780, medals (bronze for enlisted men, silver for officers) bearing their names with an image of Cliveden being fired upon on one side and the words "Germantown, October 4, 1777" on the other. This was one of the first decorations in British military history where men were honored for a specific engagement. The medal depicted the scene with great accuracy: American artillery firing from across a road lined with fences; two of the statues with which Benjamin Chew had adorned his garden; massed American troops firing a volley; and correct window placement. The Fortieth Regiment would use the image of Cliveden on medals to honor its best troops for at least another century.

Benjamin Chew was not a sufficiently obnoxious loyalist to be exiled, and he no longer lived in a house that he termed "an absolute wreck." But by 1778 he had sufficiently cleaned it up that he could rent it, and he sold it in 1779 to Blair McClenachan, a privateer and leader of Pennsylvania's Constitutionalist Party that had seized control of the state. Chew bought it back in 1797, and Cliveden remained in the family, one of Philadelphia's most prominent, until 1972.

Following the battle, the Americans retreated twenty-four miles on October 4 to Pennypacker's Mill. Private Joseph Plumb Martin, whose narrative is the best source for understanding the tribulations of the average soldier, wrote: "I had now to travel the rest of the day after marching all the day and night before and fighting all morning. I had eaten nothing since the noon of the proceeding day. . . . I was tormented with thirst all morning."[26] As exhausted as their men, General Greene fell asleep on his horse, General Conway in a barn, and Casimir Pulaski in a farmhouse as the British, stunned by the attack, remained in Germantown. One touch of civility followed: General Howe's

dog (with his master's name on his collar) had been captured by the Americans. On October 7, Washington returned him under a flag of truce.

Germantown convinced Howe that he could not fortify so extended an area, and he moved into Philadelphia itself on October 19. He moved into the substantial home of John Cadwalader, now a general in the Pennsylvania militia, while General Grey and Major John Andre—a handsome officer who became the army's most popular for his drawings, poems, and fine appearance at parties—settled into Benjamin Franklin's house. Grey took a portrait of Franklin back with him to England, which his family later returned. The British army hired the inhabitants who remained at eight shillings per day plus provisions to build their defenses.

Despite taking the city, Howe was in a tough situation. He could not receive reinforcements or provisions up the Delaware because the Americans still held Forts Mifflin and Mercer, which were supplemented by shore batteries and fireships. A siege began in early October and lasted until November 18 under the direction of Captain John Montresor, who had begun to design Fort Mifflin in 1771, although final construction was then postponed until 1776. In the meanwhile, Philadelphia came perilously close to running out of food: "provisions are so extremely scarce—bakers down to 10 days—not any wood to be had at any price—the rich have not for themselves, nor have they it in their power to relieve the cries of the poor, for money will not procure the necessaries of life." During the battle, the sixty-four-gun battleship *Augusta* ran aground: the men jumped overboard and the Americans blew it up. Joseph Plumb Martin wrote: "she blew up with an explosion which seemed to shake the earth to its center, leaving a volume of smoke like a thundercloud."[27]

The British attack lasted six weeks and was the largest bombardment of the Revolutionary War. Fort Mifflin's location was nicknamed Mud Island, as frequent rainstorms turned the land into mud. Martin remarked that "it was utterly impossible to lie down to get any rest or sleep on account of the mud, if the enemy's shot would have suffered us to do so." On November 15, the Americans blew up Fort Mifflin and retreated inland: about 250 of its 450 defenders had been killed. On November 18 General Cornwallis led two thousand men who finally captured Fort Mercer. *Common Sense*'s author Thomas Paine believed the Americans, rather than the British, came out of the battle heroically. The siege, he said, "exhibited the power of Britain in a very contemptible light.... For several weeks did that little unfinished fortress stand out against all the attempts of Admiral and General Howe.... Scheme after scheme, and force upon force were tried and defeated. The garrison, with scarce anything to cover them but their bravery, survived in the midst of mud, shot, and shells, and were at last obliged to give it up."[28]

Although the forts were ultimately lost, the six-week delay spent capturing them enabled Washington and his troops to establish impregnable winter headquarters at Valley Forge. Through most of October and November, Washington moved his army from place to place. In early December, General Howe—who had asked the secretary of state for the colonies, Lord George Germain, to relieve him of his command—made a final sortie to see if a final battle was feasible. He moved on the American encampment at Whitemarsh (several miles up Germantown Road), but after skirmishes between small advanced forces between December 4 and 6 decided the defenses were too strong and retreated to Philadelphia on December 8. Washington began moving his troops to Valley Forge on December 11; the maneuver was complete by December 19. Congress, meanwhile, found winter quarters in the distant town of York.

They had it much better than the army.

THE VALLEY FORGE WINTER, 1777–1778

Valley Forge was more than the site of the present National Park. It was the headquarters of an army that ranged as far south as Wilmington, Delaware, west to Reading, and east to New Jersey to obtain supplies and investigate loyalist activity. Some of Washington's generals suggested either Wilmington or Reading as a safer location, but Washington followed Congress's directions to remain within twenty-five miles of Philadelphia to prevent the local area from being "despoiled and ravaged by the enemy." He realized it was critical that his army receive supplies and food from Pennsylvania's interior counties, also the center of the colonial munitions industry, and Valley Forge was about thirty miles from Reading.[29]

Valley Forge is famous as the winter when the Continental army suffered the most. Surgeon Albigence Waldo wrote of the miseries of the rank and file at Valley Forge:

I am sick, discontented, and out of humor. Poor food, hard lodging, cold weather, fatigue, nasty clothes, nasty cookery, vomit half my time, smoked out of my senses, the devil in it, I can't endure it, why are we sent here to starve and freeze? What sweet felicities have I left at home: A charming wife, pretty children, good beds, good food, good cookery, all agreeable, all harmonious. Here all confusion, smoke and cold, hunger and filthiness—a pox on my bad luck. There comes a bowl of beef soup full of burnt leaves and dirt . . . away with it boys, I'll live like a chameleon upon air. . . . There comes a soldier, bare feet are seen through his worn out shoes, his legs nearly naked from the tattered remains of an only pair of stockings, his breeches not sufficient to cover his nakedness, his shirt hanging in strings, his hair disheveled, his face meager, his whole appearance pictures a person forsaken and discouraged.[30]

The problem with Valley Forge was not extreme cold: in fact, the temperature that winter was above average. Rather, the rains and snows, which meant thaws and freezing alternated, made the road and rivers to the camp difficult to use. The incompetence of the quartermaster department— which General Nathanael Greene took over later in the winter and greatly improved—was another reason. Even when the men had enough food they lacked sufficient clothing. Washington could complain to Congress on December 19 that "you might have tracked the army from White Marsh to Valley Forge by the blood of their feet" and, on December 23, that " this army must inevitably . . . starve, dissolve, or disperse." Despite his reluctance to antagonize the civilian population, Washington ordered Lord Stirling and Anthony Wayne—respectively familiar with the nearby area in New Jersey and Pennsylvania—to forage for crops and livestock.[31]

Washington realized his men needed decent housing. He had more than one thousand huts constructed, to accommodate his force of some fourteen thousand men, by January 1. They were 14 by 16 feet and 6.5 feet high, each with a fireplace and chimney, which frequently made the interiors intolerably smoky. If anything, these shelters were incubators for disease. Men died from dysentery, scurvy, consumption, cholera, typhus, pneumonia, and whooping cough. Smallpox was the number one killer—approximately 130,000 people died in the United States during the Revolutionary War from epidemics of the disease that struck repeatedly between 1775 and 1783. Washington had every soldier at Valley Forge inoculated against the disease. Unlike the

A reconstructed log cabin at Valley Forge of the type built to house Continental soldiers during the harsh winter of 1777–1778.

present-day vaccination, discovered in 1796 by Edward Jenner, in which people receive a dose of cowpox (a much less harmful disease), inoculation—introduced to America in 1722 by Massachusetts minister Cotton Mather, who had learned of the African practice from his slave Onesimus—meant injecting a small dose of smallpox itself. While usually effective, and communities that had been inoculated suffered few deaths, it could be dangerous: Jonathan Edwards, the famous minister, had died in Princeton, New Jersey, while attempting to demonstrate the value of inoculation. As a result of inoculation, almost no soldiers died of the disease for the rest of the war.

At Valley Forge, however, the figures were staggering. Muster rolls show that 1,162 out of 14,122 soldiers died of disease between December 1777 and June 1778; in contrast, about 300 Americans were killed at

the Battle of Long Island in 1776 and Brandywine in 1777, the highest totals in the war. Numbers of sick were astonishing: on January 1, 1778, 50.2 percent of the army was either "sick present" or "sick absent." The medical corps constructed "flying hospitals" in camp to quarantine and treat the sick, but these proved inadequate. Dr. Benjamin Rush of Philadelphia and a Surgeon General in the Continental army complained that they were "outrageous" and "foul" with twenty men in a space barely large enough for six; the men would sell their clothing and blankets for rum and fight among themselves. Things were better at the more distant hospitals established in Yellow Springs (a fashionable spa), Bethlehem, Ephrata, Lancaster, and Easton, where those who could be moved were sent for treatment and recovery.[32]

Arguments among both rank and file and leaders made a bad situation worse. Pennsylvania's Persifor Frazer complained that "the miserable behavior of the Yankees is enough to make me sick of the service," while Connecticut's Joseph Plumb Martin would rather "have been incorporated with a tribe of western Indians as with any of the Southern troops." Dr. John Morgan, the first professor of medicine at the College of Philadelphia, had been dismissed as the army's head physician on April 11, 1777, because of complaints from Dr. William Shippen. Shippen in turn fell afoul of Rush, who tried to have him court-martialed. When that failed, Rush left camp in disgust at the height of its troubles in January 1778. Dr. Bodo Otto of Reading then took charge of the medical department. At the same time, confidence in Washington himself eroded. General Thomas Conway praised Horatio Gates, the victor of Saratoga in October 1777, as the man heaven intended to save the country and obtained support from Lord Stirling, Richard Henry Lee, Benjamin Rush, and Thomas Mifflin to lobby Gates's case before Congress. However, Washington learned of Conway's efforts, at which time the plot ceased. Congress appointed Gates and Mifflin to the Board of War and made Conway inspector general of the army, which represented less than a vote of confidence in Washington, although it did not remove him.

February added insult to injury. The troops at Valley Forge performed a play by the British writer Joseph Addison. Even though it was designed to inculcate republican virtue based on the life of the virtuous Roman leader Cato, Congress on February 6 declared that "any person holding an office under the United States, who shall attend a theatrical performance, shall be dismissed from service." The wonder is the entire army did not use this excuse to get themselves sent home.

Then things changed for the better. Prussian drillmaster Friedrich von Steuben arrived at Valley Forge on February 23 and began to drill the troops. To be sure, Washington and his officers had done much in 1777: the army was able to perform complicated maneuvers and both attack and withdraw in good order at Brandywine and Germantown, a far cry from the rout from New York the previous year. But much improvement was still needed. Although an out-of-work captain, Steuben had managed to convince Silas Deane and Benjamin Franklin, who were in Europe at the time, that he was a baron and lieutenant general in the Prussian army. He could only speak German and French, so Colonels Alexander Hamilton and Henry Laurens translated his orders into English, while a bilingual aide would respond to his order that he swear at the men for him. He divided the troops into uniform regiments: previously, regiments had any number of companies, and officers had no idea how many men they had. He selected 120 men to be a model company, who were taught several basic commands—how to carry a musket, load, fire, fix bayonets, charge, march in step—they would then teach the rest of the army. Officers were required to account for arms, keep regular records of their troops' well-being and supplies, and inspect their troops every week. He also insisted on camp sanitation— separation of kitchens and latrines with the regular arrangement of cabins in rows.

Steuben realized his commands could be neither too complicated nor unreasonable to the average soldier. "The genius of this nation," he maintained, "is not to be compared . . . with that of the Prussians, Austrians, or French. You say to your soldier 'do this' and he does it; but I am obliged to say, 'This is the reason why you ought to do that' and *then* he does it." The soldiers appreciated the discipline, as an officer noted: "the army grows stronger every day. It increased in number . . . and there is a spirit of discipline among the troops that is better than numbers." Steuben was the first to teach the Americans how to use their bayonets properly (previously, some had used them primarily as spits to cook food on). On May 5, after a little more than two months in America, Congress appointed Steuben to replace Conway as the army's inspector general with retroactive back pay.[33]

By spring, word reached the army of the alliance France had concluded on February 6 with America, as well as news that the British (who had declared war on France on March 17) were about to abandon Philadelphia and concentrate their forces in New York. The British now had to fight the French in the West Indies and guard the homeland against a possible invasion. On May 19, Washington sent out the Marquis de Lafayette and 2,200 men to see if the British were planning to move against the American army before they left Pennsylvania. Learning the American plans from the area's numerous loyalists—as they always had since landing in Pennsylvania—General Howe persuaded his successor, Sir Henry Clinton, to give him one last chance to achieve glory. He dispatched sixteen thousand men in three columns under General James Grant to capture Lafayette. But Lafayette used five hundred of his best men, including fifty Oneida Indians, to hold off the British at Barren Hill (slightly west of Whitemarsh) while he used a little-known path to escape to the Schuylkill River. As George Washington wrote to Congress: "The Marquis, by depending on the militia to patrol the roads on his left, had very near been caught in a snare—in fact he was in it—but by his *own dexterity* or the enemy's *want of it*, he disengaged himself in a very soldierlike manner, and by an orderly and well conducted retreat got out, losing three men killed and a like number taken *only*. . . . Upon the whole the Marquis came handsomely off, and the enemy returned disappointed and disgraced; loading poor Grant with obloquy for his conduct on the occasion."[34]

The British took nearly as much time to leave Philadelphia as they had taken to get there. Only on June 18, 1778, did they leave the city; on June 23 Washington followed, recrossing the Delaware. On June 28 the Americans attacked their twelve-mile-long column at Monmouth. Proving General Howe's wisdom in not marching to Philadelphia across New Jersey, the British would have lost had not General Charles Lee, commanding the assault, withdrawn his troops when victory was at hand. No further encounters between the main American and British armies occurred in Pennsylvania.

THE BRITISH OCCUPY PHILADELPHIA, 1777–1778

Shortly after General Howe had set up his army in Philadelphia the previous October, Washington predicted that "the acquisition of Philadelphia may, instead of his good fortune, prove his ruin." Indeed, it can be argued that the British army made more converts to the American cause than all the patriotic exhortations of Thomas Paine, Benjamin Franklin, and all the rest simply by showing up. As in New York the previous year, the British army brought with it both martial law and arrogance. General Howe relied on the former Speaker of the Pennsylvania Assembly Joseph Galloway to govern Philadelphia as the superintendent of police.[35]

Galloway served efficiently. He secured horses from the surrounding area, directed a ring of about eighty spies so no movement of the Continental army escaped unnoticed, erected some new batteries that finally enabled the British to take Fort Mifflin, and administered oaths of allegiance to the British similar to those the patriots had before their departure. He appointed friends, especially Quakers, to serve under him. Abraham Carlisle, whom Galloway placed in charge of issuing passports to move outside the city (both sides allowed frequent intercourse across the lines for personal and business reasons), came to grief as he was one of two Pennsylvanians later executed for treason.

Galloway and the British also enlisted some of between 1,000 and 3,000 loyalists who made their way to British lines. Some of them joined the Philadelphia Light Dragoons, a horse brigade that supplemented the Queen's Rangers. Their principal task was to enable nearby farmers to bring produce into the city by protecting them from American soldiers who also patrolled the surrounding area, whom they confronted with mixed success.

The British brought hard money with them, which only increased the trade that had been conducted between New York and the farmers of Chester and Bucks counties along the Delaware River. Most of these were Quakers and Anglicans who did not approve of the revolution, and no one preferred depreciated Continen-tal currency to British pounds sterling. Christopher Marshall reported about 120 new stores in Philadelphia, nearly all of them kept by Scotsmen and loyalists. The town's three newspapers switched sides as well, including Benjamin Franklin's old *Pennsylvania Gazette*.

Yet within a short time, even British sympathizers were angry that the army treated those who remained in Philadelphia like conquered enemies rather than those they were sent to liberate. All patriots of any importance had left, and the 21,000 or so people who remained were loyalists and neutrals who "had too long suffered under the yoke of arbitrary power" from the rebels, according to Robert Morton. When he returned in June 1778, patriot Christopher Marshall commented on "the desolation with the dirt, filth, stench, and flies about town." The State House had been used as a hospital, its grounds as a dumping ground for dead horses. Except for the Anglican churches frequented by the British, the other religious buildings were used as hospitals, stables, and barracks: even Anglican St. Peter's had its fence torn down for firewood. On November 22, seventeen country houses near town were burned, several belonging to loyalists, which the British claimed were being used by American sharpshooters. The British imposed curfews on the citizens as they caroused at night, staging plays to which they invited their friends. As supplies ran low, Elizabeth Drinker complained of "enormities of one kind or other being committed by those from whom we ought to find protection." Joseph Galloway's wife Grace—whom the patriots later removed from her house and sent to join her husband after giving her carriage to the Spanish ambassador—believed "the greatest rebels was in the king's army," suggesting the widespread belief that General Howe—who was friendly to both Benjamin Franklin and the American cause and supported it in Parliament before the war—was a traitor at heart. With cannons and gunfire going off all the time until Fort Mifflin was finally captured in December, Hannah Griffitts composed a poem: "Wrote on the Death of a Person Who Died of a Violent Nervous Disorder Occasion'd by the Distress She Suffered in the Late Distracted Times."[36]

The loyalists were angry that the British seemed to be enjoying themselves while a wretched American army lay waiting to be destroyed. As James Allen wrote: "For 7 months Gen Washington with an army not exceeding 7 or 8000 men has lain at Valley Forge 20 miles from here, unmolested; While Sr W. Howe with

more than double his number & the best troops in the world, has been shut up in Philada where the markets are extravagantly high, & parties of the enemy all round the city within a mile or two robbing the market people. Consequently the distress of the citizens and particularly the Refugees has been very great."[37]

Nothing offended loyal Philadelphians more than the Meschianza, an extravagant party held to honor General Howe after he had been recalled and summoned to Britain to account for his behavior. His officers showed their appreciation by spending over $3,500 on a festival where a regatta on the Delaware carried the guests of honor with accompanying bands to pavilions and triumphal arches just south of the city. Local belles dressed in the Turkish costumes that were all the rage among European aristocrats sponsored officers who, dressed as medieval knights, jousted in their honor at a tournament. Dancing went on until four o'clock in the morning. Elizabeth Drinker commented: "How insensible do these people appear while our land is so greatly desolated," while Griffitts condemned the "shameful scene of dissipation."[38]

TREASON TRIALS AND DIVISIONS AMONG THE REVOLUTIONARIES, 1778–1780

Once Congress and the Supreme Executive Council returned in late July, both bodies, along with many returning Philadelphians were eager to prosecute—perhaps "persecute" might be a better word—those who had remained with the British and were not among the three thousand who left with them. A committee of 186 men, including Thomas Paine and Joseph Reed, formed an association to bring to trial those "notoriously disaffected to the American cause." Forty-five persons were accused of treason and twenty-three were brought to trial in the remaining months of 1778, although only two, both Quakers, were executed. John Roberts, a miller of Lower Merion, had tried to persuade men to enlist in the British army, and Abraham Carlisle of Philadelphia had guarded the city and issued passports under a British commission. Despite petitions from numerous people, mostly Quakers, but also including Chief Justice Thomas McKean who had delivered the sentence, the men were hanged on November 4. (The Quaker Meeting itself, which disowned those who took either side in the Revolution, did not support the petition.) McKean was hoping to control the vigilantism of the committee of 186 by showing that the courts were capable of enforcing the treason laws, and doing so against well-to-do people to show ordinary folk they were not immune because of their wealth and connections. But he had also hoped to show mercy, which Pennsylvania's president Joseph Reed and the Supreme Executive Council denied.[39]

That the treason trials were motivated more by personal animosities and general perceptions than actual actions appeared in the acquittals of William (Billy) Hamilton and David Franks, who unlike Carlisle and Roberts were brought to trial before Congress. Hamilton, who had built one of the best examples of Georgian architecture in the colonies, Woodlands (still standing at Fortieth Street and Baltimore Avenue), was a wealthy man, a friend of the Penns and much of the Philadelphia elite, but noted chiefly for his botanical gardens and experiments, which rivaled those of John and William Bartram, whose gardens a couple of miles south on the Schuylkill River (the house is preserved as a museum) were the finest in America. He left no footprint in the political world, but was accused of assisting the British and was only acquitted after a twelve-hour trial. That General John Cadwalader, a friend of Washington and commander of the Philadelphia militia, vouched for Hamilton was probably a main reason he did not suffer the death penalty. George Clymer, a signer of the Declaration of Independence but opponent of the radicals, complained of the "extremity of baseness" Joseph Reed had exhibited in the prosecution.

Also tried before Congress was the Jewish merchant David Franks, whose brother Moses was one of four British merchants in charge of supplying the army in North America. Franks had the unenviable task of being in charge of feeding and supplying the British prisoners held by the Americans. Each side paid to take care of its own prisoners, and truces and payments were arranged between the lines. Delays in payments frequently led Franks to advance his own money hoping for reimbursement from the British, which he tried to secure by stressing the urgency of the situation when, of necessity, he corresponded with the British army in New York. His principal correspondent, however, was his brother-in-law, the notorious New York loyalist Oliver Delancey, to whom Franks expressed joy over "Billy" Hamilton's acquittal. He also explained to his brother Moses that prices were high because of shortages and that there was severe division among the revolutionaries in Pennsylvania over how to govern. Although these facts were common knowledge, Franks was accused of portraying the revolution as precarious and thereby encouraging the enemy. Once again, Cadwalader attested that Franks harbored no ill feelings toward the revolution—he was the only one of about twenty-five Jews in the city who was even suspected. George Clymer also expressed his outrage that perhaps the fact that Franks's lively daughter Rebecca was one of the belles of the ball at the Meschianza and had consorted with and then married a British officer, departing with the army, also aroused suspicions. Even after his acquittal, Franks was retried in 1780 by the state of Pennsylvania: acquitted once again, he was nevertheless threatened with violence and forced to leave town. That he returned to Philadelphia in 1783 while he probably could have worked and lived with his brother in England for the rest of his life also suggests where his true allegiance lay.

The most sensational treason case in Philadelphia, however, involved the military commander of the city and, before his defection, one of the great heroes of the American Revolution. Something had snapped in Benedict Arnold. He was furious that he received little credit for the American triumph at Saratoga where he basically forced the commander Horatio Gates to assault the enemy by disobeying orders and leading the charge himself, during which he lost the use of a leg. Appointed military governor of the city on June 19, Arnold moved into the Penn family mansion and made so much money by granting permission for people to trade, as well as trading himself, that he was also able to purchase a fine country estate at Mount Pleasant. Arnold socialized freely with the loyalists who remained, such as the Chews and the Shippens, and married Peggy Shippen in March 1779 when she was eighteen and he was thirty-eight. As early as November 1778 Nathanael Greene had heard rumors from Philadelphia that Arnold was "unpopular among you owing to his associating too much with the Tories." Perhaps hoping to bring Greene over to his side, Arnold informed Greene of the "deplorable" and "horrid" situation in the nation, interpreting inflation, unrest in the army, and squabbling in Congress as signs of "impending ruin."[40]

Arnold was providing the British with secret information as early as July 1779 after the Supreme Executive Council had sought to put him on trial for his illegal gains. Peggy Shippen played an important role in his conveying his messages to the British in code in letters to her friends in New York. Arnold's court-martial was delayed until January 1780, when he was only found guilty of using government wagons for his own trading ventures. He was given command of West Point on August 3, 1780; by the end of September his connections with Major John André had been discovered and he had to flee to British lines. Arnold's treason nearly swept up his innocent aide-de-camp David Salisbury Franks, a Jewish merchant from Montreal who had moved south to participate in the rebellion. Arrested on October 2, Franks was acquitted the next day, and then insisted on complete exoneration from a court-martial, which he obtained on November 2. Franks later served as a diplomat in Europe and North Africa, securing the recognition of the United States by Morocco.

Prosecution of moderate revolutionaries and neutrals for treason revealed the desperate straits into which the Constitutionalist Party, that in 1776 had seized control of Pennsylvania, had fallen. Wealthy and influential people such as Robert Morris were joined by men such as Benjamin Franklin and Benjamin Rush who had initially supported the new government but now, as Rush stated, were appalled by its actions. The class divisions that had appeared between the Committee of Privates and other poor folk who sought to fix prices and the merchants who believed this was a guarantee that food would flow to the British instead came to a head in what is known as the "Fort Wilson Riot."[41]

In Philadelphia, on October 4, 1779, an incident broke out at the house of James Wilson, prominent lawyer, signer of the Declaration of Independence, and a principal opponent of the radical Constitutionalist government that had taken office in 1776. He had unsuccessfully defended Carlisle and Roberts, and defended others successfully, during the treason trials of the previous year. "God help us—Terrible times . . . the poor starving here and rise for redress," wrote Samuel Patterson. Critical of the unequal distribution of wealth, members of the First Company of the Philadelphia Militia Artillery had been protesting since May that while they had "cheerfully stepped forth . . . to act in a military capacity," they had to leave their families "at the mercy of the disaffected, inimical, or self-interested . . . the most obnoxious part of the community" who "had taken advantage of our absence and enormously advanced the prices on everything."[42]

All adult men were supposed to serve in the militia or pay a fine, but the penalties were far too small—especially given inflation—to encourage the wealthy to enlist. Militiamen complained that "men in these exorbitant times can acquire more by monopolizing, or by an under[handed] trade in one day, than will defray all their expenses of fines or penalties in a whole year." Unless steeper fines were introduced, one observer noted: "the middling and poor will still bear the burden and either be totally ruined by the heavy fines, or risk the starving of their families, whilst themselves are fighting the battles of those who are avariciously intent on amassing wealth by the destruction of the more virtuous part of the community." Here, the militia took a swipe at the upper class's pretensions to "republican virtue," or the disinterested love of community, that it claimed to exemplify. [43]

As early as May 24, 1779, according to Elizabeth Drinker, a "great speculator" attempted to pull down "threatening handbills": he and several others were taken to jail by the soldiers. Merchants selling above prices the militia deemed fair were forced by "men with clubs" to lower their prices. Daniel Roberdeau, the chairman of a town meeting that met on May 25, denounced those who were "getting rich by sucking the blood of the country." "Combinations have been formed for raising the prices of goods and provisions," he charged, suggesting collusion among the wealthy, "and therefore the community, in their own defense, have a natural right to counteract such combinations and to set limits to evils."

The action of even the radical Constitutionalist government showed a split had developed between its leaders and the rank and file. The state's Supreme Executive Council insisted that all those wealthy merchants and suspected loyalists who had been jailed informally by the militia, and against whom specific charges could not be proven, were to be immediately freed, so that no "innocent persons" shall "by mistake" be victims of "the unmerited censure of their fellow citizens." The militia responded on June 28 by stating "we have arms in our hands and know the use of them . . . nor will we lay them down" until "the righteous and equitable measures" to keep prices affordable were enforced. In short, the militia claimed to step into a power vacuum formed by the impotence of the elected authorities. When General John Cadwalader, a defender of falsely accused loyalists, who opposed price fixing, attempted to speak to his troops on July 25, he was silenced "by a body of about 100 men, armed with clubs, who had marched in array, under their officers, with fife and drum, and placed themselves near the stage." They then called a meeting and "the greatest number of voters ever known on such an occasion" elected by a vote of 2,115 to 281 a committee of 120 members to enforce price regulation.[44]

Yet the committee proved ineffectual, especially as on August 18 eighty of the city's leading merchants sent it a memorial denying its authority. It collapsed soon thereafter, but the militia, unable to convince Charles Willson Peale to lead them, formed instead a resuscitated Committee of Privates to supplant the defunct committee. On October 4 they met for the first time at Byrnes's Tavern. A handbill named those profiteers they ought to seize and send to the British army in New York. The broadside urged the people "to drive from the city all disaffected persons and those who supported them."[45]

The privates then had to choose who was sufficiently obnoxious to be deported. On October 4, they began rounding up suspects: they marched past the City Tavern, where a group of twenty to forty gentlemen, suspecting that some of them were the targets, retreated to James Wilson's impressive house at Third and Walnut streets where they armed themselves. As the crowd passed, shots rang out: at least six people were killed and between seventeen and nineteen seriously wounded in the confrontation. Wealthy inhabitants blamed the democratic excesses of the Pennsylvania Constitution and the hostility of the lower class to the wealthier citizens for the uprising. Henry Laurens of South Carolina, one of the wealthiest men in his state and a former president of the Continental Congress, commented: "We are at this moment on a precipice, and what I have long dreaded and often intimated to my friends, seems to be breaking forth— a convulsion among the people." [46]

Wilson was a likely target. A signer of the Declaration of Independence, a former professor at the College of Philadelphia, and a prominent lawyer, Wilson was a leader of the Republican Society, which had formed in March 1779 to oppose the Pennsylvania Constitution of 1776, which its members considered too democratic. As Dr. Benjamin Rush, another leader, commented, its supporters were "in general the ancient inhabitants of the state . . . distinguished for their wealth, virtue, learning, and liberality of manners"—in short, they were consciously aristocratic.

It seems that the first shots were fired from within the house, probably by a Colonel Campbell who was the only person in the house to be killed. Within ten minutes, Joseph Reed,

president of Pennsylvania and a Constitutionalist leader himself, led the upper-class City Troop of Cavalry, attacked the militia, and arrested those who did not run away. Twenty-seven men were placed in jail; the militia officers wanted to jail the men in Wilson's house, but this did not happen. On October 5, Reed brokered an agreement of both sides. The militia put their grievances to the assembly, especially "the high price of flour"; the assembly responded by distributing one hundred free barrels with a preference to the families of militiamen. After charges and countercharges, the Supreme Executive Council pardoned everyone involved on March 13, 1780.

THE DECLINE OF THE CONSTITUTIONALISTS AND THE PRIVATIZATION OF THE WAR, 1780–1783

By this time, the Constitutionalists had been ousted by the "Republicans" such as John Dickinson, Wilson, and Morris. Initiatives taken by well-to-do private citizens then accomplished what the Constitutionalist government and the Philadelphia committees had failed to: protect commerce and stabilize the currency. Pennsylvania had a colonial (later state) navy as early as October 1775, designed to secure Philadelphia and its trade. Most of the navy was destroyed when the British attacked Philadelphia: at Washington's direction, Captain John Hazelwood had much of the fleet burned in October 1777, when it appeared the British would capture it at Fort Mifflin, and the rest (sent up river by Trenton once the British passed the fort in November) was sunk in April 1778, when the British left Philadelphia and it was feared the British navy would trap and capture it.[47]

As the state navy died, privately financed vessels took its place. In the fall of 1779 the *General Greene*, with fifteen guns, captured six prizes off Delaware Bay. When the British stepped up attacks in the spring of 1782, the privately financed *Hyder Alley*, commanded by Joshua Barney, captured the much larger ship *General Monk* and renamed it the *Washington*. But by far the most numerous and effective naval actions during the revolution were undertaken by the 448 privateers licensed by the state between 1776 and 1782. Congress licensed 83 ships from Pennsylvania out of a total of 1,697 overall. Assuming Pennsylvania ships performed typically, the roughly 5 percent of federally authorized Pennsylvania vessels would have captured a little more than 100 (out of 2,283 ships) while ultimately about three-quarters of them (1,323) were captured themselves. Most had between six and twelve guns and crews of twenty-five to fifty men (only fourteen had more than twenty guns).[48]

Turning to the Continental navy, Irish-born Philadelphia sea captain John Barry commanded the *Lexington*, the first ship launched in the Continental navy. But he is known as the "Father of the American Navy" for his extraordinary success during the war. He was so successful

John Barry (1745–1803) was born in Ireland and settled in Philadelphia. Considered a "Father of the American Navy," he was the first officer to command an American warship under the Continental flag.

in capturing British ships that he turned down an offer of £15,000 sterling and a captaincy in the British navy to change his allegiance. His prizes included the tender *Edward*, two ships named *Alert* (twenty and twelve guns), *Mars* (twenty-six guns), *Minerva* (ten guns), *Atlanta* (twenty guns), and *Trepassy* (fourteen guns). While patrolling Delaware Bay he seized large quantities of British supplies; in May 1783, he won the revolution's final naval battle by saving a convoy carrying 72,000 Spanish dollars from Cuba to the United States by seriously damaging a British warship that attacked it.[49]

To solve the problem of inflation and lack of "real" money, the first major attempt was made by Esther DeBerdt Reed, wife of the province's president Joseph Reed. She formed the Ladies' Association of Philadelphia, in which thirty-nine women collected over $300,000—much money was being made by merchants and privateers, which the government had failed to tap with tax collections. The Ladies' Association used the money to provide linen shirts for the troops, and the idea of collecting money spread to women in Maryland, Virginia, and New Jersey. Esther Reed was also probably the writer of *The Sentiments of an American Woman*, published in 1780 just before her untimely death at the age of thirty-three.

Our ambition is kindled by the same of those heroines of antiquity, who have rendered their sex illustrious, and have proved to the universe, that, if the weakness of our Constitution, if opinion and manners did not forbid us to march to glory by the same paths as the Men, we should at least equal, and sometimes surpass them in our love for the public good. I glory in all that which my sex has done great and commendable. I call to mind with enthusiasm and with admiration, all those acts of courage, of constancy and patriotism, which history has transmitted to us: The people favoured by Heaven, preserved from destruction by the virtues, the zeal and the resolution of Deborah, of Judith, of Esther!

Born for liberty, disdaining to bear the irons of a tyrannic Government, we associate ourselves to the grandeur of those Sovereigns, cherished and revered, who have held with so much splendour the scepter of the greatest States, The Batildas, the Elizabeths, the Maries, the Catharines, who have extended the empire of liberty, and con-

tented to reign by sweetness and justice, have broken the chains of slavery, forged by tryants in the times of ignorance and barbarity.[50]

Of far more lasting importance was the Bank of North America, founded in 1781 by Robert Morris. Wealthy Philadelphians purchased shares—Benjamin Franklin bought one-tenth of 1 percent to signify his approval—and thereby were able to stem the inflated currency and cycle of price fixing and gouging that had characterized the economy of eastern Pennsylvania throughout the war. It was the model for the Bank of the United States proposed by Alexander Hamilton in 1789 (who had suggested the idea to Morris in the first place). Morris, James Wilson, Benjamin Rush, and other Philadelphia Republicans were the state's prime movers in the campaign that led to the adoption of the United States Constitution in 1787.[51]

MUTINIES AND THE END OF THE WAR, 1781–1783

Noted as the first colony to send men to the Continental army, Pennsylvania also holds the more dubious honor that its troops mutinied twice, in 1781 and 1783. Still, these protests should be understood as the refusal of long-serving and suffering troops who, without adequate pay or provisions, had been in the ranks, in many cases, for between three and eight years. As early as December 1777, General Anthony Wayne complained to the state about "the naked and distressed situation of your troops"—naked meaning not properly clothed rather than without clothing altogether. He bought clothes for his men out of his own pocket.

As 1781 began, a dispute arose when men who had enlisted at Valley Forge on January 1, 1778—for three years or the duration of the war—claimed their time in the army had ended. Moreover, many of them had joined the army between 1775 and 1777. A Captain Adam Bitting was killed during the New Year's protest. Led by a board of sergeants, the mutineers agreed to meet with Pennsylvania representatives at Princeton, near where they were stationed. They demanded back pay, bounties equal to those of new troops who had enlisted, and pardon for their past offenses. General Washington warned the state governors that they could expect more mutinies, to the point where the revolution itself could be threatened, if they did not adequately pay and supply their troops. He also realized that the mutiny could not be suppressed as other troops sympathized with the Pennsylvanians. On January 6, Pennsylvania's president Joseph Reed met with the enlisted men, and on the eighth agreed to discharge any man who took an oath that he had served for more than three years. By the end of the month, 1,150 of the 2,450 Pennsylvanians in the Continental army went home.[52]

Those who remained in the ranks marched that September to confront Lord Cornwallis's army in Yorktown, Virginia. As the French and Continental troops passed through

Captain Adam Bitting of the 4th Pennsylvania Regiment was killed by a soldier during the Pennsylvania Line mutiny on January 1, 1781. Rather than threatening to defect to the British, the Pennsylvania troops would no longer serve Congress until their grievances in back payment and enlistment terms were met.

Philadelphia on September 3, bystanders showered them with flowers, and the usually austere General Washington shouted and jumped up and down for joy when he heard that the French admiral François-Joseph-Paul, comte de Grasse, had appeared to blockade the British. Charles Willson Peale designed cutout posters of Washington and French commander Rochambeau with the inscription "SHINE VALIANT CHIEFS," which people placed in their windows in front of candles. Those, mostly Quakers, who refused to display the portraits were jeered by crowds that broke their windows and, in some cases, entered their houses, wrecked their furniture, and beat up dissidents.[53]

After Yorktown, the army had little to do except wait for the final peace, and the public's willingness to pay and supply the troops waned as their active role came to an end.

The second mutiny occurred on June 21, 1783. A few hundred soldiers, mostly from the Pennsylvania line, demonstrated at the State House in Philadelphia and chased Congress out of Philadelphia—it did not return until 1790. Usually interpreted as a sign of the weakness of the national government under the Articles of Confederation and its inability to pay or control its army, the mutiny also marked the first major confrontation between a state and the national government over their respective powers. Supporters of Pennsylvania and its president, John Dickinson, blamed Congress for the soldiers' dissatisfaction with being neither paid nor released from service, whereas supporters of a stronger national government blamed the state. Each side used the protest for its own ends, but in fact Congress was not the focus of the troops' ire and did not use the incident as an argument to increase its authority. Nor were Dickinson and the state legislature intimidated by either Congress or the soldiers.[54]

The Continental army had for the most part remained idle following the Battle of Yorktown in October 1781. The troops' desire to return home was offset by the fact that they would be disbanded without receiving their back pay. The accounts posed a major problem: each soldier was owed specific back pay, bounties, clothing allowances, rations, and others were promised land bounties. Philadelphian Robert Morris, superintendent of finance under the Articles of Confederation, favored dismissing the troops as these issues would take years to sort out, even if Congress had any money, which it certainly did not. Alexander Hamilton and Washington compromised: the army would be "furloughed" pending the peace settlement that was being negotiated and discharged when the treaty was ratified. But rumors circulated that the soldiers would be furloughed without pay, and Pennsylvania troops in the Lancaster area, most of them veterans of the 1781 mutiny and who had not been paid since 1782, marched on Philadelphia. Their intention, Congress and the state of Pennsylvania believed, was to rob the Bank of the United States. Hamilton, a congressman from New York at a time when few congressmen were in the capital, recommended calling out the Pennsylvania militia to suppress the mutiny, but the Pennsylvania Council feared it would not do any good to mobilize one group of rank-and-file Pennsylvanians—in fact, the very men who had attacked "Fort Wilson" over three years before and were noted for championing the common man—against another. Challenging the authority of Congress over the police power of the state, the Pennsylvania Council replied that the soldiers had only come to settle their accounts and welcomed them into the city. When they met with Morris's assistants, they were informed they had to agree to be furloughed to be paid, a decision

Morris made that contradicted Washington's agreement with Congress, although Morris offered them a month's pay in cash if they would return to Lancaster.

Furious, on June 21 about 280 soldiers commanded by Sergeants John Robinson and Christian Nagle marched on the State House, where both a number of congressmen (summoned by Hamilton to discuss the situation) and the Pennsylvania Council were meeting. Realizing their best hope was to intimidate the state rather than the inflexible yet bankrupt national government, they directed their petition to the president of Pennsylvania, John Dickinson, and promised him that if he did not solve their problems, "we shall instantly let in those injured soldiers upon you and abide by the consequences." The men milled around for several hours, getting drunk, shouting threats, pointing their guns at the building, and accosting New Jersey representative Elias Boudinot when he left the building. While the Pennsylvania Council agreed to negotiate what it considered the soldiers' reasonable demands for back pay, Congress sent word to Washington to send troops to suppress the mutiny, and promised to leave Philadelphia for New Jersey (Princeton, as it turned out) if they could not be assured of protection. Hamilton expressed his anger at Pennsylvania's "weak and disgusting position."

Even before the negotiations began, however, Congress left. The nationalists who dominated that body were anxious to demonstrate the impotence of the government under the Articles of Confederation, and the more states' rights delegates were also anxious to disentangle the national government from that of Pennsylvania, which the nationalists had taken over in 1780. Many of the delegates also thought Philadelphia an expensive and unpleasant place to live. Hamilton's correspondence created the illusion that it was Congress, officially assembled and meeting, that had ordered the withdrawal to Princeton, but in fact it was an ad hoc, unofficial decision of those members who happened to be present. He also let it be known that Congress was the target of the protest, whereas the demands had been directed to the Pennsylvania Council.

When the soldiers met with the Pennsylvania delegates, they apologized for their unruly behavior (which they blamed on Morris's and Hamilton's insulting offer that they disperse for a small cash payment or risk being put down by force), repudiated any intention to rob the Bank of the United States or create other disorder, and agreed to disperse if they received half their back pay, with the rest to be provided in guaranteed interest-bearing certificates, and future payments of what they were owed for rations and uniforms accounts. They also demanded a pardon for the protest. President Dickinson rebuked them for their "unprecedented and heinous fault" but promised to recommend their pardons to Congress. The troops dispersed; Washington sent 1,500 Massachusetts troops commanded by

General Robert Howe to restore order in Philadelphia, although there was no longer any need, and to investigate and try the culprits. Four soldiers were sentenced to whippings, Sergeants Nagle and John Morrison to death, but all were pardoned by Congress after the wives of President Dickinson and Robert Morris (standing in for their husbands, who were anxious to forget the whole affair) signed a petition to that effect. In October, the troops were disbanded; adjustments to their accounts were still unfinished when the assigned paymaster died five years later. Although the nationalists tried to find "some capital movers in this nefarious business," as James Mercer half-humorously implied the point was that congressmen who wanted out of Philadelphia were behind the protest, Howe's investigation found no evidence that anyone besides the aggrieved soldiers were at fault.

The long-term effects of the mutiny, however, were considerable. Congress did not return to Philadelphia until 1790. The United States Constitution made the national capital subject to the jurisdiction of Congress; undoubtedly, the question of whether Congress or the state of Pennsylvania had the authority to deal with the mutinous troops raised a sore spot with the nationalists, whose refusal to negotiate had been undercut by the more accommodating state government. Elsewhere, however, as troops who have ever since misbehaved in the communities surrounding armed forces bases well know, they are subject to both local and military law.

But the mutinies were not on people's minds on January 22, 1784, when Philadelphia celebrated the end of the revolution and the formal acceptance by Britain of American independence. A triumphant arch designed by Charles Willson Peale, fifty feet wide and thirty-five feet high, adorned Market Street. A pyramid honored those who had died, a bust paid tribute to King Louis XVI of France for his aid, and the Pennsylvania coat of arms appeared alongside the figures of Justice, Temperance, Prudence, and Fortitude. More than 1,200 lamps illuminated the display. But Pennsylvania had only won one of the three wars it was still fighting. In fact, had it lost the other two, the state today would be about half its present size.[55]

CONNECTICUT YANKEES VERSUS PENNSYLVANIANS: BEFORE THE REVOLUTION, 1763–1775

On April 19, 1763, Connecticut Yankees burned twenty Delaware Indian cabins at Wyoming. Dying in the fire was Teedyuscung, who had negotiated with Pennsylvania his people's right to live on the land as a result of the Easton agreements. Within less than a month 150 Yankees were cultivating the land. They probably never learned of the British Privy Council's order of June 1763 forbidding settlement in the Wyoming Valley when Captain Bull, Teedyuscung's son, destroyed their community that October after petitioning Pennsylvania, in vain, for retaliation. Shortly after, a group of about a hundred Pennsylvanians, including a company commanded by Lazarus Stewart, sent to drive out the Yankees, came across their remains instead. A woman had been "roasted" and others "had awls thrust into their eyes, and spears, arrows, pitchforks, etc. sticking their bodies." Thus began a bloody frontier conflict in which the French and Indian War spilled over into Pontiac's War, then into the American Revolution, and finally, with the Indians eliminated, into a struggle between Pennsylvanians (Pennamites) and Yankees that only ended around 1805.[56]

Teedyuscung's death was a major landmark in this half-century struggle for what is now northeastern Pennsylvania. It began when three Connecticut land companies—the First and Second Delaware Companies, but, most important, the Susquehannah Company, were formed between 1750 and 1753. Overcrowded Connecticut's population had risen from 26,000 in 1700 to 111,000 in 1750; it would grow to over 180,000 by 1770. The colony's sons and daughters were moving west into New York and north to the "New Hampshire Grants" that later became Vermont, but its land hunger was unrequited. Based on the charter granted in 1662 by the royal government, Connecticut claimed all the land between its northern and southern boundaries—skipping over the portion deeded to New York in 1664—to the Pacific Ocean. With the blessing of the Connecticut legislature, in October 1753, the Susquehannah Company began to

survey the desirable land in the Wyoming Valley near the present-day city of Wilkes-Barre. To legalize this move, the colony bought the area from some Iroquois—who may have been drunk and definitely did not represent the Six Nations as a whole—at the Albany Congress in 1754. Pennsylvania had bought much of the same land at the same congress. In neither case were the Delaware, Munsee, and Shawnee Indians who lived there consulted. To complicate matters, the Iroquois encouraged Teedyuscung and about seventy Delawares to occupy the area, and Pennsylvania sent Conrad Weiser, its chief Indian negotiator, to build his village. Teedyuscung's occupation led to his murder despite his refusal to support the enemy in the French and Indian War.[57]

From the early eighteenth century, the Susquehanna was the "Valley of Opportunity," as historian Peter C. Mancall called his study of the region.[58] Within a decade of settlement of the river's West Branch, in 1765, missionary Philip Vickers Fithian reported that "such a fertile, level, goodly country I have perhaps never seen. Wheat and rye, thick and very high; oats I saw in many places, yet green, and full as high . . . as a six-railed fence! . . . Cows returning home; sheep and horses grazing through the woods, and these all round, in every part, make, surely, a transporting vesper!"[59] After the French and Indian War, grain destined for the West Indies could be shipped down the broad and largely navigable river, which fed directly into Baltimore, Maryland. Founded in 1729, by the late 1760s Baltimore was second only to Philadelphia as a colonial port sending grain to the sugar islands.[60]

Pennsylvania did not express much interest in the region until the Treaty of Fort Stanwix granted the land to Pennsylvania—without Connecticut's consent—in November 1768. The next month, Pennsylvania sent surveyors to the region, and by February 1769 a body of French and Indian War veterans commanded by John Jennings, the sheriff of Northampton County, were in place to repulse a new contingent the Susquehannah Company sent. Jennings built a fort at Mill Creek, arrested three of the New England leaders when they arrived, and left Amos Ogden in command and in charge of recruiting settlers and distributing the land. In March, more than one hundred Pennsylvanians met the next group of New Englanders, arresting thirty-one of forty settlers. The Susquehannah Company responded by settling 250 men, commanded by John Durkee. They chose the site of Teedyuscung's town to construct a fort Durkee named after himself. The adjoining town they named Wilkes-Barre in honor of John Wilkes and Isaac Barre, two of the most vocal supporters of the American cause in the British House of Commons.[61]

The two forts, only a mile apart, maintained an uneasy truce until September. In November 1769 Pennsylvania finally sent two hundred troops and some cannons and compelled Durkee to surrender. The Susquehannah Company did not accept defeat. It began negotiations with Lazarus Stewart, the leader of the Paxton Boys who had massacred the Conestoga Indians in 1763, and offered him choice land if he would defend its claims. Already angry at Pennsylvania for failing to support their atrocities against the Indians, in February 1770, Stewart and his men moved from Lancaster County to join forces with the Yankees, led by Zebulon Butler. There they "plundered and destroyed" those Pennsylvanians who had ventured into the disputed territory. The Yankees in the Wyoming Valley lionized Stewart and his men in poetry:

But to the voice of conscience
Some Squires are grown so deaf,
That where you'll find a [Pennsylvania]
Just-ass [Justice]
He is ten to one a thief;
For justice, truth, and peace are fled,
And honest charity is dead,
There's none for liberty to plead
But true PAXTON *boys. . . . For break?*
Shall those Jersey bankrupts our property
invade,
And fugitive pretenders make honest men
afraid?
I find we must disperse the gang,
With Yankee boys this present spring,
Who worship GOD *and serve their King*
Like true PAXTON *boys.*[62]

Stewart's efforts to relocate the Paxton Boys enlarged his history of violence. Returning to Paxton Township to gather his supporters' families, he beat "in a most unmerciful manner" with an ax handle the constable Pennsylvania sent to arrest him. Next he harangued "in the most opprobrious terms" Justice of the Peace John De Haas when he was trying to raise a posse to bring him to justice. Stewart and twenty of his men besieged De Haas's house, challenging him to arrest them, before Stewart adjourned to a tavern where he threatened to rip out the heart of the innkeeper if he joined his pursuers. When he was finally captured while ferrying across the Susquehanna, he escaped custody and made his way to Wyoming. He then sent a letter taunting the Pennsylvania Assembly: "Let him who wishes to take my life, let him come and take it," he taunted, and he berated them for his being "conveyed to Philadelphia like a wild felon, manacled, to die a felon's death."[63]

Stewart's defiance set the tone for a vicious guerrilla war that developed in the Wyoming Valley. Whites on both sides disguised themselves as Indians both to protect their identities and to indicate that they would fight their opponents with the ferocity they attributed to "savages." Yankee Chester Pearce warned a Pennsylvanian that "the woods shall be as full of White Indians this Summer as they ever were of Black ones," who would "lay in the woods" and "shoot the heads of the Pennsylvanians." Early in 1770 Yankees dressed up as Indians and drove out Amos Ogden after one of Stewart's men had been killed. That September Ogden and 150 Pennsylvanians took control of the valley. Stewart retaliated by seizing a Pennsylvania fort; when he was later surrounded and asked to surrender, he aimed his gun through a loophole

and shot Ogden's brother Nathan, the Northampton County deputy sheriff, dead. Stewart and his men escaped and ousted the Pennsylvanians the following summer, forcing Ogden to surrender on September 15, 1771. Between 1769 and 1771 control of the Wyoming Valley had changed hands five times.[64]

Pennsylvania obtained verbal support for its claims from the Iroquois, who much preferred the hitherto peaceful Pennsylvanians on their southern border to the aggressive Yankees who had killed Teedyuscung. Only nine days after Ogden's defeat, a delegation of Iroquois in Philadelphia declared that they had deeded their land "to the proprietor Onas [Penn] and to no other person." But as the Susquehannah Company continued to send in people, in the spring of 1772, the pacifist Delaware and Munsee Indians who remained in the valley, Christianized by the Moravians, realized they could depend on neither the Six Nations nor Pennsylvania for their protection. Led by Chief Logan (the son of Shikellamy, who had negotiated the Walking Purchase and then supervised Indians in central Pennsylvania under Iroquois sovereignty), they left for the Ohio Valley.[65]

In 1773, Connecticut sent emissaries to Philadelphia to negotiate control of the region with Pennsylvania's proprietor John Penn. He not only refused their offer to submit the issue to the British Crown but dismissed their claim as "without the least foundation." In turn, Connecticut responded that its inhabitants had taken possession "when the country was entirely a wilderness, under an Indian Purchase, approved of by the colony." Penn asked the Pennsylvania Assembly to counter "the insolent outrages of men" who "sally forth with arms in their hands and in a warlike manner attempt to dispossess the peaceable inhabitants."[66]

Before the Pennsylvania Assembly acted, in January 1774 Connecticut officially incorporated the Susquehannah Company's territories into its territory and colonial government, folding them into Litchfield County, the westernmost of old Connecticut. They became the township of Westmoreland, perhaps intentionally named after the county Pennsylvania had created in the Ohio Valley the year before. When it met that September, the Continental Congress, showing its approval of Connecticut's fervent patriotism and anger at the Pennsylvania government's lack of zeal, approved the county.

As a result of Congress's decision, the war for the Wyoming Valley now pitted Pennamites (Pennsylvanians) who obtained support from the British and their loyalist and Indian allies against Yankee revolutionaries. Connecticut maintained its domination over the North Branch of the Susquehanna at Wyoming while Pennsylvanians repulsed them on the West Branch. In September 1775, William Plunkett led about 200 men who defeated 150 Yankees moving west from Wyoming at Freeland Mills near Fort Augusta (present-day Sunbury, Pennsylvania's main settle-

ment). After Zebulon Butler refused a final demand that he recognize Pennsylvania authority, the Pennsylvania Assembly finally acted. It sent five hundred men to Fort Augusta where they set out for Wyoming. On Christmas Eve and Christmas Day, Butler's and Stewart's men repulsed what they called this "band of Tories," killing or wounding about six men.[67]

"Tory" was a convenient charge the Yankees applied to dispossess their Pennsylvania opponents. In March 1776, the Wyoming Committee of Inspection accused John Secord of being a spy and hiding escaped British prisoners. The Continental Congress freed him after he pleaded his innocence, but ten other people were sent to Connecticut for trial. Their cases were even dismissed in that colony, suggesting strongly that the Wyoming Yankees were unconcerned with whether the men who posed obstacles to their settlement were loyalists or not. Trying to incorporate the Pennsylvanians under his protection, Yankee Zebulon Butler constructed a fort at Wyalusing, he claimed, "for your defense as well as ours; for if [loyalist leaders John] Butler and [Sir John] Johnson do come down the River we think they will likely fall upon you." When the Pennsylvanians refused to do military training under Yankee leadership, the Yankees seized them and relocated them to Wyoming. The region's Indians, more friendly to the Pennsylvanians, insisted the men be released and threatened to complain to Congress if they were not. The Yankees acquiesced, but kept the

Pennsylvanians' property and harassed them until they left the valley. They found refuge with the Iroquois before relocating to Fort Niagara, where a British army could protect and feed them as they prepared for a counterattack.[68]

THE WYOMING "MASSACRE" AND SULLIVAN CAMPAIGN, 1777–1783

At first, the Iroquois had tried to remain neutral in the revolution. The British were reluctant to employ them, fearing they would unleash indiscriminant war on the frontier and alienate many loyal subjects. But by 1776, this strategy changed: Lord George Germain, secretary of state for the colonies, believed a frontier war would deplete the Continental army's food supply and force Washington to send valuable troops to the frontier, where he believed the Continentals' lack of respect for persons and property would aid the British cause. In May 1776, loyalist John Butler warned an Iroquois council that the Americans intended "to take all your lands from you and destroy your people, for they are all mad, foolish, crazy, and full of deceit." Although he failed to recruit them at this time, in September, at a secret meeting at Niagara, the pro-British efforts of Molly Brant, the Indian widow of Sir William Johnson, and her brother Joseph Brant, finally won over the Senecas (more than half the Iroquois' total population), Cayugas, Onondagas, and Mohawks. Most of the Tuscaroras and Oneidas sided with the Americans. In 1776, the Iroquois extinguished their council fire, indicating unity was no more.[69]

With the frontier temporarily at peace in the latter half of 1776, the Wyoming Yankees turned out for the revolution. By January 1777, they had sent three hundred men to the Continental army. But they knew something was wrong, as the Indians in the region suddenly disappeared. The Yankees were soon building or repairing forts and scouting their northern border for signs of an impending attack. The Iroquois' disposition was not improved when some Yankees killed and scalped a Seneca woman and two men just as they were planning to attend a peace conference.

The British first used the Indians during the Burgoyne campaign of 1777. Iroquois warriors and Pennsylvania refugees joined Colonel Barry St. Leger in his futile effort to connect with the army that General John Burgoyne was leading from Canada through upstate New York. They fought in the Battles of Fort Stanwix (August 2) and Oriskany (August 6) before they were turned back. After Burgoyne's surrender, loyalist leader John Butler planned an extensive series of raids along the frontier. He consolidated British friendship with the Iroquois at a meeting in December 1777; by March 1778, in company with Pennsylvania and New York loyalists, they were attacking with impunity the isolated Yankee settlements in Wyoming.[70]

The main attack came in July. John Butler and about eight hundred Indians and loyalists descended the

North Branch of the Susquehanna. After two small forts, Wintermoot and Jenkins, surrendered on July 1 without a shot, they arrived on July 3 at Forty Fort, whose four hundred Connecticut militiamen were commanded by Zebulon Butler (no relation). Setting the small forts on fire to trick the enemy into believing he was retreating, John Butler's trap was set. The Yankees rushed out to meet him, which, John Butler wrote, "pleased the Indians highly, who observed they should be upon an equal footing with them in the woods." The Yankees opened fire when they saw the enemy seeming to be running into the forest at a distance of two hundred yards away, long before they could do much damage. The Pennsylvanians and Iroquois waited until their foes were within one hundred yards, and then ambushed them from two sides. Within thirty minutes, the Wyoming Massacre was over. John Butler claimed 227 scalps and only five prisoners, suggesting that the wounded were not allowed to survive. Lazarus Stewart was among the dead. John Butler lost fewer than a dozen men. His opponent Zebulon Butler fled, and his co-commander Nathan Denison surrendered Forty Fort the next day. The terms required that the Yankees' maintain strict neutrality for the rest of the war.[71]

John Butler and his men then turned their fury on the Connecticut settlements. He had the region's eight forts, all its mills, and one thousand dwellings destroyed. Butler made sure his Indians and loyalists inflicted no further casualties, but popular rumors of murders and massacres abounded. The settlers in the northern Susquehanna Valley who had not already left joined the "Great Runaway" and only returned after the war had ended.[72]

Two retaliatory expeditions by the Yankees failed: on September 21 Colonel Thomas Hartley led the Eleventh Pennsylvania Regiment into Iroquois country but only burned an empty village at Tioga, Pennsylvania. His men contented themselves with killing and scalping a few Indians before they learned that Walter Butler, John's brother, had a force more than twice the size of theirs ready to counterattack. Then they retreated. In October, another unrelated Butler, William, led the Fourth Pennsylvania to attack the Iroquois at Unadilla in New York, with equal futility. On November 11, Walter Butler's loyalist Rangers and Senecas led by Joseph Brant destroyed a Connecticut settlement at Cherry Valley. For the first time, the Indians lost control and massacred thirty-three civilians. On the afternoon of November 11, 1778, Captain Benjamin Warren, commanding the nearby fort, observed the smoking ruins, scalped women and children, and people with their heads crushed, "a shocking sight my eyes never beheld before of savage and brutal barbarity."[73]

The disasters of 1778 finally brought the Wyoming Valley to the serious attention of Congress and the Continental army. Philip Schuyler, commanding the Northern Department, urged General Washington:

Representative of the Wyoming Massacre, a frontier community lies in ruins following a raid by Indians and their Tory allies in this period illustration.

"Destroy the Seneca towns and the Indians must fall back to Niagara. This is a long distance from the frontier. With no intermittent place to use as a supply base, no sizable body of Indians can raid the frontiers." With the British in New York forced to send much of their army and navy to the West Indies to fight the French after their alliance with the United States was announced, Washington believed that commanding general Sir Henry Clinton would not launch offensive operations against him. He therefore decided to dispatch about four thousand men, or a third of his army, to the Pennsylvania–New York frontier in the spring of 1779 to defeat the Iroquois—a risky move that worked out. After Horatio Gates, the victor of Saratoga, turned him down on the grounds that a younger man was needed for so strenuous a march, Washington selected General John Sullivan of New Hampshire to lead the campaign.[74]

Washington was less interested in fighting the Iroquois than in destroying their ability to fight. Much like Grant's orders to Sherman in the Civil War, he instructed Sullivan that the expedition's "immediate objects are the total destruction and devastation of the settlements and the capture of as many prisoners of every age and sex as possible. It will be essential to ruin their crops now in the ground and preventing their planting more." Washington held out the hope that Sullivan might take Niagara itself, but this was a slim possibility as the British had built up its fortifications and maintained a small fleet on Lake Ontario. He also warned Sullivan—perhaps remembering the failure of Braddock and the success of Forbes in the French and Indian War—to gather intelligence of the enemy, send out scouts to prevent surprise attacks, and build forts along the route at Tioga and other sites to maintain a line of communication and potential fall-back positions. Sullivan followed these warnings carefully, which explains why he moved so slowly and yet successfully.

The British were well informed of the campaign, thanks not only to Indian and loyalist sources but to Benedict Arnold, who had become their spy. But they mistrusted Indian intelligence and worried that Sullivan's force was a diversion for a possible invasion of Canada through either New York or the Connecticut Valley, where Washington gathered troops, supplies, and built roads to fool them. Colonel Frederick Haldimand, governor-general of Canada, ordered his troops to remain at Niagara, as he believed Sullivan would besiege this critical post that sheltered numerous loyalist and Indian refugees. Henry Clinton in New York only agreed to reinforce Haldimand with 1,500 men when it was far too late.

Washington's next step was to decide the best route for the campaign. He asked for precise information from Schuyler (who favored a march through New York, which he knew best), General Edward Hand, who had moved from Pittsburgh to command the Continental troops in the Susquehanna Valley, Zebulon Butler, Pennsylvania's president Joseph Reed, and Lieutenant John Jenkins, who knew the region well. Washington asked questions about the navigability of the Susquehanna and the affiliation of Indians in the

area. He considered four possible invasion routes, three of which began at Albany and Schenectady, New York, before settling on a Pennsylvania approach for the main column of 3,000 men. He informed Schuyler that the New York routes were too "circuitous" and too close to British and Indian reinforcements who might arrive from Niagara or Canada. But he appeased the New Yorker by sending another 1,600 soldiers through the Mohawk River commanded by General James Clinton to Lake Oneida at the same time. Five hundred men commanded by Colonel Daniel Brodhead would also destroy the western Iroquois towns near the northern shores of the Allegheny River. Washington believed that in the unlikely event that the Iroquois—who mustered at best two thousand warriors—defended their territory, they would be defeated. As a prelude to the campaign, Washington approved Schuyler's proposal to destroy the Onondaga village, the capital of the Iroquois Confederacy, which Colonel Goose Van Schaick and five hundred men carried out in April.

Sullivan's and Clinton's forces consisted entirely of Continental troops. Washington mistrusted the militia, which in his experience tended to desert, flee from battle, or fight poorly. They were best employed when the British appeared in their vicinity (the "Minutemen"), and the general doubted their ability to sustain a long march into hostile territory. That Sullivan's troops kept good order is a testament to the effectiveness of Baron von Steuben's drilling at Valley

Forge and the discipline the army had acquired over two years of battle.

Sullivan led his men out of Easton, Pennsylvania, on June 18. The plan was to meet Clinton's forces at Tioga, where the Susquehanna and Chemung rivers met. Sullivan spent the entire month of July in Easton, mustering teamsters, boat crews, engineers, and surveyors to build roads, 134 boatloads of supplies, 1,200 packhorses, and 700 cattle to accompany his fifteen regiments of infantry and one of artillery. Women who served as nurses, washed clothes, cooked, and sometimes fought in gun crews came along as well. The column, six miles long, finally began to march on July 31 after much prodding from Congress and Washington.

Hoping to divert Sullivan's attention from his planned mission, the loyalists and Indians attacked elsewhere. On July 20, Joseph Brant approached Minisink with a party of eighty-seven men. Chased by 120 militiamen led by Colonel John Hathor, the Indians outflanked and routed them, killing and scalping forty. Captain John McDonald, a British regular officer commanding fifty of John Butler's Rangers, joined forces with about 120 Senecas under Cornplanter and attacked Fort Freeland on July 28. Its thirty-three soldiers surrendered on the condition that they be taken prisoner and the fifty-odd women and children inside be freed. Just after the surrender, a relief force of about seventy men under Captain Hawkins Boone arrived; Boone and thirty of his men were killed, while the rest retreated to Fort Augusta. McDonald urged the Indians to push toward the fort, but "they were too glutted with plunder, prisoners, and scalps, that my utmost efforts could not persuade them." Residents of the area begged Sullivan in vain for reinforcements, but he replied, "should I comply with the requisition . . . it would effectually answer the intention of the enemy." He referred them to the state of Pennsylvania for assistance, which took so long to mobilize that most despaired of help and deserted the valley.[75]

Sullivan finally reached Tioga on August 11. It was deserted. After General Hand's advance brigade burned it, he was ambushed outside of town by twenty Delaware Indians who killed six soldiers and wounded perhaps ten more before disappearing. While waiting for Clinton, Sullivan built a fort at Tioga. Clinton finally arrived on August 22. The two columns then marched together toward the Finger Lakes, destroying the empty villages and abundant fields they encountered. The only significant resistance occurred at Newtown, near Elmira, New York. About twelve hundred loyalists and Indians commanded by Brant and John Butler attempted an ambush, but were outflanked and routed. Sullivan lost eleven killed and thirty-two wounded. Sullivan destroyed his last village near Geneseo on September 15. Meanwhile, in the west, Daniel Brodhead's force had departed from Pittsburgh on August 11. A few friendly Delaware Indians joined his militia and volunteers. He also encountered little resistance, although he brought back to Fort Pitt a few scalps as part of $30,000 worth of plunder. Overall, Sullivan reported that the expedition burned 160,000 bushels of corn and forty Iroquois towns and that there was "not a single village left in the country of the five nations."76

Forced back to Niagara to be fed for the winter, the Iroquois swore revenge. The brunt of the attacks that began early in 1780 led by John Butler, Brant, and Cornplanter fell on New York, but northern Pennsylvania also suffered. In February loyalists and Iroquois laid siege (unsuccessfully) to Fort Stanwix, and then went on to destroy 1,000 homes, 1,000 barns, and 600,000 bushels of grain, far more than Sullivan had. They also destroyed the homelands of the Oneidas and Tuscaroras who had taken the American side.77

Peace of a sort came only when the British granted American independence and ceased to promote Indian attacks. Most of the Iroquois and loyalists moved to Upper Canada, now Ontario. The Indians who remained, led by Cornplanter, negotiated the Treaty of Fort Stanwix in 1784 that gave most of their lands to the United States. Cornplanter became an advocate of reconciliation, earned the respect of Washington (who presented him with a sword), Jefferson, and other leading statesmen, and retired with the remaining Seneca to a tract of land bordering on Lake Erie. Seeking a port on that lake, in 1791 Pennsylvania bought the land known as the "Erie Triangle" for $5,000 (before paying $150,000 to whites who had purchased some of it from the Indians) and persuaded him to relocate to the north-central part of the state. There the Senecas remained until 1964, when they were removed once again—retreating to an adjacent reservation in New York—to enable the state to build the Kinzua Dam and Reservoir to supply the greater Pittsburgh region with water. The 1791 treaty guaranteeing them their land forever, the Supreme Court ruled, was not the "treaty" with an independent nation that the Constitution states is "the supreme law of the land," but rather an agreement with a "domestic dependent nation." Since then Pennsylvania has had no recognized Indian tribes or reservations, although there is a Cornplanter State Forest in Pennsylvania.78

6. Securing Pennsylvania's Sovereignty, 1768–1805

William A. Pencak ✦ Barbara A. Gannon

FROM THE NEW PURCHASE TO DUNMORE'S WAR, 1768–1775

On November 5, 1768, Pennsylvania negotiators joined those from New York, New Jersey, and Virginia and met about three thousand Indians at Fort Stanwix (now Rome), New York. There, the Iroquois accepted a present of over £10,000 from Sir William Johnson, the superintendent of Indian affairs, to cede the "New Purchase," a huge swath of land that roughly bordered a diagonal line drawn from the present southwest to northeast corners of Pennsylvania. Thanks to the largest present ever given to Native Americans, the royal Proclamation Line of 1763 was declared null and void. The Iroquois in effect accepted a fait accompli—settlers had been ignoring the line from the beginning. The objections, as with agreements from the Walking Purchase and the Albany Congress, came from the Indians living in the area—the Shawnee in the west and Delaware in the east—who again had their land sold out from under them by the Iroquois, who claimed to be their sovereigns.[1]

Over 2,700 Pennsylvanians applied for land in the New Purchase on April 3, 1769, the first day it opened for settlement. Easy terms excluded very few: the price was five pounds per hundred acres up to three hundred acres, and people could take years to pay. By October 1770, Indian trader George Croghan claimed that between four and five thousand families were heading west. Croghan had schemes of his own too: Virginia authorized his Vandalia Company—named to honor the queen of England, who was descended from the Vandals—to take possession of much of the area around Pittsburgh. In the meantime, the British military abandoned Fort Pitt, selling it to a trader named Alexander McKee. The stage was set for a confrontation between Pennsylvania and Virginia.

On February 26, 1773, the Pennsylvania legislature created Westmoreland County to administer its territory west of the Alleghenies.

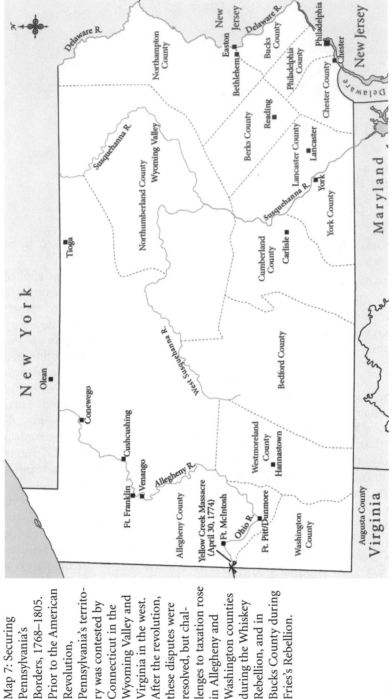

Map 7: Securing
Pennsylvania's
Borders, 1768–1805.
Prior to the American
Revolution,
Pennsylvania's territo-
ry was contested by
Connecticut in the
Wyoming Valley and
Virginia in the west.
After the revolution,
these disputes were
resolved, but chal-
lenges to taxation rose
in Allegheny and
Washington counties
during the Whiskey
Rebellion, and in
Bucks County during
Fries's Rebellion.

Robert Hanna, who founded Hannastown (or Hanna's Town), the county seat, became the justice of the peace, and Arthur St. Clair became the clerk of the court and later sheriff. A Scots army officer who had resigned his British commission after the French and Indian War, St. Clair married the niece of James Bowdoin, future governor of Massachusetts and became the largest landowner in western Pennsylvania.

Virginians were unhappy with the new Pennsylvania county, as was George Croghan, who saw his own projected colony vanishing. On January 1, 1774, Dr. John Connolly, a Pennsylvanian employed by Virginia, issued a proclamation at Pittsburgh informing the residents that Virginia's governor, Lord Dunmore, and its legislature were about to form a new county for the region. This was only a slight untruth—forbidden to create new counties by the British Crown, they instead formed the District of West Augusta with its seat at Pittsburgh, which to all intents and purposes functioned as a county. Connolly also appointed a number of justices of the peace and declared all the region's men members of the Virginia militia. He rechristened Fort Pitt "Fort Dunmore." Informed of these developments, St. Clair had Connolly arrested in Pittsburgh and talked down a crowd of eighty of his supporters.

Governor Penn remonstrated with Dunmore that the boundary between the colonies had already been settled and sent him a map and detailed explanation, suggesting that the two

colonies settle their differences peaceably. Dunmore reminded Penn that he had turned down a similar conciliatory offer from Connecticut concerning the lands in the northeast, claimed the disputed land for Virginia, demanded the release of Connolly, and insisted that St. Clair, "who had the audacity, without any authority, to commit [to prison] a magistrate acting in the legal discharge of his trust," be dismissed unless he freed Connolly and obtained his pardon.

On February 2, St. Clair did release Connolly when he promised to appear before his court at the next session, but Connolly had no intention of doing so. He returned to raise a militia of about two hundred men and marched on Hannastown, bullying and arresting Pennsylvanians and sending their justices of the peace for trial to Staunton, Virginia, the seat of Augusta County. Although Dunmore released them, Pennsylvania did nothing to counter Virginia's armed force. Pennsylvania justice of the peace William Crawford defected to Virginia when Governor Penn informed him "the Government of Virginia hath the power of raising a militia," but "there is not any such in this province." That Pennsylvania had in fact raised a militia during the French and Indian War was lost on the eastern Quaker majority in the assembly that had little desire to acquire new territory that would be filled with Scots-Irish Presbyterians who would oppose their rule.

Meanwhile, settlers continued to pour into the region. Daniel Boone, born on the outskirts of Reading, Pennsylvania, led fifty people who for the first time tried to expand the settled region to what was then Kentucky County, Virginia. On October 9, 1773, a group of Indians captured Boone's son James and tortured him and another boy to death, causing the expedition to be aborted. A surveying expedition from Virginia explored the northernmost reaches of the Ohio Valley near present-day Steubenville, Ohio, in mid-April 1774. The Indians warned it away, but Michael Cresap, son of Thomas who had instigated Cresap's War in 1731, persisted in trying to settle his Virginia grant. George Rogers Clark, the Virginia general who later defeated the British in the Northwest during the Revolutionary War, formed a settlement at the mouth of the Little Kanawha River. Troubled by reports of Indian hostilities, Cresap and the settlers met at Wheeling on April 26 and declared war. A skirmish occurred the next day at Pipe Creek when settlers opened fire on some Indian canoes. Although Connolly ordered the settlers to "hold themselves in readiness to repel any insults," many fled.

The first major action, in what is known as Dunmore's War, the Yellow Creek Massacre, occurred on April 30. John Baker, who operated a general store on the Ohio River about forty miles northwest of Fort Pitt, believed the Mingoes were preparing to attack him. He asked for help, and Daniel Greathouse arrived with twenty men. There are a number of accounts of how the fighting began. One version

is that Greathouse lured members of the nearby Indian village to the store, got them drunk, and massacred them. It is questionable if these were the Indians who were intending to attack, as they brought two women, one very pregnant, and a child with them. In any case, Greathouse and his men then attacked other Indians who appeared in two more canoes. Greathouse and his men scalped their victims, and he hung the scalps from his belt, an Indian declaration of war. Two of those murdered were the brother and sister of Chief Logan, a longtime friend of the whites. Logan's father was Shikellamy, an Iroquois who negotiated the Walking Purchase of 1737, converted to Christianity, and lived at Shamokin near present-day Sunbury to keep an eye on the Shawnee and Delaware who had been displaced in this treaty made by the Iroquois. Logan had moved west in 1772, as his lands were included in the New Purchase. His Mingo name was Tah-gah-jute; he was a Christian who took his baptismal name from Pennsylvania secretary James Logan.

A second version—which is less likely but reflects the mixture of rumor and hostilities that soon blanketed the frontier—is told in Thomas Jefferson's *Notes on the State of Virginia*:

In the spring of the year 1774, a robbery and murder were committed on an inhabitant of the frontiers of Virginia, by two Indians of the Shawanee tribe. The neighbouring whites, according to their custom, undertook to punish this outrage in a summary way. Col. Cresap, a man infamous for the many murders he had committed on those much-injured people, collected a party, and proceeded down the Kanhaway in quest of vengeance. Unfortunately a canoe of women and children, with one man only, was seen coming from the opposite shore, unarmed, and unsuspecting an hostile attack from the whites. Cresap and his party concealed themselves on the bank of the river, and the moment the canoe reached the shore, singled out their objects, and, at one fire, killed every person in it. This happened to be the family of Logan, who had long been distinguished as a friend of the whites. This unworthy return provoked his vengeance.[2]

Logan demanded vengeance for the massacre and, over the objections of Shawnee chief Cornstalk, mobilized Shawnee, Delaware, and Mingo warriors. They did not attack Pennsylvania traders, but reserved their anger for the Virginians, whom they called the "Big Knife." In response to the murders, Chief Logan killed eight and took two prisoners near the Monongahela River on June 6. On July 12, he attacked Major William Robinson and his militia force in present-day Monongalia County, West Virginia. Later that day, Logan attacked a group of settlers in Harrison County. He may have killed thirty settlers over the summer. Hundreds fled eastward, and when Connolly proved unable to defend them, most of those who remained aligned with the Pennsylvanian St. Clair, who raised an informal militia of a hundred men. On July 19, the Pennsylvania legislature finally authorized two hundred troops to join St. Clair for a period of not more

than two months, but seemed more concerned about the plight of Indians injured by settlers than the other way around. They "viewed with horror . . . the frequent murders . . . committed on some of the westward Indians" and offered a £100 reward to apprehend two whites who had killed a friendly Indian. George Croghan went to Williamsburg to try to persuade the Virginians to negotiate a peace, but Lord Dunmore was determined to conquer the Indians who had wreaked havoc on what he considered the western frontier of his province. He sent two armies to the region, each about one thousand men, one led by Colonel Andrew Lewis and the other commanded by himself. On October 10, Cornstalk, who had been persuaded to join Logan's cause, intercepted Lewis in his camp at Point Pleasant, where the Kanawha River joins the Ohio, with between three hundred and five hundred warriors. After a day of fierce fighting, with 75 Virginians killed, 140 wounded, and 33 Indians found dead on the battlefield (although many more were probably killed and wounded), Lewis was able to triumph by detaching some of his forces and attacking the Indians from the rear. Among the dead was Pucksinwah, the father of Tecumseh, who during the War of 1812 led the last confederation of Indians east of the Mississippi against the United States.

Dunmore joined Lewis and settled in at Camp Charlotte, six miles from the Shawnee encampment on the Scioto River. Eight days later, Cornstalk agreed to a peace where the

Indians agreed not to hunt any more on the south side of the Ohio River and to return all captured prisoners and black slaves. Chief Logan refused to attend the talks and sent the following message which is among the most famous examples of Indian eloquence:

I appeal to any white man to say, if ever he entered Logan's cabin hungry, and he gave him not meat; if ever he came cold and naked, and he clothed him not. During the course of the last long and bloody war, Logan remained idle in his cabin, an advocate for peace. Such was my love for the whites, that my countrymen pointed as they passed, and said, "Logan is the friend of white men." I had even thought to have lived with you, but for the injuries of one man. Col. Cresap, the last spring, in cold blood, and unprovoked, murdered all the relations of Logan, not sparing even my women and children. There runs not a drop of my blood in the veins of any living creature. This called on me for revenge. I have sought it: I have killed many: I have fully glutted my vengeance. For my country, I rejoice at the beams of peace. But do not harbour a thought that mine is the joy of fear. Logan never felt fear. He will not turn on his heel to save his life. Who is there to mourn for Logan?—Not one.[3]

Logan moved west and began to drink heavily, being killed in a Detroit tavern fight in 1781. Daniel Greathouse died of measles, aged twenty-three in 1775. Thirty-three-year-old Michael Cresap died of natural causes the same year. The Quebec Act, passed by the British Parliament on June 22, 1774, gave all Dunmore's conquests of land disputed with Pennsylvania to the province of Quebec.

THE REVOLUTION IN THE FAR WEST, 1775–1783

The main effect of the Quebec Act in western Pennsylvania was to unite most of the region's Virginians and Pennsylvanians, who met together on May 16, 1775, after they had learned of the Battles of Lexington and Concord. Blaming the Indian hostilities on Dunmore rather than their own land hunger, they agreed to oppose the loyalist governor and try to befriend the Indians in order to retain their lands. Virginia sent a hundred men to garrison Fort Pitt. Some western riflemen headed to Boston to join the Continental army, and in August the people of Pittsburgh raised a liberty pole and destroyed some tea.

Not everyone supported the American cause. In June 1775, Pennsylvania arrested John Connolly for calling a meeting with the Indians to support the British; the Virginians insisted they release him as they considered the arrest a mere pretext to gain the upper hand. Connolly promptly fled to the ships protecting Lord Dunmore off Norfolk, Virginia. Here he proposed an incredible plan for the British to win the war: he would begin at the British fort of Detroit with three hundred men, march to Pittsburgh, and then, gathering loyalists and Indians as he went, unite with British troops and vessels in Alexandria, Virginia, and thereby cut the colonies in half. Unfortunately for Connolly, he communicated his design to John Gibson in Pittsburgh, who turned out to be a patriot and informed the West Augusta Committee. Connolly meanwhile had been to Boston, where General Thomas Gage encouraged him. Unaware his plan had been leaked, Connolly was arrested when he was traveling west from Hagerstown, Maryland, and placed in the Walnut Street Jail in Philadelphia. When his wife came to join him, he proved so disagreeable to her that she told Congress he was planning to escape, whereupon he was remanded to Baltimore.

Back in Pittsburgh, the new American Indian agent George Morgan successfully negotiated peaceful relations with the Ohio Valley Indians, led by White Eyes of the Delaware and Cornstalk of the Shawnee. This lasted until early 1777, when the Iroquois, in company with loyalists led by Colonel John Butler at Niagara, devastated northern and western Pennsylvania. Thus began the "Great Runaway." The region around the West Branch of the Susquehanna and the Juniata rivers lost nearly all its settlers. On June 19, 1777, the town of Standing Stone (on the present site of Huntingdon)—where the Indians had erected a mysterious monument with petroglyphs—was destroyed. The region's principal garrison, Fort Roberdeau, established in 1778 near present-day Altoona to mine lead for the Continental army, was abandoned two years later. In 1780, the Bedford County commissioners explained to the state of Pennsylvania that they could not collect much revenue: "in some townships no assessment has been made since the Revolution began." The next year, Lieutenant George Ashman wrote that "if immediate assistance is not sent to this county . . . the whole of the frontier inhabitants will move." Most of them did.

On June 1, 1777, Congress sent General Edward Hand to Pittsburgh to defend the frontier. He failed to do so. Colonel Henry Hamilton, the British commander at Detroit, launched Indian raids with impunity and spread rumors that a huge Indian force of at least ten thousand would soon attack. Virginia and Pennsylvania militia refused to cooperate in a common expedition. Anger on the frontier revived the sort of warfare the Paxton Boys had waged: all Indians were considered hostiles and fair targets, there were no friends, only foes. In November 1777, Virginia militia killed Cornstalk, a friendly Shawnee, thereby turning the rest of his people against the Americans. Unable to find real enemies, an expedition General Hand led to the Cuyahoga River in February 1778 killed a few women, a boy, and an old man. It became known as the "Squaw Campaign." Similarly, Hamilton's agents urged the Indians to kill all rebels; when an Indian asked if that meant children, the response was: "Kill all! Destroy all! Nits breed lice."[4]

The revolutionaries had loyalists as well as British troops and Indians to worry about. John Crawford later recollected a large "conspiracy" in the Monongahela Valley whose members took a secret oath to George III. Rumors spread that General Burgoyne, invading New York from Canada in the summer of 1777, would send a force to Pittsburgh and kill all those who were disloyal. But the western Pennsylvania loyalists were repulsed with remarkable ease. Twice in August 1777, patriot militia forced much larger bodies of loyalists to disperse without firing a shot. They then imprisoned the leaders and forced the rank and file to swear allegiance to the United States. Only one person was killed in this face-off, a loyalist named Higginson who drowned after being captured; he was probably pushed off a boat by drunken soldiers.

In February 1778, however, three leading loyalists at Fort Pitt, Alexander McKee, Simon Girty, and Matthew Elliott, escaped before Hand could have them arrested when he returned from the "Squaw Campaign." (George Croghan, suspected of loyalism but not accused, fled to Philadelphia where he died bankrupt in 1782, supported by the generosity of two of his employers, Barnard and Michael Gratz.) Having lived and sympathized with the Indians, the three men's allegiance to Britain stemmed not only from Dunmore's land grants but from anger at the revolutionaries' indiscriminate slaughter of their Indian friends. They moved to Detroit, where Connolly joined them when he was released from prison. Into the 1790s, the quartet actively encouraged Indian raids against Pennsylvania. Girty became especially

notorious for participating in the capture, torture, and execution of Colonel William Crawford in 1782. He laughed at Crawford as he was dying, although the latter's fate was deserved. Crawford had directed the second Gnadenhutten Massacre. This one occurred in Ohio where pacifist Christian Delaware Indians, converted by the Moravians, had relocated to escape the French and Indian War. Crawford's army killed ninety-six men, women, and children indiscriminately.[5]

Meanwhile, the revolutionaries discovered more pro-British conspiracies. In April 1778, loyalists with scaling ladders planned to take Fort Pitt and raised the British flag within sight of its walls. Fifty members of the Thirteenth Virginia Regiment, angry at the ineffective Hand, an Irish-born Pennsylvanian, deserted; some planned to blow up the fort but were discovered and tried to flee to Detroit before they were captured; three ringleaders were executed, the rest flogged. The same month, at Kittanning, loyalists in the Juniata Valley were mistakenly killed by the Iroquois whom they had planned to join to march on Fort Pitt. A combined Indian-loyalist force attacked Fort Wallace near Ligonier, nearly capturing it.

The only Revolutionary success in the west, however, was spectacular. In June 1776, patriots George Gibson and William Linn floated with a small group of "Gibson's Lambs" down the Ohio and Mississippi from Pittsburgh. They bought 12,000 pounds of gunpowder, which they divided between Philadelphia and Pittsburgh when they finally returned a year later. In January 1778, Captain Thomas Willing repeated the trip. After leaving New Orleans he attacked the British colony of West Florida, capturing Natchez and making life miserable for loyalists in the southwest for the rest of the war.[6]

Back in Pittsburgh, Hand resigned in early 1778 after which frustrated commanders followed and quit in rapid succession: Lachlan Mackintosh from April 1778 to early 1780; Daniel Brodhead until November 1781; and then William Irvine. In a harrowing winter march, Virginian George Rogers Clark surprised and captured Henry Hamilton at Vincennes in the Illinois Country in February 1779. Despite the praise he earned, his expedition did little to stop the perpetual threat of loyalists and Indians.[7] On July 11, 1782, Colonel John Butler and his Rangers bypassed fortified Pittsburgh and destroyed Hannastown, the capital of Pennsylvania's Westmoreland County. Today, it is an archaeological site.[8] The conclusion of the United States' war with Britain by no means ended the fight with the mother country's western allies. The Indians, in fact, believed the British had sold them out and had given away the Northwest Territories—land that belonged to the Indians—at a time when the Indians were winning against the Americans.

DEFEATING THE WESTERN INDIANS, 1784–1795

Once the revolution ended, neither Pennsylvania nor the United States had an army to secure this western territory that was theirs in theory. On June 3, 1784, after six months of arguing, Congress "recommended" that the states of Connecticut, New York, New Jersey, and Pennsylvania raise seven hundred militiamen who would serve on the frontier for a year. The Continental army on that date consisted of eighty men guarding Fort Pitt and West Point. Taking oaths of allegiance to both the state and national government, Pennsylvania officers led by Lieutenant Colonel Josiah Harmar—a "fighting" Philadelphia Quaker who had served with distinction in the Revolution— recruited the First Regiment. Their task was to escort west delegates Arthur Lee and Richard Butler, whom Congress appointed to end hostilities with the Indians. The other states did not cooperate, and the 260 men Harmar enlisted were pathetic: on their way to Pittsburgh, they were frequently drunk and destroyed civilian property; sixty deserted; and they even dismantled and stole the contents of an entire store at Bedford. They quarreled with each other all winter at Pittsburgh, perhaps because Congress owed them over $4,000 in back pay. Their only accomplishment was to rebuild Fort McIntosh at the present-day Beaver Falls on the Ohio, which settlers moving westward had stripped of wood and even nails.[9]

In the spring of 1785, Harmar undertook his first offensive, not against Indians but rather the first of several attempts to burn out squatters who were in danger of starting an uncontrollable Indian war. But he

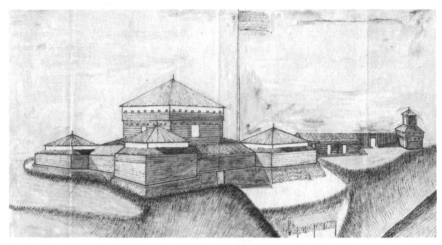

A sketch of Fort Franklin on the Allegheny River, drawn by Jonathan Heart in 1787 and part of the Josiah Harmar papers. Note that the sides were built using horizontal logs to resist light artillery since the proximity of the fort to Lake Erie meant that the fort could come under attack by either Indians or British forces using cannon.

claimed he could not even make a dent in their "immense" numbers and burning easily rebuilt log cabins mattered little. Harmar built several forts—Fort Finney (Louisville, Kentucky), Fort Steuben (Steubenville, Ohio), Fort Knox (Vincennes, Indiana), Fort Franklin (on the Allegheny River, near modern-day Franklin, Pennsylvania), and finally Fort Harmar on the Muskingum in Ohio—to try to keep the peace between the settlers and the Indians, just as the British had been doing since the 1760s and with as little success. Harmar's small force had to remain close to these posts for its own protection. "They are rather prisoners in that country, than in possession of it," "A Citizen" lamented in the *Maryland Journal.*

"The emigration is almost incredible," Harmar wrote as settlers contin-ued to move west, over 6,000 through Fort Harmar alone from December 1787 to June 1788; another estimate was that 70,000 New Englanders moved into western Pennsylvania and Ohio from 1786 to 1790. Indians and settlers clashed, and by 1788 Harmar's men had become targets. He negotiated two treaties in 1789, but the aftermath confirmed Lieutenant Ebenezer Denny's verdict: "One half [the Indians] will . . . sign articles and receive presents, while the others are killing, savaging, and doing us every possible damage." The Maumee, Wabash, and Shawnee Indians failed to sign, and hostilities increased. Arthur St. Clair, governor of the Northwest Territories, complained that the settlers "are in the habit of retaliation . . . without attending precisely to the nations from which injuries are received."

Realizing the whites were responsible for provoking the Indians, the Washington administration hoped for peace and the purchase of Indian lands. That many important politicians, including Washington himself and St. Clair, had bought huge tracts of land in the Ohio Valley on speculation was another reason they hoped to avoid conflict—it would be harder to secure titles against the actual settlers if war occurred and the frontiersmen physically took the lands from the Indians. But as the situation worsened, in June 1790, Secretary of War Henry Knox urged Harmar to "exhibit to the Wabash Indians our power to punish them for their positive depradations, for their conniving at the depradations of others, and for their refusing to treat with the United States when invited thereto. This power will be demonstrated by a sudden stroke, by which their towns and crops may be destroyed." Clearly, the model was the Sullivan Expedition that had wreaked similar havoc on the Iroquois in 1779.

Harmar's 320 regulars were supplemented by 1,100 militiamen from Kentucky, Pennsylvania, and Virginia, but Harmar doubted their ability: "it is a lamentable circumstance that instead of calling for militia the government is so feeble as not to afford three or four regiments of national troops properly organized, who would soon settle the business with these perfidious villains upon the Wabash." Harmar's force set out from Fort Washington on September 26, moving only ten miles a day with a train of artillery and six hundred

pack animals. Between October 17 and October 20 he destroyed five towns (about 250 dwellings) and 20,000 bushels of corn. But realizing he had to retreat or face a winter campaign after reaching his goal of the Wabash village at the head of the Maumee River (Fort Wayne, Indiana), Harmar headed south. During the campaign, three times he detached smaller units in the hope of enticing the Indians into battle. On October 21, the third such unit, under Major John Wyllys, was ambushed and over fifty men killed. Harmar returned to Fort Washington and counted 183 men killed and 31 wounded; a court of inquiry judged that "the conduct of the said Brigadier General Josiah Harmar merits high approbation," but historians have disagreed. He suffered heavy losses and did nothing to reduce the Indian menace or coerce them into signing a peace treaty.

Arthur St. Clair, governor of the Northwest Territories, took Harmar's place and suffered an even worse defeat in 1791. Marching north from Cincinnati with about 1,400 men, he was ambushed with 600 men killed and 300 wounded in a three-hour battle. Fifty camp followers (wives and friends of soldiers who came to cook and clean, rather than the proverbial prostitutes) were also killed, "some of them cut in two, their bubbies cut off." Emboldened by their victory, the Indians led by Shawnee chief Blue Jacket refused any point of negotiations except complete American withdrawal from the Ohio Valley, the original terms of the Treaty of Fort Stanwix in 1768. Ironically, Seneca chief Joseph Brant, now living in Canada and the Americans' fiercest foe during the revolution, unsuccessfully urged compromise. As one chief stated, based on documents taken from St. Clair's army, the United States intended to "drive all the Indians out of the country," then "give them hoes ... to plant corn and make them labor, like beasts." As the Americans soon learned, the British in Canada were encouraging and assisting the Indians; in 1793, they built Fort Miami on the Maumee River to supplement their other posts on American soil at Detroit and Niagara.[10]

The main effect of St. Clair's defeat was that Congress finally approved the Washington administration's request for a sizable regular army of about five thousand, although that figure represented a wishful target. That the British in Canada were proven to be supporting and encouraging the attacks was another reason the Legion of the United States, as it was called, came into existence. Anthony Wayne of Chester County, Pennsylvania, was chosen to command it. Wayne had a mixed record as a general during the revolution—he successfully surprised and defeated the British at Stony Point below West Point, New York, in 1779 after having been surprised himself and lost many troops at the "Paoli Massacre" outside Philadelphia in 1777. He was elected to Congress in 1790—which gave him immunity to return to his native Pennsylvania as he was subject to arrest for debt in that state—although his election was later declared irregular.

Wayne failed to mount a campaign in 1793; frontier militia did not turn out and the regular soldiers were struck by a flu epidemic. But in 1794 he finally brought peace to the Pennsylvania frontier after forty years of war. He led over 4,600 men north from Cincinnati, using Choctaw and Chickasaw Indians as his scouts. In June, the Indians repeatedly attacked Fort Recovery, the post he had built at the site of St. Clair's defeat, thereby squandering much of their manpower. Wayne marched north, burning uninhabited villages and targeting the British Fort Miami. On August 20, he encountered a coalition of Shawnee, Delaware, Miami, Ojibwa, Ottawa, Pottawatomi, and Mingo Indians along with a company of Canadian militia. They had taken shelter behind some "fallen timbers"—hence the name of the battle. After a fierce struggle, in which Wayne's infantry attacked with bayonets while his cavalry assaulted their flank, the Indians were chased back to the British fort, which closed its gates to their retreating allies. Wayne lost thirty-three killed and about a hundred wounded; Indian losses are unknown. Wayne next dared the British to attack him by marching his troops around the fort and burning their storehouses and neighboring Indian villages. They evacuated the fort the following year as the Jay Treaty stipulated all British troops withdraw from United States territory. On August 3, 1795, at the Treaty of Greenville, the Indians who had kept the settlers of western Pennsylvania and Ohio in fear agreed to withdraw from all except the northern third of Ohio.[11]

YANKEES VERSUS PENNSYLVANIANS ONCE AGAIN, 1783–1805

The revolution had devastated the Susquehanna Valley and much of the northern Pennsylvania frontier. French immigrant Hector St. John de Crèvecoeur, author of the famous *Letters from an American Farmer*, which proclaimed his new home as the land of opportunity where people of different nations lived in peace, wrote a much less famous book, *Sketches of Eighteenth-Century America* (unpublished until 1925), about the horrors he experienced there during the war:

The people of Susquehanna . . . rapidly launched forth into all the intricate mazes of this grand quarrel as their inclinations, prepossessions, and prejudices let them. [It was] a fatal era, which has since disseminated among them the most horrid poison; which has torn them with interesting divisions; and has brought on that languor, that internal weakness, that suspension of industry, and the total destruction of their noble beginning.[12]

Timothy Pickering, the future Federalist leader and a Massachusetts native who had lived in the valley since 1772, agreed that the region's civil war had rendered what had been the "Valley of Opportunity" "wretched beyond description. . . . Indeed, I did not imagine such general apparent wretchedness could be found in the United States."[13]

The fighting between Yankees and Pennsylvanians that Crèvecoeur observed continued after the Iroquois left. In November 1782, after three years of prodding, Connecticut finally agreed to a Pennsylvania proposal to have Congress decide the dispute. On December 30, with what is known as the Trenton Decree, Congress ruled that the Wyoming Valley was part of Pennsylvania but at the same time permitted individual Connecticut settlers to keep their lands. This opened a can of worms: Connecticut speculators claimed large tracts, and many lands were disputed by inhabitants of the two states. In March 1783, Pennsylvania appointed magistrates for the region who began suits of ejectment against the Yankees. They did not go willingly. By the fall, Wyoming was garrisoned with Pennsylvania troops whose leaders claimed large tracts of land for themselves, assaulting Yankees, throwing them in jail, destroying their fences and livestock, burning their homes, and dispossessing 150 farm owners. Connecticut leader John Franklin objected that a "whole herd of Pennsylvania landjobbers were set loose upon the inhabitants to exercise their wonted avaricious and hellish practices." The "Wild Yankees" responded with tactics reminiscent of the American Revolution—frequently disguising themselves as Indians and using humiliating and symbolic punishments such as whipping and tarring and feathering against their opponents.[14]

Even Pennsylvanians who had lived in the Wyoming Valley objected to the garrison's high-handed methods. Northampton County, dominated by the Yankees, sent its own deputy sheriffs to support them, capturing, and convicting forty-two Pennsylvanians for assault, riot, and other charges. In June 1784, Pennsylvania's president John Dickinson shut down the Wyoming garrison. To add to the general misery, a flood in March left many settlers on both sides homeless.[15]

As men joined marauding bands, they left women to protect their homesteads and trusted their opponents would respect the female sex. Sometimes they did, but frequently they did not. Court depositions spoke of women being "abused," a euphemism for rape. Women were beaten, and men threatened to tomahawk children. In July 1785, it appeared the Yankees had won: they drove out Pennsylvania justice of the peace David Mead and a large force he had gathered to fortify his residence at Sunbury. Connecticut's Susquehannah Company promptly began renewing its efforts, promising lands to "half share" men who remained on their grants for three years and who agreed to defend the company's claims. By the end of 1786, it had created eight new towns.

Pennsylvania cleverly responded by adopting the Confirming Act in March 1787. Now, claims to lands occupied before the Trenton Decree on both sides would be honored, while those (nearly all settled by Yankees) that came later were annulled. Splitting the Yankees with this ruling, Pennsylvania commissioned Timothy Pickering to establish order. In October, Yankee leader John Franklin attempted to organize his "completely armed and equipped"

followers to expel the "loyalists," as he termed the Pennsylvanians. Pickering beat him to the punch, arrested him, and sent him to Philadelphia. The Wyoming Valley's inhabitants in turn elected Pickering to the Pennsylvania State Convention that met in November to ratify the United States Constitution, not because they liked him or approved of his pro-ratification stance, but simply to get him off their backs. With Franklin in jail for nine months, in June 1788, the insurgent Yankees responded by kidnapping Pickering, who had returned, in the hopes of exchanging him for Franklin. But they were disappointed. In general, the Yankees who lived in the southern part of the valley had their titles validated by Pennsylvania, supported that state, and joined the militia that searched for the kidnappers, who lived in the northern, more newly settled region where the claims remained questionable. By late September, Pickering was free, his captors' weakness evidenced by the fact that they could not even compel him to intercede for pardons on their behalf.[16]

It was now Pennsylvania's turn to take the offensive. In 1790, it repealed the Confirming Act. Yet the state lacked the force to eject the Yankees, whose numbers increased during the nineties in far greater number than the Pennsylvanians'. As they formed majorities in counties and townships, Yankees attacked rival claimants with impunity as they dominated courts and juries. John Franklin, after serving five years in jail, was elected sheriff of Luzerne County in 1792, colonel of its militia in 1793, and finally its representative in the state legislature.

But as the land boom came to an end, Pennsylvania's strategy again split the Yankees. The Compromise Act of 1799 once again legalized Connecticut (as well as Pennsylvania) claims that predated the Trenton Decree. In return, Connecticut owners whose purchases were confirmed had to pay taxes to compensate Pennsylvanians who lost their land. Pennsylvanians formed the Pennsylvania Landholders Association where wealthy speculators imitated the Susquehannah Company's tactic of exchanging land for allegiance. Under the leadership of English-born Thomas Cooper—a Jeffersonian writer and politician who had been imprisoned under the Sedition Act for his harsh criticisms of the Federalists—peace at last came to the valley. Pennsylvania's Intrusion Act of 1801 provided for the imprisonment and fining of those Yankees who refused to yield property that belonged to Pennsylvanians. Resistant Yankees continued to attack those "dastardly souls who are intimidated by the Intrusion law . . . [and] creep and cringe to the agents of Pennsylvania land jobbers [and] abandon their lands . . . such men are not worthy to be called Yankees." But as the state of Pennsylvania built roads connecting communities and encouraging the production of surplus agriculture that traveled far more easily down the Susquehanna (thanks to the Conewago Canal, south of Harrisburg, opened in 1797 by the state) to the rapidly growing city of Baltimore, more and more Yankees realized that prosperity lay in accommodation. By 1805, northern Pennsylvania was at peace.[17]

THE EXCISE TAX AND THE WHISKEY REBELLION, 1791–1794

Anthony Wayne's victory over the Indians came at the very moment another American army, this one commanded at first by President George Washington himself—the only sitting American president to lead troops in the field—was marching into western Pennsylvania to suppress what is known to history as "The Whiskey Rebellion." The coincidence was serendipitous. The frontier settlers of western Pennsylvania were unable to market their corn for a profit: it was a two-week trip over numerous mountain ranges from Philadelphia to Pittsburgh; the port of New Orleans was closed to Americans by the Spanish; and the Ohio Indians had made navigation of the Ohio River perilous if not impossible. Subject to an excise tax on distilled whiskey, the western Pennsylvanians (along with Kentucky settlers who had just begun distilling the whiskey known today as bourbon) wondered what the government was doing for them in return for a new tax that small distillers disproportionately shouldered. Why, they asked, should they be unfairly taxed to pay interest on the national debt that lined the pockets of wealthy easterners and foreigners? To be collected at the place of manufacture, the tax amounted to fifty-four cents annually per gallon for those who operated

A period cartoon showing an "Exciseman," or tax collector, carrying two kegs of whiskey while being pursued by irate farmers who want to tar and feather him. Small producers of whiskey in western Pennsylvania felt a new national excise tax that included whiskey designed to pay off debt from the Revolutionary War placed an unfair burden on them compared to larger whiskey producers in the East.

stills under four hundred gallons, while owners of larger distilleries could pay a flat tax based on their stills' capacities and thus undersell those with fewer resources.[18]

Only in the late 1780s had the Scots-Irish farmers of Allegheny and Washington counties begun to make a decent living by selling grain as both whiskey and foodstuffs to the army in the West and to immigrants passing through Pennsylvania to the Ohio Valley. They remained excluded, however, from the rich lands of the Ohio Valley, still controlled by Native Americans that the federal government had been unable to defeat. And they had no access either to the rich markets in Europe and the West Indies as Spain prevented them from using the Mississippi River to float their grain down to New Orleans and the Caribbean sugar islands.

Western Pennsylvanians were not used to paying taxes. Occupied with the British invasion of Philadelphia

and opposition to their rule by loyalists, pacifists, and conservative revolutionaries, the radical revolutionaries who had taken power under Pennsylvania's Constitution of 1776 had failed either to defend or to collect taxes in much of the western part of the state. Even in the eastern counties, unhappy inhabitants destroyed roads—in one case filling a mountain pass with dung—so tax collectors could not reach courthouses, and formed crowds to prevent foreclosures on the estates of those who owed back taxes or private debts. The only reason Pennsylvania did not suffer something like Shays' Rebellion in Massachusetts (1786–1787) was that the state government was both unable and unwilling to raise an army to enforce the laws. Instead, given the vast amount of land the state owned, unlike thickly settled Massachusetts, Pennsylvania raised almost all its revenue in the 1780s and 1790s by selling state lands, thereby relieving its population of taxation and its government of potential unrest.[19]

At issue, however, was Secretary of the Treasury Alexander Hamilton's national excise tax that included whiskey, which Congress approved in 1791. Western Pennsylvania's political leaders, former Anti-Federalist champions John Smilie and William Findley and the future secretary of the treasury under Jefferson and Madison, Albert Gallatin, agreed with their constituents that the tax was unfair but urged them only to oppose it in every legal way possible. The western farmers presented a petition written by Gallatin to the House of Representatives:

That your Petitioners have been greatly alarmed by a law of Congress which imposes a duty on spirituous liquors distilled from produce of the United States. To us that act appears unequal in its operation and immoral in its effects. Unequal in its operation, as a duty laid on the common drink of a nation, instead of taxing the citizens in proportion to their property, falls as heavy on the poorest class as on the rich; immoral in its effect, because the amount of the duty chiefly resting on the oath of the payer, offers, at the expense of the honest part of the community, a premium to perjury and fraud.

Your Petitioners also consider this law as dangerous to liberty; because the powers necessarily vested in the officers for the collection of so odious a revenue are not only unusual, but incompatible with the free enjoyment of domestic peace and private property; because these powers, to prevent evasions of the duty, must pursue the endless subtleties

of the human mind, and be almost infinitely increased; and because we are apprehensive that this excise will by degrees be extended to other articles of consumption until everything we eat, drink, or wear be, as in England and other European countries, subjected to heavy duties and the obnoxious inspection of an host of officers. . . .

Our peculiar situation renders this duty still more unequal and oppressive to us. Distant from a permanent market, and separate from the eastern coast by mountains which render the communication difficult and almost impracticable, we have no means of bringing the produce of our lands to sale either in grain or in meal. We are therefore distillers through necessity, not choice, that we may comprehend the greatest value in the smallest size and weight.

The inhabitants of the eastern side of the mountains can dispose of their grain without the additional labor of distillation at a higher price than we can, after we have bestowed that labor upon it. Yet with this additional labor we must also pay a high duty from which they are exempted, because we have no means of selling our surplus produce but in a distilled state.

Another circumstance which renders this duty ruinous to us is our scarcity of cash. Our commerce is not, as on the eastern coast, carried on so much by absolute sale as by barter, and we believe it to be a fact that there is not among us a quantity of circulating cash sufficient for the payment of this duty alone.

We are not accustomed to complain without reason; we have punctually and cheerfully paid former taxes on our estates and possessions, because they were proportioned to our real wealth. We believe this to be founded on no such equitable principles, and are persuaded that your Honorable House will find on investigation that its amount, if duly collected, will be four times as large as any tax which we have hitherto paid on the whole of our lands and other property.

Submitting these considerations to your honorable body, we respectfully apply for a total repeal of the law, or for such modifications thereof as would render its principles more congenial to the nature of a free government, and its operation upon us less unequal and oppressive.[20]

When the federal government refused to honor farmers' petitions for repeal of the measure, they not only refused to pay the excise tax but threatened bodily harm to the tax collectors.

Few Americans, east or west, liked the new federal tax. In fact, the Pennsylvania legislature, anticipating the Virginia and Kentucky Resolutions of 1798 and South Carolina's nullification of the tariff of 1828, declared that only the state could levy an excise tax. No whiskey taxes were collected in western Pennsylvania in 1792 or 1793. In 1794, Governor Thomas Mifflin arranged for Pennsylvania courts to hold their sessions in the west and to hear cases involving the excise tax. However, a federal marshal ordered that farmers who refused to pay would have to stand trial in Philadelphia. The marshal met no difficulty collecting the tax as he passed through Somerset, Bedford, Washington, and Fayette counties. In Allegheny County, however, he tried to obtain payment from a farmer who had no intention of paying. When the farmer turned belligerent, the marshal ordered his arrest and sent him to stand trial in Philadelphia, to the great displeasure of local residents who believed that a "fair trial" had to occur in the immediate jurisdiction where a jury of one's peers who understood the circumstances of the case could be summoned.

The locals responded on July 16 by marching to Bower Hill, probably the finest structure in Pennsylvania west of the Alleghenies. It was the home of the Revolutionary War general John Neville, a prominent landowner, Virginian, and friend of President George Washington, who had agreed to take the job of tax collector. That a member of Virginia's planter elite was chosen to enforce a law repugnant to Pennsylvania farmers only a decade after the two states had ceased fighting over the region added yet another class dimension to the struggle. There, Neville's supporters and his armed slaves fired on the crowd, killing popular Revolutionary War veteran John McFarland. The crowd returned the next day, demanded that Neville resign his commission, and when he refused, they burned his house to the ground. The rebellion was on.

Within a week of the sacking of Neville's house, David Bradford became the rebellion's principal spokesman. Born in Maryland sometime around 1760, he had immigrated to Pennsylvania and been admitted to the Washington County bar in 1782. Serving as deputy attorney general for the county since 1783, Bradford was an extremely successful lawyer and businessman. His attractive residence, completed in 1788, reflected his high social standing in the community. Bradford led tax protests at the Mingo Creek Church on July 23, at Braddock's Field near Pittsburgh on July 28, and at the Bonnet Tavern near Bedford in early August. There the more radical insurgents repudiated the calls for nonviolent protest by Albert Gallatin and Judge Hugh Henry Brackenridge (the author of *American Chivalry*) and resolved to resist any armed force sent to enforce the excise tax. At the Bonnet Tavern they swore death to tax collectors and withdrawal from the Union if President Washington tried to enforce the despised tax. When Bradford learned, on August 6, that federal authorities were planning a large-scale invasion, he stood firm. "We have fully deliberated," he wrote in a recruiting letter to Virginians, "and have determined with head, heart, hand and voice that we will support the opposition to the excise law. The crisis is now come: submission or opposition."[21]

Westerners intercepted federal mails and destroyed letters exposing the names of rebels. In mid-August, Governor Mifflin and President Washington appointed a joint state/federal peace commission to make a final effort to end the conflict without a military invasion. Lieutenant Governor Thomas McKean and General William Irvine represented Pennsylvania; the federal government was represented by William Bradford, U.S. attorney general, Senator James Ross, and Jasper Yeats, a Pennsylvania Supreme Court justice. All five were Pennsylvanians, and they attended mass meetings at Parkinson's Ferry and Redstone Old Fort, with David Bradford and other rebel leaders. When they reported back that there was no hope of settlement, Washington prepared a military invasion.

Western Pennsylvania's resistance was not that distinctive. It was also impossible for the federal government to collect the tax in western Georgia, the Carolinas, Virginia, Tennessee, Maryland, and Kentucky. It probably only chose to enforce it in western Pennsylvania because that was the easiest region to approach, and resistance in the very state with the national capital of Philadelphia would signify the new government had inherited the "impotence" and "imbecility"—two words much in use at the time—of the Articles of Confederation.[22]

Most early histories of the Whiskey Rebellion characterized the rebels as an unruly mob that had little, if any, respect for private property or law and order. Written in the early 1800s by Federalist sympathizers, they echoed the sentiments of the nation's political leaders, who depicted rebels as people of no significance in order to minimize the effect of suppressing the rebellion. However, things were not that simple. Four colonels of the Washington County militia were among those arrested as principal rebels, as was respected Baptist minister John Corbley. And

David Bradford was a leading lawyer and the county's deputy attorney general. When they heard an army was about to attack them, some seven thousand western Pennsylvanians marched on Pittsburgh, intimidated its residents, threatened to take control of the federal arsenal at Fort Pitt, which was pretty much in ruins, and destroyed several private properties. They also threatened but did not harm Fort Lafayette, the supply depot for the federal army that was even at that moment fighting the Indians who threatened their security and trade to the west. Sympathetic "friends of liberty," who viewed the rebellion as a struggle against the eastern political powerbrokers, arose in Carlisle, Pennsylvania, and in the backcountry of Kentucky and Virginia. In Philadelphia and other eastern communities, the Democratic Societies that had formed in 1793 to support the French Revolutionary Republic formally repudiated the rebellion, as did Republican leaders Thomas Jefferson and James Madison. But many members privately expressed their support.[23]

On August 14, 1794, state representative Albert Gallatin met with the rebels at what is now known as Whiskey Point and, so he informed the federal government, convinced them to submit to the federal laws as resistance to the overwhelming force about to invade the west would be futile. David Bradford's "eight-page account of the rebellion—never published—that he dictated to officials in Spanish Louisiana in January 1795" gave a different account of the meeting. "Perhaps to tell his hosts what they wanted to hear—that there was a real possibility Spain could take over the western parts of the United States"—he claimed that the August 14 meeting declared for western independence (it did approve a flag that represented the six counties whose people showed up) and "that only under coercion did a populace nearly universally against the whiskey tax submit to federal authority." Bradford "asserted that the people in western Pennsylvania and beyond had declared the tax 'annulled,'" and formed councils, publishing notices in the *Pittsburgh Gazette* recommending to the public officials that they abstain from respecting as members of society the officials for collecting the excise tax, considering them as contemptible men, thinking by that method that no one would receive a similar official."[24]

Bradford's interpretation was the one adopted by the national government. Reports of the violence in western Pennsylvania had already reached the federal government, and it was also rumored—correctly, it appears in Bradford's case—that the rebels were asking representatives of Great Britain and Spain to aid in a frontier-wide separatist movement. Fearing the secession of western territories President Washington ordered Governor Mifflin to send the Pennsylvania militia to enforce the law. But Mifflin declined, asserting that a president in peacetime and in the absence of any local request for help had no authority to direct a state governor to use a state militia for any

A painting circa 1795 by an unknown artist depicting George Washington and his troops preparing to supress the Whiskey Rebellion. The presence of Washington's army was enough to end the rebellion. He ended up pardoning the perpetrators.

purpose whatsoever. In the process, Mifflin established a precedent that is still honored today.

Rebuffed by Pennsylvania's governor, Washington drafted a proclamation requesting that the states of Pennsylvania, New Jersey, Maryland, and Virginia raise a force of 13,000 men who would be enlisted into federal service. Washington had reasons of his own to be angry at Pennsylvania's western farmers that preceded the excise tax. Back in the 1780s, a group known as the Covenanter Squatters had contested his land ownership in Washington County. Having provoked wars with the Indians and ignored treaties respecting their lands, these western Pennsylvanians now seemed unwilling to pay a tax largely enacted on their behalf to rid the Ohio Valley of these Indians, even as the government was negotiating with the Spanish and the British to make sure the Ohio

region could be settled and its products shipped down the Mississippi.

While Secretary of the Treasury Alexander Hamilton and some Federalists were eager to use the rebellion to demonstrate the power of the new nation to raise armies and suppress insurrections, Washington simply wanted western Pennsylvanians to make some contribution toward the government that was spending so much of its energy and money to secure their interests.

On October 4, 1794, Washington joined the troops—contemptuously dubbed the "Watermelon Army" by the rebels—near Carlisle and marched out with them to Bedford County. It was there that Washington was informed that his army had scared off the "Whiskey Boys," who would now comply with the tax. Turning over command of the troops to Governor Henry Lee of Virginia, the president then returned to

Philadelphia. On November 13, federal troops arrested 150 rebels, then sent twenty of the ringleaders to Philadelphia to stand trial, including the Reverend John Corbley.[25] The U.S. District Court of Philadelphia found most of the rebels not guilty, but in July 1795 sentenced two obscure men to death for treason. Washington pardoned both. His show of force in raising an army and compassion in pardoning the offenders strengthened the new government, which made little further effort to collect the tax after its revenues increased from other sources, notably customs duties. Bradford eluded capture by escaping south to Spanish West Florida (present-day Louisiana). In 1799, Washington granted Bradford a presidential pardon. Preferring to remain on his plantation in Spain's Louisiana territory, the rebel leader never returned to the United States.

Pennsylvania's Whiskey Rebellion was the first large-scale resistance by American citizens against the United States government under the new federal constitution. It also marked the first time the president exercised the constitutional police powers of his office to suppress domestic insurrections. Although some of the rebellion's leaders may have conceived it as an attempt to secede from the United States, the overwhelming majority of its supporters believed they were engaging in tax resistance that had begun with the revolution and continued in Pennsylvania throughout the 1780s, when large numbers of inhabitants either considered state

taxes unfair or a particular administration incompetent or misguided. The term "rebellion" was coined by the Federalists, Hamilton far more than Washington, who wished to demonstrate that the new nation was indeed capable of quelling insurrections. In any event, within two years of the rebellion, the grievances of the western farmers were quieted. Just before the outbreak of the rebellion, General Anthony Wayne had defeated the Ohio Valley Indians at the Battle of Fallen Timbers, thereby ending the raids into western Pennsylvania and opening much of what is now Ohio to white settlement. In 1796 a new treaty with Spain, which allowed American citizens to sell their goods through New Orleans, opened a grain trade to the West, and brought prosperity to the region.

FRIES'S REBELLION: THE END OF THE REVOLUTIONARY ERA, 1798–1800

Another tax resistance movement was also dubbed a "rebellion" by the Federalists: Fries's Rebellion, which centered in the town of Bethlehem in Northampton County in northeastern Pennsylvania. On July 9, 1798, to pay for a proposed army for a possible war with France, a Federalist-controlled Congress approved a new federal tax on lands and houses, the latter to be assessed by the number of windows. Many Pennsylvanians found the new tax especially obnoxious, for its percentage increased progressively in accordance with assessed value, and many farms in long-settled northeastern Pennsylvania were substantial indeed. The law also said that the tax had to be paid in gold or silver, which was at a premium, and thus might cost the taxpayers more than their assessed valuation to obtain.[26]

Congress passed the tax at the same time that the United States was engaged in an undeclared naval war with France, and at a time when the Federalists who controlled Congress viewed domestic opposition to its policies as treason rather than legitimate dissent. In addition, President John Adams made the mistake of appointing ex-Tories and Quaker pacifists to collect the tax for northeastern Pennsylvania. The predominantly ethnically German population of this region had loyally supported the revolution. Despite their reputation as the "Dumb Dutch," they were well aware of their political rights. Until 1798 they had voted Federalist for the most part.

Protests against the Alien and Sedition Acts, which Congress also passed that June to suppress dissent, flowed in from all over Pennsylvania as well. The federal government was concerned especially that newspaper editors and columnists—and those most noticeable from the national capital in Philadelphia were Pennsylvanians—did not use their papers to criticize foreign or domestic policy. Thomas Cooper, an English immigrant to Northumberland, and Benjamin Franklin Bache, the grandson of Benjamin Franklin who published the *Aurora* in Philadelphia, were two of the twenty-five people arrested for sedition. Cooper was one of ten convicted, Bache died of yellow

fever in jail while awaiting trial, and his successor William Duane was attacked by Federalists who had chased him over the city's rooftops.[27]

By early 1799, loud protests against the tax were gaining momentum in Northampton, Berks, and to a lesser degree Montgomery and Bucks counties. Angry citizens set up liberty poles, as they had back in the 1770s, in protest against the British taxes that led to the American Revolution. Others poured hot water on the tax collectors, assaulted them, and destroyed their records. When sheriffs under federal court orders from the U.S. District Court headquartered in Philadelphia arrested twenty-three ringleaders and confined them in the Sun Tavern in Bethlehem, a crowd of more than a hundred men led by John Fries of Milford Township in Bucks County, an auctioneer of Welsh descent, marched to Bethlehem and freed them on March 7. The crowd was willing for the twenty-three to be tried but, as had occurred during the Whiskey Rebellion, insisted on trials in the local community, which would have guaranteed a verdict of innocent, rather than Philadelphia, where conviction was almost certain.

The "rebellion" terrified the Federalists in Philadelphia. At first convinced that Fries and his followers had committed treason, President Adams requested that the Philadelphia militia capture them. The city's "Blues," or light cavalry, commanded by General William McPherson (son-in-law of William White, the Episcopal bishop of Pennsylvania), a group of wealthy men who paid for their own horses and equipment, moved out, rounded up the leading protesters, and tracked down Fries by following his dog Whiskey into a swamp where he was hiding.

The federal government charged forty-five of the protesters with treason, although it only prosecuted Fries and four others for treason and seventeen for lesser crimes. The courts then sentenced Fries and three others to death. President Adams pardoned them, however—against the advice of every member of his cabinet—after he changed his mind and concluded that Fries and his followers were guilty only of "riot and rescue," not of making war on the government with the intent to overthrow it, as the "high" Federalists had suggested.

Adams's pardons angered Federalists and damaged his reelection chances. Federalist Pennsylvania Germans resented what they considered an overreaction to their tax protests. As a result, Pennsylvania Germans voted for electors who supported Jefferson. Ultimately, Adams did not carry Pennsylvania; instead, he split the electoral vote with Jefferson, 7 to 8 respectively, which played a significant role in his electoral defeat.[28]

From 1754 to about 1805, Pennsylvania endured a half century of different types of warfare. Traditional armies fought at Brandywine and Germantown during the American Revolution; expeditions into the wilderness forced the French and their Indian allies to abandon Kittanning and Fort Duquesne; the Paxton Boys and revolutionary troops at Gnadenhutten massacred Indians, while loyalists and Indians did likewise to Pennsylvania frontier folk; Virginians, Pennsylvanians, and Connecticut Yankees contested the boundaries of their colonies; loyalist guerrilla units plagued eastern Pennsylvania during the revolution; Anthony Wayne finally secured the frontier at the Battle of Fallen Timbers; Pennsylvanians dissatisfied with federal taxation launched the protests remembered today as the Whiskey and Fries's Rebellions. The unprecedented three-quarter-century peace of William Penn's "Holy Experiment" had degenerated into turmoil unequaled in any colony or state.

After 1800, with the exception of the naval engagement fought on Lake Erie during the War of 1812 and the battles of Gettysburg and Chambersburg during the Civil War, military action against outside foes disappeared from Pennsylvania's soil. However, Pennsylvanians continued to fight among themselves. The violence among blacks and whites, Protestants and Roman Catholics on the streets of Philadelphia; draft resistance during the Civil War; and labor unrest in the coal, railroad, and steel industries ensured that Pennsylvania's nineteenth century, like its eighteenth, acquired a nationwide reputation for internal strife matched by few, if any, other states.

7. Pennsylvania in the War of 1812 and U.S.-Mexican War

Barbara A. Gannon

While the receding frontier and victory in the war for independence meant that Pennsylvania was not the site of any military campaigns in the first half of the nineteenth century, Pennsylvanians fought two major wars during this era—the War of 1812 and the Mexican-American War. Additionally, during peacetime, citizens of the Keystone State, like many Americans of their era, showed a great deal of interest in the militia and volunteers units. Despite this ongoing attention to military affairs, the state would be unprepared to face its greatest military challenge in the 1860s when, once again, war came home.

THE WAR OF 1812

Forty years after the revolution, Pennsylvanians were again at war with Great Britain. Ostensibly, the war was fought over impressment and maritime rights; American sailors, who may or may not have been British deserters, were impressed into the Royal Navy during the Napoleonic Wars. In reality, many Pennsylvanians supported this war because they believed that British officials in Canada used attacks by Native American tribes to prevent Americans from moving west. Just before the War of 1812, there had been a series of attacks on settlers led by the Indian leader Tecumseh. In 1811, the United States Army had won an important victory at Tippecanoe, killing Tecumseh's brother. While much of the actual combat occurred in present-day Ohio, Pennsylvanians were keenly interested in frontier security and, like many other Americans, wanted to secure the West for white settlers. As a result, despite most Pennsylvanians having little interest in maritime affairs, or concerns about impressed sailors, they went to war with enthusiasm.[1]

In some ways, the War of 1812 was one of the nation's most partisan wars; the Federalists opposed the war, while Anti-Federalists supported it. Most Pennsylvanians were Anti-Federalists; eighteen out of twenty

Pennsylvania congressmen voted for war with England. When northeastern states dominated by Federalists could not, or would not, meet their militia quotas, Pennsylvania responded by calling its militia into service. While theoretically all military-aged men served, the wealthy could hire a substitute and some did. Regardless, of members' social or economic class, the militias were poorly trained. In addition, many of these militiamen mustered into service and sent to Meadville, Pennsylvania, deserted, suggesting they were also ill-disciplined. Other Pennsylvanians served in other theaters. Some fought against the British in Canada; repeated invasions of Canada by American militiamen and regulars failed. While other Pennsylvanians served in Ohio, some soldiers stayed home and guarded Philadelphia. James Forten, a wealthy black businessman, recruited African Americans to labor on fortifications defending Philadelphia. After a series of defeats by the British, culminating in the burning of the White House in Washington, D.C., Pennsylvania militiamen joined other states' forces and fought and defeated British troops near Baltimore. The British failure to capture Baltimore combined with the victory at New Orleans by Andrew Jackson after the war had ended, left Americans with the impression that they had "won" the war. These successes obscured the failure of the militia system and meant that when war came again, ill-trained Pennsylvanian's would once again go to war.[2]

While the land-based operations of Pennsylvania soldiers were as dreadful as those in other states, naval activities were more successful. Pennsylvania was the location of the greatest naval victory of the war, the Battle of Lake Erie, which resulted in U.S. control of the Great Lakes. Saying that this was the greatest naval victory of this war is significant; the United States won a number of important victories at sea during this conflict. Stephen Decatur, captain of the USS *Constitution*, had won a victory in single-ship action against a Royal Navy ship, as had other American naval officers; no other navy in this era could make this claim. While these victories heartened Americans, they did not provide it with any long-term strategic advantage. In fact, these defeats inspired British officials to enforce a tight blockade on the American coastline to prevent the U.S. Navy from attacking its ships. In contrast, success on Lake Erie mattered and led to American control of the Great Lakes and the security of the neighboring states. One prominent naval scholar identified this engagement as one the five most important naval battles in U.S. history.[3]

To win the war at sea or on the lakes, the battle had to be won on land; in this case, a fleet had to be built in the wilderness. The only way the United States could fight the British on the Great Lakes was to build ships inland along the Great Lakes coastline. Initially, officials had built some ships near Niagara, New York, but these craft were vulnerable to British attack. When Commodore Oliver Hazard Perry was sent to over-

At the turning point of the Battle of Lake Eire, September 19, 1913, Commodore Oliver Hazard Perry is rowed in his first cutter (right of center) from the heavily damaged *Lawrence* to the *Niagara*. Taking command of the *Niagara* and advantage of a British blunder in maneuvering, Perry and his gunboats pounded the British ships into surrendering, a major American victory in the War of 1812.

see the building of these ships, he moved this effort to an area less vulnerable to British attack, Erie, Pennsylvania, specifically, the sheltered bay of Presque Isle. It would be hard to exaggerate the difficulties of building a fleet in this area. The area was a wilderness, the only resource in abundance, wood, for the ships' hulls; it had none of the resources needed to make iron fittings, naval guns, and sails. The frontier had few skilled craftsmen; instead, they were brought in from Philadelphia. Other Pennsylvanians played an important role in this effort. Perry armed the ships with guns from Pittsburgh; Pennsylvania militiamen guarded the shipbuilding operation and provided some manpower for his fleet. Despite these challenges, over the winter, spring, and summer of 1813, Perry built a fleet that was, on paper, slightly more

capable than the British forces on the lake; his fleet had larger guns, even if he had fewer ships than the British commander. By September, the British had their fleet ready to fight as did the Americans. With a pennant flying, "Do not give up the ship," the last words of his friend Captain James Lawrence who had been killed in action earlier that year, Perry and his crews prepared to fight.[4]

Perry understood that his ships' larger guns—thirty-two pounders—had more fire power but less range than the British. He would have to fight at close range, and he did. Initially, this fight went poorly, partly because only his flagship, the *Lawrence*, named for his friend, engaged the enemy. The other large ship in his fleet, the *Niagara*, was under the command of an officer who had not aggressively attacked the enemy. After the *Lawrence* had been battered and bloodied by the main British ship, Perry transferred to the *Niagara* and took command. While the *Lawrence* ultimately surrendered, it seriously damaged the British ship. Because of its poor condition, the British flagship surrendered soon after Perry attacked in the *Niagara*. Eventually, the rest of the British fleet capitulated to the American fleet. The United States now controlled the Great Lakes and with it the entire Northwest. While many Americans believed that the Battle of New Orleans was the greatest victory of the war, it had little impact on the outcome; it happened after the peace treaty was signed. The Battle of Lake Erie represents a better candidate for that honor and Pennsylvanians were critical to this important victory.[5]

Despite their poor performance in the War of 1812, Pennsylvanians, like much of the nation, retained their enthusiasm for military service in the decades after the war. While the idea that all military age men should serve was on the wane, military service as a voluntary activity rose in Pennsylvanians' esteem. Respect for volunteerism did not extend to the regular U.S. Army, all theoretically volunteers. As historian Marcus Cunliffe explained, Americans embraced military volunteerism, even as they rejected military professionalism. It is likely no surprise that Pennsylvania embraced volunteer units, since Pennsylvania was the home of the first large-scale volunteer military organization in America— the Association—discussed in earlier chapters. [6]

What might be surprising was the extent to which social elites embraced military service; often only the best class of men was accepted in its ranks. One reason that military service was popular, these volunteer units emphasized military spectacle and not military training; dressed in flamboyant uniforms, they paraded around American cities. When Marcus Cunliffe chronicled these enthusiastic volunteers, he used a description provided by a member of the Philadelphia Lancer Guard in 1835. "The dress consists of a coat of rich maroon cloth faced with buff, pantaloons of crimson with a stripe of buff on the outside seams, and a helmet of the lancer shape, the skull of beaten brass, and the crest of crimson with a radiance of silver in front surrounding a golden eagle." The volunteer explains that "the species of troops is a novelty in the city, and if gotten up with spirit, will add greatly to the splendor of our parades." When Pennsylvanians found themselves at war in Mexico their martial ardor was challenged by the harsh reality of war.[7]

THE U.S.-MEXICAN WAR

When the Mexican War came, the men who had been attracted to peacetime military service volunteered to serve overseas. Initially, more than seven thousand Pennsylvanians, organized into ninety companies, volunteered for service; however, these men were not called to service and enthusiasm for overseas service waned. Later, when it needed more units, the government called into service two regiments, or twenty companies, the First and Second Pennsylvania Volunteers, ordering these units to Mexico. The volunteer experience for these units, like that of most U.S.-Mexican War volunteers was often deadly, though not because of gunshot and shell in battle; instead, they died as a result of diseases. The Second Pennsylvania recorded the third highest number of fatalities among volunteer units; however, only four soldiers died in battle, while 225 deaths were attributed to disease or accidents. The First Pennsylvania had a lower death toll: 146 from disease and other causes, while 28 occurred on the battlefield. Partly, this was due to overseas service in an environment that promoted disease, particularly for men who were not acclimated to the climate. In addition, the primitive nature of military medicine increased mortality rates. While volunteers could not control these factors, they likely could have ameliorated some of the unfavorable conditions if the men were well-disciplined and attentive to sanitation in their camps. Volunteer soldiers' lack of discipline and train-

ing meant that they lived in unsanitary conditions conducive to the spread of disease. Thomas Barclay, Pennsylvania volunteer and lawyer, identified the link between the prevalence of disease and the lack of discipline in his unit. According to Barclay "the filth of the Reg[iment] is disgraceful and will, unless remedied, create a disease." The link to his unit's lack of discipline was clear in his mind. "An officer is daily appointed to see that quarters are policed but [soldiers] pay but little attention to it." The death rate for soldiers in Barclay's company was twice that of other similar units; however, not one of these deaths occurred in battle.[8]

Despite the experience of these units, and the mortality rates of volunteer units, little would change when, two decades later, war came home to Pennsylvania. If there was a difference, it was that Civil War combat was so lethal that the tens of thousands of men who died of disease represented only one-half of the deaths experienced by Civil War soldiers; this war, more than any other, shaped Pennsylvania's military history.[9]

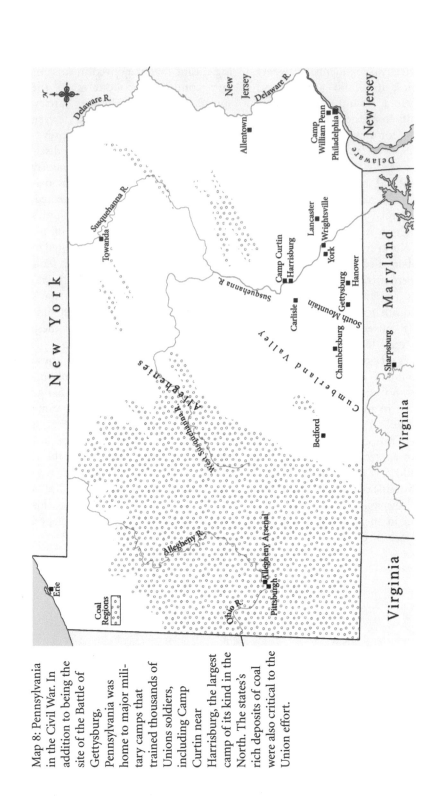

Map 8: Pennsylvania in the Civil War. In addition to being the site of the Battle of Gettysburg, Pennsylvania was home to major military camps that trained thousands of Unions soldiers, including Camp Curtin near Harrisburg, the largest camp of its kind in the North. The state's rich deposits of coal were also critical to the Union effort.

8. Pennsylvania's War for the Union, 1861–1863

Christian B. Keller

Often referred to as the "Arsenal of the Union," Pennsylvania truly lived up to its old moniker, the Keystone State, during the four bloody years of the American Civil War. It was geographically a linchpin for the Northern states, linking New York and New England with the Midwest, its railroads and canals not only ensuring peaceful commerce would continue during the conflict but also transporting hundreds of thousands of Federal troops and their equipment, ammunition, and supplies to points west and south. Its factories, arsenals, farms, and training camps produced the sinews of war during this first of modern wars, helping to clinch the Union victory by sheer logistical might. Its banking industry—although by the 1860s outpaced by that of New York—still remained a formidable weapon in its own right and lay at the disposal of the Northern war leaders, while the naval shipyard at Philadelphia retained its place as one of the country's most significant locations for construction,

outfitting, and repair of warships. If any state in the Union could fairly claim its nickname perfectly described its economic role in the war, it was Pennsylvania.

When the war broke out in April 1861, after South Carolina state forces opened fire on the Federal garrison in Charleston Harbor, it soon became apparent that the most important of Pennsylvania's contributions would not be in the realms of materiel, monetary, or maritime power (as significant as they were), but instead in men—the factory workers, farmers, miners, hospital attendants, and, most critically, the soldiers who devoted themselves to the cause of Union and liberty. Previous summaries of Pennsylvania's involvement in the Civil War, especially those written in the decades after the conflict and in the early twentieth century, tended to examine individual regiments, specific groups of people, cities, or locations, or the deeds of politicians and generals. Other, more recent chroniclers have chosen to focus on the economic, social, and cultural aspects of Pennsylvanians on the home front, sometimes to the point of inadvertently downplaying the all-critical military component. A middle ground exists, however, that offers a robust narrative of the Keystone State in the nation's greatest crisis, one that dwells on the *people* of Pennsylvania, especially the soldiers, and what they did on and off the battlefield. This chapter will peer into the lives of some of these Pennsylvanians and thereby offer a window into a time that was arguably the Commonwealth's greatest military test.

THE COMING OF THE WAR: POLITICAL BACKGROUND

The Civil War did not just burst upon Pennsylvania unexpectedly. Throughout the antebellum years, average citizens and their leaders alike increasingly became active participants in the great drama of the sectional crisis. David Wilmot, a junior congressman who had practiced law in Towanda, was probably most responsible for igniting the controversy over slavery's expansion into the federal territories with his famous "Proviso" of 1846 that demanded no slave states be created from new lands acquired from Mexico during the recent war. Southern firebrands viewed this as a death sentence to the institution of slavery, which was perpetuated by the soil-intensive cash crop economy. Cotton and tobacco, they told Wilmot and those northerners who rose to join him, needed fresh lands in order to be profitable, and thus slavery needed to expand. In many ways, this

argument against Wilmot's rider to a nondescript funding bill started the political debate in Congress that led to the demise of the national Whig Party, the rise of the Republicans, the nationalization of the abolitionist agenda, the fracturing of the Democrats, and ultimately the election of Abraham Lincoln. That event, in turn, sparked the secession of the Deep South states, beginning in December 1860, with South Carolina.

Initially, the average Pennsylvanian, guiding his plow in Perry County or offloading ships at the port of Philadelphia, followed the political events of the 1850s with marginal interest; local events and issues, such as the election of sheriffs and judges and the going price of wheat meant far more to the provincially minded citizen of the mid-nineteenth-century Commonwealth than national politics did. The problem was that the acrimony in the nation's capital over slavery increasingly spilled over into local and state politics as the last antebellum decade progressed, inciting Pennsylvanians to become more and more concerned with what happened in faraway places like Kansas, when John Brown massacred pro-slavery settlers in 1856, or in closer locales such as Harpers Ferry when he attempted to lead Virginia's slaves in rebellion in 1859. Who won local political races made a difference regarding which party, Democrat or Republican, gained an edge in the statehouse at Harrisburg, which in turn was significant for national elections. Each minor election therefore began to carry with it consequences greater than the one before it, which succeeded in politicizing the overall population in areas where political involvement had once been relegated to the upper and middle classes.

As the 1850s began to wane and the national Democrats became increasingly dominated by their southern wing, traditionally Democratic Pennsylvania found itself somewhat at odds with its sister states of the North, most of which had become strongholds of Republicanism after the election of 1856. Four years later, Lincoln carried the Keystone State, but mainly because the voters of the cities and large towns switched their allegiances, thanks to strident Republican economic appeals among working-class voters, mistakes committed by the Democrats on the national stage (such as the 1854 Kansas-Nebraska Act and the 1857 Dred Scott Supreme Court case), and a split Democratic ticket between the "northern" and "southern" presidential candidates, Stephen Douglas and John Breckinridge. Most Pennsylvania farmers, excluding the antislavery Mennonites, Amish, and Dunkers, remained loyal to the Democracy, as did the majority of the state's lumbermen, miners, and citizens dependent on those industries for their own livelihoods. Thus the stage was set for political dissent during the Civil War that mirrored a general urban-rural divide and that would occasionally manifest itself in violence. As the rest of the Southern states seceded in the winter and spring of 1861 and threatened to tear apart the old Republic, Democratic Pennsylvanians found

David Wilmot (1814–1868), a junior congressman from Pennsylvania, sponsored the "Wilmot Proviso" in 1846 that opposed the expansion of slavery into lands recently acquired from Mexico.

themselves faced with a choice: either join with their erstwhile political enemies, the Republicans, in resisting secession, taking up arms if necessary; or remain complacent, hoping the crisis would pass and allow them to continue pursuing their prewar occupations. The firing on the flag at Fort Sumter on April 12, 1861, settled the question for most, but not all, residents of the Commonwealth.[1]

MOTIVATIONS AND VOLUNTEERING: THE SOLDIERS

The most important people in Pennsylvania during the American Civil War were arguably the citizen-soldiers who volunteered or were drafted to fight for the Union. Without them, the Union war effort would have been strategically handicapped. Pennsylvania rallied more men to the national standard than any other state except New York, with a total of 427,286 soldiers and sailors having served by April 1865. This number includes militiamen temporarily called out in the emergencies of 1862 and 1863 as well as the ninety-day men who enlisted in the initial three-month regiments, most of whom later served in one of the better-known three-year regiments. It also comprises the 8,612 African American soldiers—the highest enrollment of any state—who wore Union blue. All told, these white and black Pennsylvanians filled up 270 independent regiments of infantry or cavalry and dozens of artillery batteries. Pennsylvania-born sailors sailed on countless U.S. Navy blockaders, river gunboats, and transports, some of which were constructed in shipyards in Pittsburgh and Philadelphia. Harder to ascertain are the numbers of irregular fighters, citizens from the southern tier counties who, on their own volition, took rifle or ax in hand during the Gettysburg Campaign and sniped at Confederate patrols and passing columns or attacked Confederate property. There is some evidence of this kind of armed resistance, and although the written record is sparse, it makes sense that not all Pennsylvania civilians endured the Southern invasion peacefully. The Keystone State assumed the unenviable status of being the only Northern state occupied for any length of time by the Confederate army, a distinction that in many ways made its war experience unique among all the loyal states.[2]

Among the three-month volunteer regiments that responded to Lincoln's April 1861 call for 75,000 troops to suppress the rebellion were the famous "First Defenders," five large companies of prewar militiamen from communities across the state who immediately made themselves available for Federal service and literally became the first Union volunteers to reach Washington, D.C. In so doing, they earned Pennsylvania the distinction of being the first Northern state to respond militarily to the national crisis and the plea for assistance from the Federal government. In 1861, the regular U.S. Army was small, approximately 16,000 troops, and scattered across the continent. Washington itself lay essentially bereft of troops and was vulnerable to attack. It became abundantly clear that the old army would be inadequate to meet the likely task of reuniting the country, and so the president and his cabinet had no other choice but to call on the states, as in previous wars. The First Defenders proved that Pennsylvania would heed that call, and quickly. Hailing from Pottsville, Reading, Lewistown, and Allentown, these 475 soldiers arrived in Washington on April 18, just a week after Fort Sumter had fallen. Patriotic and enthusiastic, some of them veterans of the Mexican War, they were glad to be there: one company, Pottsville's National Light Infantry, actually telegraphed Secretary of War Simon Cameron about their readiness to depart for the capital the day before Sumter was fired upon. These men realized that time was of the essence and intended to move fast.[3]

Opened near Harrisburg, Pennsylvania, on April 18, 1861, and named in honor of Pennsylvania governor Andrew Curtin, Camp Curtin became the largest Federal camp during the Civil War. More than 300,000 soldiers passed through the camp until it was closed on November 11, 1865.

After a quick mustering in at Camp Curtin in Harrisburg on April 17, the volunteers boarded trains that would take them south to the Potomac and a grateful Abraham Lincoln, who reportedly shook the hands of every one of them upon their arrival. But first they had to transit on foot through pro-secessionist Baltimore to change trains, where, according to James L. Schaadt of the Allen Infantry, "roughs and toughs, longshoremen, gamblers, floaters, red-hot secessionists, as well as men ordinarily sober and steady, crowded upon, pushed and hustled the little band and made every effort to break the thin line. . . . It was a severe trial for the volunteers with not a charge of ball or powder in their pockets." Perhaps triggering the mob of approximately 2,500 to greater violence was the presence of Nicholas Biddle, an African American orderly serving Captain James Wren of the Pottsville Washington Artillery. He wore the company's uniform and this likely enraged the locals. Bricks, bats, cobblestones, and other flying missiles soon started falling on the small group of Pennsylvanians, who had no means of protecting themselves (they were ordered to leave their outmoded weapons at home in expectation of being armed with modern ones in Washington). Luckily, unlike the Massachusetts regiments that would follow them the next day, the First Defenders suffered no fatalities in Baltimore before boarding the freight train at Camden Station that would take them the final leg of their journey. Bruised and a bit battered, including Biddle who had suffered a severe head injury, they immediately commenced their three months of service protecting the capital and its environs, marching and camping as far afield as Harpers Ferry. When their terms of service expired after seeing no real action, the vast majority of the men reenlisted in three-year regiments. As Heber Thompson of the Washington Artillery later put it, "hardly a single great battle was fought in the four years of the war . . . in which the First Defenders were not represented. Their individual war records would fill volumes of history." These first Pennsylvania soldiers to defend the cause of Union were clearly among its most ardent and faithful.[4]

They would be followed by thousands upon thousands more, men who shared with them a devotion to the sanctity of the flag, the Union, and the laws, all of which had been sullied—in most Pennsylvanians' opinion—by the secession of the Southern states. The desire to eradicate slavery was not an early motivation to fight for most of Pennsylvania's three-year enlistees, although a majority of them would later come to approve of Lincoln's Emancipation Proclamation as a means by which the war might be ended more quickly and the rebellious South suppressed. Like other Northern soldiers, men from Pittsburgh, Philadelphia, Harrisburg, Lancaster, Bedford, Erie, and countless other towns and villages fought first and foremost to preserve the Union and uphold the Constitution, which they believed (in contradiction to their Confederate counterparts) disallowed secession. The *Carlisle American* represented the thoughts of many early enlistees in its editorial of April 24, 1861: "There is but one escape from the impending ruin. To swear devotion to our coun-try, fidelity to the Constitution, and to live or die beneath the noble shadow of our country. Now is the time for Union men to prove their devotion to the Union." This sentiment was echoed by a trooper in the Eighth Pennsylvania Cavalry, who wrote his mother, "first my God, second my country, third my mother. Oh my country, how my heart bleeds for your welfare. If this poor life of mine could save you, how willingly would I make the sacrifice." Many men also initially joined as volunteers because their male relatives, friends, and neighbors enlisted, or because female relatives and friends urged them to do their duty (Civil War regiments were raised locally, most composed exclusively of men from the same community). As in all military conflicts, some Pennsylvanians also enlisted out of a sense of adventure. For them, the war would quickly end any delusions of grandeur or excitement, as soldier life consisted of seemingly endless days of drill, monotony, and camp life punctuated occasionally by a few short moments of extreme fear, adrenalin, and bravery in battle. A few other Pennsylvanians apparently donned Union blue out of concern that the Southern "slaveocracy" intended, as one soldier told his wife, to make "perfeck slaves" out of all free Northern men by subverting free government and expanding slavery into the West, thereby reducing the options available to the white working class.[5]

Immigrant Pennsylvanians, born in Germany or Ireland or the sons of the foreign-born, shared all of these motivations with their Anglo-American comrades, but some added distinctly ethnic reasons for joining up. A sense that they needed to "prove" their loyalty to their adopted homeland to skeptical Anglo-Americans, or that defending the Union struck a blow for international freedom and democracy—which had been subverted by 1860 in both Ireland and Germany—often joined the previously mentioned motivations in the hearts of immigrant soldiers. Urban-raised regiments, such as the German Twenty-Seventh, Seventy-Fifth, and Ninety-Eighth Infantries from Philadelphia, demonstrated a resolve among the Commonwealth's city immigrants to serve together in all-ethnic units to preserve their ethnic identity, whereas foreign-born soldiers living in smaller towns and rural communities tended to enlist in local regiments composed of both ethnic and nonethnic troops. Irish soldiers, such as those in the Philadelphia-raised Sixty-Ninth Pennsylvania, sometimes also joined up to gain military experience that could be used later in a potential Irish uprising across the Atlantic. These "Fenians," as they were called, were essentially Irish nationalists who, although naturalized American citizens, retained a "dual loyalty" to their old homeland and new country, a sentiment that would only fade as the postwar decades progressed.[6]

For the Keystone States's African American volunteers, who were first permitted to organize into regiments in May 1863, the war represented a real opportunity to strike boldly for the freedom of their enslaved brethren in the South, increase their own standing as loyal citizens, and in so doing assist in restoring the Union. Captain Samuel Sanders of Pittsburgh's "Hannibal Guards," an early-war company that was not allowed to muster into service since it predated the Emancipation Proclamation (which not only freed slaves in the Confederacy but also set the legal groundwork for the enlistment of black troops), still captured well the motivations of Pennsylvania's black soldiers, nearly all of whom enlisted in the federally raised United States Colored Troops (USCT) regiments: "We consider ourselves American citizens and interested in the Commonwealth of our white fellow citizens. Although deprived of all political rights, we yet wish the government of the United States to be sustained against the tyranny of slavery, and are willing to assist in any honorable way or manner to sustain the present administration." Black Pennsylvanians, once unleashed into the recruiting offices by the Emancipation Proclamation, thus shared some ideological motivations with their white compatriots, but possessed a uniquely African American reason for becoming soldiers.[7]

After a few months in the army, Pennsylvania's three-year volunteers, regardless of prewar political affiliation, tended to become strong supporters of the Federal government and the Republican administration. They knew that Lincoln was devoted to defeating the Confederacy and preserving the Union, a cause all could

An early war recruiting poster for the 75th Pennsylvania Infantry, a German-American three-year regiment raised in Philadelphia. Note the extra fifty cents bounty offered veterans of the three-month regiments.

believe in. In reply to his recalcitrant wife, who questioned if her husband had left her for a worthy cause, James S. Colwell of the Seventh Pennsylvania Reserves wrote, "You don't think him competent. It would not make any difference to me if he was not competent. For as I have often told you I care nothing about Lincoln individually, more than any other honest man, but it is the government that I hold must be maintained." Months and years of long, arduous service in camp and on the march taught Colwell and his comrades that the fastest way home lay in total support of the government in power and its military triumph over the rebellion. Compromise with the South, a

topic toyed with by many Northern civilian Democrats in the first three years of the war, became almost unthinkable to those who campaigned in the field. Unlike other Northern states, such as Illinois, which witnessed the desertion of several regiments after the announcement of emancipation, Pennsylvania experienced few significant problems with its regiments stemming from political disagreement. In 1864, its soldiers voted overwhelmingly to reelect Lincoln. The big issues confronting Governor Andrew Curtin, and ones he shared with most of his fellow loyal governors, regarded how to sustain home-front support for the war, provide replacements for those who had fallen to bullets or disease, and manage internal civilian dissent and corruption. James Colwell and the other "boys of '61," fighting primarily in the eastern theater of operations, would create little cause for concern among Pennsylvania's politicians. These soldiers' steadfast belief in the cause they were fighting for coupled with some remarkable achievements in the field made them the backbone of the principal Union army in the East, the Army of the Potomac.[8]

SACRIFICE AND VALOR, 1862

The blue flag of the Commonwealth fluttered alongside the Stars and Stripes in every engagement, large and small, of that dogged, often-defeated, but ultimately triumphant army. From the initial, shocking defeat at First Manassas in July 1861 to the carnage at Fredericksburg, the wholesale slaughter of Gettysburg, the Wilderness, and Spotsylvania, and finally the last skirmishes of the Appomattox Campaign in April 1865, Pennsylvanian valor made a name for itself and Pennsylvania blood watered the battlefields. In the western theater, too, but in far fewer numbers, the Commonwealth's infantry, cavalry, and artillery regiments could be found marching in various armies under Generals Ulysses S. Grant, William T. Sherman, and their predecessors. The Ninth Pennsylvania Cavalry, for instance, compiled one of the most enviable war records of any of the state's regiments and won notoriety as the only eastern cavalry to participate in Sherman's famous March to the Sea. The Seventy-Ninth Pennsylvania Infantry, recruited in Lancaster, participated in the climactic campaigns of Perryville, Murfreesboro, and Chickamauga, losing almost half its original number, marched through Georgia to the Atlantic, and then fought at Bentonville, North Carolina, in the last significant battle of the western Union armies. The deeds of these two units were representative, if not duplicative, of the experiences of Pennsylvanians who fought west of the Alleghenies. Other regiments were sent to the southern Atlantic coastline at various points in their wartime service, such as the Fifty-First Pennsylvania Infantry that helped secure the Outer Banks of North Carolina for the Union in 1862, or the Seventy-Fourth Pennsylvania, raised primarily among Pittsburgh's German communities, which fought

Governor Andrew Curtin (1817–1894) as he appeared during the September 1862 conference of loyal state war governors, convened in Altoona, Pennsylvania, at his invitation. This conference confirmed Curtin's and the other governors' support for Lincoln's war policies.

steadfastly in the Mid-Atlantic before being deployed to the Sea Islands off of Charleston in the fall of 1864.[9]

It was in Maryland, Pennsylvania, and especially Virginia, however, where most of the Commonwealth's sons saw action, and it was there that the fate of the nation was decided between 1862 and 1864. Only in the East could the Confederacy win its independence after suffering catastrophic losses in Tennessee and the Mississippi River valley in early 1862. In the East, also, were the two capitals of Washington, D.C., and Richmond, positions of great strategic importance, and most of the Confederacy's industrial, agricultural, and demographic means for supporting its war effort. Unfortunately for many Penn-

A scene from the 31st Pennsylvania Infantry camp near Washington in 1862. Candid photographs of camp life such as this one offer rare windows into the everyday lives of soldiers and camp followers.

sylvanians, it was in the East that the Army of the Potomac and its series of commanders squared off against the finest Southern army and general, the Army of Northern Virginia led by General Robert E. Lee.

Lee assumed command in late May 1862 after the wounding of General Joseph E. Johnston at Seven Pines, outside of Richmond on what was known as the Virginia Peninsula. At first questioned publicly in the Confederate press about his ability to lead, and not especially esteemed in the North, by the end of the Seven Days Campaign in early July Lee had saved Richmond from capture, bloodied the Army of the Potomac into retreat, and stood as the beau

ideal of his countrymen and a frightful nemesis to the men in the Northern army. Pennsylvanians who had marched to the outskirts of the rebel capital with their army commander, Philadelphia-born Major General George B. McClellan, only to be inexplicably driven back, were left both saddened by the outcome of the failed Peninsula Campaign and awed by their new adversary. Many had thought the war would end the summer before, but their hopes were dashed by the Confederate victory at First Manassas in July 1861. After a long period of reorganization, reinforcement, and restoration of morale in camps outside of Washington—all undertaken by McClellan after

Lincoln appointed him the army's new chief—the soldiers of the Army of the Potomac sailed down the Chesapeake to the peninsula in the late spring of 1862, full of renewed hope and expectation. Lee's generalship in the Seven Days shattered both; the war, most eastern Union soldiers now believed, would truly be long and bloody. The overwhelming majority of Pennsylvanians who had volunteered in 1861 resigned themselves to this belief and girded themselves to see the contest out to its finish. Despite all the sacrifice and personal loss thus far, and perhaps because of it, many soldiers probably thought as Captain Alfred Hough of Philadelphia did when he wrote his wife, "sick as I am of this war and bloodshed, as much oh how much I want to be at home with my dear wife and children . . . every day I have more religious feeling, that this war is a crusade for the good of mankind. . . . I cannot bear to think of what my children would be if we were to permit this Hellbegotten conspiracy to destroy this country." Lee could—and would—do his worst, and general after Union general would come and go as commander of the Army of the Potomac after facing him and losing. The rank and file from Pennsylvania would not, however, give up the fight.[10]

After another shattering victory at Second Manassas in August 1862, in which Pennsylvania troops again fought and fell in great numbers to no avail, Lee decided to take the strategic initiative and strike into the North, determined to decisively defeat the

The Allegheny Arsenal in Pittsburgh was one of several U.S. Army manufacturing facilities or depots located in Pennsylvania. Employing at its peak over 1,100 workers, the arsenal produced over 14 million rifle cartridges in one year alone. Along with the Fort Pitt Iron Works and foundries such as Smith, Park, and Company, the arsenal represented the industrial might the Keystone State provided the Union cause. On September 17, 1862, the same date as the Battle of Antietam, an explosion killed seventy-eight workers, mostly young women, the single largest civilian disaster during the war.

Army of the Potomac, irrevocably demoralize the Northern population, live off Northern farms and towns, and force Lincoln to accept the separation of the Confederate states. McClellan, still in command of the Federal army, moved fast to intercept him and, despite some lost opportunities to do Lee even more damage, fought the Confederates to a bloody standstill at Antietam Creek, just south of Hagerstown, Maryland, on September 17. Pennsylvanians, both in the army and at home, were more actively engaged in this campaign than in any previous, and due to the battle's proximity to the state border,

Major General George B. McClellan (1826–1885) was born in Philadelphia to a prominent family. He graduated second in his class from the United States Military Academy in 1846. He served with distinction during the U.S.-Mexican War and, due to his political connections and fluency in French, became an important military observer for the United States, most notably during the Crimean War. Resigning his commission in 1857, he became involved in the railroad industry. He returned to military service at the outbreak of the Civil War, accepting the position of major general of Ohio volunteers and soon was given the Federal appointment of commander of the Department of the Ohio on May 3, 1861. In July, he was promoted to commander of the Military Division of the Potomac.

felt a special sense of anxiety about its outcome that would not be superseded until the Gettysburg Campaign the following summer. Samuel Cormany of Chambersburg, a committed evangelical of the United Brethren faith,

finally decided that the time had come to set aside his pacifism and enlisted in the Sixteenth Pennsylvania Cavalry on September 10. His diary entry for that day reads, "NEWS! The Rebels are surely advancing on Hagerstown—Today—P.M.—I enlisted in Capt. W. H. Sollenberger's Cavalry Company. . . . Considered it a duty to serve my country in her time of need." Lying just a few miles above the Mason-Dixon Line in the fertile Cumberland Valley, Chambersburg now found itself in the projected path of the invading Southern army. Not all residents reacted as Cormany did. Two days later he wrote, "People are awfully scared—Many are leaving town—poor fools." In Carlisle, just thirty miles northward, rumors that the Confederate general Stonewall Jackson's command was coming to pillage and burn created great excitement: "We are constantly in receipt of wild rumors about Jackson's approaching us but I do not feel afraid," one woman wrote her husband in the army, "yet many are very uneasy and are packing up their valuables lest they may be destroyed. I cannot think the Rebels would burn our town or interfere with the women and children." Flight was an option exercised by many residents of the southern tier counties that September, but an equally large number resolved to remain at home and meet any Southern invaders with steely grit. Luckily for all, unlike ten months later when Lee and his army threatened Pennsylvania again, the Southern advance was halted shy of the Commonwealth's borders.[11]

Samuel Cormany and his small family were fortunate to remain unharmed in Chambersburg. For Pennsylvania's soldiers in the ranks of the Army of the Potomac, Antietam proved to be a test unlike any they had yet endured, and a deadly one for many. Serving in almost every division and in every corps of the army, men from the Commonwealth fought in all three major phases of the battle, from the North Woods, Cornfield, and West Woods; to the Sunken Road in the middle of the Confederate line; and at Rohrbach's (later Burnside's) Bridge in the south. James Colwell of the Seventh Reserves, now a captain, was one of hundreds of Pennsylvanians to fight in farmer Miller's famous cornfield. The Cumberland County-raised Seventh was part of the Second Brigade, Third Division of the vaunted First Corps, commanded by Major General "Fighting" Joe Hooker. Hooker had been instructed by McClellan to lead off the Union attacks on Lee early in the morning, around six o'clock. His target was a small, white, nondescript church building about a mile south of his position in the North Woods. If Hooker's corps could reach that building, a structure later seared in American memory as the Dunker Church, his men would effectively break the Confederate line in half and threaten its destruction. To get there, though, they had to pass through Miller's cornfield. Hunkered down in the corn the outnumbered Confederates waited for them, and there Colwell and dozens of other Pennsylvanians met their deaths.

Hooker's official report included a description of the scene: "In the time I am writing every stalk of corn in the northern and greater part of the field was cut as closely as could have been done with a knife, and the slain lay in rows precisely as they had stood in their ranks a few moments before." Colonel A. G. Magilton, commanding Colwell's brigade, wrote that the men came "under a dreadful fire," appeared to falter, but then "rall[ied] immediately, afterward advanc[ing] to the front, and drove the enemy after an obstinate resistance." The Seventh and its sister regiments in the other brigades of the First Corps' Pennsylvania Reserves Division (commanded by native Philadelphian George Gordon Meade) had to overcome terrific Confederate small arms and artillery fire. Leading his company early in the fighting, Colwell and three other Carlisle men were felled by a single artillery shell that burst in the midst of the regiment. Meade's division, Pennsylvanians all, made a gallant showing that morning in the corn, but in the end the sacrifice of Colwell and his comrades was for naught, as Hooker's grand assault was counterpunched by the Texas brigade of John Bell Hood, which itself suffered mightily. The Federals retreated to the safety of the North Woods as the blood trickled in rivulets between the corn rows.[12]

The fighting now shifted to the southwest, as first the Union Twelfth and then the Second Corps strove to break Lee's thin, barely holding line. The First Brigade, First Division of the Twelfth contained several new

A portion of the 7th Pennsylvania Reserves standing at ease. The 7th Reserves suffered grievous casualties at Antietam and Fredericksburg.

Pennsylvania regiments, such as the 125th and 128th Infantries, freshly raised nine-month units that had had precious little time to train before being sent to the army. The Berks and Bucks county men of the 128th faired poorly in their corps' attack, thrown into it before they could adequately form into regimental line and exposed to a murderous fire. "The loss was beyond measure severe," a historian of the regiment wrote, "being thirty-four killed, and eighty-five wounded, of which six subsequently died of their wounds. In addition to the Colonel, Captain William H. Andrews, under whose command the regiment was originally led to the field, and who had exhibited the most determined courage in the fight, was among the dead." Joining them would be the Twelfth Corps' commander, Major General Joseph K. F. Mansfield, whose death early in the attack broke some of his corps' momentum and, along with the repulse of the First Corps, prompted McClellan to send in the Second Corps.[13]

One of the most-respected and veteran organizations in the Federal Second Corps was the "Philadelphia Brigade," comprised of regiments raised in and around the city (69th, 71st, 72nd, and 106th Infantries). Personally leading his corps toward the Dunker Church and the West Woods beyond it, Major General Edwin V. Sumner literally lost two of his divisions en route when they were mistakenly deflected south by the position of other Federal troops and terrain difficulties. These divisions, commanded by Major General Israel B. Richardson and Brigadier General William H. French, eventually found their way to the famed "Sunken Road" in the very middle of the Confederate line and assaulted it. Major General John Sedgwick's Second Division, which included the Philadelphia Brigade, thus unknowingly moved forward alone to what became a death trap in the West Woods. Corporal Jacob Pyewell of the 106th Infantry wrote his mother three days later, "I tell you we had a Hot time of it here. The Bullets wissed thick around us—I hope this will be the last of the Fighting, I tell you it is awfull to think of and see the men getting killed off. Our Col.'s Horse was shot from under him, and also our adjutant's horse. . . . There were a great many out of our Regiment Killed and Wounded." The Philadelphia Brigade was literally cut to pieces by the makeshift but deadly trap sprung by various Confederate brigades Lee had frantically thrown into the woods; the 106th lost a third of its men and the Philadelphia Brigade overall suffered 545 casualties in less than thirty minutes, one of the highest casualty rates of any brigade engaged at Antietam. Staggering out of the West Woods, the brigade's survivors ran across the Cornfield to the safety of the artillery of their fellow Pennsylvanians in Meade's Pennsylvania Reserves Division.[14]

As the Philadelphians were extricating themselves from their unhappy predicament at about half past nine in the morning, Sumner's other two divisions started to assault the Sunken Road, which lay at the center of Lee's defensive position and connected the Hagerstown Pike with the Boonsboro Pike. What became one of the bloodiest episodes in the entire Civil War was the result of chance—both Richardson and French were supposed to follow Sedgwick—and almost broke the Confederate army in two. Four Pennsylvania regiments (53rd, 81st, 130th, and 132nd Infantries), scattered in separate brigades among the two divisions, participated in the series of uncoordinated Union attacks that witnessed the decimation of the famous Irish Brigade and, later, the christening of the road as "Bloody Lane." This farm path, used by locals in their wagons as

a shortcut between the two main roads, had over the years become depressed several feet deeper into the ground than the surrounding countryside; it was therefore a perfect "trench" from which the defending Southern infantry could fire with relative cover upon the exposed Federals. It was also a potential trap, a veritable shooting alley, if any of the Unionists could flank the position. After several failed assaults and a misunderstood order that caused two of the defending Southern regiments to leave their positions, that is exactly what happened. Once flanked, the North Carolinians and Alabamians still in the lane received the punishment they had dealt out for almost three hours.[15]

Both sides expended an immense amount of ammunition as they fired at each other, often at point-blank range. A soldier in the 130th Pennsylvania in French's division wrote his parents after the battle: "I took eighty-three Rounds on the field with me it not being enough to last until the Rebs skedaddled. I took twenty-eight Rounds out of a dead man's cartridge box. . . . I would have fired them but I got into a cornfield, and had the pleasure of taking a Rebel Second Lieut. and two privates. The Lieut. seen me leveling my Gun on him, he threw away his Sword in order to get me to go after it so that he could escape, but I took him and let the Sword lay. . . . We were under fire for five hours." Another Keystoner in the rookie, nine-month 132nd Infantry wrote compellingly of what it was like to approach the Sunken

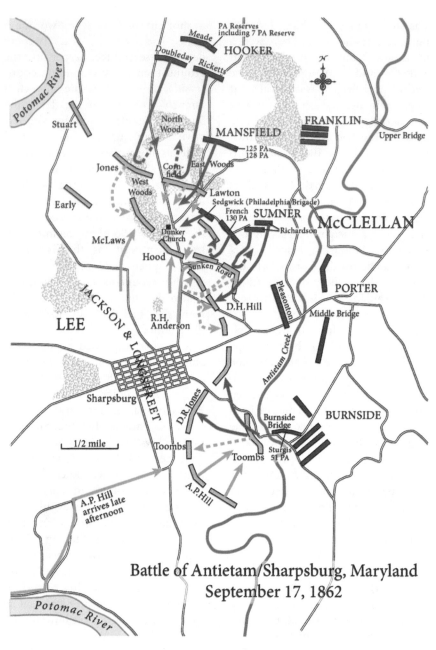

Battle of Antietam/Sharpsburg, Maryland
September 17, 1862

Road: "The compressed lip and set teeth showed that nerve and resolution had been summoned to the discharge of duty. A few temporarily fell out, unable to endure the nervous strain, which was simply awful." A private soldier's perspective on Bloody Lane was different from a

The 51st Pennsylvania and 51st New York storming the lower bridge over Antietam Creek, September 17, 1862. Sketch drawn on site by a war artist traveling with the Union army.

general's, especially a Confederate one. Regarding the precarious situation the rebels faced after the lane had fallen to the Unionists, General James Longstreet, whom Lee assigned tactical control of the position, later exclaimed, "The Confederate army would [have been] cut in two and probably destroyed, for we were already badly whipped and were only holding our ground by sheer force of desperation." A few hundred disorganized rebel infantrymen and a few cannons coalescing in Daniel Piper's cornfield were all that stood between the surviving Pennsylvanians and their Northern comrades and a crushing victory. Two entire Union corps and most of McClellan's cavalry stood ready on the other side of Antietam Creek. The cautious commanding general, on bad advice from one of his corps commanders, decided not to push his advantage, and Lee's army was saved. Once again Pennsylvania blood had been shed to no decisive end.[16]

About the time that Bloody Lane fell to Richardson's and French's mauled commands, Pennsylvanians in the southernmost sector of the battlefield were distinguishing themselves. Starting around ten o'clock, the Ninth Union Corps, under the overall command of Major General Ambrose Burnside, had fruitlessly attempted to cross Antietam Creek and create what McClellan had originally intended to be a "diversion" to keep Confederates on the other side from reinforcing their beleaguered comrades to the north. Twice Burnside had ordered weak, piecemeal assaults against Rohrbach Bridge; twice they had been repulsed. Concerned about phantom divisions of the enemy that might now be thrown against the worn-out Second Corps in the center, McClellan sent a personal aide to Burnside and demanded that the bridge be immediately taken and the Confederate right threatened. Burnside selected two regiments in Brigadier General

John F. Hartranft (1830–1889) was born near Pottstown, Pennsylvania. In 1861, he raised a three-year-regiment, the 51st Pennsylvania Infantry. The regiment notably led the charge across "Burnside's bridge" during the Battle of Antietam, suffering heavy casualties. The regiment was later transferred to the Western Theater where it fought at Vicksburg and other campaings. Hartranft was elected governor of Pennsylvania in 1872. During his second term labor unrest led to a number of violent confrontations across the state and Governor Hartranft called out both the state militia and regular army troops to restore order. His firm response eased tensions while advancing the rights of labor unions.

Edward Ferrero's brigade of Brigadier General Samuel Sturgis's division, the "twin Fifty-Firsts" of the 51st Pennsylvania and 51st New York Infantries. Both regiments had a hard-fighting reputation and were thought to be among the best in the corps, but the men looked fearfully at the high banks on the other side of the creek from which the rebels had easily repelled the morning's attacks. About four hundred Georgians under the command of Brigadier General Robert Toombs still fired at them from those heights, each soldier with a clear shot of the narrow causeway of the bridge over which the two Federal regiments would have to cross. Corporal Lewis Patterson of the 51st Pennsylvania finally shouted out to Ferrero, "will you give us our whiskey, General, if we take it?" Ferrero, a former dance instructor from New York who had recently restricted the regiment's liquor supply for bad behavior, bellowed back, "Yes, by God! . . . You shall have as much as you want if you take the bridge," and was greeted with a cheer. With that, the two regiments prepared to rush the bridge. They had about three hundred open yards to cover from the hilltop that protected them to the bridge itself, and at first the Georgians' musketry fire proved too much. Supporting artillery fire from Battery D of the Pennsylvania Light Artillery failed to suppress it, and the two infantry regiments found themselves pinned against a fence and a stone wall that bordered the creek bank. Suddenly the enemy's fire slackened, and Colonel John F. Hartranft of the 51st Pennsylvania realized the time had come to rush the bridge. His men and the New Yorkers simultaneously rose up from behind their protective cover, their regimental and national colors in the lead, and together stormed the bridge side by side. The Georgians, low on ammunition after hours of continuous firing, put up a token hand-to-hand resistance and then fled. Finally, what became known as "Burnside's Bridge" had fallen, but the cost had been high: the Montgomery and Snyder County men of the 51st Pennsylvania suffered twenty-one killed and ninety-nine wounded, many of the latter later succumbing to their injuries. Hartranft survived and was promoted to brigadier general, and his regiment got its whiskey.[17]

Burnside required another two hours to move the rest of the Ninth Corps across the Antietam. McClellan, himself accused of "the slows" by President Lincoln, was impatient with the slow progress and again demanded his corps commander take action and continue the attack in his sector. About three o'clock he did so, with all four divisions in his powerful corps. Five Pennsylvania regiments of both infantry and artillery were among this vast force that finally lumbered in the direction of the town of Sharpsburg and Lee's escape route across the Potomac River. If Burnside took the town and cut the Confederates off from the ford across the river, the Army of Northern Virginia once again would be in a position to be destroyed. Perhaps 2,800 Southerners stood in the way—hardly enough to stop the Union goliath. Yet again, however, chance seemed to favor the rebels, as a half hour into the advance Confederate general A. P. Hill's "Light" Division, freshly arrived from the capture of Harpers Ferry to the south, slammed into Burnside's flank with the power of a sledgehammer that belied their inferior numbers.

Satterlee General Hospital in Philadelphia was the largest Union army hospital during the Civil War. By the spring of 1864, over 12,000 wounded soldiers—both Union and Confederate—had been treated there. The hospital was razed soon after the war and is now a residential area next to the University of Pennsylvania.

The shock and fury of the attack, coupled with the loss of key officers at the divisional and brigade level, rocked the Federals back on their heels. At five o'clock Burnside ordered a retreat back across the creek, allowing a small force to hold a bridgehead on the western side of the creek. No one yet knew it, but the Battle of Antietam was over. The next day, Lee and McClellan watched each other from their respective positions as the stretcher parties and ambulances hurried about the fields in search of wounded men who could survive the ordeal of transportation to a field hospital. In the early morning of September 19, Lee retreated across the Potomac, his army badly damaged but alive enough to recover in the safety of Virginia.[18]

Antietam was among the top three costliest Civil War battles for the Keystone State. Total casualties are difficult to estimate but had to number at least 2,500 dead, wounded, and missing, based on the percentage of troops Pennsylvanians constituted in the Army of the Potomac at the time, where they were located organizationally, and which corps bore the brunt of the fighting (total Federal casualties topped 12,000).[19] As a general rule, one in seven wounded during the Civil War died of their wounds afterward, and at Antietam it has been suspected that that rate was higher due to the still developing condition of Union medical care and the sheer ferocity of the fighting. Hundreds of Pennsylvania husbands, fathers, sons, and brothers suffered in the crude hospitals hastily set up in barns, farmhouses, and under tents in the fields. Many lost legs or arms to amputation; some lost both. For them, the war was over. For their unscathed comrades in both the three-year and nine-month regiments, the war would continue, but it would be a different kind of war now: Lincoln, buoyed by the "victory" at Antietam, took the opportunity to issue the Emancipation Proclamation, forever altering the character of the Federal war effort and adding liberation of an enslaved people to the original strategic objective of preserving the Union. In late October, the Union army finally crossed its namesake river, much too late for the president, who had decided McClellan was no longer the man for the job. He replaced him in early November with none other than Ambrose Burnside (who, to his credit, tried to dissuade Lincoln of his fitness for the position). Burnside headed east, intent on

beating the reconstituted Confederate army to the Rappahannock River at a town called Fredericksburg. From there, he would march again on Richmond.

Lee got to Fredericksburg first and, coupled with a bureaucratic bungle that deprived Burnside of the pontoons he needed to cross the river, ensured that when the Federals did cross the Rappahannock their enemy had perfected their defensive positions on high ground and in the shelter of woods and deployed their artillery to create "killing zones" of deadly crossfire. The attacks began on December 13, a day that dawned foggy and chilled. The fog soon cleared and the temperatures rose, offering a rare opportunity for battle in the winter. Burnside's plan was to assault simultaneously both flanks of the rebel army lined up on the other side of the town and exploit any contingencies that arose with his vast reserves. He assigned Sumner control of one wing of the assaulting troops and Major General William Franklin, whose corps had been only slightly engaged at Antietam, the other. These "Grand Divisions" were probably too bulky organizationally to be as effective as the commanding general hoped, but the real problems lay in their leadership and imprecise orders from army headquarters—and superb Confederate preparations that took full advantage of the terrain.[20]

George Meade's battle-tested Pennsylvania Reserves Division was part of Major General John Reynolds's First Corps of Franklin's wing and, thanks to Burnside's muddled orders and Franklin's plodding lack of ingenuity and initiative, was sent alone against the right of Lee's battle line, commanded by Stonewall Jackson. Jackson's men were not entrenched and did not have quite the terrain advantages as Longstreet's half of the rebel line, but they did enjoy the cover of woods, a few small hills, and a long, flat plain across which the Keystone men would have to march, under artillery fire. They also had ample reserves hidden behind the front lines. Franklin dispatched two other divisions to support Meade, but they failed to do their job adequately, delayed and halted by well-placed Southern artillery rounds and confused by the location—or lack thereof—of both the enemy and their own blue-coated comrades. The result was that the Pennsylvania Reserve regiments would endure another very bloody day just three months after they had suffered so heavily at Antietam. One Southerner described their approach, with banners flying and bayonets glittering, as "one of the most imposing sights ever beheld on the American Continent." Meade protested to Franklin that his division alone would not break the rebel line; Franklin replied falsely that these were Burnside's orders. A nearby staff officer who overheard the exchange and watched the Pennsylvanians launch their attack toward Prospect Hill wrote, "Meade went in by God and he went in like a gentleman."[21]

Immediately the artillery of both sides opened up. Supporting their fellow Keystoners in Meade's infantry were several Pennsylvania batteries,

George Gordon Meade (1815–1872) was the son of a Philadelphia merchant. He attended the United States Military Academy and graduated nineteenth in his class in 1835. Aside from a brief stint as an engineer, Meade became a career military officer. He fought in the Second Seminole War and the U.S.-Mexican War, and soon after the outbreak of the Civil War he became a brigadier general of Union volunteers. He was promoted during the course of the war, and fought in the Seven Days Battles (where he was severely wounded), Antietam, Fredericksburg, and, three days after taking command of the Army of the Potomac, at Gettysburg, where he successfully thwarted the Confederate offensive into Pennsylvania. After the war he commanded several departments during Reconstruction, but ultimately succumbed to his war wound.

including Lieutenant John Simpson's Battery A of the 1st Pennsylvania Light Artillery, which lost most of its artillery horses before the infantry had even closed with the enemy. Pressed to keep firing and maneuvering his guns against the Confederate counterbattery fire, Simpson ordered his men to move the guns by hand themselves. Another Pennsylvania battery suffered fewer losses among its horses but expended an incredible 346 rounds of case shot and 236 of shell before nightfall. Although the rebel guns suffered greatly in this exchange of iron, they still managed to continue pouring it into Meade's men and the two other divisions that had been ordered to support him. As the enemy fire slackened around noon, however, Meade recognized his chance and drove his brigades forward from their temporary shelter behind the raised railroad bed of the Richmond, Fredericksburg, and Potomac Railroad. Over the crest of the bed, across the tracks, and up the gentle, wooded slope of Prospect Hill charged the Pennsylvania Reserves. Watching them move past, Meade nervously joked with Colonel William McCandless of the Second Pennsyl-vania Reserves that if his men did their duty, he might win himself a star for his woolen overcoat. McCandless sarcastically replied before moving on, "more likely a wood overcoat." Unfortunately, his prediction would prove all too true for many of his soldiers, but not until chance, once again, intervened and for a moment in time held the fate of both armies in the balance.[22]

Meade's lead brigade angled directly into a 600-yard gap mistakenly left unaccounted for by Confederate general A. P. Hill, under whose control fell this part of Jackson's line. The First Reserves, composed of men from the southern tier counties, and the Sixth Reserves, whose soldiers hailed from all over the state, uneasily entered the woods and kept on walking. No Confederate musketry greeted them and the deeper they went into the trees, the quieter their surroundings became. The wet, swampy ground pulled at their shoes and defiant saplings slapped their cheeks, and soon the military formation started to break down. In the dense underbrush vision was limited to about fifty yards. Men clumped together in companies and squads. Suddenly they came upon a row of stacked rifles, dead ahead. A few companies' worth of Pennsylvanians quickly lined up, advanced, and unleashed a ferocious volley into the surprised ranks of Brigadier General Maxcy Gregg's South Carolinians. Utter bedlam broke out as the rebels tried to form up and resist, but after their commander fell from his horse mortally wounded, command and control devolved and Gregg's entire brigade fled to their rear and left. Regiments from Meade's other two brigades had now entered the woods and began to overlap the exposed flanks of the neighboring Southern brigades, who themselves were surprised by the sudden appearance of the enemy. A sergeant in the Seventh Reserves exhorted, "Wide awake, fellows, let's give them hell!" and indeed they did. Three Confederate brigades— Gregg's, J. J. Archer's, and J. H. Lane's—were threatened with destruction by the combined but disjointed and disorganized firepower of Meade's division. Staggering from

Company C, 110th Pennsylvania Infantry after the Battle of Fredericksburg, where they sustained heavy losses.

their losses, the rebels in these brigades managed to regroup in bits and pieces, counterattacked, and began to pour in a "terrific and most galling fire," according to one Pennsylvanian. Although the Third Reserves penetrated to within sight of the Confederate ambulance train, their experience was emblematic of the plight of the entire division: without immediate and powerful support, the break in the enemy line would be sealed and retreat would become inevitable.[23]

That support was coming in the form of Brigadier General John Gibbon's division, which finally moved forward to support Meade. Because of a disagreement within Gibbon's command, they were a half hour behind the Pennsylvanians, and that half hour proved critical. Moving out briskly on the reserves' right,

Gibbon's brigades, which included several veteran Pennsylvania units in their own right (such as the 11th, 88th, 90th, and 107th Infantries), met with some initial success and dearly punished a few North Carolina regiments but, without support of their own, were unable to make progress and fell back, suffering fearful casualties. Their ammunition almost exhausted, hemmed in on three sides now and facing a counterattack from reinforcements Stonewall Jackson had thrown in to plug the gap, the Pennsylvania Reserves were also compelled to retreat. Flag bearer Reuben Schell of the Seventh Reserves wrote his father a few days later, "You can hardly call it a battel it was more like a Butcher Shop then any thing els." Meade, aware of how close his men had come to victory and the high price in blood they had paid for the miscarriage, fumed and raged, unleashing profane invective first on Brigadier General David Birney, whose division composed the other promised support Franklin had mentioned, and then on corps commander Reynolds. "My God, General Reynolds, did they think my division could whip Lee's whole army?" he asked.[24]

According to one historian, the Pennsylvania Reserves Division was never the same after Fredericksburg, losing at least a third of its number in casualties. "Ten of the fifteen regiments suffered more than 100 casualties," the most egregious loss absorbed by the Thirteenth Reserves, which witnessed 161 soldiers shot down in only two hours. Officers at all ranks, dozens of noncommissioned officers, and hundreds of enlisted men never returned home to Pennsylvania. It was Antietam all over again, but worse. Local newspapers across the state printed the casualty lists underneath editorials bemoaning the bungling of the generals and the seeming invincibility of Lee and his army. But Pennsylvania would not be alone in mourning the loss of her sons. About the same time as Meade's boys scored their initial breakthrough, Burnside had launched an even more ill-fated assault on the other flank of the rebel army at Marye's Heights, about three-quarters of a mile beyond the town of Fredericksburg. It failed, too, and worse, General Sumner, in charge of the sector, continued to allow several more attacks to follow that simply compounded the Union casualty rate.

Secure behind a stone wall at the foot of the heights that bordered yet another sunken road, Longstreet's Confederate infantry and artillery literally dissolved entire Federal regiments that charged against them. Among them was the 116th Pennsylvania Infantry, the newest addition to the famous Irish Brigade that had been so decimated at Antietam's Bloody Lane. A freshly recruited regiment, the Philadelphia Irishmen displayed nothing but courage as they dashed forward with their kinsmen from New York and Boston. Private William McCarter later recalled that "it was simply madness to advance as far as we did and an utter impossibility to go further. . . . We lost nearly all of our officers. . . . In this assault, lasting probably not over 20 minutes, our division lost in killed and wounded over 2,000 men." The Irish Brigade overall essentially disappeared as a viable fighting unit, becoming a mere shell of its former self. Heros von Borcke, foreign-born aide to Confederate cavalry chief James Ewell Brown (J. E. B.) Stuart, marveled at the spectacle: "The Federals certainly behaved with the utmost gallantry. Line after line moved forward to the assault, only to recoil again and again from the murderous tempest of shot, shell, and bullets." Burnside, overcome with despair at his headquarters on the other side of the river, wanted to lead a final charge himself, perhaps yearning for a soldier's death. His staff held him back, and Lincoln actually held back for a few months before replacing him as army commander with

Joseph Hooker. The fallout from the stinging defeat at Fredericksburg plunged not only Pennsylvania but also the entire North into despondency and gloom. The end of the war seemed more distant now than it had ever been. Lee and the Confederate high command rejoiced; perhaps they would win their independence after all.[25]

DEFEAT, DISAPPOINTMENT, AND OCCUPATION, 1863

During the winter months Civil War armies tended to hunker down in semipermanent camps close enough to depots and railheads for supply but also within watchful distance of the enemy. Rivers often served as convenient borders between the two sides. Such was the case in the winter of 1862–1863 in the Fredericksburg area. Burnside tried one more time to engage Lee and retrieve his fallen reputation and the country's spirits, but the resulting "Mud March" up the Rappahannock River turned into a fiasco. The soldiers' spirits fell further. Joseph Hooker had been petitioning Lincoln for command of the Army of the Potomac since the failure on December 13, and on January 26 the reluctant president, with no one else to turn to, relented. Over the winter and into the early spring of 1863, the boastful new commander reorganized the army back into its traditional corps structure, instituted reforms for the sanitation and well-being of the troops, created a Bureau of Military Intelligence, consolidated the Federal cavalry into one large corps under Major General George Stoneman,

and restored self-esteem in the ranks. By the time he opened the campaigning season in late April 1863, crossing the Rapidan and Rappahannock rivers well upstream of Fredericksburg, the Federal army was renewed in spirit, physically strengthened, and hankering for another go at the rebels. Confidence in the ranks ran high. Hooker boasted that they would make Lee "ingloriously fly" or force him to fight on ground of the Federals' choosing, "where certain destruction awaits him."[26]

Hooker's plan was simple: flank Lee with the bulk of the Federal infantry upriver from Fredericksburg, then advance with those corps on the southern side of the Rappahannock toward the town while several other Union corps crossed directly below it. The cavalry would penetrate deep behind Confederate lines, tearing up communications and supply networks. With Federal forces to his immediate west and east closing in like a vise and the Northern cavalry to the south, the Southern general would have no choice but to retreat, and hastily. Hooker intended to smash him during the retreat and then march freely into Richmond. The problem with the plan was that it assumed Lee would do nothing while all of these movements were occurring or would be smitten with paralysis. Neither were likely considering Lee's recent record. It was a dangerous assumption.

The first day of the Battle of Chancellorsville opened auspiciously for the Army of the Potomac. Few Pennsylvania troops were involved on

May 1, when the vanguard of the vast flanking force, Major General George Sykes's division of George Meade's Fifth Corps, collided with Confederate general Lafayette McLaws's division in the open, rolling fields west of Fredericksburg near the Zoan Church. For the first time in the war, a Union general had caught Robert E. Lee napping, and only the fast and accurate reconnaissance by J. E. B. Stuart's troopers allowed Lee enough time to react to the threat to his flank. McLaws initially gave ground, but bolstered by the arrival of Jackson's corps, began to stiffen his resistance and, by the afternoon, began to flank Sykes, who called for reinforcements. Because this Federal division contained some of the best fighting regiments in the Army of the Potomac (the U.S. Regulars, who rarely needed help) and because Hooker was not expecting such aggression from an opponent who was supposed to be "flying," the Union commander was psychologically rocked back on his heels. He had enough men to overwhelm McLaws and more than match Jackson: the Eleventh and Twelfth Corps were directly behind Sykes and the Third Corps was en route. But Hooker was so shocked and surprised by the turn of events that he ordered a general retreat, back into the tangled, second-growth forest called the "Wilderness" and a small crossroads estate named Chancellorsville. His corps had just marched through there, and the good road network offered ample opportunities for resupply and reinforcement. After regrouping, entrenching, and absorb-ing the new troops, Hooker would either await Lee's attack and thrash him or renew the offensive. Few in the Union high command swallowed this line of reasoning, believing Hooker had lost his nerve. Major General Darius Couch of the Union Second Corps, visiting with Hooker that night, left his camp "believ[ing] my commanding general a whipped man."[27]

The operational pause proved disastrous to the Federals, for it relinquished the initiative to the Confederates. Lee and Jackson wasted no time in designing a plan to make the best use of the gift Hooker had given them. Late on May 1 they agreed upon a bold plan that would send Jackson's entire corps of three divisions on a wide flanking march to the west of Hooker's new position at Chancellorsville. Stuart reported that the Federals' right flank was "hanging in the air" and prone to surprise attack. Jackson intended to destroy that flank, cut the Union army off from the fords of the Rappahannock, and then throw it into such a panic that it could be destroyed piecemeal. Lee would "fix" Hooker at Chancellorsville with just two divisions and keep him occupied while the march transpired.

The flanking movement began on the morning of May 2 and was promptly discovered by Union lookouts on a hill called Hazel Grove, southwest of Chancellorsville, but Hooker could not decide if the enemy was retreating (as he hoped) or flanking him, so he hedged his bets. He allowed Major General Daniel

Sickles's recently arrived Third Corps to leave its position at Hazel Grove and "pursue" the enemy while simultaneously ordering Eleventh Corps commander Major General Oliver Howard—whose soldiers composed the right flank and thus Jackson's target—to secure his western approaches. Sickles's departure isolated the Eleventh Corps from the rest of the Army of the Potomac, leaving a mile-long gap between them and the next sizable body of troops near Chancellorsville. That, and the fact that Howard ignored the spirit of Hooker's order by only repositioning two regiments and two cannons to face west, set up many Pennsylvanians for one of the worst days of their lives.[28]

The Eleventh Corps was over 50 percent German-born or ethnically German in May 1863. The great majority of the North's German-speaking regiments were purposefully congregated in the organization, including nearly all of those recruited from the German-speaking wards of Philadelphia and Pittsburgh. Five Pennsylvania infantry regiments (the 27th, 73rd, 74th, 75th, and 153rd Infantries) were scattered in various brigades along the Orange Turnpike, encamped in the thick woods on either side of the road. All but one faced to the south where Sickles, Howard, and (by this time of the day) Hooker all believed the rebels were either retreating to or would attack from. The 153rd, a nine-month regiment freshly assigned to Brigadier General Leopold von Gilsa's brigade of Brigadier General Nathaniel

Adolph von Hartung (1832–1902) was born in Germany and recruited by fellow expatriate, Alexander Schimmelfennig. He mustered in as a captain in the Union army in August 1861 and became an officer in the 74th Pennsylvania Infantry. Promoted to colonel and command of the 74th in May 1863, he led his regiment at Chancellorsville and Gettysburg, receiving a serious wound in the latter battle. Due to this injury, he was discharged with a disability in 1864.

McLean's First Division, was the only Pennsylvania unit actually facing west as the sun began to set in the late afternoon. The men of the 153rd, nearly all Northampton County and Lehigh County natives, were actually of "Pennsylvania Dutch" extraction, descended from colonial-era German immigrants, and thus thought of themselves as "Pennsylvanians with a difference" and referred to their comrades recently arrived from the old country as "Germany Germans." Few thoughts of ethnicity entered the minds of these soldiers around half past five that day, however, as a travel-

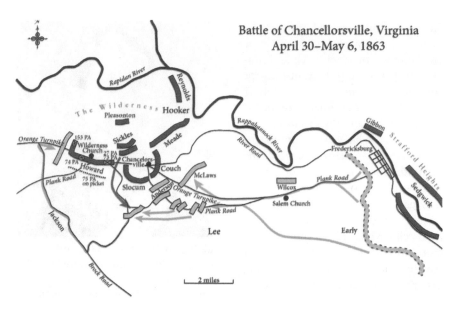

Battle of Chancellorsville, Virginia
April 30–May 6, 1863

ing feast of rabbits, quail, deer, and squirrels came scurrying through their camp, closely followed by wild-eyed pickets from the regiment, who shouted for all to grab their muskets and form up immediately. Before the men could do so, however, the bone-chilling rebel yell rent the air from front and both flanks in such volume that some men failed to notice the first flying bullets. Jackson was upon them.[29]

The 153rd and its sister regiment, the 54th New York, barely had time to form a regimental line before being overwhelmed, stationed as they were at the very point of the Confederate flank attack. Astonishingly, the 1,000-odd men of the two regiments managed to hold for perhaps ten minutes against the 26,000-strong host that assailed them from three directions. Rebel musketry was so powerful that the leaves of the trees "flutter[ed] down upon us as though a thunder

storm had broken loose," claimed Private Francis Stofflet. Captain Theodore Howell of Company D recognized that immediate withdrawal was necessary if the bulk of the regiment was to escape: "I know if our regiment had stood 3 minutes longer we would all have been cut to pieces," the Southerners coming so close that "they struck some of the men with the butts of their rifles." Before the 153rd disintegrated into chaos, every man running for his life, the regiment did manage to fire off four to five volleys in this, its literal baptism by fire. Afterward, Colonel Charles Glanz wrote proudly, "I stood with 7 companies of brave Pennsylvanians, fighting as old veterans for the honor of their state and their country."[30]

The Confederate charge lost little momentum as it plowed through the rest of the Eleventh Corps' First Division, primarily composed of Anglo-American regiments. Soon most of the division had abandoned their positions, unable to hold for more than a few minutes against the mighty onslaught, and fled down the road to Hooker's headquarters at Chancellorsville. Next in line along the turnpike were the regiments of Major General Carl Schurz's Third Division, nearly all foreign-born Germans. The Pittsburgh-raised 74th and the Philadelphia-recruited 75th Pennsylvania were not surprised by the rebels' sudden appearance, as Schurz had sent out scouts on his own initiative early in the afternoon; they reported back to him that the enemy was massing in large numbers in the woods to the west. When Schurz brought this information to Howard he was brushed off, as were some of his scouts, who also tried to warn General Hooker. The commanding general's staff sent them away, lampooning them as "excitable Dutch-men." Nonetheless, Schurz allowed camp rumor to do its work, so that by the time the refugees from the First Division hove into view, most of the Third Division had formed up, rifles in hand, and some of its regiments had even faced to the west. The problem was that they were still too few to effectively stop Jackson and now had to deal with the added problem of First Division soldiers, horses, and batteries crashing through their lines in their crazed attempts to escape capture. Lieutenant Colonel Adolph von Hartung of the 74th exclaimed that "the different regiments on our right were in a few minutes all mixed up with the Seventy-Fourth," making a

Soldiers of the 74th and 75th Pennsylvania regiments during a twenty-minute stand against the Confederate onslaught at Chancellorsville, May 2, 1863. The action of these "German regiments" and others provided time for a more substantial Union line to form in opposition.

"restoring of order an utter impossibility." Private Martin Seel wrote his brother that "bullets came from somewhere behind us. The rebels took advantage of the confusion, they charged ahead with all their might." The soldiers of the 74th, veterans of the bloody Valley Campaign and Second Manassas, found they could not effectively resist the Confederates without shooting their own fleeing countrymen, and thus began to join them. The understrength 75th Pennsylvania had been deployed on picket duty to the south of the turnpike, and thus missed some of the shock of the rebel attack along the road, but likewise was compelled to retreat in some disorder to what became a new line of defense at the Wilderness Church.[31]

In this first sizable clearing in the woods west of Chancellorsville itself, large fragments of the Third Division, including the 74th and 75th Pennsylvania, and perhaps even some rallied squads from the stampeded First Division, made a desperate twenty-minute stand. Martin Seel claimed, "We fire[d] ferociously and stopped their quick advance from continuing" unabated. Although ultimately overrun by the Confederates, the bravery of these Pennsylvanians and their Northern brethren stalled the enemy long enough to allow another battle line to be drawn up and to enable the corps baggage train and reserve artillery to escape. Colonel Friedrich Hecker of the Chicago German 82nd Illinois lay wounded in a nearby field and witnessed the scene: the German regiments "fought as long as possible against superior numbers that would have snuffed out resistance from any other troops." The next battle line, a few hundred yards to the rear, was dubbed the "Buschbeck Line" after the former colonel of the 27th Pennsylvania Infantry Adolphus Buschbeck, who now commanded a brigade in Brigadier General Adolph von Steinwehr's Second Division. Buschbeck and his soldiers from some of Philadephia's best immigrant families had had enough time to prepare behind a loose line of earthworks facing to the west and, along with the veteran 73rd Pennsylvania, another half-German regiment from the same city, stood firm with rifles cocked as the survivors of the Wilderness Church line filed in beside them, their jaws set and determined, faces smudged with powder. This time the rebels would pay dearly to dislodge them.[32]

All together it is likely that around four thousand Federals lined up for a thousand yards, shoulder to shoulder, at the Buschbeck Line. It was now half past six in the evening, with daylight fading fast and Jackson's chances of achieving a complete rout of the Union army fading with it. The longer the Eleventh Corps delayed him, the more likely the Army of the Potomac could successfully react to the shock of the flank attack. Accounts vary, but the twenty-five-odd minute final stand of the "German Corps" achieved that end. John Haingartner of the 29th New York, a regiment that was actually half Philadelphia German, described the fighting as "desperate," the Unionists striving hard to "check the impetuous attack of a victorious foe." Private Adolph Bregler of the 27th Pennsylvania wrote, "We held firm as long as we could, and pushed them back hard several times." In his official report, General Steinwehr left a vivid account of the fighting:

When I arrived upon the field I found Col. A. Buschbeck, with three regiments of his brigade (the 27th and 73rd Pennsylvania and 154th New York Volunteers), still occupying the same ground . . . and defending this position with great firmness and gallantry. . . . The attack of the enemy was very powerful. They emerged in close columns from the woods. . . . Colonel Buschbeck succeeded in checking the progress of the enemy, and I told him to hold his position as long as possible. The men fought with great determination and courage.

The Confederates managed to overlap both flanks of the line, however, and opened up with an enfilading fire that "killed and wounded nearly one-third of its whole strength," forcing the Federals to retreat. One wry soldier put it best: "before we run we g[ave] the rebs enough."33

The cost of valor for Pennsylvania's German sons at Chancellorsville was high. The 75th Pennsylvania lost 24 percent of its strength, fifty-nine men, most of them captured. The 74th absorbed fifty-two casualties, 15 percent of its total number, but twenty-two had been killed or wounded. The 73rd paid dearly for its stand on the Buschbeck Line, losing its colonel, lieutenant colonel, major, and four of its captains, almost the entire color party, and over a third of its sergeants. A total of seventy-four dead and wounded and twenty-nine missing depleted its ranks at battle's close, whereas the 27th Pennsylvania suffered fifty-six casualties out of 345 engaged, thirty-seven of whom were dead or wounded. The 153rd lost eighty-five men out of its initial seven hundred, split evenly between captured and dead and wounded.34

After being driven from their initial positions to the west of Chancellorsville, the Pennsylvania German regiments of the Eleventh Corps reformed along the Mineral Springs Road to the northeast of Hooker's

headquarters. For them and their German *Kameraden* the battle was over. For many other Keystoners in the other corps of the Army of the Potomac, the fight had just begun. The 8th Pennsylvania Cavalry, for instance, one of the few cavalry units retained with the infantry, was ordered to assault Jackson's legions along the Orange Turnpike by itself as the final light faded on May 2. In this desperate but unnecessary attempt to stem the power of the Confederate assault—night alone would stop the rebels in their tracks—the regiment was all but destroyed. Cavalry attacks against infantry rarely succeeded in the Civil War, and this action was no exception. The next day witnessed over thirty Pennsylvania infantry and artillery regiments in the Third, Twelfth, and Second Corps battle it out with Jackson's veterans, who pushed in toward Chancellorsville from the west and southwest, and the divisions of General Richard Anderson and McLaws, personally directed by Lee from the south and east. There was one major difference from the evening before, however: the vaunted Stonewall Jackson was not in charge of his wing of the Southern army, having been accidentally shot by his own troops while on a night reconnaissance. J. E. B. Stuart temporarily took over for him and, by sheer psychological force and some tactical blunders committed both by Hooker and various subordinates, the rebels gained the upper hand by ten o'clock. Hooker was knocked unconscious when a pillar he was leaning against on the Chancellorsville porch

Broadside from June 1863 declaring the approach of the Confederate army and calling out the Pennsylvania state militia.

was struck by a Confederate shell. He left no coherent orders for the senior corps commander, Darius Couch, to follow except to retreat the Federal army, which still outnumbered the enemy over two to one, to a defensive line hugging the Rappahannock. Inconclusive fighting by the wing of the Union army near Fredericksburg on May 4 effectively ended the campaign, which saw over 17,000 Union casualties (including thousands of Pennsylvanians). On the night of May 4, a recovered and chastened Joe Hooker decided to recross the river against the advice of his corps commanders. Once again, the Confederates were victorious. Once again, morale in the Federal ranks plummeted. Captain Francis Donaldson of

the 118th Pennsylvania Infantry, a regiment that had been hammered hard on May 3, wrote his brother, "The army is in a very unsettled condition. The men are morose, sullen, dissatisfied, disappointed, and mortified." Blamed for the overall defeat in the Northern press, the German soldiers of the Eleventh Corps, including those from Pennsylvania, felt a double dose of depression that made Donaldson's comment appear sanguine. Their letters home reveal a painful indignation at being scapegoated (frequently called "damn Dutch") for mistakes committed by Hooker, Howard, and others. Some officers resigned in protest, but for the men in the ranks there was no recourse but to stiffen their resolve, thicken their skin against the prejudicial remarks, and grimly look forward to the next fight.[35]

In retrospect, there was one positive strategic result of the failed Chancellorsville Campaign for the Union cause: it prompted Lee to think about bringing the war into the North a second time. This time the rebels actually made it into Pennsylvania and brought the war home to the Keystone's citizens, but the ordeal was relatively short-lived, considering the potential for a longer occupation (which was a goal Lee desired), and ended with the Federal triumph at Gettysburg. After that battle, the offensive power of the Army of Northern Virginia was broken and, coupled with the capture of Vicksburg, Mississippi, signaled the beginning of the end of the Confederate bid for independence.

In mid-May 1863, no one north or south of the Mason-Dixon Line knew what was to come. For two more months the fate of the Republic trembled in the balance in the fields and villages between Fredericksburg and southern Pennsylvania as the two armies maneuvered, probed, skirmished, and finally battled against each other in Adams County. For Pennsylvanians, both those serving in the army and their loved ones at home, the Gettysburg Campaign came to define their Civil War experience. It was seared in their memory unlike any other event of the conflict and ultimately represented the overall sacrifices of all residents of the Keystone State for the Union. Although over twenty-one more months of fratricidal warfare followed that would deeply test the resolve of the Commonwealth's citizens, Gettysburg truly became the high-water mark of their War of the Rebellion.

As it became clear that the Army of Northern Virginia was targeting Pennsylvania in its latest offensive move, Governor Andrew Curtin formally appealed for 60,000 troops "to prevent serious raids by the enemy." He believed it "necessary" to "call upon the citizens of Pennsylvania, to furnish promptly all men necessary to organize an army corps of volunteer infantry, cavalry, and artillery, to be designated the Army Corps of the Susquehanna." The June 12th proclamation was unfortunately ill-timed, however, as the rebels were still in northern Virginia and the immediate threat to home and hearth was not yet

felt by most in the Keystone State. It also came too late to effectively raise and train a force even a fraction of the size requested. A few thousand residents turned out in response to the governor's call and were mustered into primarily ninety-day emergency militia regiments that saw little service and were generally deemed useless (with a few exceptions); ironically, New York sent more men for the defense of its sister state and its militia saw considerable service in the upcoming campaign.[36]

Within a week, though, as the Confederate threat neared and the likelihood of significant occupation by the main enemy army became more imminent, an increasing stream of refugees fled their homes in the lower Cumberland Valley and rushed to safety beyond the Susquehanna. Wagon after wagon, loaded to the brim and accompanied by various numbers of farm animals, could be seen moving north and east. The gender imbalance in towns like Greencastle, Chambersburg, and Gettysburg became embarrassingly noticeable as many male heads of household gathered up their livestock, money, and other valuables and left their families behind, secure in the knowledge that their wives could hold their own against the invaders. Doubtless these decisions made good sense to those who made them at the time, but to outside observers from the Northern press and passing Confederate and, later, Union soldiers, it gave Pennsylvania a black eye. Virginian Hodijah Lincoln Meade noted the absence of men and described residents of the Commonwealth he encountered as "simple ignorant and degraded," and General Dorsey Pender of A. P. Hill's corps termed them "the most miserable people . . . coarse and dirty," with large numbers of "dirty-looking children." Private Samuel Hurst of the 73rd Ohio Infantry recalled passing through a beautiful farming area on the way to Gettysburg, but was surprised that the few men he found were not enthusiastic: "We expected to see [them] rising as one man, and rushing to arms to defend their homes" but instead "saw them rush to the fields with scythe, and reaper, and leave the work of driving back the foe undivided to ourselves."[37]

For many southern Pennsylvanians, a good percentage of whom were of Pennsylvania Dutch ethnicity, avoidance of military service and/or securing one's valuables and escaping the onslaught of enemy occupation may have been a practical response to a potentially life- and culture-threatening problem: if horses needed to plow fields and harvest crops were taken by rebel raiding parties (and paid for in worthless Confederate scrip), for instance, families might face severe hardships later or have to sell the farm. If the male head of household was killed while in military service, a given family might starve or be forced to rely on the charity of neighbors or relatives, something shunned by most Dutch communities and religious denominations. Agricultural independence was a key component of the Pennsylvania Dutch way of life, also, and so ensur-ing the future viability of the family farm was the first responsibility most men thought of, not defense of the state or the Union. Add to these prag-matic considerations a strong Democratic and anti-Republican political stance among many in the southern tier counties, and it made additional sense to take care of one-self and let the armies battle it out, but hopefully not on one's own prop-erty.[38]

To the horror of Gettysburg's resi-dents, that was exactly what hap-pened, and they were left with the added burden of thousands of dead and wounded men and the stench of rotting corpses (both animal and human) after the armies departed. For most of the citizens of Franklin County, and for many in Fulton, Cumberland, Adams, and York coun-ties, the presence of thousands of troops and military animals from both armies, off and on through June and July 1863, meant trampled crops, pillaged pantries, wells drunk dry, fences burned for campfires, and roads so badly rutted by the passage of heavy vehicles that they would remain unusable for months after-ward. A thin layer of fine dust, stirred up by the constant marching of thou-sands of feet and the trundling of thousands of wagon wheels, coated the towns and villages of these coun-ties that would take weeks to wash away. Chambersburg and its sur-rounding area, occupied the longest by the Confederates, was picked clean by rebel requisitioning parties, some of whom ventured as far west as Mercersburg. Rachel Cormany, whose

A wartime sketch of the Wrightsville bridge over the Susquehanna River in flames. The deliberate destruction of the bridge denied the Confederates access to Lancaster County and Harrisburg.

husband Samuel had enlisted in a local cavalry regiment during the invasion scare of the previous fall, wrote that local merchants in Chambersburg were "ruined" by the Confederates. Henry Hege of Marion "handed bread out the door" to passing rebels to discourage them from entering his home, but still lost all his horses to Southern foragers. "It was awful," he said, to watch the Confederates go "through the fields to hunt [hidden] horses." He regretted having not fled with his livestock earlier. Carlisle was actually bombarded by J. E. B. Stuart's horse artillery when New York militia holding the town refused to surrender, and Hanover witnessed a spirited, if brief clash between Southern and Northern cavalry just a few days before the main battle at Gettysburg. Camp Hill experienced a small skirmish between rebel horsemen and defending Pennsylvania militia in what became the northernmost penetration of Confederate forces, and another contingent of militia belied their overall reputation by stoutly defending the great wooden bridge across the Susquehanna at Wrightsville, and then burning it to prevent its use by General Richard Ewell's troops—who would have afterward proceeded to capture the state capital at Harrisburg. York, the largest Pennsylvania town occupied by the rebels, was also well plundered by official Southern foraging parties, who, although strictly governed by Robert E. Lee's General Order 73 not to molest civilians and to "pay" for all goods taken, nonetheless purloined countless objects of value and edibility. Southern Pennsylvania groaned under the weight of enemy occupation.[39]

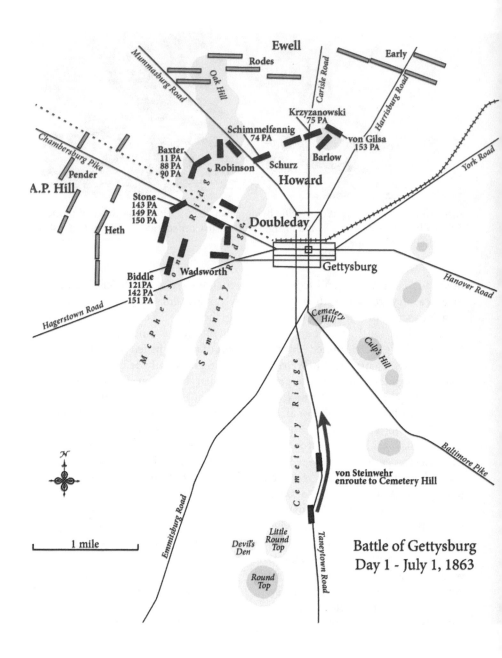

Ewell

Rodes

Early

Mummasburg Road

Oak Hill

Carlisle Road

Harrisburg Road

Krzyzanowski
75 PA

Schimmelfennig
74 PA

von Gilsa
153 PA

Chambersburg Pike

Baxter
11 PA
88 PA
90 PA

Robinson

Schurz

Barlow

York Road

A.P. Hill

Pender

Howard

Stone
143 PA
149 PA
150 PA

Doubleday

Gettysburg

Heth

Hanover Road

Biddle
121 PA
142 PA
151 PA

Wadsworth

McPherson Ridge

Seminary Ridge

Hagerstown Road

Cemetery
Hill

Culp's Hill

Baltimore Pike

Cemetery Ridge

von Steinwehr
enroute to Cemetery Hill

N

1 mile

Emmitsburg Road

Devil's
Den

Little
Round
Top

Taneytown Road

Battle of Gettysburg
Day 1 - July 1, 1863

Round
Top

9. Pennsylvania's Fight to Win the Civil War, 1863–1865

Christian B. Keller

DEFEAT AT GETTYSBURG, JULY 1, 1863

If civilians in southern Pennsylvania suffered property losses, enemy occupation, and the occasional military action during the Gettysburg Campaign, the Commonwealth's soldiers in the Army of the Potomac fared significantly worse, some units devastated in the three-day battle. The Union army, following orders from Washington to stay between the national capital and Baltimore and the Confederate army, arrived in the Keystone State over a week after the Southerners crossed the state border in force in late June. Thus, the Northern army approached from the south and the Southern army from the north and west, an oxymoronic situation but one that made geographical sense considering the routes of march of both armies and where they had been prior to engaging at the small, quiet, crossroads town of Gettysburg. Among the Pennsylvania regiments, an anxious excitement pervaded the ranks: they were coming

"home" to defend their state against rebel despoliation and to crush the rebellion once and for all. There was a common belief among the soldiers that the next great engagement might decide the outcome of the war and that they would have to fight harder than they had ever fought before. In many ways they were right.

Neither side planned for the Battle of Gettysburg to occur when and where it did. Philadelphian George Meade, now commander of the Army of the Potomac after Lincoln sacked sullen, unresponsive Joe Hooker just days before the first Federals crossed the Mason-Dixon Line, expected the fight to occur in northern Maryland and had prepared a defensive line along Pipe Creek to that end, but under political pressure to eject Lee from Pennsylvania, he hastened north to find the rebels and defeat them. As his leading corps, the First and the Eleventh, led the way from Frederick, Maryland, he dispatched a third of his cavalry, under Brigadier General John Buford, to scout out the enemy dispositions. Lee, bereft of most of his cavalry after J. E. B. Stuart had departed with its best brigades on a ride around the Union army, had only rudimentary intelligence on Federal whereabouts, and thus was surprised on June 28 to discover how close the bluecoats had come to his scattered army, which was engaged in foraging across four counties and attempting to cross the river to capture Harrisburg. He ordered a general concentration at Cashtown, a small village hugging the eastern slope of the South Mountain, just on the other side of the pass that led to Chambersburg and the rich Cumberland Valley. If he could concentrate his army faster than Meade, he could theoretically "bite off" the advancing Federal corps one at a time as they marched north from Maryland. The result would be a series of small victories amounting to one, long, running battle that would ultimately cause the decisive defeat of the Unionists.

On June 30, Lee permitted a brigade from A. P. Hill's corps to venture to the nearby town of Gettysburg to search for supplies. When the Southerners encountered the lead elements of Buford's cavalry division, they turned back without a fight, something Lee wanted to avoid until he had the army completely concentrated. The next day, July 1, Hill decided to move with two of his corps' divisions back to Gettysburg to disperse what was assumed to be a "nuisance force" of enemy cavalry; Lee acquiesced in this decision but soon got more than he bargained for.

Buford refused to be dispersed and in the process had gathered an immense amount of information about the Confederate forces on their way to the Cashtown-Gettysburg area. Thus, Meade was gifted with an unusually large amount of information about his adversary going into the main battle, whereas Lee, normally well informed by Stuart about the Federals, was going in almost blind. He also did not have all of his army ready and on the field when General Henry Heth's division of Hill's corps first traded shots with Buford's pickets about five miles west of Gettysburg at half past five in the morning. The battle had begun.[1]

Among those pickets were the troopers of the 17th Pennsylvania Cavalry, a regiment raised from counties all around the state and representative of the Keystone's population. The 17th, part of Colonel Thomas Devin's Second Brigade of Buford's division, was posted north of town to watch the approaches to Gettysburg from the north, northwest, and northeast. For a time some of its companies occupied Oak Hill while others advanced up the Mummasburg, Carlisle, and Harrisburg roads. Encountering the vanguards of Ewell's approaching rebel corps on the latter two thoroughfares, the men of the 17th gave Buford and First Corps commander Major General John Reynolds, a native of Lancaster, ample warning of the accidental Confederate envelopment that would soon engulf the Union First and Eleventh Corps. Before that occurred, however, the 17th, the only cavalry unit from the Commonwealth in Buford's command, saw several of its companies standing side by side with other cavalry regiments in the initial fight against Heth's Confederate infantry division, the dismounted men firing their .44-caliber Merrill and Smith carbines as fast as they could load them. Because Buford's men were all armed with breech-loaded carbines, they were able to shoot six to seven shots per minute compared to the Southern infantry's two to three rounds. That firepower advantage helped nullify the rebels' local numerical advantage, but quickly the weight of numbers began to tell. Buford, aware that he was buying time for the rest of the Army of the Potomac to arrive on the field, had to hold long enough to make a rebel seizure of the key hills south of town—Cemetery and Culp's hills—unlikely. Just as he was losing hope, Reynolds and the First Corps arrived, bolstering the battered cavalrymen who had fallen back to McPherson's Ridge.[2]

The initial clash of Union versus Confederate infantry occurred on that ridge, as Reynolds led his First Division, which included the famous Iron Brigade, into the fight. Only one Pennsylvania regiment marched in that division, the 56th Infantry, which was part of Brigadier General Lysander Cutler's brigade. Cutler's regiments, like the Iron Brigade, suffered tremendously as they managed to repulse Heth's North Carolinians, Tennesseans, and Mississippians, but then were forced to retreat when Heth regrouped and attacked again with

Private Levi Hocker of the 17th Pennsylvania Cavalry. The 17th was the only Pennsylvania cavalry unit in John Buford's command when his Division clashed with leading elements of Harry Heth's Confederate Division on July 1.

another Confederate division later in the morning. Colonel William Hoffmann wrote of his Centre, Indiana, and Luzerne County troops, "my officers and men did all that could be asked of brave men," a humble statement that belied the heavy 51.6 percent casualty rate. Such percentages were not uncommon in the First Corps on July 1. General Reynolds himself was one of the casualties, shot dead from his horse as he led the Iron Brigade into McPherson's Woods. Leadership of the corps devolved onto Third Division commander Major General Abner Doubleday.[3]

Of the thirty-two infantry regiments in the First Corps, eleven hailed from Pennsylvania, and the majority of them marched in

Major General John F. Reynolds (1820–1863), born in Lancaster, Pennsylvania, attended the United States Military Academy and graduated twenty-sixth in 1841. He served with distinction in the U.S.-Mexican War and, with the outbreak of the Civil War, was given command of a brigade of Pennsylvania Reserves in the Army of the Potomac. Reynolds served with distinction at Second Bull Run, Fredericksburg, and Chancellorsville, rising steadily in the army's leadership. Prior to Gettysburg, he was offered command of the entire army following Hooker's resignation, but declined in favor of his friend Georg Meade. At Gettysburg he led the Union First Corps into action on the morning of Jul 1, personally leading the famous Iron Brigade into McPherson's Woods, where he was fatally shot from his horse.

Doubleday's division. Colonel Chapman Biddle's brigade included the 121st, 142nd, and 151st Infantries, and Colonel Roy Stone's, nicknamed the "Bucktail Brigade" for the deer tails the men pinned on their caps, was completely a Keystone organization comprising the 143rd, 149th, and 150th Infantries. Both brigades fought fiercely in the McPherson's Ridge–Chambersburg Pike sector of the battlefield against Heth's men before being forced to retire to Seminary Ridge, where they made a stand with the remnants of other First Corps regiments. There they again made the enemy pay dearly in blood before retreating to Cemetery Hill: A. P. Hill's two divisions aggregately suffered about 30 percent casualties to achieve their tactical victory. The price in Pennsylvanian blood in these delaying actions, however, was astounding. When Captain William Gray of the 151st's Company I rushed to Lieutenant Colonel George McFarland in front of the Lutheran Seminary, shouting, "Colonel, my men are nearly all killed and wounded, what shall I do?" McFarland answered, "Fight with what is left." The Berks and Juniata County men did just that. Lieutenant William Blodget wrote his wife afterward that the 151st had, indeed, fought almost to the last man, and that "our poor boys fell around me like apples in a rain storm." In his official report, McFarland, who was shot, captured, and lost a leg at Gettysburg, exclaimed, "I know not how men could have fought more desperately, exhibited more coolness, or contested the field with more determined courage." His regiment entered the battle with 467 effectives and lost 51 killed, 211 wounded, and 75 missing, most of the latter at the seminary where the 151st was the last Federal unit to retire. The regiment's astonishing casualty rate earned it the unenviable recognition of second in total aggregate losses in the battle (after the 24th Michigan of the Iron Brigade), fifth in total killed, and ninth in total percentage lost (72.2 percent). Other units in Biddle's and Stone's brigades suffered similar devastating losses: the 142nd, for instance, left 68 percent of its troops on the field; the 149th, 74.7 percent; and the 150th, 66 percent. Colonel Stone summarized the actions of the Commonwealth's sons in Doubleday's division: "They fought as if each man felt that upon his own arm hung the fate of the day and the nation."[4]

Other Pennsylvanians fought with valor on the first day at Gettysburg. The 11th, 88th, and 90th Infantries in Brigadier General Henry Baxter's brigade in the First Corps' Second Division made a stubborn stand on Oak Hill Ridge, the northern extension of Seminary Ridge, that at first repulsed the rebel brigades of General Robert Rodes with heavy loss, but then were forced to retreat under enormous pressure from renewed and better-organized Southern assaults. The Berks County and Philadelphia men of the 88th and the multicounty-raised Eleventh at first could not believe their good luck: the inexperienced North Carolina brigade of Alfred Iverson approached their position as if on parade, seemingly unaware of the Pennsylvanians ensconced behind a low stone wall. The Southerners had no skirmishers out in front, a calamitous mistake, as suddenly the 750 men rose up and delivered a crashing volley at one hundred paces. Hundreds of rebels fell in that one volley, lying in even rows in the corn, shoulder to shoulder, as they had been moments before. The survivors ran for safety to a small depression in the field, but found no respite; several companies from all three Keystone regiments jumped over the wall, firing as they went, and captured several enemy standards and hundreds of prisoners in a short-lived but successful counterattack. It was one of the Commonwealth's most successful moments in the entire battle and one of the few on the fateful first day.[5]

The long-suffering German regiments of the Eleventh Corps, arriving in the early afternoon and posted to the right of the First Corps to meet Richard Ewell's oncoming Confederate legions (that the 17th Cavalry had detected earlier) fought almost as tenaciously as their comrades in the First Corps and likewise suffered heavy casualties, approximating 35 percent between the 74th and 75th Pennsylvania alone. As Lieutenant Colonel Alexander von Mitzel of the Seventy-Fourth wrote later, "things were getting hot, I had two horses shot under me but I held my position with the bayonet, and though being pressed harder and harder by the Rebels yet I held the position up to the last." Unfortunately, though, the two regiments were again poorly deployed as at Chancellorsville and, stretched to the breaking point by poor tactical decision making on the part of a neighboring Anglo-American division commander, Brigadier General Francis Barlow,

The monument for the 153rd Pennsylvania Volunteer Infantry at Gettysburg was dedicated in 1899.

were ultimately flanked and forced to hastily retreat. Barlow, a prejudiced New Englander who held the foreign-born in contempt and was in turn disliked by his German and Pennsylvania Dutch troops, foolishly extended his line to include a small hill to his front, later known as "Barlow's Knoll," without adequately covering the approaches from the Harrisburg Road. As a result, the hapless 153rd Pennsylvania, posted on the hill, once again found itself flanked and overwhelmed by superior numbers of the enemy as it had in Virginia, but not before it had seriously bloodied the Georgia brigade of John B. Gordon, who later wrote that the blue-coated enemy had behaved with gallantry and élan. Such reports were of little use to the Common-wealth's ethnic German soldiery, who, in another unhappy Chancellorsville redux, were assaulted by a second enemy after the smoke of battle had cleared away: the nativistic prejudice of fellow Northern soldiers. Among the worst was Barlow, who doubtless did their reputation great harm as one of their commanders: "But these Dutch won't fight. Their officers say so and they say so themselves and they ruin all with whom they come in contact," he complained to a Harvard College classmate. The Northern English-language press was more charitable this time, mainly because Gettysburg ended in Union victory, but perhaps as "punishment" for the widely held but inaccurate perception that they had again fought poorly, the Eleventh Corps, including all its Pennsylvania troops, was transferred out of the Army of the Potomac and sent to the Western Theater, where it managed to brush off earlier calumnies and earn the respect of its new comrades in the Chattanooga Campaign. For their part the German American and Pennsylvania Dutch soldiers were as glad to be rid of the prejudiced eastern army as it was happy to see them go.[6]

As night fell on the blood-stained plains, hills, and ridgelines west and north of Gettysburg, the regiments of the First and Eleventh Corps licked their wounds, counted their losses, and managed to regroup on the heights of Cemetery Hill, just south of town. General Howard, still in command of the Eleventh Corps but overall commander of Union forces on July 1, had prudently left one of his divisions to safeguard the hill and provide a rallying point in case of defeat. That foresight, the failure of the Confederates to attack the position, and the arrival of most of the rest of the Army of the Potomac overnight ensured that the best high ground in the area remained in Northern hands when the sun's first rays illuminated the fields on July 2. Army commander George Meade, who arrived at Gettysburg around midnight, acclaimed the Union position as it was developing a good one and decided to await the renewal of battle that he was certain Lee would proffer him.

VICTORY AT GETTYSBURG, JULY 2–3, 1863

Lee had achieved a considerable tactical victory on the first day but did not succeed in destroying the two Federal corps that had stood against him. True, they had been badly mauled in their fights against A. P. Hill's and Ewell's corps and in their hasty retreat through town to the high ground beyond it. But Ewell's failure to assault either Cemetery Hill or Culp's Hill on the evening of July 1 meant that his commanding general would now have to develop a plan to drive the reinforced enemy either directly or indirectly off those heights and the long ridgeline that stretched southward from them, Cemetery Ridge. In doing so, Lee hoped to make the most of this battle at Gettysburg that fate had presented him. It was not the fight he wanted nor where he wanted it, but he now had accepted battle and was determined to extract a decisive

victory from it, one that could alter the strategic course of the war. The next morning, with all but one of his infantry divisions at his disposal, Lee ordered General James Longstreet's corps to assault the southern end of the Union line along Cemetery Ridge and Ewell to attack Cemetery and Culp's hills. The simultaneous pressure on both ends of his line should either crumble Federal resistance or force Meade to make a mistake, which Lee could then take advantage of. The continued absence of J. E. B. Stuart and the bulk of the Confederate cavalry, a factor that had instigated the battle in the first place, still troubled Lee, but supremely confident in his soldiers, he expected victory.[7]

Longstreet's July 2 assault started late in the day around four o'clock and promptly ran into the Union Third Corps, commanded by Major General Daniel Sickles, at the Peach Orchard, Wheatfield, and Stony Hill, locations far to the front of where the Confederates expected the Union line to be. Sickles had essentially moved his corps forward to the Emmitsburg Road ridge, which, like Barlow the day before, he deemed better ground to defend from than the lower terrain Meade had assigned him at the southern end of Cemetery Ridge. Also like Barlow, however, his move threatened the viability of other Union positions and, in this case, the safety of the entire Federal line. It also sealed the fate of hundreds of Pennsylvanians. His corps, which included Brigadier General Charles Graham's all-Pennsylvania brigade of Major General David B. Birney's First

Col. Andrew Tippin and his wife. Tippin, a veteran of the U.S.-Mexican War, lived in Pottstown, Pennsylvania, at the time of the Civil War. As commander of the 68th Pennsylvania Volunteers, he and his men saw heavy fighting at Fredericksburg, Chancellorsville, and Gettysburg, where Tippin had his horse shot out from under him.

Division, would suffer terribly for Sickles's decision. Graham commanded six regiments raised in the Commonwealth (the 57th, 63rd, 68th, 105th, 114th, and 141st Infantries). Together, the men in the ranks represented nearly every Pennsylvania county and nearly all had seen substantial service in the Army of the Potomac's previous campaigns. This was truly a veteran organization, and had a less-seasoned brigade been stationed at the Peach Orchard, where Graham's regiments stood, fought, and bled, it is quite possible Sickles's entire line would have collapsed before substantial reinforcements reached it from the Second and Fifth Corps. The brigade suffered severely from Longstreet's pre-assault bombardment in its exposed forward position, but that punishment was only a foretaste of the carnage to come at the hands of General Lafayette McLaws's rebel division, which, although disorganized in its cohesion by the unexpected location of Sickles's corps, still hit Graham with the force of a tidal wave. Andrew Tippin, colonel of the 68th, assumed command of the brigade when Graham fell wounded and later wrote of the ferocity of the fighting:

It was a terrible afternoon, and all were anxious for the Fifth Corps to come up, as we were being decimated by their artillery. . . . In that orchard, the Lieutenant Colonel and Major were wounded and ten other officers killed or wounded, leaving with me but four to bring the regiment out of the fight, having had in all but seventeen present for duty. Just at sunset the rebel infantry charged upon the position with great impetuosity, and the brigade, greatly weakened by its losses and exhausted by frequent manœuvrings, outflanked and vastly outnumbered, was forced to yield; but not in disorder, retiring slowly and contesting the ground inch by inch.

The 68th lost a catastrophic 60 percent of its total strength at the Peach Orchard, a percentage representative of the casualties suffered by the brigade. The Third Corps as a whole was so badly damaged at Gettysburg that a few months later it was amalgamated into the Second Corps, but its sacrifice—and, according to some historians, Sickles's unauthorized advance—may have saved the Union

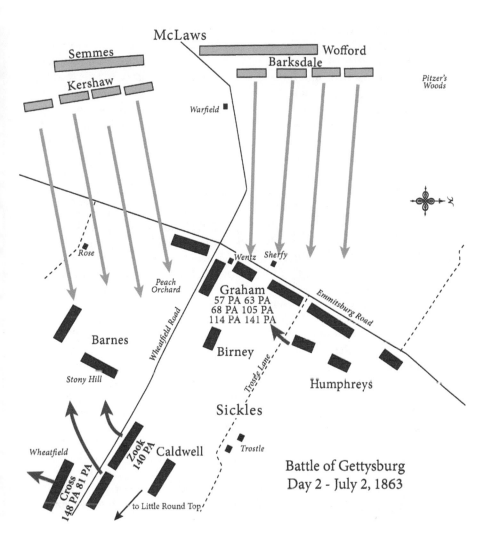

McLaws

Semmes

Kershaw

Wofford

Barksdale

Pitzer's Woods

Warfield

Rose

Wentz   Sherfy

Peach Orchard

Graham
57 PA 63 PA
68 PA 105 PA
114 PA 141 PA

Emmitsburg Road

Wheatfield Road

Barnes

Birney

Trostle Lane

Humphreys

Stony Hill

Sickles

Wheatfield

Zook
140 PA

Caldwell

Trostle

Cross
148 PA 81 PA

Battle of Gettysburg
Day 2 - July 2, 1863

to Little Round Top

army from being rolled up on its southern flank.[8]

It was a close-run thing, however, and had George Meade and Second Corps commander Winfield Scott Hancock not strenuously supported Sickles, Lee may still have achieved his goal. Thrown in to support the crumbling Third Corps in the Wheatfield sector was Brigadier General John C. Caldwell's First Division of the Second Corps. Six Keystone regiments were peppered throughout the organization, and all engaged in the seesaw battle of the bloody Wheatfield. Colonel Edward Cross's First Brigade included the 148th and 81st Infantries, recruited in Centre, Luzerne, and Philadelphia counties. The two regiments entered the waist-deep wheat side by side and, with a loud huzzah, crashed into the flank of a Georgia brigade and sent it reeling. But the Southerners, reinforced with fresh regiments, stopped their next attack cold, throwing them and several other Pennsylvania units out of the field. One Georgian, exhilarated with victory, cursed them as they retreated, shouting, "Go to the rear you d—d Yankee son of a b—h!" The two Pennsylvania regiments together left about 30 percent of their men dead and wounded on the ground. Supporting their brigade was Caldwell's Third Brigade, led by Brigadier General Samuel K. Zook of Chester County. Just as Zook led his brigade, comprising the 140th Pennsylvania and three New York regiments, into the Wheatfield he was shot from his horse, mortally wounded. Removed from the field, Zook would never know that his brigade's sacrifice and that of several others in the wheat would successfully sap enough of Longstreet's striking power that his command would be too weak to capture Little Round Top—a hill at the extreme southern end of the Union line that now assumed a position of vital significance.[9]

The timely involvement of the Pennsylvania Reserves Division, now part of the Fifth Corps, probably kept that key eminence from falling before the Twentieth Maine and its sister regiments in Colonel Strong Vincent's brigade (including the Eighty-Third Pennsylvania Infantry) arrived there. Meade, realizing that the Wheatfield sector still trembled in the balance and that yet more Federal power would be necessary, turned to his old division, under the command of Brigadier General Samuel Crawford. Crawford, a native of Franklin County, hardly had to give the order to charge into what was later called the "Valley of Death"—the low ground between Little Round Top and Houck's Ridge, which bordered the Wheatfield. A *New York Tribune* reporter wrote of the Reserves' attack:

The onset was terrible. The rebel generals threw themselves at the head of their troops, and, with sword in hand, urged them to the conflict. They well knew the ground must be held, or the advantages gained must be lost. The Reserves, however, were fighting on their own soil, with their backs to their homes; it was a battle for the safety of their families, the defence of their State, the honor of their country, the glory of their unsullied banner, and the reputation of their most beloved commander. What motives these, for men to die bravely, or to survive an honorable death with an untarnished fame! No foe could withstand a charge impelled by hearts thus nerved to the combat. First, the officers cheering on their rebel hosts, fell beneath the unerring fire of the Bucktails, and the hostile column was speedily broken and hurled back by the bayonets of the First brigade.

Although a bit embellished with flowery language, the account captured the spirit with which the all-Pennsylvania division charged into the fray. Most historians agree that the reserve regiments' attack bought the time necessary, and attenuated just enough Confederate strength, to permit the Federals to occupy Little Round Top first and defend it successfully. The fight for that hill,

Wartime sketch of Hazlett's battery in action on Little Round Top, July 2, 1863. The artist made the small hill appear higher in elevation than it actually was.

immortalized in historical fiction and film focusing on the Maine troops, also included several hundred Pennsylvanians in the Eighty-Third Infantry. Private Oliver Willcox Norton, who survived the ordeal, wrote his sister on July 12 that his regiment and brigade "fought like demons, took four hundred prisoners, and laid the rebels in heaps before them. We were splendidly posted behind rocks and trees and you may judge of the fight when I tell you that of thirteen hundred men in such a position we lost three hundred and fifty-nine and no prisoners. . . . There are thousands of things I could tell you that I cannot write. The main thing is to tell you that I am still safe and well, doing my duty the best I can."[10]

The fighting at Little Round Top, the Wheatfield, and the Peach Orchard occurred more or less simultaneously. Meade's resources were stretched to the breaking point, but at the end of the second day he had suc-cessfully redeemed Sickles's folly, held on to the key ground on the southern end of his line (Little Round Top), and maintained the integrity of his army's position. He had also wrecked most of the best remaining brigades in the Confederate army. An attack on the center of Cemetery Ridge late in the day by General Richard Anderson's division of A. P. Hill's corps almost achieved the break-through Lee had hoped for, but in the end hard fighting by the Philadelphia Brigade and the sacrifice of other Federal units, such as the First Minnesota, had staved off defeat. In the northern part of the field, Ewell's assaults on Cemetery and Culp's hills, which Lee had expected to occur at the same time as Longstreet's attacks to the south, did not occur until the latter's corps had pretty well shot its bolt. Poor coordination among the Confederate leaders was primarily to blame for that, but strong Federal leadership and intrepid resistance by the Union soldiery ensured that rebel

Matilda "Tillie" Pierce Alleman (1848–1914) was a teenage resident of Gettysburg in July 1863. Her 1885 book, *At Gettysburg, What a Girl Saw and Heard of the Battle*, is recognized as a valuable primary source account of the civilian experience during the battle. In it, Tillie describes her evacuation to a neighbor's "safe" house which was then converted into a make-shift hospital. She helped tend the wounded and, after the battle, noted the Confederate dead still strewn across the battlefield.

successes on the northern end of the Union line met the same fate as those in the south. Two of Ewell's divisions temporarily gained the summits of both Cemetery and Culp's Hills in the evening, but once again the timely arrival of counterattacking reserves (including many Pennsylvania regiments, such as the 27th and 73rd Infantries on Cemetery Hill) pushed the Confederates back. The cost in blood had been astronomical—the majority of the Army of the Potomac's 23,000 casualties at

Gettysburg were sustained on July 2—but the men in blue had held. Pennsylvania's sons had played a spectacular role in that defense.

Meade called for a council of war among his corps commanders and chief divisional officers that night in his headquarters at the Leister House. All voted to "stay and fight it out" and await Lee's next move. Meade accurately predicted what it would be: a grand assault against the middle of his line on Cemetery Ridge. For the first time in the war, a Federal army commander, and a Pennsylvanian to boot, had gotten into the head of Robert E. Lee, and at the meeting he warned the Norristown-born Winfield Scott Hancock and his Second Corps division commanders that the blow would fall on them. Meade promised them every available support for the next day. For his part, Lee initially proposed to continue the tactical plan of July 2, but Longstreet's unwillingness and unreadiness to continue the attacks in the south in the early morning scuttled that idea. Arriving at a new plan, Lee logically deduced that the Federals had reinforced their northern and southern flanks and therefore should be weakened in their center. If he could better time and execute an attack there on July 3 than the ill-coordinated attacks of July 2, success might yet perch on his banners. The plan for what became "Pickett's Charge" came together in the midmorning of July 3 and involved three major working parts: first, General George Pickett's division of Longstreet's corps, freshly arrived from Chambersburg, along with the remnants of Pettigrew's (Heth's) and Trimble's (Pender's) divisions of A. P. Hill's corps, would conduct an infantry charge against the Union center at a copse of trees, about a mile away from their starting points on Seminary Ridge. Second, prior to that assault, every available Confederate cannon would open up on the target position in a great bombardment, hopefully disabling or destroying most of the Union artillery and infantry units there. Third, as the Confederate infantry hit the copse of trees, the Confederate cavalry—now up to strength with the arrival of tardy J. E. B. Stuart and his three brigades—would crash into the Federal rear behind Cemetery Ridge, wreaking as much havoc and sowing as much chaos as possible. As the Confederate infantry broke the Union line, the horsemen would be perfectly situated to run down the routed enemy and complete the victory. Additionally, Ewell would strongly "demonstrate" against the two hills in his sector to distract Meade from the main effort.[11]

It was an ambitious plan, but had every potential for success if the three principal parts moved in a coordinated manner and if the Federals remained more or less passive. Neither happened.

In a grim harbinger of events later in the day, the Union Twelfth Corps stationed at Culp's Hill, including several Pennsylvania infantry regiments, attacked Ewell's men in their advanced positions early in the morning and threw them off the hill entirely. Bloody Confederate counterattacks

Winfield Scott Hancock (1824–1886) was born in Montgomeryville, Pennsylvania, and attended the United States Military Academy, where he graduated eighteenth in his class in 1844. A skilled and respected army officer, Hancock took over General Reynolds's command at Gettysburg after that officer had been killed, and successfully organized the Union defense on Cemetery Hill on the evening of July 1 and along Cemetery Ridge on July 2 and 3. During Pickett's Charge, Hancock received a grievous wound, yet survived the battle and war to be the Democratic nominee for president in 1880. Another Civil War veteran, James A. Garfield, narrowly defeated him in that election.

were to no avail, but drained the remaining fighting power in most of Ewell's corps. Lee would not have the demonstration in the north he had wanted. Further, the titanic artillery bombardment, which occurred around one o'clock in the afternoon (and could be heard in Harrisburg), created a great deal of noise and awe among the Northern troops but far

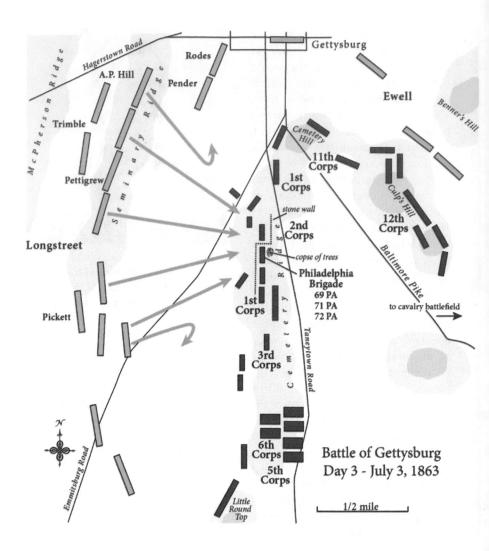

Battle of Gettysburg
Day 3 - July 3, 1863

fewer casualties in their ranks than expected. A soldier in the Philadelphia Irish 69th Pennsylvania Infantry, part of the Philadelphia Brigade stationed at the copse of trees, described the scene: "The air is filling with the whirling, shrieking, hissing sound of the solid shot and bursting shell; all threw themselves flat upon the ground, behind the little stone wall; nearly 150 guns belched forth messengers of destruction, sometimes in volleys, again in irregular, but continuous sounds, traveling through the air, high above us, or striking the ground in front and ricocheting over us, to be imbedded in some object to the rear." This cannonade, which was replied to by about eighty Federal guns, did succeed in killing or wounding several hundred infantrymen and knocking out the better part

Edwin Forbes's wartime sketch of the climax of Pickett's Charge, July 3, 1863. Ziegler's Grove, a prominent feature on Cemetery Ridge, is to the left of center. Despite the assault by almost 13,000 Confederate troops, the Union line in the foreground held.

of two batteries, but a crushing, catastrophic blow it certainly was not. The Confederate cavalry also underperformed, stopped cold by unexpectedly stout resistance by the Federal troopers in a great cavalry fight several miles to the east of Cemetery Ridge. Credit is often given to Brigadier General George Armstrong Custer and his Michiganers for stopping the Southern horsemen, but key roles were also played by the 1st, 3rd, 14th, and 16th Pennsylvania Cavalries. A member of the 3rd Pennsylvania Cavalry, writing his parents the day after the battle, summed up the Union perspective. "In the incoming charge of Stuart we had a main part. He came in all dressed like he was ready for a parade, and looked very tall and gallant in the saddle, with a might pretty horse under him. After about 3 hours the rebels retreated. . . . By doing this we had kept the Rebel cavalry out. . . . I sure think that this has just about finished Lee."[12]

When the 13,000 Confederate infantrymen stepped out of the shelter of the trees and ridgeline of Seminary Ridge about two o'clock, none of them knew much about the other parts of their commanding general's plan, nor that they had failed. Rebel battle flags unfurled in the gentle breeze and the drums and fifes struck up lively, cheerful cadences that belied the serious expressions found on most faces. For the men in the ranks, all they knew that afternoon was that the day was humid and hot and they had a mile of open ground to cross, that Lee had never failed them before, and that they trusted him to lead them to victory. Lee also had no idea that the artillery barrage had been essentially ineffective and Stuart had been stopped. His ears informed him that Ewell was inactive, and that that part of his plan had misfired. But he was still very hopeful. His subordinate Longstreet was not as sanguine, so convinced the infantry assault would fail that he could only nod his assent that launched Pickett's division across the field. A mile away, the men of the Philadelphia Brigade and other regiments in (Pennsylvania-born) Brigadier General John Gibbon's division of the Union Second Corps crouched in amazement, some with mouths agape at the imposing sight, others gritting their teeth in grim determination, still others with heads bowed in fervent prayer for their souls, which they feared might soon depart their bodies.

About a quarter of the way across the field it became apparent to all present, both Union and Confederate, that the Federal artillery had not been suppressed. Screaming agents of death went soaring through the air toward the dense ranks of gray and butternut, nearly every shot killing or wounding scores of Southern husbands, brothers, and sons. About the halfway mark, nearing the Emmitsburg Road, the bulk of Pettigrew's and Trimble's contingents retreated, unable to withstand such punishment after their rigorous bloodletting against the Union First Corps two days prior. Pickett's three brigades continued onward, suffering horrific casualties to the Union guns, which then opened up with canister as the rebels crossed the road. At 250 yards out, the 69th and 71st Pennsylvania opened fire with their .58 caliber Enfield and Springfield rifled muskets and .69 caliber smoothbores. Survivors who later witnessed early machine guns in action claimed that the effect on the advancing Virginians was similar,

men simply crumpling up and falling in rows as the bullets flew into them. The two Pennsylvania regiments had been ordered to scour the field for any serviceable guns left by Anderson's men the evening before, and, along with extra Federal weapons secured here and there, thus managed between two and five loaded weapons per man on the firing line at the wall. Those using the smoothbores loaded their guns with as many as twelve buckshot rounds per shot. The result was sheer carnage for the Southerners. Battle standards advanced and fell multiple times, commands of regiments devolved onto captains, and all military organization began to disappear. Yet still the battered rebels surged onward, a good number of men in General Richard Garnett's brigade actually reaching the low stone wall and finding a modicum of shelter there. Then they poured it into the Pennsylvanians. William Burns of the 71st wrote in his diary, "The fight soon became awful. We mowed the rebs right and left but still they came on. We had to retreat." The 71st fell back, exposing the right flank of the 69th as they went and allowing an opening for the Confederates to exploit.[13]

Brigadier General Alexander Webb, commanding the Philadelphia Brigade, later wrote that he believed all was lost at that moment. "When they came over the fences, the Army of the Potomac was nearer being whipped than it was at any time of the battle. When my men fell back I almost wished to get killed." He tried to bring the 72nd Pennsylvania, which had originally stood behind the copse of trees, into a charge to force back Garnett's men, but these bluecoats would not budge, simply standing at the crest of the ridge, delivering and receiving crushing volleys with the enemy. Then General Louis Armistead's brigade arrived, damaged from its transit across the field but still mainly intact. Leaping on top of the stone wall, he yelled, "Come on boys, give them the cold steel! Who will follow me?" Several hundred of his men and Garnett's survivors followed him directly into the vacuum left by the 71st, heading straight for the now wavering 72nd. Had the 72nd collapsed, Meade's entire center could have unraveled. At that moment, however, the 69th refused the right half of its battle line, bending it back almost to a ninety-degree angle, and thereby maintained its position while firing into the flank of Armistead's charging mass. Desperate hand-to-hand fighting ensued with rifles being used as clubs and rocks and stones flying alongside bullets. The 72nd also held its ground and, joined by the timely arrival of two neighboring regiments from Colonel Norman Hall's brigade, mortally wounded Armistead and mauled his followers. But the close-quarters fighting still continued, and the rebels refused to give up. Major Samuel Roberts of the 72nd recalled what happened next: "The color bearer, seizing the stump of the staff of the colors, whirling his hat around his head, moved with the regiment down to the wall; many of our men being wounded or killed in the advance and

The 72nd Pennsylvania Infantry monument, dedicated in 1891, is located on Cemetery Ridge and memorializes the 72nd's stand against Pickett's Charge. It depicts a soldier of the regiment in partial Zouave equipage using his rifle as a club. The monument appears on the obverse side of the United States Gettysburg commemorative quarter dollar coin.

the men behind that wall, besides men out in the field surrendered." William Burns of the 71st wrote that his rallied regiment also joined the charge, which he claimed was led by General Webb. Regardless of whether a general or a flag bearer led the counterattack, the shock of it expelled Armistead's and Garnett's survivors

The Great Central Sanitary Fair was erected on present-day Logan Circle in Philadelphia in June 1864 to raise funds for soldiers' relief. One of the most notable civilian accomplishments of the war, the fair raised the astonishing sum of $1,261,822.52 for the U.S. Sanitary Commission, a civilian-operated benevolent organization devoted to easing the discomfort of Union soldiers in the field and in hospitals. Such charities were integral to Pennsylvania's war effort in 1864–1865.

from behind the wall and made most of them prisoners. Pickett's Charge had failed, and with that failure Robert E. Lee lost his offensive punch; from that time onward he could only parry the blows delivered by the Federals. The Confederate bid for independence reached its high-water mark and receded. Pennsylvania valor had won the day for the Union—on Pennsyl-vania soil.[14]

The price to defeat Lee was steep. The Philadelphia Brigade, most responsible for the repulse of the charge on the third day, lost 418 men out of 862 present for duty, a staggering 49 percent casualty rate. Total Pennsylvania casualties at Gettysburg are difficult to calculate without a methodical check of every regiment's reported losses, but like Antietam, had to compose a significant percentage of the Union army's overall killed, wounded, and missing since the Keystone had the highest number of soldiers engaged in the battle after New York. Likely losses amounted to well over four thousand souls, the majority of whom were wounded, but a percentage of whom would perish after the battle from their injuries. A smaller number, amounting in the hundreds, were taken prisoner and experienced the humiliation of being marched south from their native state where their army had won a victory. One entire company of the Sixty-Ninth, for instance, was captured at the stone wall in front of the copse of trees and sent under guard back to Seminary Ridge. The feelings those men must have felt can only be imagined.[15]

BEYOND PENNSYLVANIA: DETERMINATION, DESTRUCTION, TRIUMPH, 1864–1865

After Gettysburg the fighting in the Eastern Theater shifted back to Virginia, where almost two more years of horrific casualties would ensue in some of the war's bloodiest battles: the Wilderness and Spotsylvania (May 1864), just to the west and southwest of Fredericksburg; the North Anna and Cold Harbor (May–June 1864), north of Richmond; the relentless siege of Petersburg (June 1864–April 1865); and finally Appomattox and Lee's surrender (April 1865). More Pennsylvanians fell in this last phase of the Civil War than in its first years, due mainly to the new military strategy created by Abraham Lincoln and his new general-in-chief, Ulysses S. Grant, whom the president brought east after his victory at Chattanooga. The strategy called for "simultaneous advances" all across the rebellious states, in order to place insurmountable pressure on Confederate resources and armies. Sherman's March to the Sea was part of this overall strategy, and only this Western army met with general success. Everywhere else the rebel forces succeeded, either through their own determination or Union bungling, in stalemating the Federals until early 1865.

In the end, Grant's plan worked because of Sherman's progress and his own supervision of the Army of the Potomac in its relentless "Overland Campaign" in Virginia that ground down Lee's army in the aforementioned battles. But those engagements could hardly be called "victories," as the Union army lost over 60,000 troops in that process of grinding Lee down. The rebel commander tactically won at the Wilderness, North Anna, and Cold Harbor, and fought Grant to a bloody draw at Spotsylvania and at Petersburg until the very conclusion of the siege. Grant, who permitted Meade to remain in operational control of the Army of the Potomac, realized that the numerical calculus of men, money, and materials, coupled with increasing Federal military competence, would ultimately result in final Northern victory. It was an accurate but brutal analysis. The Pennsylvania three-year regiments raised in 1861, such as the 51st, 56th, 74th, and 75th Infantries, the Philadelphia Brigade units, and the brave Reserve regiments—each filled with the enthusiastic patriots who responded to their country's call for aid—were all but destroyed by the time Grant's strategy had succeeded on April 9, 1865, at Appomattox Court House.

The Army of the Potomac that witnessed the surrender of the Army of Northern Virginia in that small village was a new army, composed primarily of regiments raised from 1862 onward in subsequent calls for volunteers, men who still felt a need to preserve the Union but also joined to avoid being drafted and often received large bounties from their states and localities for doing so. By 1865 small but viable segments of all the Federal armies were likewise composed of drafted men and substitutes hired by those drafted who could afford the commutation fee. Yet the valor of those Keystoners who fought in the war's last campaigns should not be diminished by these facts. It was just as sacrificial, just as significant as those who fought earlier, and demonstrates the perseverance of Pennsylvanians' devotion to seeing the war out to the end. Among these soldiers were the Commonwealth's black troops, proud members of the newly raised USCT regiments. Without them, it is possible Grant's strategy may have been stymied, or even failed. By the end of the war, 12 percent of all Union soldiers had been African American. Without their participation, the Union may simply have not had enough men at critical junctures late in the war, especially in the East.[16]

Camp William Penn, in northern Montgomery County just eight miles outside of Philadelphia, was one of the North's major training camps for the USCT regiments. Eleven regiments marched out of its gates in 1863 alone, only months after the Federal government authorized the enlistment of black troops following the Emancipation Proclamation. Many more would follow, and although not all the regiments trained there were composed of Pennsylvanians, a good percentage of them were. One of them was the Forty-Third USCT, composed of black men (and white officers, which was required army policy) from all over the Commonwealth but primarily from Philadelphia. It and its sister USCT regiments in the First Brigade, First Division of the Ninth Corps, under the command of the politically resuscitated Ambrose Burnside, were among the first black regiments to join the Army of the Potomac as it pounded against Lee in the Overland Campaign of May–June 1864. Serving as the army's rearguard and protecting its vast wagon train during that campaign prevented the 43rd from engaging in direct combat with the enemy—something some of the troops complained about—but the staggering casualties among white soldiers obliged Grant and Meade to permit the limited use of Burnside's USCT regiments in operations around Petersburg. On the way there, the men of the 43rd rejoiced at the opportunity of emancipating slaves by their very presence. Commissary Sergeant John C. Brock, a native of Carlisle, wrote the editor of Philadelphia's *Christian Recorder* on June 5 that "we have been instrumental in liberating some five hundred of our sisters and brethren from the accursed yoke of human bondage. The slaves come flocking to us from every part of the country. You see them coming in every direction, some in carts, some on their masters' horses, and great numbers on foot, carrying their bundles on their heads. They manifest their love for liberty by every possible emotion. . . . What a glorious prospect it is to behold this glorious army of black men as they march with martial tread across the sacred soil of Virginia!"[17]

By July 1864 the men of the 43rd had not yet seen more than minor skirmishes, still "shoulder[ing] their shovels and picks merrily every day. . . [going] out front to the trenches,

A wartime photograph of Camp William Penn. Located in Cheltenham Township outside of Philadelphia, the camp was constructed in 1863 to train African American soldiers to serve in the Union army. The camp trained more than 11,000 free blacks and escaped slaves, including nearly 9,000 recruited in Pennsylvania, the largest number of any northern state.

ready and willing to do everything in their power that will lead to the capture and overthrow of the rebel stronghold." The daily routine of trench construction came to an abrupt end on July 30, however, when the regiment and several other USCT units participated in the bloody attack on the "Crater," a huge hole blown in the Confederate defensive works by erstwhile white coal miners in the 48th Pennsylvania Infantry. At the last minute, Burnside's specially trained black troops were disallowed by Meade from exploiting the breakthrough (for fear of public backlash about "sacrificing" black soldiers as cannon fodder) and white troops sent in their place. The result was a debacle for Federal arms and Pennsyl-vania. Not only were several white regiments, including the Second Pro-

visional Heavy Artillery, 45th, 50th, 51st, and 100th Infantries mauled in the botched assault, but so were most of the black regiments who were belatedly ordered in after the untrained white brigades had failed. The 43rd suffered only forty-seven total casualties but the USCT division to which it was attached lost a total of 1,327 men out of 4,500 engaged. One surviving white officer lamented to a friend, "I felt like sitting down and weeping on account of our misfortune." Grant himself was crestfallen, writing shortly afterward, "It was the saddest affair I have witnessed in this war."[18]

After licking their wounds, the USCT regiments in the Army of the Potomac, joined by those in the Army of the James that had marched up the Virginia Peninsula from Fortress

Monroe, were itching for another shot at the rebels. On September 24, at New Market Heights, on the eastern side of Richmond's defenses, they got their chance. The Philadelphia-raised 6th and 22nd USCT regiments participated in this bloody attack, the brainchild of the abolitionist politician turned major general Benjamin F. Butler. Butler knew Grant was determined to break into Richmond and came up with a plan to showcase the fighting power of his African American troops in what he hoped might be the climactic (and concluding) chapter of the Petersburg siege. At dawn on September 24, Brigadier General Charles Paine's USCT division moved out from the shelter of neighboring woods, the morning air crisp and fog-ridden, the men alert, breakfasted, and ready to fight. Paine was to be supported by other, white divisions, but inexplicable delays and miscommunications held them up. As the sun began to rise, the USCT division attacked, but again coordination proved problematic. The 4th and the 6th went in alone, the other regiments bogged down in swampy terrain. The defending Confederates of the famous Texas Brigade were not surprised by the Unionists' sudden appearance, and waited, rifles cocked, neighboring artillery primed. The result was utter slaughter for the Philadelphians, who lost 62 percent of their men in this initial attack. One sergeant, who won the Medal of Honor that day (one of fourteen awarded to black soldiers in the battle), wrote in his diary, "When the charge was started, our Color guard

was full; two sergeants and ten corporals. Only one of the twelve came off that field on his own feet. Most of them are there still. . . . It was a deadly hailstorm of bullets sweeping men down as hail-stones sweep the leaves from trees. . . . It was very evident that there was too much work cut out for our two regiments. . . . We struggled through two lines of abatis, a few getting through the palisades, but it was sheer madness." As the remaining USCT brigades emerged out of the swampy terrain, they, too, were sent in piecemeal because of where and when they came out, the Union commanders becoming desperate to redeem something from the carnage. They also suffered catastrophically, some of the men forced to surrender after they were trapped in a swale directly below the rebel ramparts. Yet, the Southern fire seemed to slacken, and suddenly a few companies gained the enemy trenches and found most of the Confederates gone. Lee had ordered his defenders to pull back to a second line of defense in case this attack was simply the first wave of a grander assault. Thus, Pennsylvania's African American sons could finally claim a substantial victory, but the cost had been enormous: the 6th had suffered 209 casualties out of 377 men engaged; and the division, 842 casualties total, with a high percentage of those killed. General Butler wrote Secretary of War Edwin Stanton, "My colored troops under General Paine . . . carried entrenchments at the point of a bayonet. . . . It was most gallantly done, with most severe loss. Their praises are in the mouth of every officer in this army. Treated fairly and disciplined, they have fought most heroically." Even more reflective of the 6th's and 22nd's courage was a pithy observation from one of their enemies in the Texas Brigade, who claimed, "In my opinion, no troops up to that time had fought us with more bravery than did those Negroes."[19]

Robert E. Lee, his army now tied-down to the defenses of Petersburg and Richmond with bleak prospects for final victory, had little time to cogitate on the deeper meaning of the Battle of New Market Heights. Instead, he dwelled on opportunities to "strike those people a blow," as he put it, in hopes of influencing the upcoming Federal presidential election. Southern hopes now hung on the defeat of Lincoln in November 1864; if the Northern Democrats could elect their candidate, former commander of the Army of the Potomac George B. McClellan, there was a fair chance of negotiating at least an armistice with the North. To get McClellan into the White House, Lee and the Confederacy needed victories to demoralize the Northern people and make them lose hope that the Republicans could preserve the Union. To that end, and in order to restore the recently raided Shenandoah Valley to rebel control (from which many of Lee's supplies emanated), the rebel chieftain dispatched General Jubal A. Early and 18,000 men to the valley with orders to safeguard that "Breadbasket of the Confederacy" and, if possible, push into Maryland and Pennsylvania and

threaten Washington, D.C. Early's campaign met with considerable initial success, his small army winning several minor engagements, redeeming the Shenandoah Valley, and marching to the doorstep of the Union capital at Fort Stevens, where it engaged Union defenders and then wisely pulled back. Grant was so concerned he sent the better part of two corps from his army at Petersburg to defend Washington. On the way back to the Shenandoah, pursued now by several angry Federal corps, Early unleashed his cavalry for a raid into Pennsylvania.

Chambersburg had been occupied briefly by the Confederates twice before. In mid-October 1862, following the Battle of Antietam, J. E. B. Stuart's cavalry swept across the Potomac River, through Maryland, and into the Franklin County seat in a stunt designed to knock Northern public opinion and the Army of the Potomac off balance. It temporarily worked, but soon southern Pennsylvanians relaxed in the knowledge that the enemy army was deep in Virginia again, the only damage done to Chambersburg being the loss of some Pennsylvania Railroad property, army stores, and unpaid-for commercial merchandise. The rebels returned again in force in late June 1863 and stayed for the better part of two weeks, picking local farms and merchants clean, but again not purposefully destroying private property. On July 30, 1864, Brigadier General John McCausland's two cavalry brigades struck, bent on revenge for the burning of parts of Lexington, Virginia, a few months earlier, including the venerable Virginia Military Institute. Early had given McCausland orders to demand $500,000 in Federal currency or $100,000 in gold as ransom money. If the town fathers failed to come up with the required amount, he was to burn the town.[20]

About half past five in the morning the rebels posted six pieces of artillery on hills overlooking the sleeping town and then rode into it as a body, immediately demanding the ransom from the abruptly awakened residents. Rubbing their eyes in disbelief, a few leading citizens legitimately claimed the town had no such amount of money. McCausland's men then commenced two hours of looting, taking what they wanted from the townspeople without offering compensation. At nine o'clock the cavalry leader ordered the torch applied, to the glee of some of his subordinates. Lieutenant Fielder C. Slingluff recalled, "We had come to the conclusion that it was time for us to burn something in the enemy's country." Early, learning of the deed later, exclaimed, "it was time to open the eyes of the North." Fleeing his burning home with his family, storekeeper Jacob Hoke, a pacifist Dunker, turned around outside town and saw "four hundred buildings in flames, two hundred and seventy-four of which were dwelling houses, the affrighted occupants running wildly through the streets, carrying clothing and other articles, while screams of anguish from lost children in pursuit of their parents, the feeble efforts of the old and infirm to carry with them

On July 30, 1864, Confederate brigadier general John McCausland and his cavalry raided Chambersburg, Pennsylvania, setting parts of the town on fire. The photograph at top shows the ruins of the Bank of Chambersburg, while the one below reveals the destruction along Main Street. It took decades for the town to rebuild.

some endeared article from their blazing homes, the roaring and crackling flames, falling walls and blinding smoke, all united to form a picture of horror." Bookseller John K. Shryock wrote the Philadelphia *Lutheran and*

Missionary a detailed account of the burning, claiming "the conduct of the rebel soldiery was barbarous in the extreme, though there were many honorable exceptions. Bundles were fired upon women's backs; ladies were forced to carry back into the houses articles of clothing they had saved from the flames; drunken wretches danced upon the furniture and articles of value and ornament." He added, "everything was done to add to the terror of the panic-stricken women and children." Rachel Cormany was shocked at the aftermath, writing in her diary, "The whole heart of the town is burned. They gave no time for people to get anything out." With the fires still raging, and alerted that tardy Union cavalry was on the way, McCausland and his troopers departed. It was the end of the last Confederate incursion in Pennsylvania.[21]

It took Chambersburg thirty years to fully rebuild, and in many cases the new structures were shoddily built compared to the old ones that burned. In all, 559 buildings were lost, amounting to over $783,950 in real-estate damages alone. Yet the spirit for revenge or for giving up, either personally or politically, was absent among most Chambersburg residents. The Reverend T. G. Apple preached to a local congregation the day after the fire, astonished to witness "such resignation, such quiet, gentle submission, and such calm endurance, amid the loss of all things, as in this instance." Regarding "the feeling of revenge, so natural to the human heart, I have been gratifyingly

disappointed," Apple added. The large numbers of pacificist Mennonites and Dunkers in the area, and the influence they doubtless had on neighboring Lutherans and German Reformed congregations, probably had much to do with this remarkable reaction.[22]

McCausland was relentlessly pursued by Union cavalry, and his command ultimately paid a high price a few weeks later at the Battle of Moorefield, in modern West Virginia. Jubal Early's small army was also forced back down the Shenandoah Valley and decisively defeated by Major General Philip Sheridan in a series of battles, most notably at Cedar Creek, near Strasburg, Virginia, in October, in which more than twenty Pennsylvania infantry, artillery, and cavalry regiments participated. Sheridan's Army of the Shenandoah would now lay waste to the valley, depriving Lee of one of the very last regions to supply his dwindling army. His gamble to influence northern voting in the 1864 election had failed. The refusal of a majority of Pennsylvanians to be intimidated by the destruction of Chambersburg, coupled with heartening military victories such as Cedar Creek and the capture of Atlanta, Georgia, in September, ensured that Abraham Lincoln would not only win Pennsylvania's electoral votes but also the majority of those across the Northern states. It had been close in the Keystone, however, the president only winning by 20,000 votes, two-thirds of which were soldiers' absentee ballots. With his reelection, the

"A thrilling incident during voting,—18th Ward, Philadelphia, Oct. 11." An 1864 anti-Copperhead print depicting an elderly Jacksonian Democrat condemning a Copperhead poll worker and his support of reconcilliation with the Confederacy. The older man, who has lost a son in the war, exclaims, "Do you expect me to dishonor my poor boy's memory, and vote for men who charge American soldiers, fighting for their country, with being hirelings and murderers?"

fate of the Confederacy was sealed. The Civil War would be won by the Union.[23]

Not all in the Keystone State rejoiced at his reelection, a fact evidenced by the close results at the polls. Franklin County, for instance, despite the observations of Reverend Apple, would have gone Democratic but for the soldiers' votes. The border counties of Adams, York, Cumberland, and Fulton all turned in majorities for McClellan, as did most of the counties in the northeast and central regions of the state. War weariness, dissatisfaction with intrusive federal policies such as the draft, ethnic perceptions of resurgent nativism among the Republicans, and outright "Copperheadism"—Southern sympathy—were the culprits. If Lincoln

had not been convinced at the last minute by Republican Party stalwart and Chambersburg native Alexander McClure (whose home had been burned) to furlough 10,000 Pennsylvania soldiers to come home and "lean" on their families, some historians theorize the Commonwealth as a whole may have voted Democratic by a paper-thin margin. That would not have altered the result of the national election, but would have had a profound effect on postwar Pennsylvania politics.[24]

Throughout the war, coal miners in Schuylkill and Luzerne counties, lumbermen in Clearfield and Jefferson, Pennsylvania Dutch farmers in Lehigh and Berks, and Irish immigrants in Pittsburgh and Philadelphia resisted the draft and resented emancipation. For diverse reasons, these minority populations came to believe the Republican administration in Washington had overstepped its authority with these and other measures, trampling on the Constitution and unnecessarily prolonging an unwinnable, bloody conflict. Some came to believe that big business was in league with the government, spawning a distrust of both that would linger for decades. Open or even covert Copperheadism was rare in these counties but did exist; the main threat to the Union war effort lay in obstruction of federal policies and the societal chaos that could ensue. For a short time in 1863, for instance, miners in the northeast of the state shut down coal extraction, and their wives actually assaulted provost marshals attempting to enforce the draft. In August of that year the situation became so serious that the governor permitted the organization of Schuylkill, Carbon, and Luzerne counties as a military district and Federal troops were sent in to quell the disturbances. In Berks County, draft officials were shot at along country lanes with rock salt, and African American neighborhoods in Pittsburgh and Philadelphia lived with the constant fear of urban riots—and likely violence against them—perpetrated by angry immigrants unhappy with the prospect of freed slaves coming north and taking their jobs. Even in seemingly quiescent Centre County, the recruiting ground of the stolid 49th and 148th Infantries, apathy and then vocal opposition to the war became con-

spicuous. Writing to the colonel of the 148th on March 18, 1863, a worried citizen asked if the regiment might not come home and take care of the disloyalty: "We have . . . a good many copperheads in the country that your Centre County Regiment should by all means send their respects to. Whilst you have led a thousand of our bravest young men to face the daring rebels, a . . . thousand more traitors than the rebels you are now confronting remain at home to thwart the government in all its endeavors to crush the rebellion." Such letters often pained the men in the ranks, even those who were politically Democratic, as there was little they could do to address such concerns short of desertion, but in the end it would be their deeds on the battlefield that would truly quell the anxieties of home-front Republicans. By April 1865 they had accomplished that, despite the croaking of antiwar partisans.[25]

At a small Virginia hamlet on Palm Sunday 1865, the starving but proud veterans of Lee's once formidable Army of Northern Virginia, only 28,000 strong, surrendered to the finally victorious Army of the Potomac. Present with the army at the time were eighty-nine Pennsylvania regiments or fragments of regiments.[26] Artillerists, cavalrymen, and infantrymen from every county in the Commonwealth and every walk of life imaginable—older and younger, grizzled veteran and fresh recruit—all could now proudly claim that they had served their state and their country. It had been a long, hard war, fraught with more defeat than victory, more disappointment than joy, but as the word circulated around the campfires that their enemy had finally given up, the surviving Civil War soldiers of the Commonwealth must have smiled, shook their heads in disbelief, shouted with joy, and embraced their comrades: it had all been worth it. They had won the war. They would be going home to Pennsylvania.

10. Pennsylvania and the Birth of a World Power

Barbara A. Gannon

After the Civil War, no large-scale military mobilization occurred in Pennsylvania for fifty-two years; however, in these years America began its rise to world power. Between the end of the Civil War and the beginning of World War I, some Pennsylvanians served in the small regular army or navy with great distinction, winning the Medal of Honor in many postwar skirmishes. Others joined militias or volunteer units; these organizations would evolve into the Pennsylvania National Guard. In the twentieth century, Pennsylvania's participation in the National Guard became one of the most important aspects of the state's military history. While an improvement in military readiness, the development of the National Guard made little difference in the Spanish-American War; ill-trained Pennsylvanians would again be mobilized to fight and, instead, these men died of disease, just as they had five decades earlier in Mexico. In this conflict's aftermath, the United States became an imperial power; however,

no one anticipated the challenges of the twentieth century engendered by this new status, including the Great War, the "war to end all wars."

Almost immediately after the Civil War, the great volunteer armies were demobilized and most Pennsylvanians returned home to civilian life. Some soldiers did not and these men joined the small regular United States Army or Navy. Despite the notion that this was "peacetime," the army was still fighting. In the decades after the Civil War, Native Americans fought a number of small-scale insurgencies trying to stop western settlement. Overseas, the army and the navy became involved in a number of smaller skirmishes; the United States' first steps onto the world stage included small-scale wars in places like Korea (1871), China (1900), Haiti (1915), and Mexico (1916).[1]

At home and overseas, Pennsylvanians distinguished themselves in the post–Civil War army and navy; one indicator, seventy-five Pennsylvanians won the Medal of Honor, the

Following torrential downpours, a dam above the town of Johnstown, Pennsylvania, burst on May 31, 1889, and destroyed most of the town, killing more than two thousand persons. As part of the relief effort, the Pennsylvania National Guard deployed soldiers to assist in rescue operations and maintain order in the area. Here, a post was established overlooking the devastation.

highest award for heroism bestowed by the government. This award was relatively new; it had been created during the Civil War to recognize soldiers and sailors who "shall most distinguish themselves by their gallantry in action, and other soldier-like qualities." Since the Civil War, Pennsylvanians have received more than 10 percent of the medals awarded, second only to New York, which has the highest percentage of medals awarded to an individual state.[2]

Some of these medals were awarded for heroism in the decades between the Civil War and World War I, some in well-known actions. Henry W. Mechlin served as a blacksmith in the Seventh U.S. Cavalry. Born in Mount Pleasant, Westmoreland County, Pennsylvania, he survived the ill-fated regiment's campaign that ended at the Little Big Horn. He received his award because he and three other soldiers "courageously held a position that secured water for the command." African Americans also served in the peacetime regular army; the army had four black regiments, the 9th and 10th Cavalry and the 24th and 25th Infantry. Pennsylvanian Benjamin Brown served as a sergeant in the 24th Infantry; his citation was more specific than most other awards from this era; perhaps, an African American needed to demonstrate more than simple "gallantry." According to his award, "although [he was] shot in the abdomen, in a fight between a paymaster's escort and robbers, [he] did not leave the field until again wounded through both arms." Pennsylvanians served with distinction in the navy. In 1871, John Andrews of York, Pennsylvania, and his shipmates responded to the sinking of an American ship and the murder of

U.S. citizens in Korea. According to his citation, he served "on board the U.S.S. *Benicia* in action against Korean forts on 9 and 10 June 1871"; specifically, "stationed at the lead in passing the forts, Andrews stood on the gunwale on the *Benicia*'s launch, lashed to the ridgerope. He remained unflinchingly in this dangerous position and gave his soundings with coolness and accuracy under a heavy fire."[3]

While winning the Medal of Honor makes you exceptional, one Pennsylvanian was awarded it twice. Smedley D. Butler of West Chester, Pennsylvania, began his Marine Corps service at sixteen in the Spanish-American War. While he did not see combat in Cuba, he did serve in other overseas operations. He was wounded twice during the Boxer Rebellion in China when the United States joined other Western nations to suppress the Boxers, an organization that targeted Westerners and Christian Chinese. He also participated in a number of small actions in Central America, specifically Honduras and Nicaragua. In 1914, as Europe descended into madness, the United State fought small-scale incursions overseas; the United States occupied Vera Cruz, Mexico; in 1915, U.S. forces were engaged in Haiti. Butler received his first medal for his performance in Vera Cruz for "courage and skill in leading his men." His citation for action in Haiti is more specific:

Following a concentrated drive, several different detachments of marines gradually closed in on the old French

Smedley D. Butler (1881–1940), from West Chester, Pennsylvania, served in the Marine Corps for thirty-four years and was awarded the Medal of Honor two times for valor. He retired as a major general.

bastion fort in an effort to cut off all avenues of retreat for the [enemy]. Reaching the fort on the southern side where there was a small opening in the wall, Maj. Butler gave the signal to attack and marines . . . poured through the breach, engaged the [enemy] in hand-to-hand combat, took the bastion and crushed the [enemy's] resistance. Throughout this perilous action, Maj. Butler was conspicuous for his bravery and forceful leadership.

He finished his service as a major general and was a well-known advocate for veterans' interests. Ironically, later in life, Butler would oppose small wars that led to the soldiers' deaths merely to defend business interests.[4]

Pennsylvanians did not need to leave home in this era to defend commerce. Instead, they could serve in the

Pennsylvania National Guard. The militia had played only a small role during the Civil War; instead, the army relied on volunteer units. When the war ended, militia funding dropped precipitously. In 1870, Pennsylvania officials decided to reorganize and reinvigorate the militia and created a National Guard composed of volunteers, though men who did not join were subject to a special tax.[5]

While today the National Guard is best known for disaster relief or its wartime service, in this era, one of its primary purposes was responding to labor unrest and strikes. Nineteenth-century labor unions had emerged as one way to improve wages and working conditions. These organizations were sorely needed after a financial panic and depression in the 1870s led to higher unemployment and lower wages. In 1877, labor unions led a series of strikes to address workers' desperate conditions. The largest of these actions started as a railroad strike against the Pennsylvania Railroad Company, which had increased employees' workloads and cut their pay. It quickly spread to a number of industries around the country. Fairly quickly, these labor stoppages became violent; Pennsylvania experienced some of the bloodiest incidents. While union members were responsible for some violence, business owners and their employees killed and injured workers.[6]

Initially, business owners tried to use local police to fight strikers; often these men refused to open fire on their neighbors. In response, industri-

Governor Robert E. Pattison authorized Pennsylvania State Militia to take control of Homestead and its local Carnegie Steel Works that was currently under the control of pro-trade union workers who had gone on strike. The militia arrived on July 12, 1892, and quickly seized control of the steel plant. It would be another four decades before the government would recognize trade unions.

alists asked the governor to call the militia into service. In some cases, the militia refused to fire on strikers. In response, militia units were transferred to other locations. The Philadelphia militia was sent to Pittsburgh to deal with strikers who blocked the railroad tracks. When these Philadelphians tried to clear the obstructions, the crowd attacked with stones, coal, and other objects. Someone, no one knows who, fired a pistol. In response, the militia fired and approximately twenty citizens were killed. After, this incident, the rampaging crowd destroyed property both at the rail yards and in other parts of the city. The mob cornered the militiamen and only the use of Gatling guns stopped them from being overrun, though four militiamen were killed. The violence spread to Reading, where militiamen shot and killed eleven citizens.[7]

As a result of this new role, businessmen supported the Pennsylvania National Guard in this era. Once again, as they had in the antebellum era, middle-class men and the elites joined local military units; one reason for their enthusiastic service was fear of communism. According to one contemporary account describing the critical role played by Scranton militia in suppressing labor, "the infamous tenets of communism began to be discussed in the shops ... and their announcements were now and then heard as an ominous rumble on the public streets, portending the social earthquake, by which the social foundation should be removed, leaving no standing place for the righteous." Regardless of the reasons for these riots, the participation of the National Guard in suppressing labor unions meant that the National Guard's peacetime domestic role had the support of social elites during the decades after the Civil War.[8]

Breaking up strikes did little to prepare the Pennsylvania National Guard for its next great challenge, the Spanish-American War. The United States and Spain had long been at odds over remnants of the Spanish Empire in the New World. Native-born Cubans had revolted against colonial rule and the Spanish government had taken a number of harsh measures to squash this revolt. Many Americans objected to this cruel treatment and wanted the government to punish Spain. In February 1898, the battleship USS *Maine* sank after an explosion in Havana Harbor. While Americans believed that Spanish officials had blown up the ship, most experts believe it was an accident. When efforts to mediate this dispute failed, the United States declared war on Spain. The United States attacked the Spanish Empire, specifically, Cuba, Puerto Rico, and the Philippines.[9]

After war was declared, the entire National Guard, including Pennsylvania, was mobilized; however, the law did not permit these reservists to be federalized for overseas service. Instead, after going to camps, these men were asked to enlist as federal volunteers, and many of them did so. Overall, more than 700 officers and almost 17,000 enlisted men volunteered, serving in fourteen infantry regiments, three field artillery batteries, and three troops of cavalry. Only some of these men served overseas; most either remained in training camps or guarded facilities at home. Service at home may seem to be safe duty; however, in this war disease killed more than combat. Camp Thomas, at the Chickamauga, Tennessee, Civil War battlefield, was particularly notorious because so many soldiers suffered and died in training. Overall, sixteen Pennsylvanians were killed in action or died of wounds, seventy-four were wounded and survived; however, like most American soldiers in this war, the majority of deaths resulted from disease (226) and other causes, including accidents (7).[10]

Some units did serve overseas. Elements of the Fourth and Sixteenth Pennsylvania Infantry, the First Troop Philadelphia City Cavalry, and some Pennsylvania-based artillery units were sent to capture Puerto Rico from the Spanish. While most Pennsylvanians saw little action on Puerto Rico, the 16th Infantry had one major firefight that resulted in one man killed and five wounded, another Pennsylvania unit saw longer and more difficult service when it was sent to the Philippines. Arriving at the end of July 1898, the 10th Pennsylvania responded to an attack by Spanish forces and suffered eight dead and twenty-seven wounded. The campaign against the Spanish was short; after U.S. and Spanish officials agreed to a stage-managed battle to protect Spanish honor, the enemy surrendered.[11]

Unfortunately, victory over Spanish forces did not signal the end of the war. The Philippine campaign continued even after Spain signed a peace treaty with the United States in December 1898. While the Spanish agreed to give the Philippines to the United States, Philippine citizens, who had been fighting Spanish rule, did not agree to be given away. By February 1899, war had broken out between the U.S. Army and Philippine insurgents. Because the army was stretched thin—most regular army units were in Cuba—the 10th Pennsylvania remained on duty in the Philippines and participated in

the first offensive against local forces, an attack on their capital, Malolos. After a week of hard fighting, the 10th and other American forces occupied the insurgent city. During this short span, the unit suffered severe casualties; at the end of this campaign, the Tenth had only one-third of its members fit for duty—about 250 of 750. Most of these casualties resulted from disease and exhaustion; only six soldiers had been killed in action and another fifty-one wounded. Since combat operations did not end until two years after the last Pennsylvania volunteers returned home, the army recruited four more regiments in Pennsylvania—the 27th, 28th, 41st, and 47th U.S. Volunteers—to serve in this brutal struggle. Ultimately, more than 100,000 Americans served in the Philippines, a campaign that killed more than 7,000 Americans and at least 100,000 Philippine soldiers and civilians.[12]

Pennsylvanians did not always serve in their state National Guard or volunteer units; some served in the regular army, while others served in the navy and Marine Corps. Some men received the Medal of Honor for valor; overall, seventeen Pennsylvanians were awarded the medal for service in the Spanish-American War and the Philippine-American War. The actions of Philip Gaughan, a Pennsylvanian and marine, were recorded on his citation for his medal: "On board the U.S.S. *Nashville* during the operation of cutting the cable leading from Cienfuegos, Cuba, 11 May 1898 [and] facing the heavy fire of the enemy, Gaughan set an example of extraordinary bravery and coolness throughout this action." Sailors also received recognition. Pennsylvanian Peter Johnson was "on board the U.S.S. *Vixen* on the night of 28 May 1898. Following the explosion of the lower front manhole gasket of boiler A of the vessel, Johnson displayed great coolness and self-possession in entering the fireroom." Pittsburgh native Louis Gedeon served in a regular army unit in the Philippines and received his medal after he, "singlehanded, defended his mortally wounded captain from an overwhelming force of the enemy."[13]

While Pennsylvanians were proud of their citizens who fought with volunteer units, or in the regular army, navy, and Marine Corps, they were, like other Americans, concerned with the war's toll and frustrated by the deaths of so many soldiers at home in training camps. In the immediate aftermath of the war, the new secretary of war Elihu Root instituted a number of reforms to improve military preparedness. One of the organizations created was the United States Army Reserve, an organization that would later allow the army to enhance its medical capability in time of war. While the National Guard performed well given its limited wartime role, many issues were identified, including the inability of the federal government to send its members overseas. An Ohio National Guardsman and congressman, Charles Dick, spearheaded laws to improve National Guard readiness: the federal government would provide pay and equipment to National Guard units; in return, these units were required to train and attend regular drill and summer camps. The National Guard was also subject to federal call-up for active service, though initially this was only for operations within U.S. borders. In 1908, even more limitations were removed from the National Guard, allowing it to better serve as the main army reserve force. Despite the importance of these reforms, nothing could really prepare Pennsylvania for its next challenge— the Great War—when Pennsylvanians mobilized all of their resources for war.[14]

11. Pennsylvania in the First War to End All Wars

Barbara A. Gannon

The United States' rise to world-power status in the twentieth century had a number of consequences. First and foremost, the United States became involved in European affairs, including World War I, which killed millions of soldiers and civilians and destroyed much of the European social and political order. Even before the United States became involved in Europe in 1917, the Pennsylvania National Guard deployed to the border in Texas, responding to a violent incursion by partisans in the Mexican Civil War. When the Pennsylvania National Guard came home from Mexico, it was immediately called to active duty in Europe. Pennsylvania contributed more than its National Guard to the fight; as part of the full mobilization of American society, hundreds of thousands of Pennsylvanians, including African Americans and women, served overseas and on the home front. While Pennsylvanians in the army and navy contributed to the war effort, civilians working in critical industries were also vital to American victory. Not all Pennsylvanians supported the war effort, however, and the government used its war powers to attack any group it considered subversive. Pennsylvanians went to jail because of their antiwar political views. When the war ended, a different political agenda shaped the postwar experience of many veterans; former soldiers joined veterans' groups, such as the American Legion and the Veterans of Foreign Wars, which advocated for veterans' benefits. The men who joined these groups may have been surprised that their sons and daughters would have to go "over there" and fight on the same battlefields, some in the same National Guard units, because the first "Great War" would not be the last.

Ironically, the reforms that followed the Spanish-American War hurt the National Guard. It was more difficult to recruit because soldiers spent more time training and frequently received little or no compensation for this additional commitment. Moreover, these reforms had an unintended side effect; in the South, states used the new law to disband black militia units. In addition, while federal assistance increased, these new resources were not enough; the state still had to fund armories (unit headquarters). In 1903, Pennsylvania allocated $407,000 to its National Guard, second only to New York State. By 1913, Pennsylvania's support of its National Guard had declined to $392,500; it ranked sixth among the states in funding. In contrast, some states, such as Massachusetts and New York, increased their support for the National Guard during this period.[1]

This is an appropriate year to examine National Guard funding, the last year of peace, before the beginning of the war in Europe. While Europe seemed far away, Americans were affected by this war; German submarines attacked ships and killed American citizens. Three months after Germany had declared unrestricted submarine warfare against Allied ships, and warned citizens of neutral nations about traveling on these ships, a U-boat attacked the RMS *Lusitania*, a British passenger liner, and killed more than one hundred Americans—men, women, and children. Among the dead were at least fifteen Pennsylvanians. Four members of a Philadelphia family were lost—mother, father, and two children, aged eight and five. After the United States government protested this action and threatened to go to war in response, the German government temporarily ended its policy of unrestricted submarine warfare.[2]

While the United States avoided war with Germany in 1915, this crisis prompted American officials to examine their military establishment. In response to the war in Europe and problems south of the border in Mexico, Congress passed the National Defense Act of 1916, which increased federal funding and strengthened federal control of the National Guard. Members of the National Guard would now take dual oaths to both the federal government and their state governments, one way around the restriction on overseas deployment of National Guard units. (In the Spanish-American War, National Guard members joined volunteer units to serve overseas.) Moreover, recruits who swore this dual oath would have to meet federal enlistment standards and train longer each year. In return, the federal government paid citizen-soldiers to attend training. While these reforms improved the Pennsylvania National Guard, they proved inadequate for the challenges facing it in World War I.[3]

Before the boys were sent "over there" to fight Germans, the U.S. government dealt with a crisis over here—the Mexican Civil War. This was not the first or only Mexican civil war. During the U.S. Civil War, Mexicans had their own internecine conflict, which was, in many ways, much more brutal than its northern counterpart. In 1910, Mexicans were once again at war. Initially, this was purely an internal matter, insurgents attempting to overthrow the government. The United States first became involved in 1914 when military and naval forces occupied Vera Cruz, in response to the presence of a German ship, which had been arming the Mexican government. Smedley Butler won his first Medal of Honor in this action. As a result of American intervention, the Mexican government fell and its leader was sent into exile. Though the rebels won, they started to fight among themselves; Pancho Villa controlled one of the rebel factions. In response to American support for his rival, Villa's men attacked a town in New Mexico and killed American soldiers and civilians. In retaliation, President Woodrow Wilson ordered General John Pershing, who would later command the American forces in Europe, to lead a punitive expedition into Mexico.[4]

With the regular army chasing Villa, Wilson called up the entire National Guard, including the Pennsylvania National Guard, to protect the U.S. border. Overall, about 158,000 National Guardsmen served on the Rio Grande during this campaign. The Pennsylvania National Guard was called into service and served as the 7th Division; approximately 15,000 Pennsylvanians were stationed at El Paso, Texas. While the National Guard was likely better in 1916 than it had been in 1898, it had not yet benefited from the reforms of the National Defense Act of 1916, passed two weeks before the president called units into federal service. Overall, this mobilization did not go well. It took six weeks from the call-up on June 18, 1916, until the Pennsylvania Guard arrived at the border on July 25. This operation

The 28th Infantry Division arriving in France in May 1918.

revealed some of the shortcomings of National Guard reform. Many National Guardsmen believed that they were only volunteers in state service and rejected a mandatory federal call-up. Regulars, who worked with the National Guard observed the level of training in these units and decided that all of the money spent to reform the National Guard had been wasted. National Guardsmen resented border service: they had hoped for a quick war with Mexico that ended in victory; instead, they guarded the border and trained. To many of these men, the mission of protecting the border was not worth being taken away from their civilian pursuits and families. Eventually, the crisis passed, and the Pennsylvania National Guard returned from Mexico in early 1917, a few short months before the United States declared war on Germany.[5]

Despite misgivings about their performance on the border, the National Guard would play a critical role in World War I, though Pennsylvanians would also serve in other military units. The army in World War I was composed of three different types of combat divisions. First, the army created regular army divisions, built from preexisting regular units augmented by new recruits. Second, it called National Guard divisions to active duty. Finally, new divisions were built from scratch using volunteers and draftees as part of the national army. While these were initially organized as distinct organizations, eventually all of these units were considered divisions in the United States Army.[6]

While many served in regular and national army divisions, Pennsylvanians' most famous contribution to the war effort was the 28th Infantry Division, their National Guard unit; it became one of the hardest fighting and distinguished units in the U.S. Army. The Pennsylvania National Guard had always been designated a "division," but this was not a division in the modern sense. The modern division—a military unit composed of combat and supporting elements that operates independently—was a product of World War I. A comparison of the 7th Division, the Pennsylvania National Guard division on the Mexican Border, and the 28th Infantry Division shows how the Great War changed the National Guard. The 28th Infantry Division added machine gun battalions to its infantry brigades; a trench mortar battalion had been added to the artillery brigade. The organization of the division changed as did its leadership; the division commander, a National Guard officer, was relieved for medical reasons. National Guard division commanders were often replaced by regular army officers

before overseas deployment. All of these changes delayed the 28th's deployment overseas; ten months after mobilization, the division sailed to Europe.[7]

By the time Pennsylvanians arrived in Europe, the war had been in a virtual stalemate for almost four years. The overwhelming firepower of World War I armies created by the proliferation of machine guns, combined with the relatively limited speed of ground forces moving mostly on foot, meant that forward, offensive movements incurred heavy casualties. The advent of chemical warfare, such as the use of mustard gas, made the experience of combat even worse for soldiers. Just before most U.S. forces arrived in the summer of 1918, the German army went on the offensive in an attempt to break the stalemate caused by these developments. Two factors made this offensive possible. First, the German army was able to move forces from the east because of the Russian Revolution, which led to the withdrawal of Russia from the war. Second, German officials formulated a new style of attack that emphasized using elite forces to infiltrate the enemy's line under an artillery barrage, attacking at weak points in the line, and bypassing stronger positions. Using these new tactics in the spring and early summer of 1918, the German army advanced in a number of places on what had been a stagnant front line. Once again, as they had in 1914, Germans threatened Paris. While some U.S. Army units helped stop these advances, most American sol-

Soldiers of the 28th Division and some French Poilus rest upon a German dugout recently captured in the Argonne. The battle lasted until the armistice on November 11, 1918.

diers went into action after the Allies stopped the Germany army's offensive and participated in Allied counteroffensives.[8]

The 28th Infantry Division's Pennsylvanians fought in these critical campaigns; by the end of the war, this unit had sustained among the highest casualties of any National Guard division—14,000 dead, wounded, and missing. This record may explain the 28th's nickname, the Iron Division. General Pershing, the commander of the American Expedition-ary Force, was purported to say about its members, "you are not soldiers, you are men of iron." The Iron Division participated in three major campaigns including the Aisne-Marne offensive and the battle at Château-Thierry. Similarly, Pennsylv-anians served in national army divisions, including the

79th and 80th Infantry Divisions. The 80th Division arrived in France in June, and the 79th in August. All three units served in the American Expeditionary Force, the American army in France, arriving in time to fight in the final battles of the war. The 80th fought in the Saint-Mihiel Campaign, the largest operation solely fought by U.S. forces. Later all three units fought in the last great offensive of the war—the Meuse-Argonne Campaign—the most deadly battle ever fought by the U.S. Army. Over 1.2 million Americans fought in this campaign that produced half of the total casualties experienced by the American Expeditionary Force. By the end of this campaign, German officials realized that they could not continue the fight. It was the arrival of fresh, though inexperienced,

American soldiers that turned the tide against the German army and led to the armistice on November 11, 1918.[9]

One of these Pennsylvanians left behind a memoir of his service. Lieutenant Hervey Allen of the 28th Infantry Division described the utter horror of war on the western front in one of the best-known American memoirs of World War I—*Toward the Flame*. While this represents the experience of one officer in one unit, it reflects the experience of many American soldiers. Allen describes a German artillery barrage and how he and fellow soldiers survived the attack. "To be shelled is the worst thing in the world. It is impossible to imagine it adequately. In absolute darkness we simply lay and trembled from sheer nervous tension." He explains what happens when the shells hit their target. "We pulled out men that were smothered in the dirt; some were cut in pieces by the shell fragments and came apart when we pulled them out of the bank. Lieutenant Quinn, a Pittsburgh boy, who had just got his commission a week before, was so mixed with the two men who had lain nearest to him that I do not know yet whether we got things just right." The memoir abruptly ends when his unit is attacked by Germans with flame-throwers and overrun. He survived his injuries and lived to tell the story of Pennsylvanians at war.[10]

Pennsylvanians served in other capacities, including the newest military branch, the Air Service. Some of these men became aces, shooting down more than five enemy aircraft.

An 80th Division machine gun position near the Meuse River in 1918.

Philadelphian Charles Biddle, a graduate of Princeton and Harvard Law, left his practice and joined the French air force; he later flew in the American Air Service. He was recognized by the United States, France, and Belgium for his service. Though wounded, he survived the war and returned to practice law in Pennsylvania.[11]

The war at sea was often as brutal as the war on land. Pennsylvanian Oscar Schmidt was awarded the Medal of Honor for

gallant conduct and extraordinary heroism while attached to the U.S.S. *Chestnut Hill*, on the occasion of the explosion and subsequent fire on board the U.S. submarine chaser 219. Schmidt, seeing a man, whose legs were partly blown off, hanging on a line from the bow of the 219, jumped overboard, swam to the sub chaser and carried him from the bow to the stern where a member of the 219's crew helped him land the man on the afterdeck of the submarine. Schmidt then endeavored to pass through the flames amidships to get another man who was seriously burned. This he was unable to do, but when the injured man fell overboard and drifted to the stern of the chaser Schmidt helped him aboard.

Oscar Schmidt, left, of Philadelphia was awarded the Medal of Honor for rescuing seamen aboard a burning submarine chaser. Alice Weld Tallant, center, professor at the Woman's Medical College of Pennsylvania, was awarded the Croix de Guerre for her medical work in France. Philadelphian Loretta Walsh, right, was the very first woman to enlist in the United States Navy, and the first woman to join any service in any capacity other than a nurse.

Two Pennsylvanians who served as navy medical personnel also received the nation's highest honor for saving lives in World War I. Joel Thompson Boon was recognized for service with the U.S. Marine Corps. (The U.S. Marine Corps uses navy personnel to meet its medical needs.)

With absolute disregard for personal safety, ever conscious and mindful of the suffering fallen, Surg[eon] Boone, leaving the shelter of a ravine, went forward onto the open field where there was no protection and despite the extreme enemy fire of all calibers, through a heavy mist of gas, applied dressings and first aid to wounded marines. . . . When the dressings and supplies had been exhausted, he went through a heavy barrage of large-caliber shells, both high explosive and gas, to replenish these supplies, returning quickly with a sidecar load, and administered them in saving the lives of the wounded. A second trip, under the same conditions and for the same pur-

pose, was made by Surg. Boone later that day.

Philadelphian Orlando Henderson Petty was cited for similar actions while serving with another navy medical unit in Europe.[12]

The need for medical services allowed women to serve. Pennsylvania contributed a number of hospitals to the war effort; Philadelphians organized four of these units and women served as doctors and nurses in these hospitals. Dr. Alice Weld Tallant, a professor of obstetrics at the Woman's Medical College of Pennsylvania (now the Medical College of Pennsylvania), served in France and was awarded the Croix de Guerre for her work in a French hospital. Helen Fairchild, a nurse from Milton, Pennsylvania, died while serving in one of these hospitals and was buried with full military honors. One of the handful of women wounded in combat, Isabelle Stambaugh of Philadelphia received the Distinguished Service Cross for her work under fire in a British hospital. Two women were awarded the Navy Cross posthumously for their service at the Philadelphia Naval Hospital during the flu pandemic.[13]

Women served in other capacities. The very first woman to enlist in the United States Navy was born in Philadelphia; Loretta Walsh was the first woman to join any service in any capacity other than a nurse. Women in the World War I navy served as yeomen (F), nicknamed "yeomanettes," and provided primarily clerical services. Walsh achieved the rank of chief yeoman, a navy petty officer, the first woman to serve as a noncommissioned officer in any service. At least 11,000 women served in this capacity; one postwar history estimated that at least 2,000 Philadelphians served as yeomen; some died due to disease and accidents. Philadelphians served as women marines, assisting with recruiting and clerical work. The service and sacrifice of Fairchild, Walsh, and other Pennsylvanians represented major milestones on the road to gender-based equality in the armed services.[14]

While women in the navy might represent progress, the record for African American Pennsylvanians was more mixed. All of these men served in segregated units; some black soldiers served in combat organizations, others in support units. While these men were not allowed to serve in white divisions, they served in the mostly African American 92nd and

An African American unit digging a trench in France to bury American soldiers killed during the Meuse-Argonne Campaign and Belleau Wood.

93rd Divisions. One regiment, the 368th Infantry of the 92nd Division included black draftees from Pennsylvania. Despite virulent racism and poor equipment and training, this unit was credited with capturing a French city, Binarville, in the last week of the war. African Americans served as officers in these units and some of these men were Pennsylvanians. Many black Pennsylvanians belonged to support units, including the 813th Pioneer Infantry. These men had a difficult task after the war; they reinterred American dead who fell in the Meuse-Argonne Campaign and at Belleau Wood. Overall, almost 6,000 Pennsylvanians, black and white, men and women, died in World War I; overall, the state suffered almost 30,000 casualties.[15]

While Pennsylvanians' efforts on the front line were critical, the contribution of civilians at home, particularly in Pittsburgh-based factories, may have been even more important to the war effort. During World War I, Pennsylvania was the world's greatest center for steel production; the state's abundant iron ore and coal explained this dominance. Additionally, after the Civil War American industry adopted the Bessemer process, which injected air into molten iron to remove impurities and make cheap steel. Andrew Carnegie, industrialist and philanthropist, was one of the first to adopt this British process, making his western Pennsylvania mills the center of world steel production. As a result, when war came, Pittsburgh became the "Arsenal of the World." As early as December 1914, the British government contracted with Pittsburgh-based Westinghouse Electric and Manufacturing for millions of rounds of ammunition, including naval and artillery shells. Once the United States joined the war, Pittsburgh became an arsenal for U.S. forces, producing millions of artillery shells, including 600,000 high-explosive shells for howitzers— a large artillery piece. In addition to making shells, Pittsburgh-based industries made naval guns, gas masks, railroad cars, armor plating, and other critical military and naval equipment.[16]

Some of this steel likely ended up in ships made in Philadelphia. Because of attacks on merchant shipping and the expansion of the navy, the United States needed more ships, and Pennsylvania-based operations were critical to these shipbuilding efforts. An entire new shipyard was built at Hog Island, near Philadelphia; it stretched over two and one-half miles and housed the infrastructure to build fifty ships, making it the largest shipyard in the world. While an impressive accomplishment, the war ended before the first ship built at this facility went into service.[17]

While most Pennsylvanians supported the war, others did not, and the government took extraordinary action to suppress dissent on the home front. Prior to the United States' entry into the war, some Pennsylvanians of German descent supported Germany and opposed American involvement in the war. Once war came, this type of opposition ceased; however, individuals who opposed the U.S. involvement for either religious or ideological reasons continued to object. Pennsylvania had been founded by pacifist Quakers, later Mennonites arrived in the state; both groups objected to World War I military service for religious reasons. When war came, some Pennsylvanians claimed conscientious objectors' status to avoid the draft; however, Americans who claimed this status were sometimes treated harshly by military authorities. Those who objected for political reasons, such as Socialists, were often targeted by both civilians and government officials. In Philadelphia, mobs attacked Socialists handing out material opposing the draft. In response, police arrested the men distributing this material. A few days later,

Philadelphia police raided a socialist organization and arrested many of its members. This was not merely a local effort; the United States government used a number of legal measures, including the Espionage Act (1917) and the Sedition Act (1918), to outlaw any antiwar speech—spoken and written—to target those who were opposed to the war.[18]

One of the most significant Supreme Court cases related to civil liberties in wartime involved a Pennsylvanian jailed under the provisions of the Espionage Act. Philadelphian Charles Schenck was a Socialist charged with writing, printing, and distributing leaflets questioning the constitutionality of the draft. Despite the failure of the government to provide any evidence that this appeal inspired any potential recruits to avoid service, Schenck was found guilty in federal court of violating the Espionage Act. The case was appealed to the U.S. Supreme Court; however, in the landmark case *Schenck v. United States*, the court ruled against Schenck. Justice Oliver Wendell Holmes Jr. wrote the majority opinion, citing the needs of the government in wartime to justify upholding this conviction. In his decision, Holmes articulated a "clear and present danger" argument, which justified limiting civil liberties in wartime, comparing these leaflets to "a man shouting fire in a theater and causing a panic." Others, who opposed the decision, questioned the analogy, arguing that Schenck was really running in the "theater between the acts and inform[ing] the audience honest-ly but perhaps mistakenly that the fire exits are too few or blocked." Despite some controversy over this decision, Schenck went to prison for six months.[19]

The Schenck case represented just one epilogue of the Great War; providing another legacy were the veterans of the conflict. When the war ended, the dead were buried and survivors came home. Some of these men had served in combat, others had not; the United States had millions of men in camps waiting to go overseas when the war ended. Regardless of their wartime experiences, when these men returned to Pennsylvania, they, like their fathers and grandfathers, formed veterans' organizations. Civil War veterans had formed the Grand Army of the Republic (GAR), the Northern army's largest veterans' organization. Veterans of the Spanish-American and Philippine-American Wars had their own groups. In 1913, the Veterans of Foreign Wars formed, welcoming all soldiers who had served overseas. After World War I, veterans organized the American Legion for all soldiers, including those who had served at home, which its founders envisioned as the GAR of the Great War.[20]

Pennsylvanians were among the founding members of the American Legion, and less than one year after the armistice—June 1919—the Pennsylvania American Legion formed. The American Legion, in this state and in others, saw itself as performing two distinct but interrelated functions. First, the organization advocated for veterans and their interests, including benefits for disabled veterans. The men who had served in the 28th, 79th, 80th, 92nd, and 93rd Divisions needed the services provided by the newly formed Veterans Bureau, which would later evolve into the Veterans Administration. During the early years of the Pennsylvania American Legion, its members focused on ensuring that this agency and the rest of the federal government aided disabled and unemployed veterans.[21]

Second, the American Legion advocated what it termed "one-hundred percent Americanism." Partially, this idea originated in the war itself; anti-German sentiments prompted some Americans to advocate abandoning ethnic identities that might encourage foreign allegiances. When the war was over, "one-hundred percent Americanism" became less about any single ethnic group and more about emerging "-isms," such as socialism and communism. In the aftermath of the Russian Revolution, veterans and other Americans turned against socialist and communist organizations in the United States as demonstrated by the "Red Scare" of 1919. The American Legion's particular target was the International Workers of the World (IWW). Legionnaires participating in a 1919 Armistice Day parade had been killed by IWW members in Centralia, Washington. The conviction of the IWW members in this attack remains controversial to this day. What is not a matter of dispute is that the American Legion saw itself as a bulwark against commu-

nism, socialism, radicalism, and other organizations that they believed supported these groups, such as the American Civil Liberties Union. In 1927, some members of the Pennsylvania American Legion protested a club at West Chester State Teacher's College (now West Chester University) that declared U.S. intervention in Nicaragua imperialistic. The instructors who organized the club were fired. The Legion denied its involvement in this personnel action, but congratulated the school on removing these men.[22]

Even more controversial than the fate of two college professors, some elements of the Pennsylvania American Legion became involved with labor disputes supporting business interests. The Legion in Centralia had opposed the IWW strike by loggers and lumbermen and that played a role in the Armistice Day attack. It must be emphasized that these were actions at the local level that did not reflect the views of the state or national organization. The national American Legion mandated neutrality in labor disputes, the national commander asserting that "the Legion was not a strike breaking organization." Despite this official position, Legion members often became involved in strikes as part of an effort to enforce "law and order" measures. In 1934, members of the American Legion supported the Laughlin Steel Company that fought efforts to unionize its workforce. An attack by a group of armed men on steelworkers killed one and wounded many others. Legionnaires who were union members often rejected their organization's involvement in these activities. As one scholar of the Legion argued, "efforts by many Legionnaires to remain neutral in labor struggles that did not threaten community safety, and divided opinion within the ranks (even when some of their comrades acted legally as special deputies), demonstrate that the Legion as a whole did not act as a tool of business, even if it did in some localities."[23]

Regardless of the action of some local groups, the Pennsylvania American Legion played a positive role in the community. Legion officials considered one of its most important community activities, American Legion Baseball, to be the "greatest Americanizing influence on the young manhood of America." At the height of the Depression, Pennsylvania American Legion Baseball sponsored 150 teams. These kinds of community activities reflected the value of this organization to the citizens of Pennsylvania.[24]

Veterans did more than organize baseball teams in the 1930s; they fought for veterans' bonuses. The government agreed to pay World War I veterans a bonus in 1945. Veterans economically devastated by the Depression wanted the government to give these bonuses a decade earlier. When veterans formed a "Bonus Army" to march on Washington in 1932, President Herbert Hoover ordered army chief of staff Douglas MacArthur to break up their protest. MacArthur used the army to attack and destroy the veterans' encampment. While this constituted a setback for these men, by 1936 Congress approved a bonus for soldiers; however, President Franklin D. Roosevelt vetoed this measure. Congress was able to override his veto because of the support of Pennsylvanian James Van Zandt, national commander of the Veterans of Foreign Wars. While World War I veterans were critical to the development of the American Legion and the Veterans of Foreign Wars in the 1930s, in the next decade another, larger, generation of veterans joined these organizations. Before these men could become veterans, Pennsylvanians had to face their greatest twentieth-century challenge—World War II.[25]

12. Pennsylvania in World War II: Total Mobilization for Total Victory

Barbara A. Gannon

Despite misgivings about involvement in another European war, Pennsylvanians mobilized for total war two decades after the Great War. Many factors that made Pennsylvania vital to victory in World War I were critical in World War II; it provided military manpower and military material to the war effort. Over 1.25 million Pennsylvanians served in the armed forces, of these approximately 33,000 men and women died. Moreover, Pennsylvania provided the nation with some of its most senior wartime leaders. While leadership is critical, victory was the product of many lesser-known Pennsylvanians who distinguished themselves in a variety of military and naval units; the 28th Infantry Division once again fought in some of the toughest and most important battles of the war. On the home front, Pennsylvania factories produced vital war material; African American men and women participated in the industrial workforce that produced these critical sup-

plies. Industrial expansion represented only one aspect of the home front; Pennsylvanians were fully mobilized for war. Some Pennsylvanians volunteered as civil defense workers and others entertained soldiers and sailors; virtually every citizen was affected by rationing; many citizens bought war bonds. When the war ended, Pennsylvanians came home. In the aftermath of war, the United States emerged as a great power. The decades that followed the end of the war included a long cold war and a number of shorter hot wars; however, Pennsylvanians would never be as unready for war as they were in 1941.

It is hard to understand why Americans in 1941 were surprised by Pearl Harbor; much of the world had already been engulfed by war. As early as 1931, Japan had invaded Manchuria. By 1935, Italy's Mussolini had invaded Ethiopia as a way of realizing his imperial ambitions; one year later, Germany and Italy signed an alliance. In 1937, on the other side of the world, Japan invaded China; eventually, soldiers of the Land of the Rising Sun would occupy parts of China, including the city of Nanking. The subsequent rape and murder of Chinese men, women, and children in this city horrified the world. In Europe, the Austrian people voted to join Germany and the Third Reich. In 1938, the people of Czechoslovakia (the Czech and Slovak republic) ceded part of their nation to Germany when France and Britain forced them to do so; less than a year later, Germany took the rest. Seizing the opportunity provided by Western inaction, Italy invaded Albania. A few months later on September 1, 1939, Germany invaded Poland. Britain and France guaranteed Poland's border and went to war, though they could do very little to help and Poland fell quickly. After a short respite, in spring 1940, Germany attacked France; it capitulated quickly to the German blitzkrieg—an attack using motorized forces, such as tanks, in concert with aircraft, to achieve a quick and decisive victory. While Britain stopped the German juggernaut with its navy and the Royal Air Force, most of the continent, including Norway, Denmark, and Greece, fell to the Nazis; only neutral nations, Spain, Portugal, Sweden, and Switzerland, survived. While Hitler signed a nonaggression treaty with Stalin, this was null and void when Germany invaded the Soviet Union in the summer of 1941. In the Pacific, Japan used the occupation of France to expand its empire and took over French Indochina. It was Japanese expansion

and the American response, economic sanctions including an oil embargo, that led to Pearl Harbor. Given the state of the world in late fall and winter of 1941, the United States might have been more prepared for war.[1]

One reason Pennsylvanians were not ready before Pearl Harbor is that they did not want to be ready; many Americans rejected U.S. involvement in European or Asian troubles. In the interwar period, Americans believed that they had been dragged into World War I by munitions makers motivated by greed, the so-called "Merchants of Death." Moreover, many German Americans and others rejected involvement in a war against Germany. Some Americans admired Hitler; in some instances, they agreed with his anti-Semitic views. Among those who opposed such overseas involvement were the Mothers and Daughters of Pennsylvania. A man attending an August 1941 meeting of the group expressed his admiration for Hitler. On another end of the political spectrum, Pennsylvanians objected to war regardless of its justification. Some of these pacifists continued to reject war even after Pearl Harbor; some performed alternate service in the military as medics or remained at home, performing alternate community service. Still others like Larry Gara of Reading were jailed for their refusal to serve and were treated poorly as prisoners. Regardless of Pennsylvanians' desire to avoid war, in December 1941, the Japanese attacked Pearl Harbor and other U.S. possessions in the Pacific; almost immediately, Germany declared war on the United States.[2]

The 28th Infantry leading the American contingent in the victory parade in Paris, August 1944.

When war came, neither the regular United States Army nor the National Guard was ready, though a prewar draft and mobilization of the National Guard helped. In 1939, the U.S. Army was smaller than the Belgian army; however, the outbreak of war in Europe and Japanese expansion prompted the United States government to expand available military resources. In 1940 the first peacetime military draft was implemented, and soon thereafter the National Guard was mobilized. Initially, National Guard units were trained by regular army officers and retained their distinct identity; eventually, National Guard divisions were assimilated into the U.S Army. When this occurred, recruits who had been drafted or volunteered were sent to these units, regardless of their state of origin. The 28th Infantry Division was mobilized in February 1941, and it would not come home until it had fought four long years of hard combat in the European theater.[3]

While the European combat experience was brief in the First World War, it was not in the Second. The first American combat unit invaded North Africa in November 1942; from this initial campaign in Africa, the United States and its allies fought across Sicily, Italy, France, and into Germany and victory. The 28th Infantry Division's record in World War II is even more impressive than it was in World War I, though over time it lost much of its Pennsylvania identity. The 28th began its combat service in July 1944, after the invasion of Normandy. It had trained in the United States and in Great Britain since its mobilization. When it arrived, the United States and its allies were attempting to move farther inland; the 28th and the rest of the Allied armies sustained high casualties as they fought through the thick,

Soldiers of the 110th Infantry Regiment, 28th Infantry Division, moving cautiously through the Hürtgen Forest. The battle between American and German forces for the forest lasted from September 1944 to February 1945, with the Americans alone suffering more than thirty thousand casualties.

tall bushes of hedgerows. Though breaking through to open country helped, the 28th still had a tough fight; in August 1944, the new division commander was killed only hours after he had taken command. After this hard campaigning, the division received a unique award: it was the only U.S. division to march in the parade celebrating the liberation of Paris. By the time victory was won in Europe, the 28th had participated in a number of campaigns, including Northern France (after the Normandy breakout), the Rhineland, and Ardennes-Alsace. As part of its service, it participated in two of the hardest fought battles in Europe, the Battle of Hürtgen Forest and the Battle of the Bulge, the last great offensive by the German army in the west.[4]

It is appropriate that Pennsylvanians fought in the Battle of the Bulge; it was the greatest battle the U.S. Army fought since Gettysburg. After suffering severe casualties in the Hürtgen Forest, the 28th Infantry Division needed to rest and recuperate. In December 1944, the division was sent to what officials considered a quiet sector in the Ardennes Forest. Unfortunately, the German High Command targeted that area for a major offensive. German officials hoped that a breakthrough in this area would split Allied forces and allow their army to advance on Antwerp—a critical Belgian port. German forces surprised U.S forces, including the 28th, advancing during bad weather when U.S. aircraft were unable to fly. While another division surrendered, the 28th managed to delay German forces long enough for reenforcements to arrive and the weather to clear, allowing U.S. aircraft to attack German units, forcing the German army to retreat. By war's end, the division had suffered almost

25,000 casualties; more men died or were wounded or missing than were authorized for this unit. This experience explains the new nickname of the unit, the "Bloody Bucket," based on the red keystone, the divisional patch, worn on the soldiers' uniforms.[5]

Not everyone in the 28th was from the Keystone State, nor did Pennsylvanians only serve in in this unit. Pennsylvanians were represented in all of the military services and in all the war's theaters. Some of these Pennsylvanians were among the most senior military and naval officials. The general of the army George C. Marshall, chief military adviser to President Roosevelt, was born and raised in Uniontown, Pennsylvania. Though he never had a combat command, he was considered the architect of victory over Germany and Japan. After the war, he would be appointed secretary of state; it was the Marshall Plan that rebuilt war-torn Western Europe. While Marshall was considered an elder statesman, Pennsylvania also provided the army with its youngest general, James M. Gavin, commander of the 82nd Airborne Division. In addition to his wartime leadership, in the postwar era, he pioneered efforts to integrate the military; he incorporated the all-black 555th Parachute Infantry Battalion into his division.[6]

Pennsylvanians led American forces on the sea and in the air. Overall, five full admirals, seven vice admirals, and seventeen rear admirals were Pennsylvanians; among these flag officers was Harold R. Stark, chief

of naval operations and later in charge of naval forces in Europe. The vice admirals included Alan G. Kirk of Philadelphia, who commanded amphibious forces during the Normandy invasion. Pennsylvania was represented in the Pacific theater by Vice Admiral John H. Newton of Pittstown who served as deputy to Admiral Nimitz, commander of all Allied forces in the South Pacific. Perhaps even more impressive, the general of the army Henry "Hap" Arnold was born in Gladwyne, and led the U.S Army Air Corps. When he completed his tour, he handed over the command to General Carl Spaatz of Boyertown, who had served as his deputy during the war.[7]

While it is difficult to track the service of all Pennsylvanians in the different services across the many theaters of war, a sampling of Medal of Honor winners who were either born in Pennsylvania or credited to the state demonstrates both the wide variety of Pennsylvanians' experience and the exceptional nature of their service and sacrifice. During the attack on Pearl Harbor, Philadelphian Edwin J. Hill, chief boatswain, "led his men of the line-handling details of the U.S.S. *Nevada* to the quays, cast off the lines and swam back to his ship" in an attempt to move the ship to safety. Sadly, he received this medal posthumously; when he was "attempting to let go the anchors, he was blown overboard and killed." In later Pacific campaigns, Pennsylvanians distinguished themselves as well. The twenty-one-year-old U.S. Marine Corps corporal Anthony P. Damato of

Pennsylvanians assumed key positions during World War II, including, from left to right, top to bottom, U. S. Army Chief of Staff George C. Marshall, from Uniontown; Major General James M. Gavin, from Mount Carmel; Chief of Naval Operations Harold Stark, from Wilkes-Barre; senior U.S. naval commander during the Normandy invasion, Alan Kirk, from Philadelphia; commanding general of U.S. Army Air Forces Hap Arnold, from Gladwyne; commander of Strategic Air Forces in Europe Carl Spaatz, from Boyertown.

Shenandoah, was cited for his service on one of the many island campaigns in the Pacific. He was manning a lightly held perimeter on the front lines. According to the citation for his award, "when [one] of the enemy approached the foxhole undetected and threw in a hand grenade, Corporal Damato desperately groped for it in the darkness. Realizing the imminent peril to all [three men] and fully aware of the consequences of his act, he unhesitatingly flung himself on the grenade and, although instantly killed as his body absorbed the explosion, saved the lives of his [two] companions."

Among the Pennsylvanians who served in army units assigned to the Pacific campaigns was Staff Sergeant Robert E. Laws of Altoona, who fought in the final campaign to liberate the Philippines. His Medal of Honor citation reads like a movie script and demonstrates Americans' hostility to the Japanese:

He led the assault squad when [his company] attacked enemy hill positions. The enemy force, estimated to be a reinforced infantry company, was well supplied with machineguns, ammunition, grenades, and blocks of TNT and could be attacked only across a narrow ridge 70 yards long. . . . Covered by his squad, S/Sgt. Laws traversed the hog-back through vicious enemy fire until close to the pillbox, where he hurled grenades at the fortification. Enemy grenades wounded him, but he persisted in his assault until [one] of his missiles found its mark and knocked out the pillbox. With more grenades, passed to him by members of his squad who had joined him, he led the attack on the entrenched riflemen. In the advance up the hill, he suffered additional wounds in both arms and legs, about the body and in the head, as grenades and TNT charges exploded near him. Three Japs rushed him with fixed bayonets, and he emptied the magazine of his machine pistol at them, killing [two]. He closed in hand-to-hand combat with the third, seizing the Jap's rifle as he met the onslaught. The [two] fell to the ground and rolled some 50 or 60 feet down a bank. When the dust cleared the Jap lay dead and the valiant American was climbing up the hill with a large gash across the head.

Staff Sergeant Laws survived his injuries and returned home.[8]

Pennsylvanians served in the Army Air Corps in both theaters. In the Pacific, two Pennsylvanians won the award for the same mission. Second Lieutenant Joseph R. Sarnoski of Simpson, volunteered to serve as a crew member on a vital reconnaissance mission over a heavily defended island in the Solomon Islands. The pilot was Major Jay Zeamer of Carlisle. According to the citation explaining Sarnoski's award, "When the mission was nearly completed, about 20 enemy fighters intercepted [his aircraft]. At the nose guns, 2d Lt. Sarnoski fought off the first attackers, making it possible for the pilot to finish the plotted course. When a coordinated frontal attack by the enemy extensively damaged his bomber, and seriously injured 5 of the crew, 2d Lt. Sarnoski, though wounded, continued firing and shot down 2 enemy planes." Sarnoski "crawled back to his post and kept on firing until he collapsed on his guns." Meanwhile, Zeamer, "sustained gunshot wounds in both arms and legs, [one] leg being broken. Despite his injuries, he maneuvered the damaged plane so skillfully that his gunners were able to fight off the enemy during a running fight which lasted 40 minutes. . . . Although weak from loss of blood, he refused medical aid until the enemy had broken combat." This aircraft and Zeamer survived because he "continued to exercise command despite lapses into unconsciousness, and directed the flight to a base 580 miles away." While Zeamer survived, Sarnoski did not live to receive his medal.[9]

Similarly, in Europe, Pittsburgh-native Sergeant Archibald Mathies did not survive his final mission. Mathies served as an engineer and gunner on a mission over Europe when enemy fighters attacked his aircraft and wounded his fellow crew members; the copilot was killed and the pilot wounded. Despite the fact that no one onboard was able to fly the aircraft, the surviving crew managed to get the aircraft to their home station. According to the citation, upon arrival home, "Sergeant Mathies and the navigator volunteered to attempt to land the plane. Other members of the crew were ordered to jump, leaving Sergeant Mathies and the navigator aboard." Mathies's commanding officer determined that the surviving crew could not land the damaged aircraft and ordered the crew to jump. "Sergeant Mathies and the navigator replied that the pilot was still alive but could not be moved and they would not desert him. They were then told to attempt a landing. After two unsuccessful efforts, the plane crashed into an open field in a third attempt to land. Sergeant Mathies, the navigator, and the wounded pilot were killed." Unlike many Medal of Honor citations, there is no last sentence justifying this award, for example, that it reflected the "highest credit" upon the recipient or that it was in the "highest traditions" of the service. This type of courage and self-sacrifice was exceptional even by Medal of Honor standards.[10]

Pennsylvanians also received this medal serving in other ground combat units in Europe. At least five Pennsylvanians were awarded this medal for service with the 1st Infantry Division; these awards were for their conduct in campaigns across Europe including Sicily, France, Belgium, and Germany. Others received this award for service in Italy with the 3rd, 36th, and 88th Divisions. While most of these men received it for taking lives, one Pennsylvanian received it for saving lives. Technician Fifth Grade Alfred L. Wilson of Fairchance, served as a medic in the 26th Infantry Division. "While treating his comrades he was seriously wounded, but refused to be evacuated by litter bearers sent to relieve him. In spite of great pain and loss of blood, he continued to administer first aid until he was too weak to stand." These serious wounds did not stop Wilson; instead, "crawling from [one] patient to another, he continued his work until excessive loss of blood prevented him from moving . . . refusing assistance himself [until] . . . finally [he] lapsed into unconsciousness. . . . By steadfastly remaining at the scene without regard for his own safety, [he] helped to save the lives of at least [ten] wounded men." While these represent stories of exceptional heroism, they document the service of Pennsylvanians in all the theaters of war, in all services, in many different capacities including—sailors, pilots, gunners, infantrymen, medics, and others too numerous to list.[11]

Women served in the newly created auxiliary military and naval services. In World War I, women had served as nurses; only the navy and Marine Corps welcomed women and allowed them to perform other duties. In World War II, all services created auxiliaries that allowed women to perform a wide variety of tasks. The army created the Women's Army Auxiliary Corps (WAAC), later simply the Women's Army Corps (WAC);

Florence A. Blanchfield (1884–1971), who first trained as a nurse in Pittsburgh, served in the U.S. Army Nurse Corps in World War I and World War II. She was promoted to superintendent of the nurse corps in 1943. She became the first woman to receive a military commission in the regular army.

the navy, the Women's Auxiliary in Volunteer Service (WAVES); the Marine Corps, Women Marines; the Coast Guard, Women's Reserve of the Coast Guard, nicknamed SPAR, short for the Coast Guard's motto "Semper Paratus"—always prepared. Philadelphian Virginia Creed joined the WAVES, and Helen L. Snyder Streets of Harrisburg joined the marines. Mary Louise Milligan Rasmuson of Pittsburgh joined the WAC in 1942; before her retirement from the army twenty years later she commanded this organization.

Florence Blanchfield trained as a nurse in Pittsburgh and served as director of training at a hospital in Bellevue, Pennsylvania. She nursed

the sick and wounded in World War I and in World War II she directed the Army Nurse Corps. After the war, she received the first regular army commission held by a woman. Not all women lived to see the war's end; three Pennsylvanians died in the same plane crash in the Pacific, all members of the Women's Army Corps. Mary Holmes Howson of Wayne, was killed in an airplane crash serving with the Women Air Force Service Pilots (WASP). Women who served in these units were considered civilians; her family had to pay for her funeral. The government retroactively recognized them as military veterans in 1977.[12]

Like women, black Pennsylvanians were not allowed to serve in every unit; instead they joined the segregated units. Pennsylvanians joined the segregated 92nd and 93rd Infantry Divisions as they had in World War I. The 92nd served in Italy and the 93rd in the Pacific. Frank Little, a career soldier from Philadelphia, served in the 93rd. Other African Americans served in army logistic units, including critical transportation units that brought supplies to combat units. New opportunities opened in the Air Corps, the United States Air Force's predecessor. African Americans like James T. Wiley of Pittsburgh served as fighter pilots with the famous Tuskegee Airmen. Similarly, the navy and marines allowed African Americans to serve their country in new ways. Before the war, most African Americans in the navy had been waiters; during the war, black sailors were allowed to perform other roles, including as commissioned officers. In a step backward, the navy created the first segregated ships for some of these sailors. The first African American marines also served in racially segregated units. One of the first black marines was a Philadelphia native, Richard Vander-lippe Washington; later he would be the oldest surviving World War II African American marine. An African American student at Temple, Frederick C. Branch, received the first marine commission ever given to a black American.[13]

Similarly, the war and the labor shortage opened up opportunities for African Americans in Pennsylvania; however, racism made it difficult for these men to take full advantage of these openings. Even before the war, President Roosevelt issued an executive order prohibiting racial discrimination in the government and defense industry. When war came, African Americans found work in industries where they had been previously denied employment. While sometimes this was voluntary, in other instances it took a combination of the U.S. government's Fair Employment Practices Committee, and protests by African Americans to force white Americans to hire and promote black workers. Even when industries were willing to hire African Americans they sometimes failed to integrate the workplace. In Philadelphia, a shipyard segregated black workers, while a similar facility in Pittsburgh did not. In Philadelphia, white transit workers went on strike to protest the employment of African Americans as street-

James T. Wiley (1919–2000) received a degree in physics from the University of Pittsburgh. He was one of the original twenty-four Tuskegee Airmen, and he was one of the first two pilots of the 99th squadron to land in North Africa in May 1943.

car drivers. The strike ended when President Roosevelt deployed the army to protect black workers and drive the streetcars. In the strike's aftermath, more African Americans were hired by the Philadelphia transit system. Ultimately, labor shortages in Pennsylvania industries, such as in steel production, led to the employment of black Pennsylvanians in these industries.[14]

Women also benefited from the need to replace men who went into the service. All across the United States, women increased their participation in the workforce during the war. Many women had always worked outside the home; during the war, the government encouraged women who stayed at home to obtain outside employment. It was not merely numbers, but the type of jobs women held. Women did what most considered men's work. The iconic figure of "Rosie the Riveter" represented all women who did work that they had never done before the war, such as riveting together pieces of metal to make aircraft and ships.[15]

Pennsylvanians were no different; women entered the workforce in unprecedented numbers and did jobs they had never done in peacetime. The steel industry, in particular, needed female workers. Before the war, the steel industry had few women workers; they had not even been hired in clerical positions. Initially, the steel industry hired women to fill these administrative functions; however, when labor shortages became acute they began to hire women to work on the shop floor alongside men. When the war ended, all of the women who worked in the mills lost their jobs, though some were allowed to stay in clerical positions. Women worked in other industries, including manufacturing ammunition. Because this was dangerous work, minority women were often welcome; Philadelphia's Frankford Arsenal employed black women to inspect shell casings. In contrast, African American women were not hired for the type of clerical and administrative function open to white women. According to one observer, in Pittsburgh, not a single African American woman was employed in any clerical capacity in that city. Black women had been hired by that city's Westinghouse Corporation to run machinery; however, these women were segregated on

the night shift. Despite the existence of this type of discrimination, the need for more personnel in Pennsylvania industries opened up unprecedented opportunities for underrepresented groups to obtain industrial employment.[16]

These openings were created because, once again, Pennsylvania's factories provided the material needed for victory. By 1945, Pennsylvania contributed 31 percent of the steel produced in the United States, and 20 percent of all the steel produced in the world. To produce steel you need coal. Despite the shortage of mine workers, Pennsylvania produced 30 percent of the nation's coal. During the war, Pennsylvania also had a petroleum industry, though it was in decline. The state produced lubricating oil for aircraft, and gasoline and other high-powered fuel for the war effort. All of this raw material was used by the state's war factories. Steel companies provided bombs for aircraft and shells for artillery built in the state. Some of Pennsylvania's steel went to the state's shipyards that built combat vessels, including battleships, carriers, submarines, and amphibious vehicles. One company in Chester, Pennsylvania, the Sun Ship Company, was the largest producer of oil tankers in the world. Pennsylvania's factories produced weapons, including torpedoes, mortars, bazookas (antitank weapons), and rifles.[17]

Surprisingly, the most ubiquitous American vehicle in the war—the jeep—originated in Pennsylvania. While the Willys Company has been most associated with the develop-

The original Bantam "jeep" built by the Bantam Car Company of Butler, Pennsylvania, to meet the U.S. Army's requirements for a four-wheel-drive, 40 horsepower, 1,300 pound reconnaissance car. While the company's design became an iconic vehicle, most ended up being built by the larger Willys-Overland Company, obscuring the original role of Bantam.

ment of this vehicle, it was the American Bantam Company of Butler that designed the original all-terrain light reconnaissance vehicle that Americans would recognize today as the jeep. While the origin of the word "jeep" is uncertain, the origin of the vehicle is not. In the late 1930s, the army, particularly the cavalry, needed a light reconnaissance vehicle that was able to operate in all types of terrain. By 1940, the army realized it needed to accelerate the modernization of the force based on how the European war demonstrated the value of motorized units. When the army asked for companies to design a light all-terrain vehicle, the Pennsylvania-based American Bantam Company and Willys-

Overland responded. Ameri-can Bantam managed to design the reconnaissance car that met the army's needs in only forty-nine days. While the vehicle was designed by American Bantam, the army was concerned that the company was too small to meet its needs and it allowed Willys-Overland and Ford to also build this vehicle. Eventually, these larger companies took over jeep production and American Bantam's role in creating this revolutionary vehicle was lost.[18]

In addition to building war materials like the jeep, Pennsylvanians also performed a variety of war-related tasks. When the National Guard was called into service, the state had created a Pennsylvania Reserve Defense Corps for the emergency. It was called to active duty after Pearl Harbor to guard bridges and other critical assets. Pennsylvanians served in civil defense organizations; more than 600,000 belonged to the Citizens Defense Corps. These civilians supervised air-raid drills and ensured that the black out—rules to keep homes and business from showing lights—was observed. Pennsylvanians served in the Civil Air Patrol, which performed a number of functions, including submarine patrols. Other Pennsylvanians served in the Temporary Reserve of the Coast Guard, escorting ammunition ships down rivers to ports and regulating traffic at shipyards. Most members of these organizations were past military age and could not be drafted; however, they were able to perform these homeland defense missions.[19]

Since the selective service system was implemented at the local level, Pennsylvanians served on draft boards. Other civilians had a more difficult job—supervising the rationing system. Civilians needed more than money to buy some goods—gasoline, tires, meat, and sugar. Ration boards determined who received what ration based on their need; for example, a person who needed to travel for essential war work was allocated more gas than someone whose job was not considered as vital. While every man, woman, and child was affected by government rationing, some civilians went further: they bought war bonds, collected scrap metal for recycling, grew vegetables in victory gardens, or volunteered with the Red Cross. Higher education was not exempt from the war effort; thirty-eight Pennsylvania colleges and universities trained soldiers and sailors for a variety of tasks, everything from pilot to postman. On a lighter note, Pennsylvanians organized United Service Organizations (USOs) to entertain troops training in the state, creating a home away from home before they went overseas.[20]

When the war ended and the soldiers and sailors who had relaxed in these USO centers went home, the peace was relatively short-lived; six years later, Pennsylvanians fought in Korea, twenty years later in Vietnam, forty-five years later in Kuwait, sixty-five years later in Iraq and Afghanistan. Neither of the great wars of the twentieth century seemed to have created a peaceful future for Pennsylvanians.

13. The Wars that Ended No War: Pennsylvania Military History After World War II

Barbara A. Gannon

While Pennsylvanians would never again be mobilized for total war, in the decades after World War II, they would never really experience peace. In addition to a number of hot wars in these decades—including the Korean War, the Vietnam War, the Gulf War (Operation Desert Storm and Shield), the Iraq War, and the war in Afghanistan—the Cold War between the United States (and its allies) and the Soviet Union (and its allies) affected Pennsylvanians. While these hot wars were smaller than the world wars, Pennsylvanians still fought, died, were wounded, or sickened in these conflicts. Pennsylvanians continued to distinguish themselves serving in the army, navy, marines, and the newest service—the United States Air Force.

By the end of the twentieth century, the United States emerged as the most powerful nation in the world with the collapse of the Soviet Union and its allies. During this period, the military role of previously marginalized

Pennsylvanians, African Americans, women, and gays expanded; today, these men and women have the exact same opportunities as any other Americans in the armed forces. While opportunities for these groups expanded, the percentage of the population that served shrank, and the armed forces may not have been as representative of all Pennsylvanians as they had been during earlier wars. The men and women who did serve faced a new set of challenges in the twentieth century. Ironically, just as the United States dominated the world militarily at the dawn of the twenty-first century, war came home again to Pennsylvania when an aircraft hijacked as part of the terrorist attacks on September 11, 2001, crashed in Shanksville, Pennsylvania. In the aftermath of this attack, Pennsylvanians fought overseas in Iraq and Afghanistan, America's longest wars. As this is written, the outcome of these conflicts is uncertain; however, it is clear that the military history of twenty-first century Pennsylvanians will be no less distinguished than that of previous generations.

Before Pennsylvanians faced the challenges of the twenty-first century, they had to address the extraordinary challenges of the second half of the twentieth century. The end of the war in 1945 did not usher in the dawn of a more peaceful world. In the immediate aftermath of World War II, the wartime alliance between democratic nations and communist nations, including Stalin's Soviet Union, collapsed. As a result, peace did not mean a lessening of international tension. Ironically, just as the advent of the atomic bomb made the prospect of war seem more horrifying, the nuclear arms race caused by this development seemed to make it more likely. Moreover, the ideological differences between democratic countries and communist nations, combined with the fear engendered by the spread of communism, meant that for the next few decades the United States engaged in a Cold War with communist nations.[1]

Pennsylvanians' fear of communism overseas prompted them to oppose anyone they believed to be a communist at home. Much of the attention on anticommunism in this era has been at the national level, particularly the activities of Joseph McCarthy and the House Un-American Activities Committee (HUAC); however, state and local entities took action against what they believed to be homegrown security threats—communist and other leftist

groups. Moreover, while much of the focus has been on the postwar period, Pennsylvanians' fear of communist activities began even before World War II, inspired by the 1939 nonaggression pact between the Nazi and the Soviet governments. During what some have called a "little red [communist] scare," state officials formed committees that investigated communist groups, including organizations that some believed were fronts for the Communist Party. Some of these groups were actually communist affiliates, others were not. Once war came, Pennsylvanians put aside some of their concerns because the Soviet Union was our ally. Once the war was over, Pennsylvanians engaged in a vigorous campaign against communists and anyone they thought might have been a communist. As in the national campaign led by Joseph McCarthy and his allies, many Pennsylvanians' lives and careers were destroyed. While recent research had supported some Pennsylvanians' concerns that the Soviet Union used its communist allies for its own purposes, it is also clear that many innocent citizens were caught up in these investigations.[2]

THE KOREAN WAR, 1950–1953

While Americans may have exaggerated the threat of communism at home, events overseas, including Soviet domination in Eastern Europe and the victory of the Communist Chinese under Mao Zedong, supported their concern over communist expansion. In the summer of 1950, communist North Korea attacked

South Korea. These two states had been created in the aftermath of World War II when the victorious allies divided Korea, which had been part of the Japanese empire. The Soviet Union helped North Koreans establish their government and the United States assisted South Koreans; eventually, a communist government formed in the North and a noncommunist government in the South. The Soviet Union also equipped the North Korean military with tanks and other weapons; however, the United States did not fully equip the South Korean army.[3]

As a result, the North Korean army was very successful when it crossed the thirty-eighth parallel separating the two countries; it captured much of South Korea, including the capital Seoul. In contrast, the United States Army, as part of a United Nations (UN) effort to stop North Korean aggression, was unprepared for war and did not do well in the opening months of the war. Eventually, it stopped the North Korean advance at the Pusan Perimeter; among these defenders was nineteen-year-old Melvin Brown, who was born in Mahaffey, Pennsylvania. According to the citation for his Medal of Honor, after "taking a position on a 50-foot-high wall he delivered heavy rifle fire on the enemy. His ammunition was soon expended and although wounded, he remained at his post and threw his few grenades into the attackers causing many casualties. When his supply of grenades was exhausted his comrades from nearby foxholes tossed others to him and he left his

George H. Ramer (1927–1951) was born in Meyersdale, Pennsylvania, and after serving in the navy during World War II, he graduated from Bucknell University in 1950. A Marine reservist, he was called to active duty in April 1951. For his selfless actions on Heartbreak Ridge, Korea, on September 21, 1951, in which he sacrificed his life to preserve his fellow soldiers, he was awarded the Medal of Honor.

position, braving a hail of fire, to retrieve and throw them at the enemy." When he was unable to resist the enemy in any other way he "drew his entrenching tool from his pack and calmly waited until they [one] by [one] peered over the wall, delivering each a crushing blow upon the head. Knocking 10 or 12 enemy from the wall, his daring action so inspired his platoon that they repelled the attack and held their position." While the perimeter held, Brown never lived to see this victory; he was reported missing the day after this attack and later reported as killed in action.[4]

After a successful amphibious invasion at Inchon near Seoul, U.S. forces, working with their UN allies, proceeded up the peninsula into North Korea. As they came closer to the border with China, Chinese officials warned them to stop their advance; when they did not, China joined the war and pushed UN forces all the way back into South Korea, recapturing Seoul. Eventually, UN forces pushed the Chinese and North Koreans back into North Korea. One critical battle fought during this period was known as Heartbreak Ridge. During this battle, George Ramer, a U.S. Marine Corps second lieutenant, born in Meyersdale, Pennsylvania, "fearlessly led his men up the steep slopes and although he and the majority of his unit were wounded during the ascent, boldly continued to spearhead the assault. With the terrain becoming more precipitous near the summit and the climb more perilous as the hostile forces added grenades to the devastating hail of fire, he staunchly carried the attack to the top, personally annihilated [one] enemy bunker with grenade and carbine fire and captured the objective with his remaining [eight] men." Heartbreak Ridge received this name because of desperate attacks like this one that failed. As the Medal of Honor citation explains, "unable to hold the position against an immediate, overwhelming hostile counterattack, [Ramer] ordered his group to withdraw and single-handedly fought the enemy to furnish cover for his men and for the evacuation of [three] fatally wounded marines." He paid the price for this

delaying action and was again severely wounded. Despite his injuries, he "refused aid when his men returned to help him and, after ordering them to seek shelter, courageously manned his post until the hostile troops overran his position and he fell mortally wounded." His family and those of the other Pennsylvanians who died in this war likely did not forget the "heartbreak" of what has been called a forgotten war. After a prolonged stalemate, the war ended in an armistice and, at best, an uneasy peace between the warring nations.[5]

Pennsylvanians answered the call to serve in what some have called a police action, though it was as brutal as any war fought by Americans. The 28th Infantry Division was called into service, though it was sent to Europe in case the Soviet Union took advantage of the war in Asia to invade Europe. Black Pennsylvanians began to serve in newly integrated units; Harry Truman had integrated the service by executive order in 1948. Overall, more than 400,000 Pennsylvanians served, and 2,400 died.[6]

THE VIETNAM WAR, 1965–1973

While Americans may have forgotten Korea, most Americans remember the United States' next war, if for no other reason than its divisive nature. It was again fear of communism and its expansion that prompted the United States' involvement in Southeast Asia, particularly in Vietnam. Much like Korea, Vietnam was divided into a North Vietnam and a South Vietnam. It was also different from the situation in the Koreas. The North Vietnamese communists were indigenous Vietnamese nationalists who were not controlled by either the Soviet or the Chinese Communist governments, though they agreed with their views. The North's leader, Ho Chi Minh, was an enormously popular Communist who had led the resistance to Japanese occupiers during the war and the French colonial government after the war. After Ho Chi Minh and his forces defeated the French, the Geneva Accords divided Vietnam at about the seventeenth parallel. The same agreement mandated elections to reunite the two sections; however, South Vietnamese officials refused to hold these elections. Despite concerns about its commitment to democracy, the United States supported the government of South Vietnam as a bulwark against the expansion of communism. Though it was more corrupt and less democratic than Americans hoped, the South Vietnamese government represented a significant portion of the population that was anticommunist, particularly Catholics.[7]

Moreover, U.S. involvement in this conflict developed at a slower pace than it did in Korea. Initially, in 1955, the United States agreed to train South Vietnamese forces. For the next decade, most Americans in Vietnam were advisers. In 1965, President Lyndon Baines Johnson sent large numbers of ground combat troops into South Vietnam and bombed the North Vietnamese after a purported attack on U.S. Navy vessels in the Gulf of Tonkin. In the eight years between 1965 and the end of the war in 1973, Americans fought the enemy in jungles and rice paddies and in the air over North Vietnam. Eventually, the United States signed a peace treaty with the North; two years later, the South Vietnamese government fell to the North Vietnamese and today there is a single nation—Vietnam.[8]

Overall, more than 3,400 Pennsylvanians were killed in Vietnam. Second Lieutenant Carol Ann Drazba of Dunmore was one of eight women who died in Vietnam; she was killed in a helicopter crash. Some of the men who served in this conflict received the Medal of Honor for their service. Richard L. Etchberger, chief master sergeant, U.S. Air Force, born in Hamburg, Pennsylvania, was a radar technician manning a secret installation in Laos when his position was overrun by enemy forces. "Chief Etchberger's entire crew lay dead or severely wounded. Despite having received little or no combat training, Chief Etchberger single-handedly held off the enemy with an M-16, while simultaneously directing air strikes into the area and calling for air rescue." He held the enemy in check until rescue aircraft arrived and then "repeatedly and deliberately risked his own life, exposing himself to heavy enemy fire in order to place three surviving wounded comrades into rescue slings hanging from the hovering helicopter waiting to airlift them to safety. With his remaining crew safely aboard, Chief Etchberger finally climbed into an evacuation sling himself, only to be fatally wounded by enemy ground fire as he

Three Pennsylvania recipients of the Medal of Honor for service in Vietnam. Left to right: Richard L. Etchberger, U.S. Air Force, from Hamburg; Michael J. Estocin, U.S. Navy, from Turtle Creek; Michael J. Crescenz, U.S. Army, from Philadelphia.

was being raised into the aircraft." Because of the classified nature of this installation the award was delayed; in 2010, his sons received the medal from President Barack Obama in a White House award ceremony.[9]

The bombing campaign over North Vietnam was no secret when Lieutenant Commander Michael J. Estocin, born in Turtle Creek, led support missions that suppressed antiaircraft missiles in strikes against power plants in North Vietnam. He was cited for two missions, one on April 20, 1967, the other April 26 of that year. On the second mission, Estocin "in support of a coordinated strike against the vital fuel facilities in Haiphong, . . . led an attack on a threatening SAM [surface-to-air missile] site, during which his aircraft was seriously damaged by an exploding SAM; nevertheless, he regained control of his burning aircraft and courageously launched his . . . missiles before departing the area." The citation did not reveal Estocin's fate at the time he was given this award. His air-

craft crashed as a result of this damage. His wingman thought he was dead, though there was some reason to believe he was a prisoner. When U.S. prisoners were released at the end of the war, he was not among them. Later it was determined that he died when his aircraft crashed. His fate and that of other Americans missing in action remains an important issue for many Americans.[10]

A Philadelphian distinguished himself on the ground. Corporal Michael J. Crescenz, like so many other soldiers in Vietnam, was only nineteen when he was killed. One morning his unit was attacked and Cresencz took action. He

seized a nearby machine gun and, with complete disregard for his safety, charged 100 meters up a slope toward the enemy's bunkers which he effectively silenced, killing the [two] occupants of each. Undaunted by the withering machine gun fire around him, Cpl. Crescenz courageously moved forward toward a third bunker which he also succeeded in silencing, killing [two] more of the enemy and momentarily clearing the route of advance for his comrades. Suddenly, intense machine gun fire erupted from an unseen, camouflaged bunker. Realizing the danger to his fellow soldiers, Cpl. Crescenz disregarded the barrage of hostile fire directed at him and daringly advanced toward the position. Assaulting with his machine gun, Cpl. Crescenz was within 5 meters of the bunker when he was mortally wounded by the fire from the enemy machine gun.

The citation explains that his "bravery and extraordinary heroism at the cost of his life are in the highest traditions of the military service." Sadly, that could be said for many teenagers from Pennsylvania in Vietnam and other wars.[11]

So many soldiers who served in Vietnam were nineteen because young men enlisted or were drafted right after high school. In other wars, more soldiers were older because more reserve units served. Few reservists mobilized for Vietnam; government officials worried that a large-scale reserve call-up would be politically unpopular. After Korea, manpower requirements were smaller and the population larger, so a smaller percentage of Pennsylvanians served. Initially, this was accomplished by allowing individuals to be exempt from the draft. Exemptions had always existed when the United States used conscription to fill manpower needs; clergymen and essential war workers were exempt. Later these exemptions expanded to include college students. Since attending college allowed men to avoid the draft,

Pennsylvanians of higher economic and social classes were less likely to serve. This put the burden of the Vietnam War on non-college-bound, poorer Americans. While the ability to avoid military service made the war initially more palatable to some Americans, eventually this lack of fairness was another reason Americans opposed the war. As part of an effort to reform the draft, exemptions were eliminated, and a lottery system was put in place. It is difficult to decide how a fairer draft might have affected Americans support for the war since American involvement was winding down by the time these reforms were implemented.[12]

Initially, few Pennsylvanians opposed this war, though Quakers and other pacifists rejected American involvement in Southeast Asia. Based in Philadelphia, the American Friends Service Committee had always worked with conscientious objectors in earlier wars. Most of these men objected to war and military service of any sort. As U.S. involvement in Vietnam increased, the number of young men who did not reject all wars, only this particular war, increased. Objecting to a particular war, a "selective objection," was a more difficult way to avoid service. The Philadelphia-based Central Committee for Conscientious Objectors assisted young men regardless of the nature of their objection to military service. Rejecting American involvement was not restricted to pacifist groups; many Americans, particularly college students, believed that the United States should end this war. In Pennsylvania and across the nation, there were a number of protests against the war. In 1967, some students at the University of Pennsylvania protested campus recruiting by the Central Intelligence Agency and Dow Chemical (maker of the herbicide Agent Orange). Penn State did not experience these types of protest until late in the war; but, by 1970, large numbers of Penn State students had joined the antiwar movement. In the aftermath of the Vietnam War, Americans would become less willing to get involved in similar conflicts—"Vietnam Syndrome."[13]

WARS IN THE MIDDLE EAST

An aversion to overseas entanglements did not last. Ironically, despite the focus on and fears over the Soviet Union in Europe or the Chinese in Asia, the United States would find its next series of challenges in the Middle East. In some ways, this should not have surprised Americans; the political instability in the area, combined with its value as a major source of oil, meant that this region was critical to U.S. national security strategy. While the United States had always supported the nation of Israel, it was not until the early 1970s that Arab nations used their control over the world oil supply to punish the United States and its allies for this assistance. Later in that same decade, the Shah of Iran, a U.S. ally, was overthrown and replaced by a government hostile to the United States that allowed American diplomats to be taken hostage by Iranian

students. The failure to rescue these prisoners destroyed Jimmy Carter's presidency. At the same time, the Soviet Union invaded Afghanistan, and this led Carter to direct the Department of Defense to create a military force capable of responding to crises in this region. A little more than a decade later, in August 1990, the United States and its allies responded to Iraq's invasion of neighboring Kuwait, initially by defending U.S. ally Saudi Arabia, in Operation Desert Shield; later the United States initiated Operation Desert Storm to liberate Kuwait in 1991—both operations together are commonly referred to as the Gulf War. Because of the overwhelming technical advantage of allied forces, including absolute supremacy in the air, and well-trained military and naval forces, Operation Desert Storm lasted only one hundred hours. Many of the army officers who led these successful operations attended the Army War College located in Carlisle, Pennsylvania.[14]

The Gulf War represented a turning point for the National Guard and the United States Army Reserve in Pennsylvania and elsewhere. In the aftermath of the Vietnam War, the Defense Department decided on a "Total Force Policy," which made the reserve forces a more integral part of a total active and reserve force. Partly, this was done because reserve forces were cheaper and it made sense to utilize them more effectively. As a result, military officials assigned important missions to reserve forces, particularly in the area of logistics and combat support roles. These officials were less willing to use reservists, particularly the National Guard, in combat roles. Because of the Total Force Policy, large numbers of reservists were called to active duty for the Gulf War, though the 28th Infantry Division, Pennsylvania's National Guard division, was not mobilized. Instead, smaller units were ordered to active duty. One of these units, the 14th Quartermaster Detachment, a water purification detachment from Greensburg, lost nineteen soldiers killed in action and another forty-three wounded when an Iraqi missile hit their barracks. Because this represented 81 percent of the detachment, the unit experienced the highest percentage of casualties in the Gulf War.[15]

CHALLENGES FOR VETERANS

While Pennsylvanians were killed or wounded, soldiers also suffered from one of the most forgotten casualties of war—disease. The Gulf War in 1991 has had a surprisingly high number of postwar illnesses attributed to military service. A study of more than four thousand veterans of Operations Desert Shield and Storm, which included many Pennsylvanians, found that reservists who had deployed to the Middle East were much more likely to be ill after the war. Many of these symptoms, such as aching joints, are part of a cluster of symptoms associated with a new disease called Gulf War illness. Using the same data, psychologists examined the mental health of soldiers who served in this conflict. They found that soldiers who participated in the

Gulf War, including Pennsylvanians, "experienced significant levels of stress. Some saw the dead and wounded, both American and enemy. Anxiety and concern over chemical, terrorist, and . . . missile attacks were widespread. All were separated from family and friends at home. All had to adjust upon return. The vast majority worked unbelievably long hours and faced severe environmental extremes and working conditions." This likely could have been said for Pennsylvanians in all American wars, but now scientists know how to study the effects of war on soldiers and veterans.[16]

Veterans who suffered from these ailments needed the support of veterans groups. The American Legion and Veterans of Foreign Wars continued to operate, and new organizations, such as Vietnam Veterans of America, formed. The Pennsylvania American Legion lost a number of its members who attended a 1976 convention to a disease caused by bacteria in air-conditioning ducts—now known as "Legionnaires' disease." Despite this tragedy, the American Legion and other veterans' organizations prospered, partly because veterans continued to need their assistance. After World War II, the Veterans Administration built a number of new hospitals to treat veterans who were healing from their wartime experiences; later these became a lifeline for poor veterans who had no other medical options. Veterans in Pennsylvania played a key role in the fight to ensure funding for these hospitals. Veterans' organizations and hospitals will continue to be important to Pennsylvanians in the twenty-first century to meet the needs of aging Korean and Vietnam War veterans, and younger veterans who served in Middle Eastern wars.[17]

WARS IN AFRICA AND EUROPE

The type of international instability that led to American involvement in the Middle East is part of a broader pattern; the end of the Vietnam War and the Cold War did not mean an end to American involvement overseas. Whether it was in Europe, parts of the former Yugoslavia (Bosnia, Serbia, and Kosovo) or in Africa (Somalia), American soldiers found themselves in peacekeeping roles. Unfortunately, these missions were not always peaceful. In 1995, the United States sent troops to Somalia to work with the United Nations in its capital Mogadishu to address a humanitarian catastrophe occurring in a nation run by feuding warlords. The UN ordered the arrest of one of these warlords. When the United States attempted to arrest some of his senior aides, these forces were attacked by local militiamen. Helicopters supporting this operation were shot down and American soldiers attempted to protect their grounded crewmen.[18]

Among the men defending the downed aircraft was army sniper Sergeant First Class Randall D. Shughart, who entered the service in Newville, Pennsylvania. Shughart volunteered to defend the critically injured soldiers near helicopter crash sites. According to his Medal of Honor citation, though "equipped with only his sniper rifle and a pistol, Sergeant First Class Shughart and his team leader, while under intense small arms fire from the enemy, fought their way through a dense maze of shanties and shacks to reach the critically injured crew members." Upon arriving at the crash site, he "pulled the pilot and the other crew members from the aircraft, establishing a perimeter which placed him and his fellow sniper in the most vulnerable position. Sergeant First Class Shughart used his long range rifle and side arm to kill an undetermined number of attackers while traveling the perimeter, protecting the downed crew. . . . [He] continued his protective fire until he depleted his ammunition and was fatally wounded." Though most of the men he attempted to save were killed, Shughart's "actions saved the [helicopter] pilot's life." The movie *Black Hawk Down* portrays the heroism of Shughart and his comrades. The subsequent withdrawal from Somalia suggested that Americans might be unwilling to commit to overseas conflicts if such actions led to the deaths of American soldiers and sailors.[19]

THE IRAQ AND AFGHANISTAN WARS

The next decade would demonstrate that Americans were still willing to fight when sufficiently provoked. In the aftermath of the attacks on September 11, 2001, the United States went to war in both Iraq and Afghanistan. One of the attacks occurred on Pennsylvania soil. One of the planes hijacked by Al-Qaeda operatives crashed in Shanksville, after the passengers and crew decided to fight the terrorists for control of the aircraft. These men and women all died when the plane crashed, but they likely saved many more lives with their actions. In the aftermath of these attacks, the United States and its NATO allies overthrew the Taliban regime in Afghanistan, a country that hosted Osama bin Laden and his organization. In 2003, the United States government's mistaken belief that Iraq had weapons of mass destruction led to the invasion of Iraq and the overthrow of Saddam Hussein.[20]

These Iraq and Afghanistan wars spanned the first decade of the twenty-first century and became America's longest wars. While the 28th Infantry Division did not serve as a unit, many elements of this division did, as did tens of thousands of Pennsylvanians in active and reserve units. While it is difficult to tell the story of all Pennsylvanians' service in these wars, the heroism of one young Pennsylvanian deserves to be chronicled, particularly since, like too many other teenagers, Private First Class (later Specialist) Ross A. McGinnis never came home. "Private McGinnis was manning [his] M2 .50-caliber Machine Gun, [in Iraq, when] a frag-

mentation grenade thrown by an insurgent fell through the gunner's hatch into [his] vehicle. Reacting quickly, he yelled 'grenade,' allowing all four members of his crew to prepare for the grenade's blast. Then, rather than leaping from the gunner's hatch to safety . . . Private McGinnis covered the live grenade, pinning it between his body and the vehicle and absorbing most of the explosion." The Medal of Honor citation always explains that the actions worthy of the medal were in the "highest traditions of the military service." It can also be said that this was in the highest tradition of Pennsylvania military service.[21]

Looking forward, Pennsylvania will always have its defenders. Now we can say "all men and women" and not separate their contributions based on the type of service or unit; all Pennsylvanians can perform all duties, including combat roles. Moreover, neither gay men nor gay women are excluded from the military. While this represents a step forward for society and the status of previously marginalized groups, let us all hope that these men and women will not be needed; it would be enormously gratifying to end the story of Pennsylvania's military history right here, with this as its final chapter.[22]

Appendix

Pennsylvania's Military Monuments, Historic Sites, Museums, and Memorials

Pennsylvania's physically surviving military heritage dates from the French and Indian War. The war began in 1754 in what is now western Pennsylvania. **Fort Necessity National Battlefield** is a reconstruction of the small circular fort where Colonel George Washington, aged twenty-two, hoping to claim the region for Virginia, surrendered to a larger French force, precipitating the war. Programs on the site include reenactments and training for those who will be interpreters at Indian villages. The battlefield is located along Route 40 southeast of Uniontown; street address: RD 2, Box 528, Farmington, PA 15437.

The **Fort Pitt Museum**, run by the Heinz History Center in Pittsburgh following catastrophic cuts to the state budget for historical sites (which fell from over $29 million in 2005–2006 to under $3 million in 2011–2012) stands on the site of the original fort, built by the British in 1758. Of the original structure, only a small blockhouse owned by the Daughters of the American Revolution remains. The museum has dioramas and artwork on the fort's role in the settlement of the West from the French and Indian War to the Lewis and Clark Expedition of 1805, which used it as its headquarters to gather men and supplies. Videos and artwork, including paintings by Robert Griffing, the foremost painter of the French and Indian War and frontier life at the time, enhance the display of artifacts. The museum is located at 101 Commonwealth Place, Point State Park, Pittsburgh, PA 15222.

The French were defeated in the war, but not the Indians. **Bushy Run Battlefield** is the site where in 1763 Colonel Henry Bouquet and five hundred soldiers marching from Carlisle defeated the Indians who had been besieging Pittsburgh, opening western Pennsylvania to settlement after the war. The only historic site devoted to Pontiac's War, the visitors' center and museum have artifacts and a statue of a Native American warrior (fully painted in black and red); the battlefield site is well marked and an annual reenactment occurs. Also included are works by Robert Griffing. The battlefield is located along Route 993 West, three miles from Business 66 North/toll road 66 intersection near Greensburg. Address: Bushy Run Road, Jeanette, PA 15644.

Fort Ligonier is one of the best-preserved eighteenth-century Vauban forts in the world. These structures, designed by the French military engineer the Marquis de Vauban, were practically impregnable as the outer walls hid a moat, which in turn protected star-shaped interior walls. Its extensive exhibit halls set the French and Indian War in context of the world war occurring at the same time in Europe, India, Africa, and the West Indies. An art gallery has thirteen portraits of notable figures of the war. "The Hermitage" preserves the surviving parlor of General Arthur St. Clair's late-eighteenth-century mansion. The George Washington collection includes the general's pistols and his eleven-page autobiographical manuscript memoir of his defense of the frontier during the French and Indian War. The site is located on Route 30, intersection with Route 711, fifty miles east of Pittsburgh; street address: Fort Ligonier Foundation, 200 South Market Street, Ligonier, PA 75658.

Pennsylvania was both the center of the national government and the site of many military actions during the American Revolution. Most famous is **Valley Forge**, where the National Historical Park features a visitor cen-

ter, video, and costumed interpreters who tell the story of the deadly winter Washington's army spent here in 1777 and 1778. Notable sites are the Muhlenberg Brigade, a reconstruction of soldiers' quarters; Washington's headquarters (the Isaac Potts mansion); General Varnum's quarters, a typical farm house of the era; the Horace Wilcox Library (formerly the estate of Philander Chase Knox, U.S. attorney general under President Theodore Roosevelt and later President Taft's secretary of state), which has research materials on the encampment and area; and the Washington Memorial Chapel, a Gothic style functioning Episcopal church built in 1903. It has stained glass windows depicting the history of Valley Forge, a beautiful carillon with fifty-eight bells, and outside its front door a statue of William White, chaplain of the Continental army, later the first Episcopal bishop of Pennsylvania. Valley Forge National Historic Park is located near the intersection of I-76 and U.S. 202 and 422, on Route 23, at King of Prussia. Address: 1400 Outer Line Drive, King of Prussia, PA 19406.

Fort Mifflin, just south of Philadelphia, was built to defend the city in 1777 from the British. It was occupied by the U.S. Army until 1954. The fort has several buildings that tell its history and offers periodic living history reenactments. Site of the largest bombardment in the history of North America in 1777, it held off the British navy to prevent it from ascending the Delaware River and thus occupying Pennsylvania north of

Philadelphia. The site is located east of I-95, by turning on Route 15, Island Avenue, then left on Enterprise Avenue, and right on Fort Mifflin Road; address: Fort Mifflin Road, Philadelphia, PA 19153.

Most of the sites at **Independence National Historical Park**, such as Independence Hall and the Liberty Bell, concern the civilian aspects of the American Revolution and founding of the nation (such as Franklin Court). But the park also contains the New Hall Military Museum (located on Chestnut Street between Third and Fourth streets) and the reconstructed Carpenters' Hall of 1791 (the First Continental Congress met at the original building). The latter housed the offices of the War Department and Secretary of War Henry Knox when Philadelphia became the nation's capital from 1790 to 1800. Exhibits highlight the founding of the U.S. Navy and Marine Corps. The Thaddeus Kosciuszko National Memorial is the house at Third and Pine streets where the Polish patriot and Revolutionary War general lived in the 1790s after the Polish struggle for independence was defeated. Portraits of many Revolutionary War generals are in the Second Bank of the United States Building (Chestnut Street, between Fourth and Fifth). A statue of John Barry, the first captain in the U.S. Navy, is at the rear of Independence Hall. A statue of George Washington and an eternal flame commemorate the Unknown Soldier of the American Revolution at Washington Square (Pine Street and Sixth Street), where many American Revolutionary soldiers are anonymously buried. George Boudreau's *Independence: A Guide to Historic Philadelphia* (Westholme Publishing, 2011) offers a readable and thorough introduction to the National Park and its connection with Revolutionary-era events and people. The national park is located in downtown Philadelphia; mailing address: 143 South Third Street, Philadelphia, PA 19106.

Also on Independence Mall is the **National Constitution Center**, the only institution dedicated to disseminating information about the United States Constitution. It features the Museum of We the People and, with artifacts loaned from the Gettysburg Foundation, is preparing a permanent exhibit to explore the constitutional impact of the Civil War. The center is located at 525 Arch Street, Philadephia, PA 19106.

In Philadelphia's Fairmount Park, historic **Belmont Mansion**, one of the finest examples of early eighteenth-century Palladian architecture in the United States, is home to the Underground Railroad Museum at Belmont Mansion. The house is located at 2000 Belmont Mansion Drive, Philadelphia, PA, 19131.

The **Brandywine Battlefield Historic Site** offers three self-guided driving tours that provide a thorough overview of this extensive battlefield. Surviving structures include the Old Kennett (Quaker) Meeting House, whose members held their midweek meeting as the battle raged around them; the Gideon Gilpin House, belonging to a well-to-do Quaker farmer, who lost eighty-seven animals, twelve tons of hay, 230 bushels of wheat, fifty pounds of bacon, one gun, and one history book when soldiers' plundered his farm; and the Benjamin Ring House, Washington's headquarters during the battle, which has been reconstructed after extensive fire damage occurred in 1931. Reenactments occur yearly on the anniversary of the battle. Brandywine Battlefield park is located about one mile east of Chadds Ford in southeastern Pennsylvania; address: Brandywine Battlefield Park Associates, P.O. Box 202, 1491 Baltimore Pike, Chadds Ford, PA 19317.

Cliveden, the mansion built by Benjamin Chew, chief justice of the province of Pennsylvania between 1763 and 1767, is the principal surviving site of the Battle of Germantown. Here a small garrison of British soldiers fended off protracted and unnecessary assaults from the attacking Continental army, enabling reinforcements to arrive and repulse the Americans. Both original and other period furnishings, along with bullet holes, may be found in this attractive example of the country houses built by wealthy Philadelphians. The battle is reenacted the first week of every October. Cliveden is located at 6401 Germantown Avenue, Philadelphia, PA 19144.

Washington Crossing Historic Park offers a reenactment of Washington crossing the Delaware each year at Christmas along with a visitor center describing the crossing

and other educational programs throughout the year. Nearby is the **David Library of the American Revolution**, an important scholarly repository, the only library collecting books and copies of manuscripts from throughout the world concerning the Revolutionary era. The David Library is open to the public Tuesday through Saturday, 10 a.m.–5 p.m. It is closed Sunday, Monday, and holidays. Admission is free. Washington Crossing Historic Park is located at 1112 River Road, Washington Crossing, PA 18977; David Library of the American Revolution is at 11201 River Road, Washington Crossing, PA 18977.

Western Pennsylvania also figured in the War of Independence. **Fort Roberdeau** was built in 1778 under the direction of General Daniel Roberdeau to protect workers in the adjacent lead mine and smelting facility from loyalists and Indians. The reconstructed fort features a museum of contemporary artifacts in an 1860 farmhouse. Fort Roberdeau Historic Site is located at 383 Fort Roberdeau Road, Altoona, PA 16601.

The fleet that won the principal U.S. naval victory in the War of 1812 was built in Erie, Pennsylvania, with materials gathered from throughout the state. The **U.S. Brig *Niagara*** is a reconstruction of the flagship Commodore Oliver Hazard Perry used to win the Battle of Lake Erie in 1813. It is used as a training ship; there is also a museum of artifacts on the maritime history of the lake and region. The **Erie Maritime Museum** (U.S. Brig *Niagara* home port) is located at 150 East Front Street, Erie, PA 16507.

Gettysburg National Military Park, along with the town itself and Gettysburg National Cemetery, is the most extensive and famous Civil War site in Pennsylvania if not the nation. The Gettysburg Foundation operates the **Visitor Center** and 22,000-square-foot **Gettysburg Museum of the American Civil War**. Recently the now-defunct Civil War Museum of Philadelphia transfered ownership of more than 3,000 artifacts to the Gettysburg Foundation, including medical and hospital items, music and games relating to the war, weapons, flags, and the personal effects of Abraham Lincoln, Ulysses S. Grant, George Gordon Meade, and others.

Over 1,300 monuments dot the extensive battlefield: fighting began north and west of the town on July 1, 1863, moving to the south and east on July 2 and 3. Equestrian monuments to Civil War generals—George Gordon Meade, Winfield Scott Hancock, Henry Slocum, John F. Reynolds (killed at the battle), O. O. Howard, and John Sedgwick of the Union; Robert E. Lee and James Longstreet (added in 1998) of the Confederacy—particular regiments both North and South are usually found at positions associated with them during the battle. Most impressive is the Pennsylvania Monument, which contains plaques listing all 34,530 men from the state who fought at the battle. There are several New York monuments, including the castle-shaped structure on Little Round Top and the Tammany

Wigwam and Indian right at the center of the "Bloody Angle" where Pickett's Charge was repulsed on July 3. It shows that not all New York Democrats believed the state should secede and join the Confederacy as advocated by Mayor Fernando Wood. As the state with the most people and financial resources, New York's structures not only tower over those of other states—contrast its castle with the simple rock remembering Joshua Lawrence Chamberlain's Maine troops who held off the Confederates at Little Round Top—but its column at the National Cemetery is higher than that built by the nation itself. In general, the Confederate monuments—which were not allowed until the twentieth century—are in better shape than the older ones erected by the Union.

What became the **Gettysburg National Cemetery** was placed on Cemetery Hill, close to Evergreen Cemetery, the town's burying ground, which had been built in 1854. Many soldiers must have noticed the sign posted at the entrance: "All persons found using firearms in the grounds will be prosecuted using the utmost vigor of the law." Much fighting occurred in and around the cemetery and on Cemetery Ridge that towered about one hundred feet above most of the battlefield. Union soldiers noticed how the beautiful cemetery was filled with dead men and horses, abandoned equipment, and its trees and gatehouse damaged and destroyed.

Evergreen Cemetery, designed for a community of about two thousand people, was not spacious enough to accommodate thousands of bodies at once. Governor Andrew Curtin and the state of Pennsylvania soon raised money to have a larger cemetery built, rejecting the idea that family members should pay to have their kinfolk interred. State efforts, headed by Gettysburg lawyer David Wills, soon merged with those of the privately funded Gettysburg Memorial Association founded by another local attorney, David McConaughy, which hoped to gather the men buried at various sites in and near the town. They purchased about seventeen acres for $2,475.87 and hired landscape architect William Saunders to design the cemetery. He placed the Soldiers' National Monument in the cemetery's center, surrounded by semicircles of graves, all equal in size to demonstrate the equality brought by death, that were barely visible on a terraced hillside. On November 19, 1863, the cemetery was dedicated: Abraham Lincoln gave his famous two-minute Gettysburg Address following a two-hour speech by Edward Everett, a nationally famous orator and former governor and senator from Massachusetts, secretary of state, and ambassador to Great Britain, who compared the Union troops to the Athenians who defended their city against the Spartans and Persians. Lincoln considered his speech a failure. Lincoln was difficult to hear, and newspaper reports frequently got parts of the text wrong; this was only corrected when he made some copies available after newspapers began to print his talk and praise his eloquence.

By March 1864, 3,564 Union soldiers were buried in the National Cemetery: about 3,000 Confederates who had been placed in mass graves were repatriated to the South, nearly all to Hollywood Cemetery in Richmond, Virginia. In 1872, the privately funded cemetery became the Gettysburg National Cemetery under the auspices of the War Department. As space remained available, the army allowed soldiers who had served in the Spanish-American War and World War I to be buried in the cemetery.

The Gettysburg Battlefield and Cemetery soon became the site of tourism inspired by town boosters. They advertised railroad trips from Philadelphia, which could be as short as one day but were preferably longer: visitors were advised to take advantage of the healthy waters found at nearby spas. When automobiles began to supplement railroads, the town touted the various highways that provided easy access from virtually all directions. To attract visitors, local businessmen built museums—one contained a diorama of the battle that lit up to illustrate its progress, another a train ride that simulated Lincoln's trip to the cemetery—and began to hold popular ghost tours that persist today.

Townfolk also encouraged veterans to hold reunions on the battlefield. The earliest were organized by veterans of the Sixty-Ninth Pennsylvania Regiment who, in 1887, formed the Philadelphia Brigade Association and built a Philadelphia monument. They were the first to encourage Confederates to join them "in a spirit of fraternity, charity and loyalty" on the battle's twenty-fifth anniversary. A Union band played "Dixie" as Confederates marched across the field where Pickett's Charge had occurred, this time to be met by handshakes rather than bullets. The most lavish reunion was held in 1913 on the battle's fiftieth anniversary, with the state of Pennsylvania footing the lion's share of over $600,000 in costs. Over a half million veterans attended, including 22,000 Pennsylvanians, 303 of whom had fought for the Confederacy. The last major commemoration of the battle by survivors occurred on its seventy-fifth anniversary, marked on July 6, 1938: 1,359 Union and 486 Confederate veterans joined a half million spectators as President Franklin D. Roosevelt dedicated the Eternal Light Peace Memorial. Since then, yearly reenactments have occurred, usually in the sweltering weather that characterizes southern Pennsylvania in July.

One notable work of art found at the battlefield is the 1883 Gettysburg Cyclorama oil painting (27 by 359 feet) by Paul Philippoteaux, on display since 2008 at the new visitors' center. Originally shown at the Chicago Exposition of 1883 and then in Boston, it was purchased by a Gettysburg businessman who set it up for viewing just in time for the 1913 reunion. Purchased by the National Park Service in the 1960s, it offers views of the progress and leading scenes of the battle at different times. The Museum and Visitor Center at Gettysburg National Military Park is located at 1195 Baltimore Pike, Gettysburg, PA 17325.

The Cyclorama is not the only well-known work of art that offers several perspectives on the battle. For many years, the most awe-inspiring object at the State Museum of Pennsylvania has been Peter Frederick Rothermel's enormous—sixteen-by-thirty-two-foot—painting The Battle of Gettysburg. Commissioned by the Commonwealth of Pennsylvania in 1867 for the price of $25,000, it took Rothermel three years to finish the canvas that many Americans still visualize when they think of the moment when Pickett's Charge reached the Union lines at "the Angle." To accompany the massive central canvas, Rothermel also completed four smaller battle paintings. The adjacent State Capitol also has Civil War murals painted by Violet Oakley, which depict the soldiers as mostly young and, along with their commanders, as grim and battle hardened rather than triumphant. Oakley's murals of Revolutionary and World War I soldiers, along with Edwin Austin Abbey's painting of Baron von Steuben drilling troops at Valley Forge, are among many artworks related to Pennsylvania history in the Museum and State Capitol. The State Museum is located in Harrisburg, on Third Street between Forster and North streets, adjacent to Pennsylvania's State Capitol Building in the State Capitol Complex; the museum's address is 300 North Street, Harrisburg, PA 17120.

Before the arrival of epic motion pictures in the early 1900s, generations of Americans were thrilled by huge depictions of epic historical events. Rothermel's canvases toured the nation from 1870 to 1873, and during the nation's 1876 Centennial Exhibition were displayed prominently in the newly constructed Memorial Hall in Philadelphia, along with other works by American artists. There it remained until 1894, when the Commonwealth finally found a space large enough in Harrisburg to display it. The painting now sits on the floor of the State Museum, since it is too tall to be hung from the wall.

As epic and patriotic as it appears today, Rothermel's *Battle of Gettysburg* was quite controversial in the decades that followed its completion. Rothermel modeled the soldiers in the canvas on particular individuals; so others wanted to know why they were excluded or not displayed more prominently. When the painting was first shown in New York City—the nation's center for art criticism but also the leading center of Confederate sympathy in the North—critics considered it both a bloody monstrosity (although little blood is present) and a needless provocation against white Southerners at a time when the nation needed sectional harmony.

While Rothermel went out of his way to get details of faces and uniforms right, he included critical leaders and events of the battle rather than capturing a single moment. Hoping to provide a sense of the battle's import and drama rather than a literal reconstruction of the critical moment in Pickett's Charge, he included General Meade (on the left)—who was not on the scene of the battle— and action at Little Round Top (on the right), which had taken place the previous day.

Many cities and towns in Pennsylvania erected Civil War monuments: most were machine-made prefabricated columns featuring one or more soldiers. The **Smith Memorial Arch**, funded by Philadelphia inventor Richard Smith, was built between 1891 and 1912. It marks the entrance to **West Fairmount Park** in the city— Memorial Hall, where the 1876 Centennial Exhibition was held is directly behind it —and contains four statues and seven busts of Civil War generals and admirals, along with one each of Smith and the executor of his estate. Its inscription reads:

This monumental memorial presented by RICHARD SMITH type founder of Philadelphia—in memory of Pennsylvanians who took part in the Civil War

Their strife was not for aggrandizement and when conflict ceased the North with the South united again to enjoy the common heritage left by the fathers of our country resolving that thereafter all our people should dwell together in unity.

An 1887 bronze **statue of General George Gordon Meade** by sculptor Alexander Milne Calder is located behind Memorial Hall in West Fairmount Park. There is a petition drive seeking to relocate it to City Hall where it would be seen by many more people.

Other notable statues in Fairmount Park include **Randolph Rogers's** *Lincoln the Emancipator* finished in 1871 and commissioned by the Lincoln Monument Association. One of the most moving sculptures of Lincoln, it stresses the delicacy yet might of the pen with which he signed the Emancipation Proclamation. It is across Kelly Drive from the entrance to the Philadelphia Art Museum. A **Daniel Chester French equestrian statue of Ulysses S. Grant**, dedicated by President McKinley in 1899, is across the Schuylkill River from Memorial Hall on Kelly Drive. He sits on his horse in a plain overcoat and hat, suggesting his practical, no-nonsense style of generalship. **Equestrian statues of General Anthony Wayne** and **George Washington** are also located near the Art Museum entrance. Equestrian statues of leading Pennsylvania generals **John Reynolds** and **George B. McClellan** may also be found at Philadelphia City Hall, Broad and Market streets.

Two memorials in Pottsville, although modest, are most moving. The **Garfield Square Monuments** on Market Street include a plaque with the inscription: "IN MEMORY OF THE FIRST DEFENDERS AND NICHOLAS BIDDLE OF POTTSVILLE, FIRST MAN TO SHED BLOOD IN THE CIVIL WAR, APRIL 18, 1861." An African American, Biddle could not be mustered into the ranks along with his white comrades, but accompanied them as Captain Wren's orderly and was the special target of a mob in Baltimore that protested the arrival of the Union troops. **Biddle's grave marker** at the town's African Methodist Episcopal Church was desecrated over the years and had to be replaced. The cemetery is located at 816 Laurel Boulevard, Pottsville, PA 17901. There is also a **bust of General George A. Joulwan**, a Pottsville native and former supreme commander of NATO, in the town square just south of the Civil War memorial on Route 209.

Soldiers and Sailors Memorial Hall and Museum in Pittsburgh is a monumental classical structure built by the Grand Army of the Republic in the 1890s. Its four halls are available for events, and the National Military Museum tells the role of southwest Pennsylvania in America's conflicts beginning with the Civil War. The Memorial Hall and Museum are located at 4141 Fifth Avenue, Pittsburgh, PA 15213.

Harrisburg is the site of the **National Civil War Museum**, which has seventeen galleries devoted to the history of the war. Noteworthy exhibits include "Costs of the War," about medicine and mortality; "Why Men Fought"; "The Navy"; "Women in War"; "Lincoln: War and Remembrance"; "Camp Curtin" (the Union camp, located in Harrisburg, where many soldiers trained and were then shipped to the Army of the Potomac); and others on particular battles, campaigns, and the general history of the war. Markers outside record the number of men who served and died from each state. The museum is located at One Lincoln Circle at Reservoir Park, Harrisburg, PA 17103.

There are few monuments in Pennsylvania relating to the Spanish-American War, but an important one can be found in Philadelphia. Among various items relating to the naval history of the city at the **Independence Seaport Museum** is the USS *Olympia*, the flagship of Admiral George Dewey when he captured Manila in the Philippines during the Spanish-American War. The museum also features the World War II Balao-class submarine USS *Becuna*. The museum is located at 211 South Columbus Boulevard, Philadelphia, PA 19106.

For an overview of Pennsylvania's role in twentieth-century wars, the best site is the **Pennsylvania Military Museum** in Boalsburg, Centre County, about ninety miles northwest of Harrisburg. A World War I trench is a notable feature, along with weapons, uniforms, and artifacts. Adjacent is the 28th Division Infantry Shrine, commemorating Pennsylvania National Guard units mustered as part of this division that suffered heavy casualties in World Wars I and II. The facade of the museum has a wall depicting the ribbons appearing on medals issued by the United States. The Pennsylvania Military Museum is located at 51 Boal Avenue (602 Boalsburg Pike), Boalsburg, PA 16827.

World War II veterans are honored at several museums. The **Pennsylvania Veterans Museum** in downtown Media, in Delaware County, features exhibits (some interactive) on World War II devoted to the invasion of Europe, the home front (women's and children's role), and the war in the Pacific. Several films may be viewed. The museum is located at 12 East State Street, Media, PA 19063.

The **Eldred World War II Museum** contains a Hall of Flags of all the Allied powers; dioramas of the Battle of Midway, the Battle of Kursk in Russia, and General Patton's advance through Europe; large operations maps; and the story of the National Munitions Company, formerly located in Eldred, where 1,500 workers labored day and night from 1942 to 1945 and produced 8,000,000 bombs, mortar shells, and fuses. Visitors can "operate" a tank on a simulated battlefield. Exhibits are devoted to the various theaters of the war and the war's causes. The museum is located about eighty-five miles south of Niagara Falls, at 201 Main Street, Eldred, PA 16731.

Among the many exhibits at the **Carnegie Science Center** is the USS *Requin*, a World War II Tench-class submarine whose functions are explained using advanced video technology. The Science Center is located next to Heinz Field on the Ohio River, at One Allegheny Avenue, Pittsburgh, PA 15212.

Eisenhower National Historic Site, adjacent to the Gettysburg Battlefield, was the president's weekend retreat and home after he retired. He purchased it in 1950, having been stationed at Gettysburg during World War I. The home is furnished much as when he lived in it. A virtual tour is available online, and items at the house illustrate Eisenhower's military career and role as supreme commander in World War II. The site is only accessible via shuttle buses from Gettysburg National Military Park Visitor Center, 1195 Baltimore Pike, Gettysburg, PA 17325.

Philadelphia has one of the nation's more impressive Vietnam War memorials. The **Philadelphia Vietnam Veterans War Memorial** consists of two walls, one with the names of Philadelphians who died in the war, the other of eight panels designed by Temple University student Tom Rice, illustrating aspects of the war from the launching of the first air strikes to the evacuation of Saigon. The memorial is located across from Penn's Landing, in a plaza straddling the Vietnam Veterans Memorial Highway (I-95), at Columbus Boulevard and Spruce Street, Philadelphia, PA 19132.

Pennsylvania has several aircraft museums. The **Air Heritage Museum and Aircraft Restoration** facility in western Pennsylvania has several restored aircraft, some of which participate in air shows, along with artifacts related to aviation history of the region. The museum is located at Beaver County Airport, 35 Piper Street, Beaver Falls, PA 15010.

The **American Helicopter Museum and Education Center** has more than thirty-five helicopters on display, the largest number in the United States, both civilian and military, along with a research library and artifacts. Visitors can enter the helicopters. The museum is located at 1220 American Boulevard, West Chester, PA 19380.

The **Delaware Valley Historical Aircraft Association** (DVHAA) has fourteen aircraft, over two hundred models, and forty display cases focusing on World Wars I and II, Korea, Southeast Asia, women in aviation, and contemporary aircraft and space exploration. The DVHAA museum is located along Route 611 (1155 Easton Road, Horsham), three miles north of Turnpike Exit 343, adjacent to Naval Air Station–Joint Reserve Base Willow Grove, PA 19090.

The **Mid-Atlantic Air Museum** contains forty-three civilian and twenty-two military airplanes from 1928 to the present plus two Wright Brothers' replicas. Many of these are used in air shows. The museum is located at the Reading Regional Airport, off Route 183 (eighteen miles south of I-78 or just north of the intersection of Routes 422 and 183). Address: 11 Museum Drive, Reading, PA 19605.

The **Piper Aviation Museum** in Lock Haven is dedicated to the former company located on this site and contains aircraft and aircraft equipment, corporate and family records, flight journals and magazines, photographs, and memorabilia. The museum's address is One Piper Way, Lock Haven, PA 17745.

The **U.S. Army Heritage and Education Center**, adjacent to the Army War College, in Carlisle, offers rotating exhibits on different aspects of U.S. military history, but its primary function is to preserve journals, letters, and other memorabilia relating to veterans, to present lectures and other educational programs, and to facilitate research. It is located at 950 Soldiers Drive, Carlisle, PA 17013.

The **Flight 93 National Memorial** at Shanksville opened on September 11, 2015. Here, fourteen years earlier, the passengers and crew of United Airlines Flight 93 forced terrorists who had hijacked the plane with the probable intention of targeting the White House or Capitol to crash with the loss of all aboard. Authorized by Congress in 2002, the memorial was designed by Paul Murdoch Architects and Nelson Byrd Woltz Landscape Architects. Panels at a Visitor Shelter tell the story of the flight; visitors are invited to write messages and leave tributes. A Wall of Names has forty panels honoring the passengers and crew who died on the flight. Flight 93 National Memorial is located at 6424 Lincoln Highway, Stoystown, PA 15563; mailing address is P.O. Box 911, Shanksville, PA 15560.

Notes

INTRODUCTION

1 See Carolyn Weekly, *The Kingdoms of Edward Hicks* (New York: Abrams, 1999).

2 Voltaire, *Letters on the English* (Cambridge, MA: Harvard Classics, 1909), letter 4, "On the Quakers."

3 See Lucie Street, *An Uncommon Sailor: A Portrait of Admiral Sir William Penn* (New York: St. Martin's, 1988); and Richard S. Dunn and Mary Maples Dunn, eds. *The World of William Penn* (Philadelphia: University of Pennsylvania Press, 1986).

4 The standard work is E. Willard Miller, ed., *A Geography of Pennsylvania* (University Park: Pennsylvania State University Press, 1995).

5 Vikram Rao, *Shale Gas: The Promise and the Peril* (Research Triangle Park, NC: RTI Press, 2012).

CHAPTER ONE: BEFORE PENNSYLVANIA

1 Thomas J. Sugrue, "The Peopling and Depeopling of Early Pennsylvania: Indians and Colonists, 1680–1720," *Pennsylvania Magazine of History and Biography* 116 (1992): 3–31, esp. 9–12.

2 See Michael Dean Mackintosh, "New Sweden, Natives, and Nature," in *Friends and Enemies in Penn's Woods: Indians, Colonists, and the Racial Construction of Pennsylvania*, ed. William A. Pencak and Daniel K. Richter (University Park: Pennsylvania State University Press, 2004), 3–17.

3 See Carol E. Hoffecker et al., eds. *New Sweden in America* (Newark: University of Delaware Press, 1995).

4 Karen Ordahl Kupperman, ed., *Captain John Smith: A Select Edition of His Writings* (Chapel Hill: University of North Carolina Press, 1988), 160. To facilitate the reader, spelling, capitalization, and punctuation have been modernized in this and many other quotes throughout the book.

5 James F. Pendergast, "The Massawomeck: Raiders and Traders into the Chesapeake Bay in the Seventeenth Century," *Transactions of the American Philosophical Society*, n.s., 81 (1991): i–vii; 1–101.

6 Francis Jennings, "The Indian Trade of the Susquehanna Valley," *Proceedings of the American Philosophical Society* 111 (1966): 406–24.

7 Daniel K. Richter, "War and Culture: The Iroquois Experience," *William and Mary Quarterly*, 3rd ser., 40 (1983): 528–59; Jon Parmenter, "After the Mourning Wars: The Iroquois as Allies in Colonial North American Campaigns, 1676–1760," *William and Mary Quarterly*, 3rd ser., 64 (2007): 39–76.

8 Daniel K. Richter, *The Ordeal of the Longhouse: The Iroquois Peoples in the Era of European Colonization* (Chapel Hill: University of North Carolina Press, 1992).

9 Daniel K. Richter and James H. Merrell, eds., *Beyond the Covenant Chain: The Iroquois and Their Neighbors in*

North America, 1600–1800 (University
Park: Pennsylvania State University Press,
2003); Francis Jennings, *The Ambiguous
Iroquois Empire: The Covenant Chain
Confederation of Tribes with the English
Empire from the Beginnings to the Treaty
of Lancaster* (New York: W. W. Norton,
1984).

CHAPTER TWO: PENNSYLVANIA'S EARLY DEFENSE POLICY, 1682–1730

1 Jeffery M. Dorwart, *Invasion and
Insurrection: Security, Defense, and War in
the Delaware Valley, 1621–1815* (Newark:
University of Delaware Press, 2009), 52–
53; Simon Finger, "'A Flag of Defiance at
the Masthead': The Delaware River Pilots
and the Sinews of Philadelphia's Atlantic
World in the Eighteenth Century," *Early
American Studies* 8 (2010): 386–409. For
maps of the land ceded by the treaties,
see James O'Neil Spady, "Colonialism
and the Discursive Antecedents of *Penn's
Treaty with the Indians*," in Pencak and
Richter, *Friends and Enemies in Penn's
Woods*, 18–40, esp. map on 34.

2 Spady, "Colonalism and the
Discursive Antecedents of *Penn's Treaty
with the Indians*."

3 Good examples of these quarrels
include John Smolenski, "The Death of
Sawantaeny and the Problem of Justice
on the Frontier," and Louis M. Waddell,
"Justice, Retribution, and the Case of
John Toby," in Pencak and Richter,
Friends and Enemies in Penn's Woods,
104–43; and David C. Hsiung, "Death on
the Juniata: Delawares, Iroquois, and
Pennsylvanians in a Colonial Whodunit,"
Pennsylvania History 65 (1998): 445–77.

4 Dorwart, *Invasion and Insurrection*,
56–59; Joseph J. Kelley Jr., *Pennsylvania:
The Colonial Years, 1681–1776* (Garden
City, NY: Doubleday, 1980), 78–89;
Samuel J. Newland, *The Pennsylvania
Militia: Defending the Commonwealth,*

1669–1870 (Annville: Commonwealth of
Pennsylvania, Department of Military
and Veterans Affairs, 2002), 10.

5 Dorwart, *Invasion and Insurrection*,
59–60.

6 Hamilton quoted in ibid., 60; Kelley,
Pennsylvania, 119–22.

7 Dorwart, *Invasion and Insurrection*,
60–62; Kelley, *Pennsylvania*, 130–42;
Newland, *Pennsylvania Militia*, 14–16.

CHAPTER THREE: WARS IN PENNSYLVANIA, 1731–1748

1 For this and the following paragraphs, see Paul Doutrich, "Cresap's War:
Expansion and Conflict in the
Susquehanna Valley," *Pennsylvania
History* 53 (1986): 89–104; Joseph Ord
Cresap and Bernarr Cresap, *The History
of the Cresaps* (Gallatin, TN: Cresap
Society, 1987), 19–74; Patrick Spero,
"The Conojocular War: The Politics of
Colonial Competition, 1732–1737,"
*Pennsylvania Magazine of History and
Biography* 136 (2012): 365–403.

2 Newland, *Pennsylvania Militia*, 30–
32; Dorwart, *Invasion and Insurrection*,
67–68.

3 Daniel Johnson, "'What Must Poor
People Do?': Economic Protest and
Plebeian Culture in Philadelphia, 1682–
1754," *Pennsylvania History* 79 (2012):
117–153.

4 Newland, *Pennsylvania Militia*, 30–
32; Dorwart, *Invasion and Insurrection*,
67–68.

5 Thomas Montgomery, ed., "Officers
and Soldiers in the Service of the
Province of Pennsylvania," in
Pennsylvania Archives, 5th ser., vol. 1
(Harrisburg, PA: Secretary of the
Commonwealth, 1906), 3–17, has the
data on the soldiers as discussed in this
and the next paragraph.

6 Three accounts of the Association are
used for this and the next several paragraphs: Sally Griffith, "'Order, Discipline

and a Few Cannon': Benjamin Franklin, the Association, and the Rhetoric and Practice of Boosterism," *Pennsylvania Magazine of History and Biography* 116 (1992): 131–55; Barbara Gannon, "The Lord Is a Man of War, the God of Love and Peace: The Association Debate, Philadelphia, 1747–1748," *Pennsylvania History* 65 (1998): 46–61; and Jessica Choppin Roney, "'Ready to Act in Defiance of Government': Colonial Philadelphia Voluntary Culture and the Defense Association of 1747–1748," *Early American Studies* 8 (2010): 358–83. See also Dorwart, *Invasion and Insurrection*, 70–76; and Newland, *Pennsylvania Militia*, 33–45.

CHAPTER FOUR: PENNSYLVANIA IN THE FRENCH AND INDIAN WARS, 1748–1766

1 For Croghan's fascinating and colorful career, see especially Nicholas B. Wainwright, *George Croghan: Wilderness Diplomat* (Chapel Hill: University of North Carolina Press, 1959); and William J. Campbell, "An Adverse Patron: Land, Trade, and George Croghan," *Pennsylvania History* 76 (2009): 117–40; quotation from David Dixon, *Never Come to Peace Again: Pontiac's Uprising and the Fate of the British Empire in North America* (Norman: University of Oklahoma Press, 2005): 15.

2 C. B. Galbreath, ed., *Expedition of Celoron to the Ohio Country in 1749* (Columbus, OH: F. J. Herr Printing, 1921).

3 Kenneth P. Bailey, *The Ohio Company of Virginia and the Westward Movement, 1748–1792* (1939; repr., Lewisburg, PA: Wennawoods, 2000).

4 Lois Mulkearn, "Why the Treaty of Logstown, 1752," *Virginia Magazine of History and Biography* 59, no. 1 (1951): 3–20.

5 Donald H. Kent, *The French Invasion of Western Pennsylvania, 1753* (Harrisburg: Pennsylvania Historical and Museum Commission, 1954).

6 Eugene Irving McCormac, *Colonial Opposition to Imperial Authority During the French and Indian War* (Berkeley: University of California Studies in History, 1911), 16–17.

7 Hugh Cleland, ed., *George Washington in the Ohio Valley* (Pittsburgh: University of Pittsburgh Press, 1955).

8 Doug MacGregor, "The Shot Not Heard Round the World: Fort Trent and the Opening of the War for the Empire," *Pennsylvania History* 74, no. 3 (2007): 354–73.

9 "Ensign Ward's Deposition," in William M. Darlington, ed., *Christopher Gist's Journals* (1893; repr., New York: Argonaut Press, 1966), 275–78; Frederick Tilberg, "Washington's Stockade at Fort Necessity," *Pennsylvania History* 20, no. 3 (1953): 240–57.

10 Edward G. Lengel, *General George Washington: A Military Life* (New York: Random House, 2005), 33–38.

11 Ibid., 41–43.

12 T. R. Clayton, "The Duke of Halifax, the Earl of Newcastle, and the American Origins of the Seven Years' War," *Historical Journal* 14 (1981): 571–603; Thad W. Riker, "The Politics Behind Braddock's Expedition," *American Historical Review* 12 (1904): 742–52.

13 Timothy J. Shannon, *Indians and Colonists at the Crossroads of Empire: The Albany Congress of 1754* (Ithaca, NY; Cornell University Press, 2002), chaps. 3 and 6.

14 Ibid., chaps. 4 and 5; McCormac, *Colonial Opposition*, 39–40.

15 Stephen C. Harper, *Promised Land: Penn's Holy Experiment, the Walking Purchase, and the Dispossession of the Delawares, 1600–1783* (Bethlehem, PA: Lehigh University Press, 2008).

16 Frank G. Speck, "The Delaware Indians as Women: Were the Original Pennsylvanians Politically Emasculated?" *Pennsylvania Magazine of History and Biography* 70 (1946): 377–89; William A. Starna, "The Diplomatic Career of Canasatego," in Pencak and Richter, *Friends and Enemies in Penn's Woods*, 144–66.

17 See James H. Merrell, ed., *The Lancaster Treaty of 1744* (Boston: Bedford/St. Martin's, 2008).

18 Joseph R. Fischer, *A Well-Executed Failure: The Sullivan Campaign Against the Iroquois, July–September 1779* (Columbia: University of South Carolina Press, 2008), 16.

19 Paul E. Kopperman, *Braddock at the Monongahela* (Pittsburgh: University of Pittsburgh Press, 1977); Thomas E. Crocker, *Braddock's March: How the Man Sent to Seize a Continent Changed American History* (Yardley, PA: Westholme, 2009).

20 Benjamin Franklin, *The Autobiography of Benjamin Franklin*, chap. 16. There are numerous online and in print versions of the *Autobiography* with different pagination, chapters, and sometimes texts. I have cited the one found at www.readbookonline.net/title/54245/.

21 McCormac, *Colonial Opposition*, 43.

22 Kopperman, *Braddock*, chap. 9; Franklin, *Autobiography*, chap. 16; McCormac, *Colonial Opposition*, 46.

23 Franklin, *Autobiography*, chap. 16.

24 C. A. Weslager, *The Delaware Indians: A History* (New Brunswick, NJ: Rutgers University Press, 1990), 225.

25 Kopperman, *Braddock*, 103–4.

26 Franklin, *Autobiography*, chap. 16.

27 James Graham, *The Life of General Daniel Morgan of the Virginia Line of the Army of the United States* (New York: Derby and Jackson, 1856), 29–30; John Mack Faragher, *Daniel Boone: The Life and Legend of an American Pioneer* (New York: Holt, 1993), 36–40.

28 In addition to the books by Kopperman and Crocker, cited above, see good firsthand accounts of the battle: Charles Hamilton, ed., *Braddock's Defeat: The Journal of Captain Robert Cholmley's Batman; The Journal of a British Officer; Halkett's Orderly Book* (Norman: University of Oklahoma Press, 1959); Sheldon S. Cohen, ed., "Major William Sparke Along the Monongahela: A New Historical Account of Braddock's Defeat," *Pennsylvania History* 62, no. 2 (1995): 546–56.

29 "The Braddock Campaign," Fort Necessity website, http://www.nps.gov/fone/braddock.htm.

30 Paul A. W. Wallace, *Indians in Pennsylvania* (Harrisburg: Pennsylvania Historical and Museum Commission, 1981), 147.

31 Morton Montgomery, *History of Berks County in Pennsylvania* (Philadelphia: Everts, Peck, and Richards, 1909): 109–10.

32 Fred Brenckman, *History of Carbon County, Pennsylvania* (Harrisburg, PA: James J. Nungesser, 1913), 34–46.

33 Fredric Klees, *The Pennsylvania Dutch* (New York: Macmillan, 1961), 154–56.

34 Kelley, *Pennsylvania*, 335–43; Newland, *Pennsylvania Militia*, 76–79; Peters quotations from Matthew C. Ward, "An Army of Servants: The Pennsylvania Regiment During the Seven Years' War," *Pennsylvania Magazine of History and Biography* 119 (1995): 78.

35 Dorwart, *Invasion and Insurrection*, 86–88.

36 Louis M. Waddell, "Defending the Long Perimeter: Forts on the Pennsylvania, Virginia, and Maryland Frontier," *Pennsylvania History* 62, no. 2 (1995): 171–95.

37 For accounts of the Kittanning expedition, see Daniel P. Barr, "Victory at Kittanning? Reevaluating the Impact of Armstrong's Raid on the Seven Years' War in Pennsylvania," *Pennsylvania*

Magazine of History and Biography 131
(2007): 5–32; James P. Myers Jr.,
"Pennsylvania's Awakening: The
Kittanning Raid of 1756," *Pennsylvania
History* 66, no. 3 (1999): 399–420; and
William A. Hunter, "Victory at
Kittanning," *Pennsylvania History* 23, no.
3 (1956): 376–407.

38 Myers, "Pennsylvania's Awakening,"
408, 412, for Barton quotations.

39 Barr, "Victory at Kittanning," 23–24,
29.

40 John J. Zimmerman, "Benjamin
Franklin and the Quaker Party, 1755–
1756," *William and Mary Quarterly*, 3rd
ser., 17 (1960): 291–313; Matthew C.
Ward, "An Army of Servants," 75–93.

41 Fred Anderson, *Crucible of War: The
Seven Years' War and the Fate of Empire
in British North America, 1754–1766*
(New York: Vintage, 2001), 204–6.

42 John J. Zimmerman, "Governor
Denny and the Quartering Act of 1756,"
*Pennsylvania Magazine of History and
Biography* 91 (1967): 266–81.

43 McCormac, *Colonial Opposition*,
54–57.

44 Douglas C. Cubbison, *The British
Defeat of the French in Pennsylvania,
1758: A Military History of the Forbes
Campaign Against Fort Dusquesne*
(Jefferson, NC: McFarland, 2010), is the
source for all information on the cam-
paign except where noted. For
Washington's role, see Lengel, *General
George Washington*, 67–76.

45 Anderson, *Crucible of War*, 274–80.

46 Dixon, *Never Come to Peace Again*,
38–41.

47 Newland, *Pennsylvania Militia*, 91–
92; Kelley, *Pennsylvania*, 437.

48 Dixon, *Never Come to Peace Again*,
41.

49 Ibid., 62–72.

50 See Anderson, *Crucible of War*, 250–
56, 400–409, 457–75 for Amherst's career
during the war.

51 Dixon, *Never Come to Peace Again*,
57–78, quotations at 77–78.

52 Ibid., 99, 103, 105.

53 Ibid., 94–97.

54 See Francis Parkman's classic, *The
Conspiracy of Pontiac* (New York: Collier
Books, 1962); Charles S. Grant, "Pontiac's
Rebellion and the British Troop Moves of
1763," *Mississippi Valley Historical Review*
40 (1953): 75–88; as well as Dixon, *Never
Come to Peace Again*; and Gregory Evans
Dowd, *War Under Heaven: Pontiac, the
Indian Nations, and the British Empire*
(Baltimore: Johns Hopkins University
Press, 2004).

55 Dixon, *Never Come to Peace Again*,
108–21.

56 Ibid., 135–38.

57 Ibid., 147–50, 151–52.

58 Elizabeth A. Fenn, "Biological
Warfare in Eighteenth-Century North
America: Beyond Jeffery Amherst,"
Journal of American History 86 (2000):
1552–80, argues that the blankets were
the cause of the epidemic; Philip Ranlet,
"The British, the Indians, and Smallpox:
What Actually Happened at Fort Pitt in
1763?" *Pennsylvania History* 67, no. 3
(2000): 427–41, argues that not all Indian
groups who received them suffered an
epidemic, as most had been in contact
with whites a long time.

59 Dixon, *Never Come to Peace Again*,
162–68.

60 Ibid., 186–95.

61 Ibid., 199–202.

62 Ibid., 215–16.

63 For good accounts of the Paxton
Boys, Kevin Kenny, *Peaceable Kingdom
Lost: The Paxton Boys and the Destruction
of William Penn's Holy Experiment* (New
York: Oxford University Press, 2011); see
also Brooke Hindle, "The March of the
Paxton Boys," *William and Mary
Quarterly*, 3rd ser., 3 (1946): 461–86;
James E. Crowley, "The Paxton
Disturbance and Ideas of Order in
Pennsylvania Politics," *Pennsylvania
History* 37, no. 4 (1970): 317–19.

64 Statement of William Henry, Esq., of Lancaster, in *An Authentic History of Lancaster County in the State of Pennsylvania*, ed. J. I. Mombert (Lancaster, PA: J. E. Barr, 1869), 185.

65 Ibid., 185–86; Samuel Hazard, ed., *Colonial Records of Pennsylvania, 1683–1776: Minutes of the Provincial Council of Pennsylvania from the Organization to the Termination of the Proprietary Government*, vol. 9 (Harrisburg, PA: T. Fenn, 1852), 101. For this mentality, see Jeremy Engels, "Equipped for Murder: The Paxton Boys and the Spirit of Killing All Indians in Pennsylvania, 1763–1764," *Rhetoric and Public Affairs* 8 (2005): 355–82.

66 Isaac Sharpless, "A Pennsylvania Episode," *Bulletin of Friends' Historical Society of Philadelphia* 1, no. 2 (1907): 73–74.

67 [Thomas Barton], *The Conduct of the Paxton-Men, Impartially Represented* (Philadelphia, 1764).

68 The pamphlets are printed in John R. Dunbar, ed., *The Paxton Papers* (The Hague: Mouton, 1957); and thoroughly discussed in Alison Gilbert Olson, "The Pamphlet War over the Paxton Boys," *Pennsylvania Magazine of History and Biography* 123 (1999): 31–55.

69 Dixon, *Never Come to Peace Again*, 216–19.

70 Ibid., 219–21. The Conococheague massacre occurred near present-day Mercersburg, in the Cumberland Valley.

71 Matthew C. Ward, "Redeeming the Captives: Pennsylvania Captives Among the Ohio Indians, 1755–1765," *Pennsylvania Magazine of History and Biography* 125 (2001): 161–89.

72 James E. Seaver, ed., *A Narrative of the Life of Mrs. Mary Jemison* (1824; Syracuse, NY: Syracuse University Press, 1990), 19–22.

73 Daniel P. Barr, "'A Monster So Brutal': Simon Girty and the Degenerative Myth of the American Frontier, 1783–1900," *Essays in History* 40 (1998), http://www. essaysinhistory.com/articles/2012/114.

74 G. S. Rowe, "The Frederick Stump Affair, 1768, and Its Challenge to Legal Historians of Early Pennsylvania," *Pennsylvania History* 49, no. 4 (1982): 259–88.

75 Eleanor M. Webster, "Insurrection at Fort Loudon in 1765: Rebellion or Preservation of Peace?" *Western Pennsylvania History* 47 (1964): 125–39.

76 For two accounts of the Black Boys and their resistance, see Stephen H. Cutcliffe, "Sideling Hill Affair: The Cumberland County Riots of 1765," *Western Pennsylvania History* 59 (1976): 39–54; and Webster, "Insurrection at Fort Loudon."

77 Dixon, *Never Come to Peace Again*, 257.

78 The song, written by an Irishman, George Campbell, and sung to the tune of "Black Joke," is contained in a brief autobiographical account by the major figure involved in the Cumberland County riot, James Smith, *An Account of the Remarkable Occurrences in the Life and Travels of Col. James Smith* (Lexington, KY, 1799), 111–13; see also Hazard, *Colonial Records*, 9:270–72; Karen Ramsburg, "Saving the Birthplace of the American Revolution," with remarks by Patrick Spero and Nathan Kozuskanich, *Pennsylvania History* 79, no. 1 (2012): 49–64; and SavetheSmithHouse.com for efforts to save the house.

CHAPTER FIVE: PENNSYLVANIA IN THE AMERICAN REVOLUTION, 1765–1783

1 Ann Uhry Abrams, "Benjamin West's Documentation of Colonial History: *William Penn's Treaty with the Indians*," *Art Bulletin* 64, no. 1 (1982): 59–70.

2 For the Presbyterian impact on Pennsylvania politics, see Nathan R. Kozuskanich, "For the Security and Protection of the Community: The Frontier and the Makings of Pennsylvanian Constitutionalism" (Ph.D. thesis, Ohio State University, 2005); Cornell University Press is publishing a revised version.

3 The best account of revolutionary mobilization in Philadelphia is Richard Alan Ryerson, *The Revolution Is Now Begun: The Radical Committees of Philadelphia, 1765–1776* (Philadelphia: University of Pennsylvania Press, 1978).

4 Joseph Seymour, *The Pennsylvania Associators, 1747–1777* (Yardley, PA: Westholme, 2012), 60–64.

5 See Robert J. Guy Jr., "William Thompson and the Pennsylvania Riflemen," in *Pennsylvania's Revolution*, ed. William Pencak (University Park: Pennsylvania State University Press, 2010), 211–30. For the rifles themselves, see John Dillin, *The Kentucky Rifle* (York, PA: George Shumway, 1967). See also the entries for these respective counties, in John B. Frantz and William Pencak, eds., *Beyond Philadelphia: The American Revolution in the Pennsylvania Hinterland* (University Park: Pennsylvania State University Press, 1998).

6 Philip J. Swain Jr., "Bostonians Who Served in the American Revolution" (senior paper, Tufts University, 1978); Edward C. Papenfuse and Gregory Stiverson, "General Smallwood's Recruits: The Peacetime Career of the Revolutionary War Private," *William and Mary Quarterly*, 3rd ser., 30 (1973): 117–32; for donation and depreciation lands, see Donna Bingham Munger, *Pennsylvania Land Records: A History and Guide for Research* (Lanham, MD: Rowman and Littlefield, 1993); Christine Rose, *Military Bounty Land, 1776–1855* (Dunn Loring, VA: CR Publications, 2011).

7 Steven Rosswurm, *Arms, Country, and Class: The Philadelphia Militia and the "Lower Sort" During the American Revolution* (New Brunswick, NJ: Rutgers University Press, 1989).

8 John Gilbert McCurdy, "The Origins of Universal Suffrage: The Pennsylvania Constitution of 1776," *Pennsylvania Legacies* 8, no. 2 (2008): 6–13.

9 For the constitution as democratic, see Paul Selsam, *The Pennsylvania Constitution of 1776: A Study in Revolutionary Democracy* (Philadelphia: University of Pennsylvania Presss, 1936); for the view that was imposed by a frequently tyrannical minority, see Wayne L. Bockelman and Owen S. Ireland, "The Internal Revolution in Pennsylvania: An Ethnic-Religious Interpretation," *Pennsylvania History* 41, no. 2 (1974): 124–59.

10 For this and the next several paragraphs, see Francis S. Fox, "Pennsylvania's Revolutionary Militia Law: The Statute that Transformed the State," *Pennsylvania History* 80, no. 2 (2013): 204–14; see also Karen Guenther, "Berks County," in Frantz and Pencak, *Beyond Philadelphia*, 81–82; Jerome H. Wood Jr., *Conestoga Crossroads: Lancaster, Pennsylvania, 1730–1790* (Harrisburg: Pennsylvania Historical and Museum Commission, 1979), 144–53.

11 Most of the information in this section is from Wilbur H. Siebert, *The Loyalists of Pennsylvania* (Columbus: Ohio State University, 1920), archive.org/details/pennsyloyalist00siebri ch. See also Anne M. Ousterhout, *A State Divided: Opposition in Pennsylvania to the American Revolution* (Westport, CT: Praeger, 1987).

12 Most of the information in this and the following section comes from Siebert, *Loyalists of Pennsylvania*.

13 Rosemary S. Warden, "The Infamous Fitch: The Tory Bandit, James

Fitzpatrick of Chester County,"
Pennsylvania History 62, no. 3 (1995):
376–87.

14 Peter Mulcahy, "The Doan Outlaws
of Bucks County: The Life and Times of
the Plumstead Cowboys," http://hayge-
nealogy.com/hay/sources/gibson/doans.h
tml.

15 See three works by James P. Myers
Jr., "The Bermudian Creek Tories,"
Adams County History 3 (1997): 4–40;
"Homeland Security in the Pennsylvania
Backcountry: The Example of the
Reverend Mr. Daniel Batwelle, SPG,"
Pennsylvania History 78, no. 3 (2011):
247–71; and *The Ordeal of Thomas
Barton, Anglican Missionary in the
Pennsylvania Backcountry, 1755–1780*
(Bethlehem, PA: Lehigh University Press,
2010).

16 Siebert, *Loyalists*, 27–37.

17 Judith Van Buskirk, "They Didn't
Join the Band: Disaffected Women in
Revolutionary Philadelphia,"
Pennsylvania History 62, no. 3 (1995):
319–20.

18 Siebert, "Loyalists," 58–59; for general patterns of allegiance by region in
Pennsylvania, see Frantz and Pencak,
Beyond Philadelphia, esp. xix–xxv and
195–98.

19 Ken Miller, *Dangerous Guests:
Enemy Captives and Revolutionary
Communities
During the War for Independence*
(Ithaca, NY: Cornell University Press,
2014), chaps. 3 and 4; Francis S. Fox,
*Sweet Land of Liberty: The Ordeal of the
American Revolution in Northampton
County, Pennsylvania* (University Park:
Pennsylvania State University Press,
2003), 137–42.

20 The standard history of
Washington's winter 1776–1777 cam-
paign is now David Hackett Fischer,
Washington's Crossing (New York: Oxford
University Press, 2006).

21 Thomas Paine, *Thomas Paine:
Collected Writings,* ed. Eric Foner (New
York: Library of America, 1995), 91.

22 Thomas J. McGuire, *Brandywine
Battlefield Park* (Mechanicsburg, PA:
Stackpole Books, 2001), quotation at 17;
McGuire's far more detailed account, *The
Philadelphia Campaign,* vol. 1,
Brandywine and the Fall of Philadelphia
(Mechanicsburg, PA: Stackpole Books,
2006), and Stephen R. Taaffe, *The
Philadelphia Campaign, 1777–1778*
(Lawrence: University Press of Kansas,
2003), esp. 63–80, are the best discus-
sions of the Battle of Brandywine.

23 Ebenezer Elmer (1752–1843) of
New Jersey, later a U.S. congressman, has
extensive papers from the revolution at
the New Jersey Historical Society,
Newark, including journals, observations
of Indian life during the Sullivan
Expedition, and writings on medicine
and politics.

24 Thomas J. McGuire, *The Battle of
Paoli* (Mechanicsburg, PA: Stackpole
Books, 1988).

25 Thomas J. McGuire, *The
Philadelphia Campaign,* vol. 2,
Germantown and the Road to Valley Forge
(Mechanicsburg, PA: Stackpole Books,
2007).

26 Joseph Plumb Martin, *A Narrative
of a Revolutionary Soldier* (New York:
Signet, 2010), 64.

27 John W. Jackson, *The Pennsylvania
Navy, 1775–1781: The Defense of the
Delaware* (New Brunswick, NJ: Rutgers
University Press, 1974); Martin,
Narrative, esp. 76–77.

28 Paine, *Paine: Collected Writings*, 162.

29 Wayne Bodle, *The Valley Forge
Winter: Civilians and Soldiers in War*
(University Park: Pennsylvania State
University Press, 2004), 66. Bodle's study
is the most thorough account of this
winter.

30 Albigence Waldo, "Diary of Surgeon
Albigence Waldo, of the Connecticut

Line," *Pennsylvania Magazine of History and Biography* 21 (1897): 306–7.

31 James S. Bailey, "Two Winters of Discontent: A Comparative Look at the Continental Army's Encampments at Valley Forge and Jockey Hollow," in Pencak, *Pennsylvania's Revolution*, 306–34.

32 Simon Finger, *The Contagious City: The Politics of Public Health in Philadelphia* (Ithaca, NY: Cornell University Press, 2012), 86–104; Elizabeth A. Fenn, *Pox Americana: The Great Smallpox Epidemic of 1775–1782* (New York: Hill and Wang, 2004), esp. 98–102.

33 Paul Lockhart, *The Drillmaster of Valley Forge: The Baron de Steuben and the Making of the American Army* (Washington, DC: Smithsonian Books, 2008).

34 Letter from George Washington to Gouverneur Morris, May 29, 1778, in *Writings of George Washington*, electronic text, vol. 11; Taaffe, *Philadelphia Campaign*, 188–89.

35 Siebert, *Loyalists*, 40–50.

36 Van Buskirk, "They Didn't Join the Band," 307–29; Meredith H. Lair, "Redcoat Theater: Negotiating Identity in Occupied Philadelphia, 1777–1778," in Pencak, *Pennsylvania's Revolution*, 192–210.

37 Allen quote, Siebert, *Loyalists*, 48.

38 Van Buskirk, "They Didn't Join the Band," 317; for organizer John André's colorful account of the Meschianza, see Benson J. Lossing, *The Pictorial Field-Book of the Revolution*, vol. 2 (New York: Harper, 1852), 303–7n.

39 Peter C. Messer, "A Species of Treason and Not the Least Dangerous Kind: The Treason Trials of Abraham Carlisle and John Roberts," *Pennsylvania Magazine of History and Biography* 123 (1999): 303–32; for the treason trials of William Hamilton and David Franks, discussed in the next paragraphs, see M. Laffitte Vieira, *West Philadelphia*

Illustrated (Philadelphia: Avil Printing Company, 1903), 110–12 (for Hamilton); and Mark Abbott Stern, *David Franks: Colonial Merchant* (University Park: Pennsylvania State University Press, 2010), esp. 1–5, 142–57 (for both Hamilton and Franks).

40 Siebert, *Loyalists*, 69–71.

41 See generally William Pencak, "The Revolution Magnified: Pennsylvania in the Late Eighteenth Century," in John M. Coleman, Robert G. Crist, and Phillip E. Stebbins, eds., *Pennsylvania and the Federal Constitution* (University Park: Pennsylvania Historical Association, 1987), 5–20; Charles Rappleye, *Robert Morris: Financier of the American Revolution* (New York: Simon and Schuster, 2010), 181–195.

42 John K. Alexander, "The Fort Wilson Incident of 1779: A Case Study of the Revolutionary Crowd," *William and Mary Quarterly*, 3rd ser., 31 (1974): — 589, 590, 593; Rosswurm, *Arms, Country, and Class*, 205–27.

43 Alexander, "The Fort Wilson Incident," 594.

44 Ibid., 599–600.

45 Ibid., 600–601. See Russell F. Weigley, et al. *Philadelphia: A Three Hundred Year Old History* (New York: W.W. Norton, 1982), 147.

46 Ibid., 589.

47 Jackson, *Pennsylvania Navy*; Charles Oscar Paullin, *The Navy of the American Revolution* (Chicago: University of Chicago, 1906), 373–96.

48 M. Ruth Kelly, *The Olmstead Case: Privateers, Property and Politics in Pennsylvania, 1787–1810* (Selingsgrove: Susquehanna University Press, 2005)

49 Tim McGrath, *John Barry: An American Hero in the Age of Sail* (Yardley, PA: Westholme, 2011).

50 Mary Beth Norton, *Liberty's Daughters: The Revolutionary Experience of American Women, 1750–1800* (Boston:

Little, Brown, 1980), 178–86; [Esther DeBerdt Reed], *The Sentiments of an American Woman* (Philadelphia: John Dunlap, 1780).

51 Bray Hammond, *Banks and Politics in America from the Revolution to the Civil War* (Princeton, NJ: Princeton University Press, 1991), 40–64.

52 E. Wayne Carp, *To Stave the Army at Pleasure* (Chapel Hill: University of North Carolina Press, 1984), 175–87.

53 Charles Coleman Sellers, *Charles Willson Peale with Patron and Populace* (Philadelphia: American Philosophical Society, 1969), 17–19.

54 There are two good modern accounts of the 1783 mutiny: Kenneth R. Bowling, "New Light on the Philadelphia Mutiny of 1783: Federal-State Confrontation at the Close of the War for Independence," *Pennsylvania Magazine of History and Biography* 101 (1977): 419–50; and Mary A. Y. Gallagher, "Reinterpreting the 'Very Trifling Mutiny' at Philadelphia in June 1783," *Pennsylvania Magazine of History and Biography* 119 (1995): 3–35.

55 Sellers, *Charles Willson Peale*, 20.

56 Main sources for the discussion of the Wyoming Valley are Glenn F. Williams, *Year of the Hangman: George Washington's Campaign Against the Iroquois* (Yardley, PA: Westholme, 2005), Paul B. Moyer, *Wild Yankees: The Struggle for Independence Along the Revolutionary Frontier* (Ithaca, NY: Cornell University Press, 2007); Frederick J. Stefon, "The Wyoming Valley," in Frantz and Pencak, *Beyond Philadelphia*, 133–52; and Kelley, *Pennsylvania*, 649–53, 680–88; see James R. Williamson and Linda A. Fossler, *Zebulon Butler: Hero of the Revolutionary Frontier* (Westport, CT: Greenwood Press, 1995), for a fine general account of the struggle. On the death of Teedyuscung, see Moyer, *Wild Yankees*, 21–22; Dowd, *War Under Heaven*, 81–82.

57 Moyer, *Wild Yankees*, 14–21.

58 Peter C. Mancall, *Valley of Opportunity: Economic Culture Along the Upper Susquehanna, 1700–1800* (Ithaca, NY: Cornell University Press, 1991).

59 Julian P. Boyd and Robert J. Taylor, eds., *The Susquehannah Company Papers*, 11 vols. (Ithaca, NY: Cornell University Press, 1962–1971): 6:329.

60 Robert J. Brugger, *Maryland: A Middle Temperament, 1634–1980* (Baltimore: Johns Hopkins University Press, 1986), 68–70, 102–3, 152–53.

61 Moyer, *Wild Yankees*, 22–23, 28–31.

62 Moyer, *Wild Yankees*, 24–27; Kelley, *Pennsylvania*, 649–50; Williamson and Fossler, *Zebulon Butler*, 20–24; "A New Song, in High Vogue in Northampton County, in the Province of Pennsylvania" (Philadelphia, 1771).

63 Kelley, *Pennsylvania*, 650; Williamson and Fossler, *Zebulon Butler*, 22–26, 39–44.

158 Kelley, *Pennsylvania*, 650–51; Moyer, *Wild Yankees*, 7–28.

64 Stefon, "Wyoming Valley," 140–41; Williamson and Fossler, *Zebulon Butler*, 17–25; Moyer, *Wild Yankees*, 31.

65 Kelley, *Pennsylvania*, 686–88; Stefon, "Wyoming Valley," 140–41; Francis Jennings, "James Logan," in *American National Biography*, ed. John A. Garraty and Mark C. Carnes (New York: Oxford University Press, 1999), 13:836–37.

66 Stefon, "Wyoming Valley," 138–41: Moyer, *Wild Yankees*, 39–40.

67 Moyer, *Wild Yankees*, 25–29; Williamson and Fossler, *Zebulon Butler*, 55–56.

68 Stefon, "Wyoming Valley," 144, 146; for Iroquois and other Indians at Niagara, which became a refugee center during the war for pro-British Indians, see Colin G. Calloway, *The American Revolution in Indian Country* (New York: Cambridge University Press, 1995), 129–57.

69 Barbara Graymont, *The Iroquois in the American Revolution* (Syracuse, NY: Syracuse University Press, 1975), 97–99.

70 John Luzader, *Saratoga: A Military History of the Decisive Campaign of the American Revolution* (New York: Savas Beatie, 2010), 120–39; 195–97; Fischer, *Well-Executed Failure*, 25–26.

71 Accounts of the "Wyoming Massacre" include Williams, *Year of the Hangman*, 114–133; Fischer, *Well-Executed Failure*, 23; Stefon, "Wyoming Valley," 146–48; for Jon Butler's account to Lt. Col. Bolton, July 8, 1778, Frederick Haldimand Papers, British Library Additional Manuscripts No. 21,760, folios 31–34, with thanks to the British Library (London, UK) and by courtesy of the Public Archives of Canada, available online at "Battle Related Transcriptions," Rev War '75, http://www.revwar75.com/library/jkr.

72 For the "Great Runaway," see Russell Spinney, "The Sons of the Old Chiefs: Surveying Identity and European-American Relationships in the 'New Purchase' Territory (Centre County, Pennsylvania, 1769–1778," in Pencak, *Pennsylvania's Revolution*, 121–43.

73 Kelley, *Pennsylvania*, 660.

74 The source for the Sullivan Expedition discussed in the next several paragraphs is Fischer, *Well-Executed Failure*; for this paragraph, see esp. 41–44.

75 Ibid., 182–84.

76 Ibid., 193.

77 Ibid., 182, 192.

78 Thomas S. Abler, *Cornplanter: Chief Warrior of the Allegany Senecas* (Syracuse, NY: Syracuse University Press, 2001); Joy Ann Bilharz, *The Allegany Senecas and Kinzua Dam: Forced Relocation Through Two Generations* (Lincoln: University of Nebraska Press), 1998.

CHAPTER SIX: SECURING PENNSYLVANIA'S SOVEREIGNTY, 1768–1805

1 The main sources for this section are Reuben Gold Thwaites and Louise Phelps Kellogg, eds. *Documentary History of Dunmore's War* (Madison: State Historical Society of Wisconsin, 1905); Glenn F. Williams, *Dunmore's War: The Last Conflict of America's Colonial Era* (Yardley, PA: Westholme, 2016); Douglas MacGregor, "Double Dishonor: Loyalists on the Middle Frontier," in Pencak, *Pennsylvania's Revolution*, 144–67; John Connolly, *A Narrative of the Transactions, Imprisonment, and Sufferings of John Connolly, an American Loyalist and Lieut.-Col. in His Majesty's Service*, originally published in 1783, reprinted in *Pennsylvania Magazine of History and Biography* 12 and 13 (1888 and 1889); and Tim Blessing, "The Juniata Valley," in Frantz and Pencak, *Beyond Philadelphia*, 153–70.

2 Thomas Jefferson, *Notes on the State of Virginia* (London: John Stockdale, 1787), 104–6.

3 Ibid., 105–6; see also Giles Gunn, *Early American Writing* (New York: Penguin, 1994), 409–10.

4 Gregory Knouff, "Soldiers and Violence on the Pennsylvania Frontier," in Frantz and Pencak, *Beyond Philadelphia*, 180–82.

5 Ibid., 183–84.

6 James W. Raab, *Spain, Britain, and the American Revolution in Florida* (Jefferson, NC: Mcfarland, 2007), 130–34; J. Leitch Wright, *The American Revolution in Florida* (Gainesville: University of Florida Press, 1975); Joseph Barton Starr, *Tories, Dons, and Rebels: The American Revolution in West Florida* (Gainesville: University of Florida Press, 1977).

7 William Nester, *George Rogers Clark: "I Glory in War"* (Norman: University of Oklahoma Press, 2004).

8 For the destruction of Hannastown (or Hannah's Town), see John Butler to Captain Matthews, August 5, 1782, available at http://www.revwar75.com/library/jkr.

9 The information in the following section is taken mainly from Richard H. Kohn, *Eagle and Sword: The Federalists and the Creation of the Military Establishment in America, 1783–1802* (New York: Free Press, 1975).

10 John F. Winkler, *Wabash 1791: St. Clair's Defeat* (Oxford: Osprey, 2011).

11 See Alan D. Gaff, *Bayonets in the Wilderness: Anthony Wayne's Legion in the Old Northwest* (Norman: University of Oklahoma Press, 2008).

12 Hector St.-John de Crèvecoeur, *Letters from an American Farmer; and Sketches of Eighteenth-Century America* (New York: Signet, 1963), 353.

13 Paul Moyer, "'Real' Indians, 'White' Indians, and the Contest for the Wyoming Valley," in Pencak and Richter, *Friends and Enemies*, 235–36; Stefon, "Wyoming Valley," 152.

14 Moyer, *Wild Yankees*, is the general source for the rest of this discussion of the Wyoming Valley; quotation on 43.

15 Ibid., 40–49, 58–59.

16 Ibid., 65–75.

17 Quotation from *Luzerne County Federalist*, October 1, 1801; general information from Moyer, *Wild Yankees*.

18 The standard history of the Whiskey Rebellion is Thomas P. Slaughter, *The Whiskey Rebellion: Frontier Epilogue to the American Revolution* (New York: Oxford University Press, 1988); also valuable is Steven R. Boyd, ed., *The Whiskey Rebellion: Past and Present Perspectives* (Westport, CT: Greenwood Press, 1985).

19 See Terry Bouton, *Taming Democracy: "The People," the Founders, and the Troubled End of the American Revolution* (New York: Oxford University Press, 2009); and Anthony M. Joseph, "The Decline of the Cheerful Taxpayer:

Taxation in Pennsylvania, c. 1776–1815," in Pencak, *Pennsylvania's Revolution*, 282–305.

20 "Petition Against the Excise," in *The Writings of Albert Gallatin*, ed. Henry Adams, 3 vols. (Philadelphia: Lippincott, 1879), 1:3–4.

21 Slaughter, *Whiskey Rebellion*, 184.

22 Mary K. Bonsteel Tachau, "A New Look at the Whiskey Rebellion," in Boyd, *Whiskey Rebellion*, 97–118.

23 See Jeffrey A. Davis, "Guarding the Republican Interest: The Western Pennsylvania Democratic Societies and the Excise Tax," *Pennsylvania History* 67, no. 1 (2000): 43–62.

24 "Bradford House Historical Marker," ExplorePAhistory.com, at http://explore pahistory.com/hmarker.php?markerId=1 -A-29A.

25 "Rev. John Corbley (1733–1803) Historical Marker," ExplorePAhistory. com, at http://explorepahistory.com/hmarker.php?markerId=1-A-29F.

26 Paul Douglas Newman, *Fries's Rebellion: The Enduring Struggle for the American Revolution* (Philadelphia: University of Pennsylvania Press, 2004).

27 The most important books on this subject are still James Morton Smith, *Freedom's Fetters: The Alien and Sedition Acts* (Ithaca, NY: Cornell University Press, 1966); and Leonard W. Levy, *Freedom of Speech and Press in Early American History: Legacy of Suppression* (New York: Harper and Row, 1963).

28 John E. Ferling, *Adams vs. Jefferson: The Tumultuous Election of 1800* (New York: Oxford University Press, 2005), 91–93, 144–45, 156–57, 164, 168–89.

CHAPTER SEVEN: PENNSYLVANIA IN THE WAR OF 1812 AND THE U.S.-MEXICAN WAR

1 Victor A. Sapio, *Pennsylvania and the War of 1812* (Lexington: University Press of Kentucky, 1970).

2 Martin Kaufman, "War Sentiment in Western Pennsylvania: 1812," *Pennsylvania History* 31, no. 4 (1964): 436; Harold L. Myers, *Pennsylvania and the War of 1812* (Harrisburg: Commonwealth of Pennsylvania, Pennsylvania Historical and Museum Commission, 1964), 7–12; and Julie Winch, *A Gentleman of Color: The Life of James Forten* (New York: Oxford University Press, 2002), 175–76. For more on the broader war effort, see Donald R Hickey, *The War of 1812: A Forgotten Conflict* (Urbana: University of Illinois Press, 2012).

3 George C. Daughan, *1812: The Navy's War* (New York: Basic Books, 2011), 73–84; Craig L. Symonds, *Decision at Sea: Five Naval Battles That Shaped American History* (Oxford: Oxford University Press, 2005), 23–79.

4 Richard Dillon, *We Have Met the Enemy: Oliver Hazard Perry, Wilderness Commodore* (New York: McGraw-Hill, 1978), 61–127.

5 Symonds, *Decision at Sea*, 51–74.

6 Marcus Cunliffe, *Soldiers and Civilians: The Martial Spirit in America, 1775–1865* (New York: Free Press, 1973).

7 Cunliffe, *Soldiers and Civilians*, 218.

8 Randy W. Hackenburg, *Pennsylvania in the War with Mexico* (Shippensburg, PA: White Mane, 1992), 3, 4–8, 315–16; Richard Bruce Winders, *Mr. Polk's Army: The American Military Experience in the Mexican War* (1997; repr., College Station: Texas A&M University Press, 2008), 147; Allan Peskin, ed., *Volunteers: The Mexican War Journals of Private Richard Coulter and Sergeant Thomas Barclay, Company E, Second Pennsylvania Infantry* (Kent, OH: Kent State University Press, 1991), 3, 6–7, 95.

9 Allen C. Guelzo, *Fateful Lightning: A New History of the Civil War and Reconstruction* (New York: Oxford University Press, 2012), 515–16.

CHAPTER EIGHT: PENNSYLVANIA'S WAR FOR THE UNION, 1861–1863

1 Judith Giesberg, *Keystone State in Crisis: The Civil War in Pennsylvania* (Mansfield, PA: Pennsylvania Historical Association, 2013), 11–19; Christian B. Keller, "Diverse German Immigrants and Ethnic Identity on the Eve of the Civil War," in David L. Valuska and Christian B. Keller, *Damn Dutch: Pennsylvania Germans at Gettysburg* (Mechanicsburg, PA: Stackpole Books, 2004), 8–9.

2 Jim Weeks, "Pennsylvania in the Civil War," Historic Pennsylvania Leaflet No. 23 (Harrisburg: Pennsylvania Historical and Museum Commission, 1998); Samuel P. Bates, *History of Pennsylvania Volunteers, 1861–5*, 5 vols. (Harrisburg, PA: B. Singerly, State Printer, 1869–1871), 1:3; William Blair and William Pencak, eds., *Making and Remaking Pennsylvania's Civil War* (University Park: Pennsylvania State University Press, 2001), xii; Valuska and Keller, *Damn Dutch*, 68–69.

3 Bates, *History*, 1:3–4; John David Hoptak, "The Union's Forgotten First Defenders," in "*The Civil War in Pennsylvania*," special joint issue of *Pennsylvania Heritage, Pennsylvania Legacies*, and *Western Pennsylvania History* (Summer 2013): 5–9. Hoptak's book *First in Defense of the Union: The Civil War History of the First Defenders* (Bloomington, IN: AuthorHouse, 2004) is a good overview of the history of the First Defenders.

4 James L. Schaadt, "The Allen Infantry in 1861," in Heber S. Thompson, *The First Defenders* (n.p., 1910), 138; Thompson quote from ibid., 95; Hoptak, "Union's Forgotten First Defenders," 10–13.

5 James M. McPherson, *What They Fought For, 1861–1865* (New York: Anchor Books, 1994), 32–33; Reid

Mitchell, *Civil War Soldiers: Their Expectations and Their Experiences* (New York: Penguin Books, 1988), 11–15; *Carlisle American*, April 24, 1861.

6 Christian B. Keller, *Chancellorsville and the Germans: Nativism, Ethnicity, and Civil War Memory* (New York: Fordham University Press, 2007), 26–29; Susannah Ural, *The Harp and the Eagle* (New York: New York University Press, 2006), 2–4. There is substantial evidence that ethnic (and nonethnic) troops from Pennsylvania and other Northern states also enlisted for economic reasons: a steady paycheck. Economic motivations probably combined with more patriotic ones for most soldiers, especially those who enlisted after 1861.

7 George L. Davis, "Pittsburgh's Negro Troops," *Western Pennsylvania Historical Magazine* 56 (June 1953): 104–12; Sanders quoted in Eric Ledell Smith, ed., "The Civil War Letters of Quartermaster Sergeant John C. Brock, 43th Regiment, United States Colored Troops," in Blair and Pencak, *Making and Remaking*, 143. There were three USCT regiments that marched out of Philadelphia. A small number of Pennsylvania black soldiers enlisted in other states' black regiments, such as the famous Fifty-Fourth Massachusetts, prior to the official raising of USCT regiments in the Commonwealth.

8 William B. Hesseltine, *Lincoln and the War Governors* (Gloucester, MA: Peter Smith, 1972), 166–67, 344–46, 380; Giesberg, *Keystone State in Crisis*, 78; J. Matthew Gallman, *The North Fights the Civil War: The Home Front* (Chicago: Ivan R. Dee, 1994), 165; James S. Colwell to Annie H. Colwell, November 11, 1861, reprinted in David G. Colwell, ed., *The Bitter Fruits: The Civil War Comes to a Small Town in Pennsylvania* (Carlisle, PA: Cumberland County Historical Society, 1998), 85.

9 Weeks, "Pennsylvania in the Civil War"; *Pennsylvania at Chickamauga and Chattanooga: Ceremonies at the Dedication of Monuments Erected by the Commonwealth of Pennsylvania* (Harrisburg: Wm. S. Ray, State Printer of Pennsylvania, 1900), 240–50; Valuska and Keller, *Damn Dutch*, 157.

10 Hough quoted in McPherson, *What They Fought For*, 43. For a good overview of the Peninsula Campaign, see Stephen W. Sears, *To the Gates of Richmond: The Peninsula Campaign* (New York: Houghton Mifflin, 1992).

11 One of the finest compilations of scholarly thought on the Antietam Campaign of 1862 is Gary W. Gallagher, ed., *The Antietam Campaign* (Chapel Hill: University of North Carolina Press, 2007), which provides a good introduction outlining Lee's objectives and McClellan's early movements to intercept. See Samuel Cormany's diary entries, September 10–17, 1862, reprinted in James C. Mohr, ed., *The Cormany Diaries: A Northern Family in the Civil War* (Pittsburgh: University of Pittsburgh Press, 1982), 229–31; Samuel and Rachel Cormany's letters are a trove of information on Chambersburg during the war. See also Annie H. Colwell to James S. Colwell, September 12, 1862, reprinted in Colwell, *Bitter Fruits*, 131.

12 Ted Ballard, *Battle of Antietam: Staff Ride Guide* (Washington, DC: Center of Military History, U.S. Army, 2006), 22–26, 55; U.S. War Department, *The War of the Rebellion: A Compilation of the Official Records of the Union and Confederate Armies*, 128 vols. (Washington, DC: Government Printing Office, 1893), ser. 1, vol. 19, pt. 1, 218, 274 (hereafter cited as *OR*); Colwell, *Bitter Fruits*, 136–37. The Pennsylvania Reserves were unique among the units of the Army of the Potomac, regiments originally called up by Governor Andrew

Curtin in 1861 for defense of the state but shortly turned over to Federal service. They were brigaded together and formed an entire division in the Union First Corps at Antietam. George Meade's Civil War career began when he assumed command of a brigade of the reserves in 1861. Repeated bravery, competence, and steadiness in battle had elevated him to division command of the reserves by the fall of 1862.

13 Ballard, *Battle of Antietam*, 26–28; Bates, *History*, 4:166–67.

14 Ballard, *Battle of Antietam*, 28–30; Jacob Pyewell to mother, September 20, 1862, reprinted in Alan Sessarego, *Letters Home: A Collection of Original Civil War Soldiers' Letters—Antietam, Chancellorsville, Gettysburg* (Gettysburg, PA: privately printed, 1988), 3.

15 *OR*, ser. 1, vol. 19, pt. 1, 169–80, 803–10; Stephen W. Sears, *Landscape Turned Red: The Battle of Antietam* (New York: Warner Books, 1983), 245, 259–73.

16 Unknown soldier in 130th Pennsylvania to parents, September 18, 1862, reprinted in Sessarego, *Letters Home*, 2; soldier in the 132nd Pennsylvania, quoted in Oliver C. Bosbyshell, ed., *Pennsylvania at Antietam: Report of the Antietam Battlefield Memorial Commission of Pennsylvania* (Harrisburg, PA: Harrisburg Publishing Co., State Printer, 1906), 191; James Longstreet, "The Invasion of Maryland," in *Battles and Leaders of the Civil War*, ed. Robert Underwood Johnson and Clarence Clough Buel (New York: Century Company, 1887–1888), 2:669.

17 Sears, *Landscape Turned Red*, 293–95; A. M. Gambone, *Major-General John Frederick Hartranft: Citizen Soldier and Pennsylvania Statesman* (Baltimore: Butternut and Blue Press, 1995), 62–67; Bates, *History*, 2:1–2.

18 Sears, *Landscape Turned Red*, 305–10, 315–18, 322–23.

19 This is admittedly a loose calculation based on a rudimentary analysis of available Pennsylvania regimental casualty reports for the battle combined with an estimate of likely wounded who died shortly after the battle. The actual number is probably higher.

20 George C. Rable, *Fredericksburg! Fredericksburg!* (Chapel Hill: University of North Carolina Press, 2002), 190–91.

21 Ibid., 192–95; quote from R. T. Mockbee's "Historical Sketch of the 14th Tennessee" at 195. Like Meade, John Reynolds was trained at West Point and was himself a native Pennsylvanian, born in Lancaster, and had made a name for himself as a leader in the Pennsylvania Reserves. He replaced the wounded Joseph Hooker as commander of the First Corps following Antietam.

22 Ibid., 200–204; *OR Supplement*, pt. 2, 58:88; St. Clair A. Mulholland, "At Fredericksburg," *National Tribune*, October 8, 1881.

23 Rable, *Fredericksburg*, 204–9; Bates, *History*, 1:552 and 2:762.

24 Rable, *Fredericksburg*, 210–14, 216; Reuben Schell to father, December 17, 1862, Schell Letters, in archives of Fredericksburg and Spotsylvania National Military Park, Fredericksburg, VA; Isaac R. Pennypacker, *General Meade* (New York: Appleton, 1901), 102.

25 Rable, *Fredericksburg*, 217; Paul Jones, *The Irish Brigade* (Gaithersburg, MD: Olde Soldier Books, n.d.), 124, 156–57; William McCarter, *My Life in the Irish Brigade: The Civil War Memoirs of Private William McCarter, 116th Pennsylvania Infantry*, ed. Kevin E. O'Brien (Campbell, CA: Savas, 1996), 183, 226; Frank A. Boyle, *A Party of Mad Fellows: The Story of the Irish Regiments in the Army of the Potomac* (Dayton, OH: Morningside House, 1996), 215–21; Heros von Borcke, *Memoirs of the Confederate War for Independence* (1938; reprint, Nashville, TN: J. S. Sanders, 1999), 313.

26 Stephen W. Sears, *Chancellorsville* (New York: Houghton Mifflin, 1996), 140–50; Keller, *Chancellorsville and the Germans*, 49.

27 Ernest B. Furgurson, *Chancellorsville, 1863: The Souls of the Brave* (New York: Alfred A. Knopf, 1993), 334–40 ; Daniel E. Sutherland, *Fredericksburg and Chancellorsville: The Dare Mark Campaign* (Lincoln: University of Nebraska Press, 1998), 185–90.

28 Sears, *Chancellorsville*, 442–45.

29 Keller, *Chancellorsville and the Germans*, 51, 56.

30 Francis Stofflet quoted in the *Easton Daily Free Press*, May 3, 1913; Theodore Howell to wife, May 10, 1863, MPF 502, Lehigh County Historical Society, Allentown; Colonel Charles Glanz, 153th Pennsylvania to Governor Andrew G. Curtin, June 2, 1863, RG-19, 153th Pennsylvania Folder, Pennsylvania State Archives, Harrisburg, hereafter PASA.

31 Keller, *Chancellorsville and the Germans*, 59–61; *OR*, ser. 1, vol. 25, pt. 1, 665; Martin Seel to Georg Seel, May 10, 1863, copy and translation in archives of Fredericksburg and Spotsylvania National Military Park; *Pittsburgher Freiheitsfreund*, May 18, 1863.

32 Keller, *Chancellorsville and the Germans*, 65–66; Martin Seel to Georg Seel, May 10, 1863; Hecker quoted in *Pittsburgher Freiheitsfreund*, May 22, 1863.

33 Keller, *Chancellorsville and the Germans*, 67–70; John Haingartner Civil War Memoir, Historical Society of Pennsylvania, Philadelphia; Adolph Bregler to parents, May 10, 1863, Bregler Pension File, 27th Pennsylvania, App. 172.294, certify. 128.498, National Archives and Records Administration, Washington, DC, hereafter NARA; Augustus C. Hamlin, *The Battle of Chancellorsville* (Bangor, ME: privately

published, 1896), 76; *OR*, ser. 1, vol. 25, pt. 1, 645–46; James Emmons, quoted in Mark H. Dunkelman and Michael J. Winey, *The Hardtack Regiment: An Illustrated History of the 154th Regiment, New York State Infantry Volunteers* (Teaneck, NJ: Fairleigh Dickinson University Press, 1981), 61.

34 *OR*, ser. 1, vol. 25, pt. 1, 660; "Report of killed and wounded and missing of the 75th Reg't. PV," RG-19, Box 45, Folder 13, PASA; 73th and 75th Pennsylvania Morning Report Books, April–May 1863, RG-94, NARA; *Philadelphia Daily Evening Bulletin*, May 8, 1863; *Philadelphia Freie Presse*, May 17 and 18, 1863; *National Tribune*, January 12, 1893.

35 Keller, *Chancellorsville and the Germans*, 72; Sears, *Chancellorsville*, 390–98; 410–18; Donaldson to his brother, May 14, 1863, in *Inside the Army of the Potomac: The Civil War Experience of Captain Francis Adams Donaldson*, ed. J. Gregory Acken (Mechanicsburg, PA: Stackpole Books, 1998), 264. For a detailed examination of Northern Anglo-American newspapers' scapegoating of the German element of the Eleventh Corps and the soldiers' and home front's reaction, see Keller, *Chancellorsville and the Germans*, chapters 4 and 5. The Pennsylvania German regiments of the corps thus entered the Gettysburg Campaign committed to vindicating their besmirched honor and the sacrifices of their comrades at Chancellorsville.

36 Bates, *History*, 5:223; *OR*, ser. 1, vol. 27, pt. 2, 79–80.

37 Valuska and Keller, *Damn Dutch*, 56–57, 63–64; Edwin B. Coddington, *The Gettysburg Campaign: A Study in Command* (New York: Scribner's, 1968), 140–41; Hodijah Lincoln Meade to Charlotte Randolph (Meade) Lane, July 19, 1863, quoted in Mitchell, *Civil War Soldiers*, 150; William W. Hassler, ed., *The*

General to His Lady: The Civil War Letters of William Dorsey Pender to Fanny Pender (Chapel Hill: University of North Carolina Press, 1965), 254; Samuel H. Hurst, *Journal-History of the Seventy-Third Ohio Volunteer Infantry* (Chillicothe, OH: S. H. Hurst, 1866), 65; Jim Weeks, "'A Disgrace That Can Never Be Washed Out': Gettysburg and the Lingering Stigma of 1863," in Blair and Pencak, *Making and Remaking Pennsylvania's Civil War*, 190–96.

38 Valuska and Keller, *Damn Dutch*, 63–65. Accused of "Copperheadism"—anti-Union and pro-Confederate sympathies—by Republicans and War Democrats during the war, the vast majority of Pennsylvania Dutch, who accounted for a good half of the southern tier counties' overall populations, simply wished to be left alone and hoped the war would pass them by. Countless families had sent sons to fight among the volunteers of 1861, but after the indignation of Fort Sumter wore off and the reality of a long war set in, many southern Pennsylvanians began to question the increasingly intrusive and status-quo-changing Republican policies such as emancipation, the draft, and the occasional suspension of the writ of habeas corpus. In these concerns they were joined by other Pennsylvanians in the coal-mining and lumbering regions of the state, who ultimately resorted to armed resistance to federal policies.

39 Ibid., 52–54, 61, 71; Rachel Cormany diary entry, June 23, 1863, in Mohr, *Cormany Diaries*, 334; Henry B. Hege to Henry G. Hege, July 12, 1863, reprinted in W. P. Conrad, *Conococheague: A History of the Greencastle-Antrim Community, 1736–1971* (Greencastle, PA: Greencastle-Antrim School District, 1971).

CHAPTER NINE: PENNSYLVANIA'S FIGHT TO WIN THE CIVIL WAR, 1863–1865

1 Scott Hartwig, "The Campaign and Battle of Gettysburg" in Valuska and Keller, *Damn Dutch*, 78–81.

2 Valuska and Keller, *Damn Dutch*, 116–18; Richard Rollins and Dave Shultz, *Guide to Pennsylvania Troops at Gettysburg*, 2nd ed. (Redondo Beach, CA: Rank and File Publications, 1998), 4–5.

3 Rollins and Shultz, *Guide to Pennsylvania Troops*, 5.

4 Michael A. Dreese, *The 151st Pennsylvania Volunteers at Gettysburg: Like Ripe Apples in a Storm* (Jefferson, NC: McFarland, 2000), 48, 53–58; Richard E. Matthews, *The 149th Pennsylvania Volunteer Infantry Unit in the Civil War* (Jefferson, NC: McFarland, 1994), 86–89; Rollins and Shultz, *Guide to Pennsylvania Troops*, 8–12, Stone quoted at 11.

5 Harry W. Pfanz, *Gettysburg: The First Day* (Chapel Hill: University of North Carolina Press, 2001), 171–77; John D. Vautier, *History of the 88th Pennsylvania Volunteers in the War for the Union, 1861–1865* (Philadelphia: J. B. Lippincott, 1894), 1–5, 135–36.

6 Louis Fischer, "The 11th Corps at Gettysburg," *National Tribune*, December 12, 1869; Wilhelm Roth letters, Co. K, 74th PA, Civil War Misc. Collection, U.S. Army Military History Institute, Carlisle, PA (hereafter USAMHI); John P. Nicholson, *Pennsylvania at Gettysburg* (Harrisburg, PA: William Stanley Ray, 1914), 1:434; Alexander von Mitzel's account can be found in Wilhelmina von Mitzel's widow's pension file, cert. 418227, app. 367705, NARA; William Simmers and Paul Bachschmid, *The Volunteer's Manual; or, Ten Months with the 153d Penn'a Volunteers* (Easton, PA: D. H. Neiman, 1863), 26–27; Francis Barlow to Robert Treat Paine, August 12,

1863, quoted in Coddington, *Gettysburg Campaign*, 704; Valuska and Keller, *Damn Dutch*, 155–57. Adding to the lasting stigma of the Eleventh Corps' poor performance at Gettysburg was the famous "Schimmelpfennig Incident," in which Brigadier General Alexander Schimmelpfennig, who commanded a division at Gettysburg, supposedly hid in a pigsty in town after his German regiments had been pushed back from their positions. At the end of the battle, he emerged unhurt, to the derision of prejudiced Anglo-Americans, who passed down the story and embellished it out of all proportion. In fact, Schimmelpfennig exercised good judgment in hiding himself and avoiding capture while the Confederates occupied the town.

7 Hartwig, "Campaign and Battle of Gettysburg," 94–96.

8 Ibid., 97; Bates, *History*, 2:675–76; Rollins and Shultz, *Guide to Pennsylvania Troops*, 46–50.

9 Hartwig, "Campaign and Battle of Gettysburg," 100–101; J. W. Muffly, *The Story of Our Regiment: A History of the 148th Pennsylvania Volunteers* (Des Moines, IA: Kenyon Printing and Mfg. Co., 1904), 603; A. M. Gambone, *The Life of General Samuel K. Zook: Another Forgotten Union Hero* (Baltimore: Butternut and Blue, 1996), 46–50; Harry F. Pfanz, *Gettysburg: The Second Day* (Chapel Hill: University of North Carolina Press, 1987), 284–86.

10 J. R. Sypher, *History of the Pennsylvania Reserve Corps* (Lancaster, PA: Elias Barr, 1865), 461; Norton to sister, July 12, 1863, reprinted in Oliver Willcox Norton, *Army Letters, 1861–1865* (New York: O. W. Norton, 1903), 161–62.

11 Hartwig, "Campaign and Battle of Gettysburg," 104–6.

12 Anthony McDermott and John Reilly, *A Brief History of the 69th Regiment, Pennsylvania Veteran Volunteers* (Philadelphia: D. J. Gallagher, 1889), 30; Bradley M. Gottfried, *Stopping Pickett: The History of the Philadelphia Brigade* (Shippensburg, PA: White Mane Books, 1999), 167–68; "John" (unidentified trooper in the Third Pennsylvania Cavalry) to "Dear Folks," July 4, 1863, reprinted in Sessarego, *Letters Home*, 23. Although historians still debate the reasons behind the failure of the Confederate pre-charge bombardment, the leading hypothesis is that the fuses on many of the Confederate shells were faulty. The vast amount of black powder smoke obscuring the target zone also made it difficult for rebel artillerists to sight their guns.

13 Gottfried, *Stopping Pickett*, 170–72; William Burns, Seventy-First Pennsylvania, diary entry, original at USAMHI, quoted in ibid.

14 Gottfried, *Stopping Pickett*, 173–75; Coddington, *Gettysburg Campaign*, 517; Gary G. Lash, "The Philadelphia Brigade at Gettysburg," *Gettysburg Magazine* 7 (July 1992): 97–113.

15 Gottfried, *Stopping Pickett*, 178–79.

16 Noah Andre Trudeau, *Bloody Roads South: The Wilderness to Cold Harbor, May–June 1864* (Boston: Little, Brown, 1989), 11–12, 15–16. Trudeau joins other historians of the war's later campaigns by claiming that "about half" of the three-year enlistees from the 1861-raised regiments reenlisted. Regiments that were already badly reduced in numbers that did not succeed in reenlisting enough veteran volunteers were dissolved, their reenlistments amalgamated with other regiments.

17 "The Unsung Heroes of the War," accessed February 17, 2015, http://pacivilwar150.com/people/africanamericans/Overview.aspx; Smith, "Civil War Letters of Quartermaster Sergeant John C. Brock," 146–48; Brock to "Mr. Editor," June 5, 1864, reprinted in ibid., 151–53.

18 Joseph T. Glatthaar, *Forged in Battle: The Civil War Alliance of Black Soldiers and White Officers* (New York: Free Press, 1990), 150; Smith, "Civil War Letters," 157; Martin W. Oefele, *German-Speaking Officers in the U.S. Colored Troops, 1863–1867* (Gainesville: University Press of Florida, 2004), 173–74.

19 "Battle of New Market Heights: USCT Troops Proved Their Heroism," accessed February 17, 2015, http://www.civilwar.org/battlefields/new-market-heights/new-market-heights-/battle-of-new-market-heights.html; Glatthaar, *Forged in Battle*, 150–51; Oefele, *German-Speaking Officers*, 182.

20 Charles Royster, *The Destructive War: William Tecumseh Sherman, Stonewall Jackson, and the Americans* (New York: Alfred A. Knopf, 1991), 38–40. For a comprehensive overview of the burning and the effects of the raid in Franklin County, see W. P. Conrad and Ted Alexander, *When War Passed This Way* (Shippensburg, PA: White Mane, 1987).

21 Royster, *Destructive War*, 39 (Slingluff quotation); Jubal A. Early, *War Memoirs: Autobiographical Sketch and Narrative of the War Between the States* (1912; reprint, Bloomington: Indiana University Press, 1960), 401; B. S. Schneck, *The Burning of Chambersburg, Pennsylvania*, 4th ed. (Philadelphia: Lindsay and Blakiston, 1864), 46–48 (Hoke's letter to the German Baptist Brethren newspaper *Religious Telescope*, August 10, 1864) and 60–61 (quoting article by John K. Shryock in the Philadelphia *Lutheran and Missionary*, August 11, 1864); Rachel Cormany diary entry, August 6, 1864, in Mohr, *Cormany Diaries*, 446.

22 Schneck, *Burning of Chambersburg*, 74–75; Apple quoted in ibid., 38–39.

23 Arnold Shankman, *The Pennsylvania Antiwar Movement, 1861–1865* (Madison, NJ: Fairleigh Dickinson Press, 1980), 199–200.

24 Giesberg, *Keystone State in Crisis*, 77–78.

25 Ibid., 63–64, 77; William A. Helffrich, *Lebensbild aus dem Pennsylvanisch-Deutschen Predigerstand: Oder Wahrheit in Licht und Schatten* (Allentown, PA: N. W. A. and W. U. Helffrich, 1906), 301; James M. Thompson to James A. Beaver, March 18, 1863, quoted in Carol Reardon, "'We Are All in This War': The 148th Pennsylvania and Home Front Dissension in Centre County During the Civil War," in *Union Soldiers and the Northern Home Front: Wartime Experiences and Postwar Adjustments*, ed. Paul A. Cimbala and Randall M. Miller (New York: Fordham University Press, 2002), 20. It should be noted that the powerful Pennsylvania Union Leagues, pro-Republican civic organizations composed of the most politically and financially powerful Unionists in the state, also had much to do with the tamping down of antiwar sentiments through public speeches, voluminous printed materials, support of sanitary fairs and other patriotic events, and intense political patronage at the local level.

26 *OR*, ser. 1, vol. 46, pt. 1, 564–80.

CHAPTER TEN: PENNSYLVANIA AND THE BIRTH OF A WORLD POWER

1 Max Boot, *Savage Wars of Peace: Small Wars and the Rise of American Power* (New York: Basic Books, 2003), 56–98, 129–70, 182–204.

2 *The Congressional Medal of Honor: The Names, the Deeds* (Forest Ranch, CA: Sharp and Dunnigan, 1984), 3–4, 1034; and Abigail Beardsley and Alan Jalowitz, "Honorable Pennsylvanians," Pennsylvania Center for the Book, Pennsylvania State University, accessed July 21, 2013,

http://pabook.libraries. psu.edu/pal-itmap/MOH.html.

3 *Congressional Medal of Honor,* 681, 651–52, 642; Jonathan Sutherland, *African Americans at War: An Encyclopedia* (Santa Barbara, CA: ABC-CLIO, 2004), 751.

4 Justin Corfield, "Butler, Smedley (1881–1940)," in *Encyclopedia of the Veteran in America,* ed. William Pencak (Santa Barbara, CA: ABC-CLIO, 2009), 1:114–16; and *Congressional Medal of Honor,* 550–56.

5 Joseph J. Holmes, "The Decline of the Pennsylvania Militia, 1815–1870," *Western Pennsylvania Historical Magazine* 57 (April 1974): 199–217; and Frederick S. Brightley, *Annual Digest of the Laws of Pennsylvania for the Years 1862 to 1870* (Philadelphia: Kay and Brother, 1870), 1614–16.

6 Michael A. Bellesiles, *1877: America's Year of Living Violently* (New York: New Press, 2010), 145–46, 155–60; John K. Mahon, *History of the Militia and the National Guard* (New York: Macmillan, 1983), 112–13, 116.

7 Philip S. Klein and Ari Hoogenboom, *A History of Pennsylvania,* 2nd ed. (University Park: Pennsylvania State University Press, 1980), 326–28; Joseph John Holmes, "The National Guard of Pennsylvania: Policemen of Industry, 1865–1905" (Ph.D. diss, University of Connecticut, 1971), 75–91; and Mahon, *History of the Militia,* 116–18.

8 Samuel C. Logan, *A City's Danger and Defense; or, Issues and Results of the Strikes of 1877, Containing the Origin and History of the Scranton City Guard* (Scranton, PA: Jas. B. Rodgers, 1887), 9; Mahon, *History of the Militia.*

9 Allan R. Millett, Peter Maslowski, and William B. Feis, *For the Common Defense: A Military History of the United States from 1607 to 2012* (New York: Free Press, 2012), 252–68; G. J. A. O'Toole, *The Spanish War: An American Epic, 1898.* (New York: W. W. Norton, 1984), 11–12, 397–400.

10 John B. B. Trussell, "Pennsylvania Volunteers in the Spanish-American War," *Military Collector and Historian* 38, no. 3 (1986): 99–109; and Richard A. Sauers, *Pennsylvania in the Spanish-American War: A Commemorative Look Back* (Harrisburg: Pennsylvania Capitol Preservation Committee, 1998), 14–19, 82–83.

11 Sauers, *Pennsylvania in the Spanish-American War,* 59–66, 67–70.

12 Ibid., 70–79, 82.

13 Ibid., 83; and *Congressional Medal of Honor,* 613, 616, 594.

14 Michael D. Doubler and John W. Listman Jr., *The National Guard: An Illustrated History of America's Citizen-Soldiers* (Washington, DC: Brassey's, 2003), 53–57.

CHAPTER ELEVEN: PENNSYLVANIA IN THE FIRST WAR TO END ALL WARS

1 Jerry M. Cooper, *The Rise of the National Guard: The Evolution of the American Militia, 1865–1920* (Lincoln: University of Nebraska Press, 1997), 132–39, 181–84.

2 Millett, Maslowski, and Feis, *For the Common Defense,* 304; *Lusitania Claims: Message from the President of the United States . . .,* 67th Congress, 2nd Session, Senate doc. no. 176 (Washington, DC: Government Printing Office, 1922), 2–4.

3 Cooper, *Rise of the National Guard,* 153–55.

4 Mark E. Neely Jr., *The Civil War and the Limits of Destruction* (Cambridge: Harvard University Press, 2010); Millett, Maslowski, and Feis, *For the Common Defense,* 302–3.

5 Cooper, *Rise of the National Guard,* 114, 156–63; National Guard Bureau, *Report on the Mobilization of the*

Organized Militia of the National Guard of the United States (Washington, DC: Government Printing Office, 1916), 48, 61, 154; *Pennsylvania in the World War: An Illustrated History of the Twenty-Eighth Division* (Pittsburgh, PA: States Publications Society, 1921), 1:123–24, 131.

6 Richard W. Stewart, ed., *The United States Army in a Global Era, 1917–2003* (Washington, DC: Center of Military History, United States Army), 21.

7 *Pennsylvania in the World War*, 1:131, 136–42. The unit was mobilized in mid-July 1917 and most elements of the Twenty-Eighth arrived in Europe in mid-May 1918.

8 Millett, Maslowski, and Feis, *For the Common Defense*, 323, 330–38; Stewart, *United States Army*, 27–45.

9 H. G. Proctor, *The Iron Division: The National Guard of Pennsylvania in the World War* (Philadelphia: John C. Winston, 1919), 11–12; Anne Cipriano Venzon and Paul L. Miles, eds., *The United States in the First World War: An Encyclopedia* (New York: Garland, 1999), 639–41; J. Stuart Richards, ed. *Pennsylvanian Voices of the Great War: Letters, Stories, and Oral Histories of World War I* (Jefferson, NC: McFarland, 2002), 230, 234; and Millett, Maslowski, and Feis, *For the Common Defense*, 335–38.

10 Hervey Allen, *Toward the Flame: A Memoir of World War I* (New York: Farrar and Rinehart, 1926; reprint, Lincoln: University of Nebraska Press, 2003), 43, 49, 277.

11 *Philadelphia in the World War, 1914–1919* (New York: Published for the Philadelphia War History Committee by Wynkoop, Hallenbeck, Crawford, 1922), 165–68; Jon Guttman, *Groupe de Combat 12 "Les Cigognes": France's Ace Fighter Group in World War I* (Oxford: Osprey, 1914), 56, 65, 73, 84–85, 120, 122;

"Charles J. Biddle, Air Ace, Dies," *Bucks County (PA) Courier Times*, March 24, 1972, 10.

12 *Congressional Medal of Honor*, 509, 530, 535; and *Philadelphia in the World War*, 308.

13 *Philadelphia in the World War*, 201–29; Benjamin F. Shearer, ed., *Home Front Heroes: A Biographical Dictionary of Americans During Wartime* (Westport, CT: Greenwood Press, 2007), 796; *History of the Pennsylvania Hospital Unit (Base Hospital Number 10 U.S.A) in the Great War* (New York: Paul Hoeber, 1921), 88–89; and Lettie Gavin, *American Women in World War I: They Also Served.* (Niwot: University Press of Colorado, 1997), 65, 257, 268.

14 Lisa Tendrich Frank, ed., *An Encyclopedia of American Women at War: From the Home Front to the Battlefields* (Santa Barbara, CA: ABC-CLIO, 2013), 585–87; Gavin, *American Women*, 1–18, 26, 245–56; *Philadelphia in the World War*, 172.

15 Sutherland, *African Americans at War*, 282–86; *Philadelphia in the World War*, 194–98; and Klein and Hoogenboom, *History of Pennsylvania*, 430.

16 Frank R. Murdock, "Some Aspects of Pittsburgh's Industrial Contribution to the War," *Western Pennsylvania Historical Magazine* 4 (1921): 214–33. Klein and Hoogenboom, *History of Pennsylvania*, 305–8.

17 Klein and Hoogenboom, *History of Pennsylvania*, 430.

18 Frances H. Early, *A World Without War: How U.S. Feminists and Pacifists Resisted World War I* (Syracuse, NY: Syracuse University Press, 1997), 92–99; and Klein and Hoogenboom, *History of Pennsylvania*, 429–30.

19 Richard A. Parker, *Free Speech on Trial: Communication Perspectives on Landmark Supreme Court Decisions*

(Tuscaloosa: University of Alabama Press, 2003), 5, 20–33.

20 Terry Radtke, *The History of the Pennsylvania American Legion* (Mechanicsburg, PA: Stackpole Books, 1993), 3–4; and William Pencak, *For God and Country: The American Legion, 1919–1941* (Boston: Northeastern University Press, 1989), 31.

21 Radtke, *History of the Pennsylvania American Legion*, 17, 25; Pencak, *For God and Country*, 121, 159, 175–81.

22 Pencak, *For God and Country*, 3–10,149–53; and Radtke, *History*, 35–36.

23 Radtke, *History*, 48–50; Pencak, *For God and Country*, 224–34.

24 Radtke, *History*, 127–32.

25 Pencak, *Encyclopedia of the Veteran*, 2:387–88; and Pencak, *For God and Country*, 202–5.

CHAPTER TWELVE: PENNSYLVANIA IN WORLD WAR II

1 Douglas Brinkley and Michael E. Haskew, eds., *The World War II Desk Reference* (New York: Castle, 2008), 2–9.

2 H. C. Engelbrecht and F. C. Hanighen, *Merchants of Death: A Study of the International Armament Industry* (New York: Dodd, Mead, 1934); Glen Jeansonne, *Women of the Far Right: The Mothers' Movement and World War II* (Chicago: University of Chicago Press, 1996), 41; and Larry Gara and Lenna Mae Gara, *A Few Small Candles: War Resisters of World War II Tell Their Stories* (Kent, OH: Kent State University Press, 1999), 78–88.

3 Steven T. Ross, ed., *U.S. War Plans, 1938–1945* (Boulder, CO.: Lynne Rienner, 2002), 17; Michael E. Weaver, *Guard Wars: The 28th Infantry Division in World War II* (Bloomington: Indiana University Press, 2010), 10, 20, 98–99, 253.

4 Weaver, *Guard Wars*, 127–242.

5 Ibid., 173, 187–242, 256.

6 Pennsylvania Historical and Museum Commission (PHMC), *Pennsylvania at War, 1941–1945* (Harrisburg: Pennsylvania Historical and Museum Commission, 1946), 11–15; Seth A. Givens, "555th Parachute Infantry Battalion," in *Ethnic and Racial Minorities in the U.S Military: An Encyclopedia*, ed. Alexander M. Bielakowski (Santa Barbara, CA: ABC-CLIO, 2013), 226–27.

7 PHMC, *Pennsylvania at War*, 15–16.

8 *Congressional Medal of Honor*, 298–99, 345, 369.

9 Ibid., 439–40, 488–89.

10 Ibid., 381–82, 376, 379.

11 Ibid., 357, 359, 390, 394, 424, 430, 434, 460–61, 482, 484–85.

12 Doris Weatherford, *American Women During World War II: An Encyclopedia* (New York: Routledge, 2010), 154, 167, 497–503 (WAC), 480–85 (WAVES), 417–19 (SPAR), 476–80 (WASP); Mary Bacon Hale and Amy Cloud, *Women Marines Association: A Pictorial History* (Paducah, KY: Turner Publications, 1995), 97; Barbara Sicherman and Carol Hurd Green, eds., *Notable American Women: The Modern Period* (Cambridge, MA: Harvard University Press, 1980), 83–85; Frank, *Encyclopedia of American Women at War*, 393–95; and "Remembering Mary," Wings Across America, accessed March 24, 2016, http://www.wingsacrossamerica.us/wasp/memorial/mary.htm; and Joseph S. Kennedy, "Teacher Took to the Sky to Serve in WWII . . .," Philly.com (*Philadelphia Inquirer*), March 14, 1999, http://articles.philly.com/ 1999-03-14/news/25513086_1_nancy-harkness-love-women-airforce-service-pilots-wasps.

13 Ulysses Lee, *The Employment of Negro Troops* (Washington, DC: Office of the Chief of Military History, United States Army, 1966); Robert F. Jefferson, *Fighting for Hope: African American Troops of the 93rd Infantry Division in*

World War II and Postwar America (Baltimore: Johns Hopkins University Press, 2008), 31–32, 65; Charles W. Dryden, *A-Train: Memoirs of a Tuskegee Airman* (Tuscaloosa: University of Alabama Press, 1997), 88; Paul Stillwell, ed., *The Golden Thirteen: Recollections of the First Black Naval Officers* (New York: Berkley Books, 1994); Melton A. McLaurin, *The Marines of Montford Point: America's First Black Marines* (Chapel Hill: University of North Carolina Press, 2007); "Black Military History," *The Word: The Official Newsletter of Black Marine Reunions* 6, no. 8 (August 2012): 2–3; and Catherine Reef, *African Americans in the Military* A to Z of African Americans (New York: Facts on File, 2010), 39–40.

14 Merl E. Reed, "Black Workers, Defense Industries, and Federal Agencies in Pennsylvania, 1941–1945," *Labor History* 27, no. 3 (Summer 1986): 356–84.

15 Emily Yellin, *Our Mothers' War: American Women at Home and at the Front During World War II* (New York: Free Press, 2004), 39–41, 43–45.

16 Jim Rose, "The Problem Every Supervisor Dreads: Women Workers at the U.S. Steel Duquesne Works During World War II," *Labor History* 36, no. 1 (Winter 1995): 24–51; and Weatherford, *American Women*, 10, 305.

17 PHMC, *Pennsylvania at War*, 42–51.

18 Steven Zaloga and Hugh Johnson, *Jeeps, 1941–45* (Oxford: Osprey, 2005), 4–12.

19 PHMC, *Pennsylvania at War*, 32–40.

20 PHMC, *Pennsylvania at War*, 31, 35–37, 40– 41.

CHAPTER THIRTEEN: THE WARS THAT ENDED NO WAR

1 John Lewis Gaddis, *The Cold War: A New History* (New York: Penguin, 2005).

2 Philip Jenkins, *The Cold War at Home: The Red Scare in Pennsylvania, 1945–1960* (Chapel Hill: University of North Carolina Press, 1999).

3 Millett, Maslowski, and Feis, *For the Common Defense*, 453–57.

4 Ibid., 457; *Congressional Medal of Honor*, 178–79.

5 Millett, Maslowski, and Feis, *For the Common Defense*, 458–60, 467–74; *Congressional Medal of Honor*, 229; Arned L. Hinshaw, *Heartbreak Ridge: Korea, 1951* (New York: Praeger, 1989); and Clay Blair, *The Forgotten War: America in Korea, 1950–1953* (New York: Times Books, 1987).

6 William M. Donnelly, *Under Army Orders: The Army National Guard During the Korean War* (College Station: Texas A&M Press, 2001), 146; Jeffrey A. Davis, *The Pennsylvania Journey* (Layton, UT: Gibbs Smith, 2005), 201; and U.S. Department of Defense, Defense Casualty Analysis System, "U.S. Military Casualties—Korean War Casualty Type by State and Territory," accessed July 6, 2013, https://www.dmdc.osd.mil/dcas/pages/report_korea_state.xhtml.

7 Stanley Karnow, *Vietnam: A History* (New York: Viking Press, 1983), 135–48, 198–204, 218–19, 224, 234–35, 250, 257, 278–79.

8 Ibid., 676, 679–80; Larry Addington, *America's War in Vietnam: A Short Narrative History* (Bloomington: Indiana University Press, 2000), 80–174.

9 U.S. Army Center of Military History, Medal of Honor Recipients, Vietnam War, "Etchberger, Richard L.," accessed December 12, 2014, http://www.history.army.mil/moh/vietnam-a-l.html#ETCHBERGER; and Fred L. Borch III, *Medals for Soldiers and Airmen: Award and Decorations of the United States Army and Air Force* (Jefferson, NC: McFarland, 2013), 27–28.

10 *Congressional Medal of Honor*, 55; John B. Nichols and Barrett Tillman, *On*

Yankee Station: The Naval Air War over Vietnam (Annapolis, MD: Naval Institute Press, 1987), 63–65.

11 *Congressional Medal of Honor*, 43–44.

12 Addington, *America's War in Vietnam*, 87–88, 133–35.

13 Mike Wittels, *Advice for Conscientious Objectors in the Armed Forces* (Philadelphia: Central Committee for Conscientious Objectors, 1970), 35–37; Amey A. Hutchins with the University of Pennsylvania Archives, *University of Pennsylvania*, Campus History Series (Charleston, SC: Arcadia Publishing, 2004), 107; and Kenneth J. Heineman, *Campus Wars: The Peace Movement at American State Universities in the Vietnam Era* (New York: New York University Press, 1993), 26–31, 56, 59, 242–45.

14 Peter L. Hahn, *Crisis and Crossfire: The United States and the Middle East Since 1945* (Dulles, VA: Potomac Books, 2005); Judith Stiehm, *The U.S. Army War College: Military Education in a Democracy* (Philadelphia: Temple University Press, 2002).

15 Stephen M. Duncan, *Citizen Warriors: America's National Guard and Reserve Forces and the Politics of National Security* (Novato, CA: Presidio Press, 1997), 6, 35–40, 50–51, 140–42; Tim O'Gorman and Steve Anders, *Fort Lee*, Images of America (Charleston, SC: Arcadia Publishing, 2003), 111.

16 Robert H. Stretch et al., "Physical Symptomatology of Gulf War–Era Service Personnel from the States of Pennsylvania and Hawaii," *Military Medicine* 160, no. 3 (March 1995): 131–36; and Robert Stretch et al., "Psychological Health of Gulf War–Era Military Personnel," *Military Medicine* 161, no. 5 (May 1996): 261. While initially many had doubted the existence of Gulf War illness, recent studies identified a biomarker for this condition using brain scans. See Rakib U. Rayhan et al., "Increased Brain White Matter Axial Diffusivity Associated with Fatigue, Pain and Hyperalgesia in Gulf War Illness," *Plos One* 8, no. 3 (March 2013): 1–10.

17 Radtke, *History of the Pennsylvania American Legion*, 99–107.

18 Boot, *Savage Wars*, 318–35.

19 Boot, *Savage Wars*, 322; U.S. Army Center for Military History, Medal of Honor Recipients, Somalia, "Sergeant First Class Randall D. Shughart," accessed December 12, 2014, http://www.history.army.mil/moh/somalia.html#SHUGHART; Congressional Medal of Honor Society, "Shughart, Randall D.," accessed December 12, 2014, http://www.cmohs.org/recipient-detail/2198/shughart-randall-d.php;; James H. Willbanks, ed., *America's Heroes: Medal of Honor Recipients from the Civil War to Afghanistan* (Santa Barbara, CA: ABC-CLIO, 2011), 307–9.

20 Millett, Maslowski, and Feis, *For the Common Defense*, 633–80;

21 Pennsylvania National Guard, History of the PA Guard, "Twenty-First Century," accessed March 24, 2016, http://www.paguard.com/guard_basics/guard-history.html. U.S. Army, Medal of Honor, Operation Iraqi Freedom, official citation for Ross A. McGinnis, accessed July 26, 2013, http://www.army.mil/medalofhonor/mcginnis/citation/; and profile, "The Story of SPC Ross A. McGinnis," accessed July 26, 2013, http://www.army.mil/medalof honor/mcginnis/profile/.

22 J. Ford Huffman and Tammy S. Schultz, eds., *The End of Don't Ask, Don't Tell: The Impact in Studies and Personal Essays by Service Members and Veterans* (Quantico, VA: Marine Corps University Press, 2012), 2.

Further Reading

Pennsylvania: An Overview

Davis, Jeffrey A., and Paul Douglas Newman, eds. *Pennsylvania History: Essays and Documents*. New York: Routledge, 2015.

Miller, Randall M., and William A. Pencak, eds. *Pennsylvania: A History of the Commonwealth*. University Park: Pennsylvania State University Press, 2002.

Colonial Period to 1800

Bodle, Wayne. *The Valley Forge Winter: Civilians and Soldiers in War*. University Park: Pennsylvania State University Press, 2004.

Crocker, Thomas E. *Braddock's March: How the Man Sent to Seize a Continent Changed American History*. Yardley, PA: Westholme Publishing, 2009.

Crytzer, Brady. *Guyasuta and the Fall of Indian America*. Yardley, PA: Westholme Publishing, 2013.

Cubbison, Douglas C. *The British Defeat of the French in Pennsylvania, 1758: A Military History of the Forbes Campaign Against Fort Duquesne*. Jefferson, NC: McFarland, 2010.

Dixon, David. *Never Come to Peace Again: Pontiac's Uprising and the Fate of the British Empire in North America*. Norman: University of Oklahoma Press, 2005.

Dorwart, Jeffery M. *Invasion and Insurrection: Security, Defense, and War in the Delaware Valley, 1621–1815*. Newark: University of Delaware Press, 2009.

Fischer, David Hackett. *Washington's Crossing*. New York: Oxford University Press, 2006.

Fischer, Joseph R. *A Well-Executed Failure: The Sullivan Campaign Against the Iroquois, July–September 1779*. Columbia: University of South Carolina Press, 2008.

Franklin, Benjamin. *The Autobiography of Benjamin Franklin*. 2nd ed. Edited by Leonard W. Labaree, Ralph L. Ketcham, Helen C. Boatfield, and Helene H. Fineman. With a new forward by Edmund S. Morgan. New Haven, CT: Yale University Press, 2003.

Frantz, John B., and William A. Pencak, eds. *Beyond Philadelphia: The American Revolution in the Pennsylvania Hinterland.* University Park: Pennsylvania State University Press, 1998.

Jackson, John W. *The Pennsylvania Navy, 1775–1781: The Defense of the Delaware.* New Brunswick, NJ: Rutgers University Press, 1974.

Kent, Donald H. *The French Invasion of Western Pennsylvania, 1753.* Harrisburg: Pennsylvania Historical and Museum Commission, 1954.

McGuire, Thomas J. *The Philadelphia Campaign.* Vol. 1, *Brandywine and the Fall of Philadephia,* Mechanicsburg, PA: Stackpole Books, 2006.

Nagy, John A. *Rebellion in the Ranks: Mutinies of the American Revolution.* Yardley, PA: Westholme Publishing, 2008.

Nagy, John A. *Spies in the Continental Capital: Espionage Across Pennsylvania during the American Revolution.* Yardley, PA: Westholme Publishing, 2011.

Newman, Paul Douglas. *Fries's Rebellion: The Enduring Struggle for the American Revolution.* Philadelphia: University of Pennsylvania Press, 2004.

Ousterhout, Anne M. *A State Divided: Opposition in Pennsylvania to the American Revolution.* Westport, CT: Praeger, 1987.

Pencak, William, ed. *Pennsylvania's Revolution.* University Park: Pennsylvania State University Press, 2010.

Seymour, Joseph. *The Pennsylvania Associators, 1747–1777.* Yardley, PA: Westholme Publishing, 2012.

Slaughter, Thomas P. *The Whiskey Rebellion: Frontier Epilogue to the American Revolution.* New York: Oxford University Press, 1988.

Taaffe, Stephen R. *The Philadelphia Campaign, 1777–1778.* Lawrence: University Press of Kansas, 2003.

Williams, Glenn F. *Year of the Hangman: George Washington's Campaign Against the Iroquois.* Yardley, PA: Westholme Publishing, 2005.

The War of 1812

Hickey, Donald R. *The War of 1812: A Forgotten Conflict.* Urbana: University of Illinois Press, 2012.

Sapio, Victor A. *Pennsylvania and the War of 1812.* Lexington: University Press of Kentucky, 1970.

Skaggs, David Curtis, and Gerard T. Althoff. *A Signal Victory: The Lake Erie Campaign, 1812–1813.* Annapolis, MD: Naval Institute Press, 2012.

Stagg, J. C. A. *The War of 1812: Conflict for a Continent.* New York: Cambridge University Press, 2012.

The U.S.-Mexican War

Eisenhower, John S. D. *So Far from God: The U.S. War with Mexico, 1846–1848.* New York: Random House, 1989.

Greenberg, Amy. *A Wicked War: Polk, Clay, Lincoln, and the 1846 U.S. Invasion of Mexico.* New York: Alfred A. Knopf, 2012.

Hackenburg, Randy W. *Pennsylvania in the War with Mexico.* Shippensburg, PA: White Mane, 1992.

Winders, Richard Bruce. *Mr. Polk's Army: The American Military Experience in the Mexican War.* College Station: Texas A&M University Press, 1997.

AMERICAN CIVIL WAR

Blair, William, and William Pencak, eds. *Making and Remaking Pennsylvania's Civil War.* University Park: Pennsylvania State University Press, 2001.

Coddington, Edwin B. *The Gettysburg Campaign: A Study in Command.* New York: Scribner's, 1968.

Colwell, David G., ed., *The Bitter Fruits: The Civil War Comes to a Small Town in Pennsylvania.* Carlisle, PA: Cumberland County Historical Society, 1998.

Conrad, W. P., and Ted Alexander. *When War Passed This Way.* Shippensburg, PA: White Mane, 1987.

Giesburg, Judith. *Keystone State in Crisis: The Civil War in Pennsylvania.* Mansfield, PA: Pennsylvania Historical Association, 2013.

Gottfried, Bradley M. *Stopping Pickett: The History of the Philadelphia Brigade.* Shippensburg, PA: White Mane, 1999.

Mohr, James C., ed., *The Cormany Diaries: A Northern Family in the Civil War.* Pittsburgh: University of Pittsburgh Press, 1982.

Sandow, Robert M. *Deserter Country: Civil War Opposition in the Pennsylvania Appalachians.* New York: Fordham University Press, 2011.

Shankman, Arnold. *The Pennsylvania Antiwar Movement, 1861–1865.* Madison, NJ: Fairleigh Dickinson Press, 1980.

Valuska, David L., and Christian B. Keller. *Damn Dutch: Pennsylvania Germans at Gettysburg.* Mechanicsburg, PA: Stackpole Books, 2004.

POST–CIVIL WAR ARMY

Coffman, Edward M. *The Old Army: A Portrait of the American Army in Peacetime, 1784–1898.* New York: Oxford University Press, 1986.

Rickey, Don, Jr. *Forty Miles a Day on Beans and Hay: The Enlisted Soldier Fighting the Indian Wars.* Norman: University of Oklahoma Press, 1963.

Utley, Robert M. *Frontier Regulars: The United States Army and the Indian, 1866–1891.* Lincoln: University of Nebraska Press, 1984.

SPANISH- AND PHILIPPINE-AMERICAN WARS

Linn, Brian McAllister. *The Philippine War, 1899–1902.* Lawrence: University Press of Kansas, 2000.

O'Toole, G. J. A. *The Spanish American War: An American Epic.* New York: W. W. Norton, 1984.

Trask, David F. *The War with Spain in 1898.* Lincoln: University of Nebraska Press, 1996.

World War I

Coffman, Edward M. *The War to End All Wars: The American Military Experience in World. War I.* New York: Oxford University Press, 1968.

Kennedy, David M. *Over Here: The First World War and American Society.* New York: Oxford University Press, 1980.

Richards, J. Stuart, ed. *Pennsylvanian Voices of the Great War: Letters, Stories, and Oral Histories of World War I.* Jefferson, NC: McFarland, 2002.

Williams, Chad L. *Torchbearers of Democracy: African American Soldiers in the World War I Era.* Chapel Hill: University of North Carolina Press, 2010.

World War II

Kennedy, David M. *The American People in World War II: Freedom from Fear, Part II.* New York: Oxford University Press, 1999.

Murray, Williamson, and Allan R. Millett. *A War to be Won: Fighting the Second World War.* Cambridge, MA: Belknap Press of Harvard University Press, 2001.

Overy, Richard. *Why the Allies Won.* New York: W. W. Norton, 1995.

Terkel, Studs. *The Good War: An Oral History of World War II.* New York: New Press, 1997.

Korean War

Halberstam, David. *The Coldest Winter: America and the Korean War.* New York: Hyperion Books, 2007.

Hastings, Max. *The Korean War.* New York: Simon and Schuster, 1988.

The Cold War and Vietnam

Gaddis, John Lewis. *The Cold War: A New History.* New York: Penguin Press, 2005.

Herring, George C. *America's Longest War: The United States and Vietnam, 1950–1975.* 5th ed. Boston: McGraw-Hill Education, 2014.

Jenkins, Philip. *The Cold War at Home: The Red Scare in Pennsylvania, 1945–1960.* Chapel Hill: University of North Carolina Press, 1999.

Karnow, Stanley. *Vietnam: A History.* New York: Viking Press, 1983.

Radtke, Terry. *The History of the Pennsylvania American Legion.* Mechanicsburg, PA: Stackpole Books, 1993.

Recent Wars

Atkinson, Rick. *Crusade: The Untold Story of the Persian Gulf War.* Boston: Houghton Mifflin, 1993.

Filkins, Dexter. *The Forever War.* New York: Vintage, 2009.

Jones, Seth G. *In the Graveyard of Empires: America's War in Afghanistan.* New York: W. W. Norton, 2010.

Index

Abbey, Edwin Austin, 255
Adams, John, 61, 133-134
Adams, Samuel, 56
Addison, Joseph, 86
Afghanistan, 237, 244, 246-247
African Methodist Episcopal Church, 257
Agent Orange, 244
Air Heritage Museum and Aircraft
    Restoration facility, 259
Alan Seeger Park, xiii
Albany Congress, 101, 111
Albany Congress of 1754, 46
Albany Plan of Union, 5, 23
Alert, 95
Alexander, William, 74
Alien and Sedition Acts, 133
Allegheny Arsenal, 151
Allegheny Mountains, 34
Allegheny River, 39, 108, 120
Alleman, Matilda "Tillie" Pierce, 188
Allen, Hervey, 217
Allen Infantry, 145
Allen, James, 63, 89
Allen, William, 78
Al-Qaeda, 247
American Bantam Company, 234
American Chivalry (Brackenridge), 129
American Civil Liberties Union, 222
The American Crisis (Paine), 67
American Expeditionary Force, 216
American Friends Service Committee,
    xii, 243
American Helicopter Museum and
    Education Center, 259
American Legion, 212, 221-222, 245
American Revolution
  battle of Brandywine and, 71-76
  British occupy Philadelphia and, 76-83,
    87-89
  Germantown and, 76-83

  in the far west and, 116-119
  mutinies and, 96-100
  organizing and, 56-62
  origins of, 55-56
  privatization of the war and, 94-96
  suppressing opposition and, 62-67
  treason trials and, 89-94
  Washington crosses the Delaware and,
    67-71
  winter at Valley Forge and, 83-87
Amherst, Jeffrey, 34, 38-39, 42, 44, 48
Amish, xiii, 60, 143
Anderson, Fred, 19
Anderson, Richard, 171, 187
André, John, 82, 92
Andrews, John, 206-207
Andrews, William H., 154
Andros, Edmund, 6
Antietam, battle of, x, 151, 153-155, 157-
    161, 164, 194, 199
Apple, T. G., 201-202
Appomattox Campaign, 149
Appomattox Court House, 195
Archer, J. J., 162
Armistead, Louis, 193-194
Armistice Day, 222
Armstrong, Edward, 31
Armstrong, John, 30-32, 43, 45, 57, 72,
    80-81
Army Corps of the Susquehanna, 173
Army of Northern Virginia, 150, 159,
    172-173, 195, 203
Army of the Potomac, x, 148, 150-151,
    153, 160-161, 165-167, 170-171,
    177, 179-180, 182-184, 188, 192,
    195-197, 199, 203, 257
Army War College, xi, 244, 259
Arnold, Benedict, 58, 91-92, 108
Arnold, Henry "Hap", 228-229
Articles of Confederation, 98-99, 129

Illustration Credits
Drexel University: 218
Fold 3: 167
Harvard University: 17
Historical Society of Pennsylvania: 8, 126
John Carter Brown Library: 58
Library Company of Philadelphia: 3, 159
Library of Congress: 26, 41, 46, 51, 81, 97, 137, 143, 145, 149. 150, 151, 152,
154, 157, 158, 161, 163, 175. 179, 180, 187, 189, 191, 194, 197, 200, 202, 206,
207, 218, 235
Marine Corps: 239
Mercury News (Pottstown, PA): 184
Metropolitan Museum of Art: 131
Monticello: 233
National Archives: 214, 216, 217, 219, 226, 227, 229, 242
National Park Service: 85, 182, 193
Naval Historical Center: 218
New York Public Library: 28, 35, 107, 169, 172
Ontario Heritage Trust: 5
Pennsylvania State University Library: 208
Private Collection: 95
Steve Kennedy: 148
University of Pittsburgh: 39
Wikimedia Commons: 23 (Wilson 44691), 68 (Luke Jones)
William L. Clements Library: 120
Winterthur Museum: 14

About the Authors

William A. Pencak (1951–2013) was professor emeritus of history at Pennsylvania State University. He is the author of many articles and books, including *Pennsylvania: A History of the Commonwealth*, and was editor of *Pennsylvania History: A Journal of Mid-Atlantic Studies*.

Christian B. Keller is professor of history in the Department of National Security and Strategy at the United States Army War College, Carlisle, Pennsylvania. He is author of a number of books and articles on the Civil War, including *Chancellorsville and the Germans: Nativism, Ethnicity, and Civil War Memory* and, as co-author, *Damn Dutch: Pennsylvania Germans at Gettysburg*.

Barbara A. Gannon is associate professor of history at the University of Central Florida and has written on Pennsylvania and various military history subjects, including *The Won Cause: Black and White Comradeship in the Grand Army of the Republic.*, winner of the Wiley-Silver Prize.